Alexandria and
Alexandria (Arlington) County,
Virginia

Minister Returns

and

Marriage Bonds

1801–1852

T. Michael Miller

HERITAGE BOOKS
2025

HERITAGE BOOKS

AN IMPRINT OF HERITAGE BOOKS, INC.

Books, CDs, and more—Worldwide

For our listing of thousands of titles see our website
at
www.HeritageBooks.com

A Facsimile Reprint
Published 2025 by
HERITAGE BOOKS, INC.
Publishing Division
5810 Ruatan Street
Berwyn Heights, MD 20740

— Publisher's Notice —
In reprints such as this, it is often not possible to remove
blemishes from the original. We feel the contents of this
book warrant its reissue despite these blemishes and
hope you will agree and read it with pleasure.

International Standard Book Number
Paperbound: 978-1-55613-029-8

DEDICATED TO MY PARENTS:

Nathan & Mary M. Miller

ACKNOWLEDGEMENTS

I would like to express my gratitude to
the Alexandria Library
for the use of their excellent facilities.

PREFACE

Formally established as a town in 1749, Alexandria, Virginia grew from a small tobacco trading post into the economic, socio-political and ecclesiastical epicenter of Northern Virginia. Its population nearly doubled from 2,700 inhabitants in 1790 to 4,900 souls in 1800. Its harbor was filled with brigs, schooners and ships of the line which traversed the high seas and engaged in international and coastwise trade. The streets were lined with substantial brick houses and the "sound of the hammer and trowel were at work every where..." In 1796, a visitor, the Duc de La Rouce Foucauld commented that: "Alexandria is beyond all comparison the handsomest town in Virginia - indeed is among the finest in the United States."

Besides its commercial and maritime importance, Alexandria was a center of early church activity. Scottish merchants and factors brought with them the Presbyterian faith and a meeting house was erected on South Fairfax street in 1772. The Protestant Episcopal Church functioned as the official state church of Virginia until it was disestablished in 1784. As early as the mid-1760s the Episcopalians had erected a "Chapel of Ease" near Princess and Royal streets. The early church then fell into a state of disrepair and James Parsons and John Carlyle were hired by the vestry to construct a substantial new one at the head of Cameron street. Finished in 1773, Christ Church continues to serve the parish and the Alexandria community.

It was not long before other religious sects arrived at the seaport town. Catholics, although legally banned from practicing their faith settled in Alexandria in the 1770s and worshiped in several locales. A small brick structure situated on the outskirts of town on South Washington street initially met their needs. Later in 1826, St. Mary's was constructed under the pastorate of the Reverend Joseph W. Fairclough on South

Royal street. Today it is the oldest Catholic parish in the State of Virginia.

Quakers from Philadelphia emigrated to Alexandria soon after the Revolutionary War and established a meeting house in the 300 block of South St. Asaph street in 1802. Itinerant Methodist preachers also frequented Alexandria as early as 1772. Under the leadership of Ezekiel Cooper a small chapel was built off Duke street on Chapel alley in 1791. In 1804, the Methodist constructed a larger edifice on South Washington street. Known as Trinity Church, the congregation still holds services on Cameron Mills road in Alexandria. As a result of a schism over the slavery issue in 1844, the Methodist congregation splintered into two factions. The pro-North faction worshiped at Trinity while the Southerners erected the Methodist Epsicopal Church South across the street on the west side of the 100 block of South Washington street. Another Methodist assembly called the Methodist Protestant Church was founded in 1829 and constructed a church in the 100 block of North Washington street.

A similar schism in the Episcopal church resulted in the formation of St. Paul's Episcopal Church in 1808. Initially the offshoot dissenters met in a small chapel on the 200 block of South Fairfax street until a permanent church, designed by Benjamin Latrobe, was constructed within the 200 block of South Pitt street.

In 1803 a Baptist Society was formed in Alexandria. It erected a meeting house on the 200 block of South Washington street. Destroyed by fire in 1829, the church was rebuilt in 1830. Since then it has undergone extensive renovations.

Besides administering to the spirtual needs of their congregations, the Alexandria clergy were frequently requested to perform the sacrament of marriage. The record of these marriages form the basis of this volume.

Prior to 1801 Alexandria and Alexandria County were a legal and geographic component of Fairfax County. The Virginia Legislature ceded this area to the Federal Government in December 1789. Congress accepted the gift on February 27, 1801, and Alexandria town and county became a legal territory within the ten mile square District of Columbia. From 1801 to 1846 it remained under Federal jurisdiction until it was retroceded to the State of Virginia in 1847.

Few Alexandria marriage records have survived prior to 1801. Mrs. Connie Ring, Archivist at the Fairfax County

Courthouse, has prepared an excellent compilation of marriages of the county dating from its formation in 1742 until 1853. She gleaned these marriage records from the county deeds, wills, chancery suits and other archival sources. The fruits of her labor have been published in *The Historical Society of Fairfax County, Virginia, Inc.*, Vol. 16, 1980, p. 52; Vol. 17, 1981, p. 39. Another source of early marriage records may be found in the Alexandria Presbyterian Church Register. These date from 1789 to 1860. A typescript copy has been prepared by the Fairfax County Chapter of the Daughters of the American Revolution and may be viewed at the Lloyd House Library in Alexandria. The late Mary Powell, historian of the Mt. Vernon Chapter of the D.A.R., also compiled and published these Presbyterian Marriage Records, 1789-1825, in the August 1920 issue of the *D.A.R. Magazine*.

Mrs. Ruth Lincoln Kaye, historian at St. Paul's Episcopal Church, has performed a commendable service by publishing "The First Fifty-Two Years of St. Pauls Episcopal Church, Alexandria, Virginia - 1809-1861" in the June 1980 *National Genealogical Society Quarterly Magazine*, Vol. 68, p. 95. Serialized in other issues, the article notates marriages celebrated by the St. Paul clergy.

An excellent source of Quaker marriage records is William Wade Hinshaws, *Encyclopedia of American Quaker Genealogy*, (Baltimore, Md.: Genealogical Publishing Co., 1973), Vol. 6 - Virginia. The records of the Alexandria monthly meetings are replete with marriages. These are significant because it was not until 1825 that the Virginia Legislature passed a law requiring Quaker marriages to be recorded in county court houses. Even then the Friends continued to ignore this rubric.

Recently the Christ Church Vestry book, 1765-1842, and Parish Register, 1860-1878, were transcribed by Carroll Ainsworth McElligott and printed in the *Genealogical and Historical Magazine of the South*, Vol. I, No. 1, 2, 4, (1984). The transcription is pregnant with genealogical data including the marriage records of the Church.

The current list of Marriage Bonds and Minister Returns have been transcribed from ten roles of microfilm prepared by the Virginia State Library and available at the Alexandria Library, Lloyd House. They include: Minister Returns, 1801-1853 and Marriage Bonds, 1801-1852.

Bonds were first required in Virginia in 1660. All persons wishing to be married had to post a bond and secure a license from the county clerk stating that there was no legal impediment to prevent the marriage. The clerk would then prepare the license and it would be presented to a minister who would conduct the service. A list of Alexandria ministers who performed these ceremonies and their church affiliation is provided below.

Finally, it is hoped that this volume will be helpful to those whose ancestors once walked the cobblestoned streets and alleyways of old Alexandria, Virginia.

MINISTERS AND CLERGY WHO PERFORMED MARRIAGE
CEREMONIES IN ALEXANDRIA
1801 – 1852

ADAMS, SAMUEL – ?

ANDREWS, WELLS – 2nd Presbyterian Church

BARCLAY, FRANCIS – Christ Church, minister 1810-1811

BROWN, BENJAMIN N. – Methodist Episcopal

BUNN, SEELY – Trinity Methodist Church, 1810

CONE, SPENCER H. – First Baptist Church, 1816-1823

CORNELIUS, SAMUEL – First Baptist Church, 1824-1841

DANA, CHARLES B. – Christ Church, 1834-1860

DANFORD, JOSHUA N. – 2nd Presbyterian, 1838-1840

DAVIS, CHARLES A. – Trinity Methodist Church, 1833-34

DIBRELL, ANTHONY – Methodist Episcopal Church South,
      1851-52

EDWARDS, W. B. – Trinity Methodist Church

FAIRCLOUD, JOSEPH WILLIAM – St. Mary's Catholic
      Church, 1818-1830

GRIFFITH, ALFRED – Trinity Methodist Church, 1816

HANSON, J. M. – ?

HARRISON, ELIAS – Old Presbyterian Meeting House, 1817,
      1820-1863

HERNDON, T.D. – (d. 1854), Presbyterian

HILL, Wm. – 2nd Presbyterian Church, 1836-1838

JACKSON, WILLIAM (b. 1793, d. 1844), St. Paul's Episcopal
      Church, 3rd Rector, 1827-1832

JEFFERSON, HAMILTON – ?

JOHNSTON, JAMES T. (b. 1797, d. 1877), St. Paul's Epis
      copal Church, 4th Rector

KEITH, REVEL – Christ Church, 1825-1827

KINGSFORD, EDWARD – First Baptist Church, 1841-1848

LARKIN, JACOB – Trinity Methodist, 1829-1830

LIPPITT, E. R. – Protestant Episcopal Church

LOWN, JOHN M. - ?
MACARTNEY, FRANCIS - Trinity Methodist Church, 1841-42
MCMULLINS, SOLOMON - ?
MAFFITT, Wm. - Presbyterian Minister, d. 1828, resided at
    Salona in Fairfax County
MATTHEWS, THOMAS - Quaker
MORGAN, Lyttleton F. - Methodist Episcopal Church
MUIR, JAMES - Old Presbyterian Meeting House
NORRIS, OLIVER - Christ Church, 1813-1825
RICHARDSON, J. W. - ?
ROBBINS, ISAAC - Trinity Methodist
ROBY, WASHINGTON - Methodist Protestant Church, 1843,
    1844
ROSSER, LEONIDAS - Methodist Episcopal Church South,
    1849-1851
ROSZELL, STEPHEN G. - Trinity Methodist Church, 1836,
    1837, 1851
ROWEN, JOSEPH - Trinity Methodist Church, 1802
RYLAND, C.H. - First Baptist, from King and Queen County,
    Virginia
SMITH, GEORGE A. - St. Paul's Episcopal Church
VILLIGER, GEORGE - St. Mary's Catholic Church, 1852-1854
WATERS, WILLIAM - Trinity Methodist Church, 1801, 1803,
    1804
WEBSTER, AUGUSTUS - Methodist Protestant Church, 1834
WILMER, WILLIAM HOLLAND - b. 1782, d. 1827, St. Paul's
    Episcopal Church, 2nd Rector, 1812-1826

HOW TO USE THIS BOOK

This book is divided into two sections: Minister Returns and Marriage Bonds. In each section, the grooms are listed alphabetically by their surnames. To find brides, bondsmen, parents, and aliases, check the index.

The letters in parentheses following the couples listed in the Minister Returns section identify the ministers who performed the marriage ceremonies. Below are the letter codes and the ministers' names.

(AG)   Alfred Griffith
(AW)   A. Webster
(BNB) Benjamin N. Brown
(CAD) C. A. Davis
(CBD) Charles B. Dana
(?D)   ____ Dibrell
(DC)   Isaac Robbins in Alexandria, D. C.
(EH)   Elias Harrison
(EK)   Edward Kingsford
(ERL) E. R. Lippitt
(FB)   Francis Barclay
(FM)   Francis Marartney
(GAS) George A. Smith
(GW)   George Williger
(HJ)   Hamilton Jefferson
(IR)   Isaac Robbins
(JF)   Joseph Faircloud
(JHR) J. H. Ryland
(JJ)   J. Johnston
(JL)   J. Larkin
(JM)   James Muir
(JMH) J. M. Hanson

(JML) John M. Lown
(JR)   Joseph Rowen
(JWR) J. W. Richardson
(LFM) L. F. Morgan
(LHC) L. H. Cone
(LR)   Leo Rosser
(ON)   Oliver Norris
(QM)   Quaker Marriages
(RK)   Revel Keith
(RMH) R. M. Hanson
(SA)   Samuel Adams
(SB)   Seely Bunn)
(SC)   Samuel Cornelius
(SGR) Stephen G. Rozzel
(SM)   Solomon McMullins
(TDH) T. D. Herndon
(TM)   Thomas Matthews
(WA)   Wells Andrews
(WBE) W. B. Edwards
(WH)   Wm. Hill
(WHW) Wm. H. Wilmer
(WJ)   Wm. Jackson
(WM)   Wm. Maffitt
(WR)   Washington Robey
(WW)   Wm. Waters

MINISTER RETURNS

ACKER, Nicholas of Washington City to Sarah Ellen Bisbey of Alexandria, May 25, 1848 (JJ)

ADAM, John to Mary Dunlap, Feb. 22, 1816 (JM)

ADAMS, Abijah to Margaretta H. Wherry, June 12, 1821 (JM)

Francis to Mary R. Newton, Dec. 20, 1814 (JM)

George R. to Mary A. Bontz, Jan. 19, 1836 (BNB)

James L. to Sarah Y. Carson, July 29, 1852 (WBE)

James to Catherine Bruner, Feb. 25, 1802 (JM)

Leonard to Nancy Davis, March 4, 1802 (JM)

ALEXANDER, Amos to Eliza Wroe, Jan. 10, 1805 (JM)

Austin to Eleanor Sherwood, Dec. 26, 1816 (JM)

ALLEN, James to Lucretia Murray, Jan. 2, 1828 (WJ)

Reuben to Catharine Cole, Aug. 29, 1852 (WBE)

Wm. to Anna Donalson, March 20, 1803 (SA)

ALLISON, Amos to Ann Geiger, March 30, 1803 (JM)

Bryan to Ann Barr, April 8, 1801 (JM)

Daniel to Nancy Ellis, Jan.

ALLISON (continued) 7, 1845 (EK)

Elias to Nancy Kent, Feb. 17, 1803 (JM)

John to Nancy Darnes, Dec. 26, 1815 (IR)

ALTERFRI, Peter to Margaret Bartlett, Sept. 26, 1805 (DC)

AMAST, Feline to Martha Brown, Nov. 12, 1815 (WHW)

AMBUSH, Calvert to Patsey Csyer, March 22, 1834 (IR)

ANDERSON, James to Nancy Davis, Jan. 21, 1836 (BNB)

James to Nelly Weylie, Sept. 2, 1802 (JM)

Nimrod to Elizabeth Davy, Dec. 17, 1808 (IR)

Robert to Mary Black, June 5, 1837 (WH)

ANDOLE, Bernard to Eleanor Stone, Aug. 27, 1801 (JM)

ANDREWS, Elijah to Ann Wheatly, March 1821 (no date) bond dated March 1, 1821 (JF)

Jacob to Polly Baxter, April 7, 1810 (JM)

Joshua to Harriot Potts, July 4, 1822 (EH)

Wells to Nancy Harper, Sept. 14, 1819 (JM)

1

ANNIS, John to Elizabeth Baggett, July 1, 1852 (?D)

ANTRIM, Parnell to Sarah Manley, June 28,1802 (JM)

ARMSTRONG, John T. to Catherine Tennison, Dec. 23, 1827 (SC)

Samuel to Lucy Ann Mullin, Lic. Aug. 24, 1837 (IR)

ARNOLD, Garnett to Elizabeth Chisam, Dec. 23, 1803 (WW)

Harrison H. B. to Mary J. A. Brooke, June 6, 1850 (LR)

William to Ann Stevenson, Sept. 4, 1816 (See also: Stephenson) (IR)

ARTHUR, Samuel to Catharine Trescott, Dec. 3, 1817 (AG)

ARUNDELL, John to Catherine Boyd, July 23, 1818 (WHW)

ASHBY, Turner H. to Elizabeth L. Gregory, June 1, 1853 (EH)

ASHFORD, George to Susanna Compton, Dec. 25, 1806 (JM)

ASHTON, Thomas to Elizabeth Wallace, Nov. 17, 1836 (WH)

ATKINSON, Guy to Albina Birch, April 7, 1803 (JM)

ATWELL, Manly of Loudoun County, Virginia, to Rebecca S. Berry of Alexandria, D.C., June 12, 1834 (JJ)

Richard to Elizabeth Meads, May 30, 1811 (IR)

AUDLEY, Thomas to Catharine Javins, March 18, 1816 (IR)

AULD, David to Mary E. Kidwell, Dec 11, 1851 (?D)

AVERY, Philip to Sarah Slatford, Dec. 7, 1809 (IR)

Thomas to Margt. Walker, Sept. 4, 1850 (LR)

BADDIN, Sainttobin to Mary Ann Ball, Jan. 16, 1804 (WM)

BAGGET, Wm. to Elizabeth Brown, July 28, 1825 (SC)

BAGGETT, Charles to Elizabeth Baggett, March 24, 1804 (JM)

BAGGOT, Thomas to Nancy Henry, Dec. 6, 1842 (Also: Baggett) (FM)

BAILISS, Robert to Peggy Porter, Feb. 12, 1801 (JM)

BAKER, Carroll to Mary Chitis, Feb. 27, 1817 (WHW)

Samuel to Susan Gladdin, May 30, 1815 (JM)

BALDWIN, George to Jane Hayes, July 24, 1801 (WM)

BALE, Richard to Sally Nelson, May 26, 1810 (IR)

BALL, Allen to Ann Wiley, Dec. 31, 1801 (JM)

Spencer to Eliza Luke, Feb. 25, 1814 (ON)

Thomas to Jane Mackelroy, Dec. 1815 (ON)

BALLENGER, James to Ann Stepheson, Nov. 14, 1816 (JMH)

BANK, Hugh to Rhoda Nollowood, Jan. 2, 1816 (JM)

BARBER, Peter to Patty Kennedy, Aug. 12, 1811 (IR)

BARCROFT, Testus to Maria Piercy, June 6, 1820 (JM)

BARKLEY, Reszin to Julia Morris, July 20, 1816 (JMH)

BARNES, Jesse to Susanna Green, Jan. 9, 1803 (JM)

BARNETT, George to Mary Ann Cranston, March 15, 1810 (JM)

Isaac to Lucy Burgess, August 4, 1803 (JM)

BARRY, David to Mary Ann Foster at Mrs. Fosters' Oct. 3, 1834 (AW)

Richard to Patty Marshall, June 2, 1835 (BNB)

Robert to Amelia Ramsay, Oct. 21, 1824 (WA)

Wm. to Mary Cooke, May 20, 1803 (JM)

BARTLE, Samuel to Susan Rhodes, March 24, 1814 (JM)

BASSETT, W. H. to Eleanor O'Neille, Jan. 22, 1822 (JF)

BAUGH, Lewis K. to Eliza Ann Beedle, 1817 (LHC)

BAVERS, Thomas to Delilah Davis, Nov. 21, 1815 (JM)

BAYLISS, Daniel to Sarah Swann, May 23, 1833 (CAD)

BEACH, Noah of Alex. to Lucretia Cooke of Alexandria, May 11, 1852 (JJ)

BEAKLEY, John to Sophia Whitney, May 7, 1828 (SC)

BEALE, John to Mary McKerven, May 24, 1812 (JM)

BEAN, Benjamin to Matilda Lee Hughley, Aug. 18, 1823 (Also: Hughnely) (IR)

Rev. Henry H. of Alexandria, D. C. to Matilda Talbot of Alexandria, Dec. 5, 1833 (JJ)

BEARCROFT, Domini to Sa-

BEARCROFT (continued) rah Watson (coloured), Dec. 20, 1811 (IR)

BEARD, George to Elizabeth Berry, Sept. 13, 1818 (ON)

BEAVERS, John to Ellen Lee, Feb. 19, 1852 (EH)

BECKLEY, Wm. to Ann Watson, Nov. 8, 1827 (SC)

BEECH, John to Mary Glasgoe, Jan. 7, 1801 (JM)

Thomas to Cordelia Smith, Oct. 2, 1812 (JM)

BEHIER, Peter to Ann King, April 15, 1806 (JM)

BELL, Alexander to Susanna Evans, Nov. 23, 1830 (JL)

George to Sally Waugh (coloured), Aug. 17, 1820 (WHW)

Robert to Jane L. Hamilton, Lic. June 29, 1837 (IR)

William to Maria Hines, Lic. July 28, 1836 (IR)

BENNETT, John to Ann Perry, August 3 , 1804 (JM)

Mordecai to Milly McCarty, Oct. 16, 1817 (JMH)

BENSON, James to Elizabeth Dorsey, Jan. 24, 1828 (SC)

BENTER, Wesley to Ann Bontz, Dec. 12, 1816 (IR)

BENTLEY, Robert to Kitty Longden, Oct. 9, 1817 (WHW)

BENTON, Samuel to Elizabeth Vowell, July 8, 1805 (DC)

BERNARD, John to Sarah Dove, May 30, 1807 (IR)

BERRY, C. C. to Elizabeth Campble, Jan. 6, 1842 (See also: Campbell) (FM)

George to Mary Ann Gofson, Jan. 3, 1842 (See also:

BERRY (continued)
Gossen) (FM)
James to Ann Davies, March 14, 1811 (JM)

BIGGS, James to Nancy Talbutt, Feb. 4, 1804 (WM)
James to Rebecca Talbott, Dec. 28, 1801 (JM)

BINES, David to Margaret M. Cannon, Oct. 23, 1817 (JMH)

BIRCH, Isaac to Elizabeth Walker, Sept. 8, 1815 (JM)
Joseph to Sarah Posey, Jan. 22, 1818 (IR)

BISHOP, John S. to Amanda R. Horwell, April 23, 1829 (JL)

BLACK, James of Alexandria to Helen Talbott of Alexandria, Aug. 3, 1831 (WJ)

BLACKFORD, Henry to Sarah Parsons, March 27, 1815 (JM)

BLACKLOCK, Nicholas F. to Eliza Ramsay, Dec. 9, 1813 (JM)
Robert J. to Ann M. Ramsey, April 16, 1816 (JM)

BLACKSBURN, James to Milly Ann Brown, June 2, 1853 (WBE)

BLACKWELL, Lewis to Milly Bennett, July 19, 1834 (SM)

BLADEN, Thomas (Jr.) to Ann Caroline, Sept. 4, 1811 (IR)

BLAKE, James H. of North Carolina to Sarah F. Contee of Alexandria, Apr. 22, 1852 (JJ)
William of Whitehall, New York to Nancy Keene of

BLAKE (continued)
Alexandria, D. C., Oct. 17, 1842 (ERL)

BLAKENEY, John to Jane Spriggs, Dec. 24, 1803 (WW)

BLUE, John to Catharine Evans, March 27, 1806 (JM)

BODKIN, Washington L. of Alexandria to Catherine A. Harper of Alexandria, Dec. 14, 1837 (JJ)

BOGUE, Francis S. to Elizabeth Boyd, March 4, 1830 (IR)

BOISEAU, Joseph to Mary Ann Jenkins, Feb. 19, 1819 (JF)

BONTS, George to Mary Benter, June 25, 1818 (IR)

BONTZ, Jacob to Sarah Carlin, March 11, 1818 (AG)

BOOTH, Wm. J. to Christiana Lowe, Sept. 20, 1843 (WR)

BORSET, Fielder to Ann A. M'Rea, June 19, 1817 (WHW)

BOSS, Abraham to Ann D. Hickey, Oct. 15, 1815 (WHW)

BOSTON, Samuel E. to Julia Ann Love, Feb. 28, 1828 (date of license) (IR)

BOURNE, William to Margaret Nairn, Oct. 13, 1836 (See also: Neale) (WH)

BOWERS, Jacob to Eliza Mills, July 9, 1853 (WBE)

BOWLER, John to Frances Leary, Feb. 10, 1822 (ON)

BOWLES, Thomas to Susan Sales (both coloured), June 9, 1813 (IR)

BOWLING, Ambrose G. to

BOWLING (continued)

Margaret James, July 29, 1808 (IR)

George to Elizabeth Veitch Feb. 26, 1805 (JM)

George to Sarah Staples, March 18, 1801 (JM)

John to Frances Griffin, Feb. 11, 1818 (IR)

Robert to Jane Christie Neal, Nov. 28, 1816 (See also: Neille) (JMH)

BOYD, John to Delila Slater, Lic. June 15, 1836 (LFM)

John to Mary Kirk, June 30, 1810 (IR)

Robert to Betsy Bailey, Nov. 20, 1810 (IR)

BOYER, Elias to Ann Bruce, August 16, 1803 (JM)

John to Martha Ann Reynolds, Nov. 9, 1812 (IR)

Joseph to Ann Kirk, Jan. 20, 1840 (EH)

BOYLE, John to Julia Ann Hudson, Feb. 25, 1830 (JL)

BRADLEY, Harrison to Elishaba Harris Huguely, April 23, 1816 (IR)

BRADY, John S. to Susan Brown, Jan. 22, 1828 (date of license) (IR)

BRAINSITE, Wm. to Eliza. Corry, Aug, 15, 1802 (JM)

BRAMEL, Wm. W. to Mary H. Jones, Sept. 20, 1827 (SC)

BRANDAS, John to Mary Cole, July 7, 1853 (EH)

BRANDT, Richard H. to Ann Caroline Smoot, Jan. 8, 1828 (WJ)

BRANNON, Wm. to Joicey Forest, April 24, 1833 (IR)

BRAWNER, Henry to Eliza-

BRAWNER (continued)

beth Anness, June 25, 1815 (WHW)

Henry to Kitty McRea, June 9, 1815 (JM)

Wm. H. to Mary G. Speake, Sept. 15, 1840 (EH)

BREAST, James A. to Eliza Talbot, Nov. 30, 1826 (Also: Talbott) (SC)

BRENT, Henry to Elizabeth Evans, Dec. 27, 1818 (See also: Blue) (WHW)

BRIGHT, John to Nancy Young both of Alexandria, Dec. 23, 1823 (WA)

BRISCOE, Warner W. to Jane H. Slacum, Nov. 16, 1825 (WHW)

BRISON, John to Mary McKinney, April 16, 1818 (ON)

BRITTINGHAM, Jas. to Polly Brown, July 3, 1803 (JM)

BROAD, Michael to Jane Martin, Jan. 14, 1804 (WM)

Thomas to Mary May, Dec. 28, 1820 (JM)

BROADWATER, William E. to Margaret Darne, Nov. 22, 1816 (IR)

BROCCHUS, Thomas to Rachel Ashton, Nov. 5, 1801 (JM)

BROCKETT, Robert Jr. to Elizabeth Longdon, Dec. 14, 1815 (JM)

Walter B. to Elizabeth Byrne, Nov. 18, 1815 (JM)

BRODERS, James to Elizabeth Curtain, Jan. 29, 1814 (IR)

BROGDON, George to Sarah Solomon, August 24, 1809

BROGDON (continued)
(free blacks) (JM)
BROMLY, Joseph to Mary
Smith, March 5, 1801 (JM)
BRONAUGH, Casey to Ann
G. Jacobs, Jan 27, 1814
(ON)
BRONGH, Heppel to Betsey
Lunt, Feb. 4, 1804 (WW)
BROOKE, Rev. Robert D. of
Iowa to Mary W. Smith of
Fairfax County, Virginia,
(Lic. from Clerk of Fairfax
County), Oct. 16, 1850
(CBD)
Thomas to Sarah Coffin,
Sept. 5, 1809 (JM)
BROOKES, David to Mary
Jones both of Alexandria,
Sept. 13, 1829 (WJ)
BROOKS, Hanson to Peggy
Fuggit, Dec. 4, 1819 (JM)
James to Sarah Johnson,
July 27, 1817 (AG)
John of Prince George's
County, Maryland, to Es-
ther Jane Fowle of
Alexandria, D. C. Apr. 23,
1846 (JJ)
John of Prince George's
County, Maryland, to Sarah
F. Daingerfield of Alex-
andria, Jan. 12, 1830 (WJ)
BROTHERS, John Fair to
Elizabeth Ends, May 30,
1805 (JM)
BROWERS, John to Mary
Mahanny, March 9, 1820
(JF)
BROWN, Alexander to Mary
Jane Billingsly (coloured),
Nov. 25, 1841 (JWR)
Henry C. to Mary E.
Travers, March 23, 1852
(WBE)
Henry to Sarah A. Piper

BROWN (continued)
(both coloured), June 25,
1813 (ON)
James to Susan Martin, Nov.
15, 1817 (WHW)
John to Margaret Coates,
Aug. 2, 1812 (JM)
John to Maria Leathrum,
Aug. 25, 1823 (JF)
John to Martha Bolen, June
3, 1816 (JM)
John to Mary G. Gretter,
Oct. 22, 1811 (JM)
M. to M. Catharine Bradley,
June 24, 1852 (?D)
Wm. O. to Sarah J. Lang-
ford, May 18, 1852 (WBE)
BRUCE, Aaron to Nancy
Smith, Sept. 2, 1815 (JM)
BRYANT, George W. to Jane
Eliza Beokly, July 29,
1852 (JHR)
BUCKINGHAM, Isaac to
Mary Brown, July 15, 1821
(ON)
BUCKLER, James to Mary
Gilbreth, Aug. 27, 1812
(IR)
BUCKLEY, John D. to Mar-
garet Legg, Aug. 25, 1817
(AG)
BUNUFF, John to Elizabeth
Keach, Sept. 14, 1815 (IR)
BURAGE, Thomas to Hannah
Simms , May 20, 1834
(See also: Burrag) (CAD)
BURBY, Joseph to Mary
Major, June 6, 1833 (CAD)
BURCHELL, Edward to Ann
Bates, Feb. 20, 1821 (IR)
BURFORD, John A. to Han-
nah Dyson, Feb. 23, 1804
(JM)
BURKE, Delany to Sarah
Jane Berry (coloured) Oct.
31, 1850 (CBD)

BURKE (continued)
Henry to Francis Ann Anderson, Dec. 17, 1842 (FM)
Richard S. to Ann McDemick, Feb. 18, 1830 (Also: McDennick) (EH)
BURNET, Francis to Elizabeth Stewart, March 1, 1818 (Also: Bennot) (WHW)
BURSON, Stephen F. to Rebecca Myers, Jan. 14, 1822 (ON)
BURWICK, James to Margaret Adams, June 16, 1834 (IR)
BUSH, Nathaniel of Alexandria to Jane Chatham of Alexandria, July 3, 1838 (JJ)
BUTLER, James to Flora Jackson, Oct. 5, 1839 (IR)
BUTTS, L. W. to Mary E. Wells, Dec. 12, 1844 (WR)
CABLE, George to Polly Stott, June 16, 1810 (IR)
CADDIS, David to Sarah Henderson, July 5, 1820 (ON)
CADEN, James to Ellen White, May 18, 1820 (JF)
CAIN, John to Lucy Hamilton, Nov. 15, 1817 (WHW)
CALDER, John A. to Endora A. Jackson, Nov. 3, 1853 (WBE)
CALDWELL, Josiah F. to Maria Magruder, Nov. 27, 1815 (JM)
CALVERT, Henry to Ellenor Willis, July 6, 1821 (IR)
CALVIN, George to Mary Ann Crany, Lic. April 4, 1837 (IR)
CAMPBELL, William to Elizabeth Smedley, July

CAMPBELL (continued)
27, 1818 (IR)
CANNON, John Newton to Ann Wattles, June 5, 1802 (JM)
CARBILL, John to Joanna Manough, Oct. 31, 1852 (GW)
CARLIN, George W. to Elizabeth Harris, April 20, 1810 (IR)
CARNE, Richard L. to Cecelia Shakes, July 3, 1821 (JF)
CARNES, Wm. D. to Catherine Deneale, 1826 (RK)
CARPENTER, Randall to Sophia Williams, May 28, 1816 (JMH)
CARRINGTON, Eli to Alesanna Kell, Aug. 31, 1815 (IR)
CARROL, Sinclair to Agnes Johnston, May 9, 1802 (JM)
Thomas L. to Mildred Thompson, March 23, 1841 (IR)
CARSON, John to Elizabeth Jerome, May 21, 1809 (JM)
Samuel to Jane Hamilton, Nov. 28, 1806 (JM)
CARTER, Richard to Sarah Armitage, Lic. July 30, 1836 (LFM)
Robert to Sarah Taylor, Jan. 25, 1834 (IR)
CARTWRIGHT, Jonathan to Eliza L. Dade, Aug. 15, 1833 (CAD)
CARUSI, Nathaniel to Jane Hollywood, Nov. 16, 1830 (EH)
CARY, Nicholas to Isabella Armstrong, Dec. 14, 1808

7

CARY (continued)
(IR)
CATTERTON, Thomas Ward
to Linn y Finnik, Feb. 23,
1804 (WM)
CATTS, Samuel to Elizabeth
Legg, Dec. 27, 1815 (JMH)
CAWOOD, Benjamin H. to
Mary Ann Magie, July 9,
1829 (JL)
Benjamin to Anna Ferguson,
Nov. 12, 1814 (JM)
Daniel to Mary M'Faw,
March 18, 1816 (WHW)
Grafton to Sally R. Madden,
Feb. 24, 1824 (WA)
Moses O. B. to Deliah
Robinson, Jan. 13, 1818
(AG)
CHAMBERLAIN, Lincoln to
Mary Harris, Nov. 3, 1822
(EH)
Luther to Jane S. Adams,
Jan. 18, 1825 (WA)
Wm. G. to Margaret Mus-
grove, (both of Alexandria
County), Dec. 14, 1843
(EK)
CHANCE, John to Mary
Paget, March 14, 1814
(WHW)
CHASE, Henry to Rachel
Magruder, Oct. 6, 1852
(WBE)
CHEFSON, Lewis to Ann
Freeman, Oct. 4, 1801
(JM)
CHICK, Wm. M. to Ann
Smith, April 9, 1816 (JMH)
CHILDS, David to Mary Mit-
chum, Jan. 22, 1806 (DC)
CHIPLEY, Samuel to Sarah
M. Bayliss, July 4, 1833
(CAD)
CHISOLM, John to Mary Ann
Grigsby, Jan. 5, 1801 (JM)

CHRISTMAN, John to Eliza-
beth Barr, Nov. 26, 1804
(JM)
CHURCH, Henry to Margaret
M'Callester, May 7, 1802
(JM)
John to Mary Ann Heth-
rington, Dec. 19, 1833 (IR)
CLAGETT, Davis to Louise
Thompson, Jan. 18, 1818
(ON)
James A. to Mary F. Minor,
Sept. 12, 1844 (ERL)
Richard H. to Sarah Ramsay
both of Alexandria, Nov. 1,
1823 (WA)
CLAGGETT, Wm. W. to Ann
Page, June 15, 1815
(WHW)
CLAPDORE, Jacob L. of
Alexandria to Louisa Bos-
well of Alexandria, Jan.
10, 1837 (JJ)
John M. to Eliz. A.
Frederick, Dec. 29, 1833
(CAD)
CLARK, Edward to Maria
Fletcher, Lic. April 8,
1844 (IR)
Isaac to Mary Smith, Oct.
10, 1815 (JM)
James C. of Chester County,
Pennsylvania, to Hannah
E. Taylor of Alexandria,
D. C., Oct. 19, 1842 (JJ)
John M. to Nancy King, Nov.
2, 1815 (WHW)
Peyton to Emiline Mullen,
Lic. May 21, 1836 (IR)
Robert C. to Hester E. Gib-
son (coloured), Sept. 26,
1844 (WR)
CLARKE, Elias to Catherine
Mitchell, Jan. 6, 1825
(WHW)
Horatio D. to Nancy Wil-

8

CLARKE (continued)
liams, Aug. 26, 1821 (ON)
John C. to Adaline Carlin, April 14, 1853 (WBE)
Joseph to Harriet. A. Kidwell, Jan. 9, 1853 (WBE)
CLARKSON, Edward to Elizabeth H. Green, Nov. 28, 1827 (WJ)
CLARRIDGE, James H. to Mary P. Padget, Sept. 8, 1842 (FM)
CLEMENTS, Henry to Elizabeth Jones, Aug. 16, 1817 (AG)
Robert H. to Alice L. Ramsay, July 19, 1825 (SC)
William to Sarah Booth, June 2, 1802 (JM)
CLIFFORD, Nehemiah to Nancy Nelson, Aug. 21, 1805 (DC)
CLIFT, Edward B. to Elizabeth Clark, June 15, 1853 (WBE)
COCKRILL, Marlin to Mary Stonemet, Jan. 1, 1805 (DC)
COFFIN, Daniel to Sarah Findley, Dec. 17, 1801 (JM)
John to Elizabeth Bennett, June 10, 1802 (JM)
COHAGAN, John to Elizabeth Bowie, May 24, 1812 (JM)
COHEN, William to Catharine Cary, April 30, 1801 (JM)
COLDMAN, Wm. Smith to Nancy Somby (coloured), March 14, 1826 (SC)
COLE, James to Lucy Bayle, 1826 (RK)
Thomas to Tryphasa Hand, Nov. 6, 1806 (JM)
William to Mary Ann Baker,

COLE (continued)
Jan. 13, 1842 (FM)
COLLIN, William A. to Sarah Slatford, June 13, 1802 (JM)
COLLINGWORTH, A. D. to Mary Tennison, Sept. 14, 1827 (SC)
COLONE, Vincent to Catharine Donaldson, March 17, 1810 (IR)
COLSTON, Anthony to Priscilla Merrick, Lic. 2 April 1835 (IR)
COLUMBUS, Charles to Eliza Rixter , Nov. 2, 1820 (JF)
COLYER, John to Elizabeth Mullen, April 15, 1833 (IR)
CONRAD, Charles Magill of New Orleans to Mary Elisa Angela Lewis of Fairfax County, Virginia, July 30, 1835 (JJ)
CONWAY, Robert to Margaret Sweet, May 22, 1809 (JM)
COOK, John F. P. to Mary A. Clements, April 21, 1835 (EH)
Joseph to Anna Baggott, July 10, 1827 (SC)
Lewis to Lydia Bailey, Nov. 30, 1809 (IR)
COOKE, Joseph to Jane Gilbreth, Dec. 19, 1810 (IR)
COOLY, Azar... to Susan Taylor, April 6, 1828 (SC)
COOPER, Joseph to Ann Morris, April 7, 1821 (WHW)
Wm. to Sally Dove (coloured), Dec. 9, 1830 (JL)
CORDERY, Henry to Elizabeth Green, Dec. 7, 1813

CORDERY (continued)
(ON)
CORE, Daniel to Mary Lambert, Aug. 5, 1815 (IR)
CORSE, M. Percival of Alexandria to Margaretta Fitzhugh of Alexandria, Jan. 10, 1849 (JJ)
CORWIN, Stephen to Julia Hopewell, June 26, 1806 (DC)
COWING, Robert to Sophia Ann Biggs, June 26, 1829 (JL)
COX, William to Mary Curtis, May 8, 1811 (IR)
COXEN, Nathaniel to Catharine Gullat, Oct. 18, 1821 (IR)
CRABTREE, Eleazer to Elizabeth Belcher, Aug. 5, 1816 (JM)
CRAGGINS, Charles S. to Mary Hillyard, May 28, 1830 (JL)
CRAM, Samuel to Mary Hickman, Jan 1, 1812 (JM)
CRANDELL, Phillip to Catherine A. McKnight, March 17, 1834 (EH)
CRANDLE, Thomas to Sarah Strait, Jan. 21, 1802 (JM)
CRANSTON, Samuel to Miss Sarah Varnell, Oct. 1, 1822 (WA)
CRAWFORD, William to Elizabeth Higdon, Nov. 12, 1822 (JF)
CREASE, John Hipsley to Jane Newton, Oct. 20, 1813 (JM)
CREDIT, Harry to Ann Cole (coloured), April 27, 1820 (ON)
CREIGHTON, Thomas B. to A. Roberta English both of

CREIGHTON (continued)
Alexandria, May 21, 1846 (JJ)
CREMITTAND, Ebenezer to Margaret Stewart, July 28, 1801 (WM)
CRISTOPHE, Christian to Harriott Cox, April 16, 1811 (JM)
CROOK, Thomas to Polly Philips, June 10, 1818 (IR)
William to Mary King, Nov. 16, 1809 (IR)
CROSBY, Lewis to Sarah Ann Russell, May 17, 1809 (JM)
CROSS, Richard of Alexandria to Lucinda Baliss of Alexandria, Jan. 3, 1836 (JJ)
Wm. J. to Susanna Cash, April 10, 1853 (WBE)
CROWDER, Thomas to Ellenor P. L. Franklin, June 15, 1841 (IR)
CRUPPER, John A. to Ellen Ann Oakley, May 11, 1840 (JML)
CUNNINGHAM, William to Ann Fitzgerald, May 13, 1812 (IR)
CUPIT, Robert to Phebe Franklin, Dec. 9, 1852 (JHR)
CURBY, Thomas to Susan Best, Aug. 10, 1820 (IR)
DADE, Charles Stuart to Jane Adam, May 23, 1809 (JM)
Francis to Harriot Shepherd, Dec. 12, 1811 (JM)
Langhan to Eliz. Scott, July 10, 1815 (WHW)
DAINGERFIELD, Edward to Margaret B. Vowell, Oct. 20, 1827 (WJ)
John B. of Alexandria, D. C.

DAINGERFIELD (continued)
to Rebecca H. Grew of
Alexandria, June 29, 1841
(JJ)
DALTON, Daniel to Margaret
Emmit, June 11, 1801
(JM)
DANIEL, James to Catharine
Balis, Jan. 2, 1831 (JL)
DARLEY, Thomas to Chloe
Kidwell, Feb. 19, 1807
(DC)
DARLY, Charles to Sarah A.
Cook, March 24, 1850 (LR)
DARNEL, John to Rhodey
Taylor, Aug. 16, 1810 (JM)
DARNELL, Henry to Letty
Grason, May 17, 1815
(Also: Grayson) (IR)
DAVENPORT, Samuel B. to
Mary A. Hunt, May 18,
1841 (FM)
DAVIDSON, Francis R. to
Jane Wellborne both of
Alexandria, March 24,
1831 (WJ)
John D. to Mary Ann Rosh,
April 27, 1837 (WH)
DAVIS, Benjamin to Mary
Turner, Sept. 24, 1812
(WHW)
Cornelius to Maria Stanton,
Dec. 30, 1813 (IR)
Cornelius to Polly Bolling,
April 12, 1821 (IR)
Daniel to Nancy Grimes,
May 14, 1802 (JM)
Henry W. of Alexandria, D.
C. to Constance T. Gar-
dener of Alexandria, D. C.,
Oct. 30, 1845 (JJ)
James to Susan E. Morris,
Dec. 17, 1833 (CAD)
John to Elizabeth Throop,
July 11, 1820 (IR)
John to Matilda Kiteley,

DAVIS (continued)
June 20, 1818 (ON)
John to Sally Wright, March
21, 1816 (WHW)
John to Sarah Crandele, Aug.
1, 1801 (WM)
John to Sarah Taylor, June
18, 1803 (WW)
Moses to Elizabeth Heisson,
Aug. 30, 1827 (SC)
Noah to Mary Young, both of
Alexandria, July 10, 1823
(WA)
Washington to Lucinda Pip-
sico (coloured), Sept. 13,
1821 (ON)
Wm. to Catharine Coxe,
June 1, 1830 (JL)
DAVY, Davy to Betsy Bowl-
ing, Aug. 21, 1806 (JM)
Thomas to Mary Glauville,
Nov. 1, 1820 (WA)
DAWSON, Philimon to Nancy
Ord, May 12, 1818 (ON)
DAY, Baldwin of Fauquier
County, Virginia, to
Lucretia Guthrie of
Alexandria, Jan. 20, 1828
(WJ)
Hanson to Peggy Fullerton,
Oct. 17, 1822 (JF)
Horatio to Martha Dun-
nington, May 17, 1815
(JM)
DEAKINS, Francis W. to
Christiana Jane Cook,
April 16, 1835 (SM)
DEARBORN, Charles to
Elizabeth Markly, April
22, 1830 (EH)
George to Mary L. Markley,
Sept. 10, 1835 (EH)
DEEBLE, Edward to Mar-
garet McCleish, June 11,
1816 (See also: McClish)
(JM)

DEIZ, Adam to Eva Fredericksen, April 13, 1820 (WHW)

DEKRAFFT, F. C. to Harriot Scott, Feb. 13, 1812 (JM)

DELPHY, Bartholomew to Mary Cravell, Sept. 2, 1817 (JMH)

DEMAINE, William to Sarah Hamack, Sept. 4, 1834 (IR)

DENNIS, James U. of Somerset County, Maryland, to Jane Cecelia Hooe of Alexandria, Oct. 8, 1846 (JJ)

Littleton of Accomac County, Virginia, to Anne Caroline Fowle of Alexandria, Oct. 10, 1843 (JJ)

DENTY, Samuel to Nancy Bailess, Nov. 6, 1830 (IR)

DERRICK, William to Margaret Franklin (both free coloured people), Feb, 27, 1851 (CBD)

DESHIELDS, Joseph to Sarah A. E. G. Monroe, March 24, 1825 (WA)

DETERLY, Michael to Mary Coones, April 1, 1804 (JM)

DEVAUGHN, John to Catharine Workman, May 8, 1816 (JMH)

John to Mary Churchman, June 29, 1815 (WHW)

John to Nancy Cady, July 10, 1816 (WHW)

DEWETT, Aaron to Eliza Mark, July 11, 1814 (JM)

DICK, David to Sarah Ann Posey, Sept. 18, 1810 (JM)

Joseph to Catherine Pipsics (coloured), July 3, 1817 (WHW)

DIFFENDAFFER, John to Barbary Wilkes Jan. 7, 1816 (JMH)

DIMENTS, Richard to Violetta Shannon, Nov. 17, 1814 (WHW)

DIXION, John A. of Alexandria to Fanny Chatham of Alexandria, Nov. 17, 1847 (JJ)

DIXON, David to Celia Fitzgerald, Lic. March 11, 1835 (IR)

John to Mary Jerro, April 14, 1805 (JM)

DOANE, Samuel to Semphonica Hugnely Dec. 1, 1853 (WBE)

DOBIE, William to Nancy Jefferson, June 25, 1817 (Also: Ann Jefferson) (AG)

DOE, Josiah H. to Mary R. Butler, May 13, 1818 (WHW)

DOERR, Conrad to Elizabeth Reynolds, June 18, 1814 (IR)

DOGAN, Anthony to Maria Rooe both of Alexandria, April 7, 1823 (WA)

DOLEMAN, William to Matilda Nichols, Lic. Dec. 31, 1834 (IR)

DONALDSON, Thomas to Matilda Gregory, Nov. 2, 1819 (WA)

DORLAND, Wm. L. to Mary E. Tyson at the house of Lucas Gillingham, May 2, 1850 (QM)

DORSEY, Edward to Ann Lee, July 23, 1834 (SM)

Rev. Thomas J. to Jane P. Robbins, Dec. 24, 1829 (JL)

DOUGHARTY, Arthur to Re-

DOUGHARTY (continued) becca Smith, June 27, 1801 (JM)

DOUGHTERTY, Daniel to Jane M. Summers, Dec. 14, 1818 (JF)

DOUGLASS, George to Harriet B. Chapman (coloured) Nov. 14, 1850 (CBD)

Jacob to Mary Gutherie, Dec. 19, 1815 (WHW)

James Jr. to Margaret Fleming, Oct. 25, 1826 (WA)

James to Eliza Kincaid, Nov. 17, 1812 (JM)

Richard L. to Maria Blacklock, Dec. 31, 1815 (WHW)

DOWDALL, Colin to Margaret Stokoly, April 23, 1804 (JM)

DOWELL, Albert H. of North Carolina to Rosena Duffy of Alexandria, March 30, 1847 (JJ)

DOWNS, Ignatius to Eliza Chrise, Sept. 19, 1818 (IR)

DREW, Charles to Polly Hubble, Dec. 9, 1804 (JM)

DROWN, John to Sally Higdon, Dec. 30, 1805 (DC)

Thomas to Ebby Goods, Nov. 29, 1806 (DC)

DUDLEY, James to Margaret A. Shield, Feb. 23, 1831 (JL)

John to Elizabeth Ward, Feb. 15, 1821 (IR)

Joseph to Mary D. Simmes, Feb. 7, 1828 (SC)

Wm. to Nancy Credit, 1826 (RK)

DUFFEY, George H. of Alexandria, D. C. to Sarah C. Steele of Alexandria, D. C., July 1, 1845 (JJ)

DUNBAR, Peter to Ann R. Cracroft, June 27, 1816 (ON)

DUNCAN, Charles (coloured) to Allevy Snowden (coloured), June 2, 1808 (IR)

Robert to Hannah Burnett, Dec. 17, 1801 (JM)

Samuel to Elizabeth Price, Aug 10, 1833 (IR)

DUNN, James to Penelope Cayton, Oct. 21, 1810 (JM)

DuVALL, Edmund B. of Prince George's County, Maryland, to Caroline D. Lansdale of Alexandria, Oct. 28, 1846 (JJ)

Wm. to Sarah A. Grundell, May 20, 1852 (WBE)

DYE, Amos to M. Parsons, Jan. 4, 1844 (WR)

Reuben to Elizabeth Turner, July 17, 1804 (JM)

DYER, Francis to Margaret Hunter, March 18, 1813 (WHW)

Walter to Deborah Dyer, June 21, 1815 (JMH)

William to Mary Skinner, March 17, 1831 (IR)

DYKES, Andrew to Ann Lutz, Oct. 31, 1816 (ON)

DYRE, Thomas to Margaret Grumble, May 10, 1842 (See also: Dyer) (FM)

EARLE, Samuel to Margaret Way, Jan. 4, 1813 (IR)

EARP, Simon to Mitty Scott, November 2, 1803 (WW)

EASTON, Tildon to Rebecca Clare Cook, July 30, 1834 (SM)

ECKLE, Charles of Georgetown, D. C. to Charlotte Perry of Alexandria, May 19, 1818 (WA)

EDELIN, Edward to Sarah Moore, Jan. 6, 1802 (JM)

ELLIOT, John to Amelia Mills, Dec. 20, 1812 (JM)

ELLIOTT, Silas to Ann Bradly, Sept. 2, 1812 (IR)

ELLIS, Edward of Alexandria to Mary E. Smoot of Alexandria, Dec. 7, 1852 (JJ)

Joseph to Sarah Emerson, May 18, 1812 (IR)

EMBERSOY, Richard D. to Catherine William, Nov. 14, 1815 (IR)

EMERSON, Aquila to Drury Coade, Nov. 26, 1818 (ON)

George W. to Endocia C. Suter, Jan. 20, 1842 (JWR)

Harrison A. to Fanny Deblance, Jan. 13, 1831 (JL)

Harrison to Jane Watson, Jan. 6, 1820 (JM)

John L. to Catherine Ball, May 24, 1822 (EH)

John L. to Sarah Coade, Dec. 24, 1818 (ON)

William D. to Ellen Dowell, June 21, 1825 (SC)

EMMERSON, Wm. R. to Isabella V. Daley both of Alexandria, May 9, 1848 (JJ)

ENDICOT, Samuel to Polly Call, October 1, 1805 (JM)

ENGLISH, James to Ann Richards, June 8, 1820 (WHW)

ENTWISLE, Isaac to Ann Ryan, Jan. 13, 1806 (JM)

James Jr. of Alexandria to Catherine A. Radcliff of Washington City, Jan. 17, 1849 (JJ)

Wilmer J. of Alexandria to Mary Mills of Alexandria, March 10, 1853 (WBE)

ERVINE, David to Sarah Lanham, August 6, 1806 (JM)

ESHON, George to Aliddy Blakeleig, Aug. 1, 1801 (WM)

EVANS, Edward to Letty Waugh (coloured), April 7, 1834 (CAD)

Ephraim to Jane L. Wadsworth both of Alexandria, June 6, 1823 (WA)

Samuel to Elizabeth Shule, Oct. 25, 1837 (See also: Shute) (SGR)

Simon to Ann Jackson, July 13, 1853 (WBE)

EVELETH, Ebenezer of Elizabeth City, Virginia, to Mary W. Butts of Alexandria, April 27, 1827 (WJ)

EWART, Horatio to Cloanna Dudley, July 11, 1803 (JM)

EWELL, Charles to Bridget Borrowdale, Feb. 19, 1812 (JM)

Charles to Maria D. Craik, Oct. 1, 1818 (ON)

FADLEY, James to Ann Robinson, May 24, 1832 (IR)

FAIRFAX, Archibald B., United States Navy, to Eliza W. Norris of Alexandria, March 2, 1852 (JJ)

FARMER, Edm. to Ann E. Drake, Aug. 16, 1850 (LR)

FAW, Abraham to Sarah Moody, April 20, 1806 (JM)

FELL, Christopher to Guertrude Smallridge, Nov. 26, 1823 (JR)

FEUGIT, James to Susan

FEUGIT (continued)
Javins, May 15, 1821 (See also: Fugett) (IR)
FIELD, Horatio to Elizabeth Boyer, Nov. 4, 1804 (JM)
Stephen to Mary Ann Whitington, June 14, 1821 (Also: Whittington) (IR)
FitzGERALD, James to Mary Ann Robinson, 21 Aug. 1833 (IR)
FitzHUGH, John T. of King George County, Virginia, to Rachel M'Cobb of Alexandria, Feb. 5, 1828 (WJ)
Norman to Mary Anne Vowell both of Alexandria, April 8, 1823 (WA)
FITZUGH, Wm. to Jane Halley, Nov. 9, 1815 (WHW)
FLEET, Charles to Malinda Kent, Dec. 24, 1801 (JM)
FLEMING, Thornton to Sally Cohagan, Jan. 8, 1806 (DC)
FLETCHER, Charles to Marie Taylor, Aug. 21, 1828 (IR)
FOOTE, Frederick of Prince William County, Virginia, to Verlinda Ashton of Alexandria, May 15, 1838 (JJ)
Frederick to Catharine R. Ramsay, Oct. 20, 1825 (WA)
FORCE, Peter to Hannah Evans, 1817 (LHC)
FORD, Danial to Louisa Hatton (coloured), Jan. 24, 1843 (Also: Foard) (FM)
West to Precilla Bell, Aug. 14, 1812 (JM)
William to Eunice Arrington, Sept. 30, 1818

FORD (continued)
(ON)
FORREST, David M. to Mary Clagett, Feb. 1, 1820 (ON)
FORTUNE, Ashbell R. to Mary A. Hills, Aug. 19, 1833 (CAD)
FOWLE, George D. of Alexandria, D. C. To Sarah Ellen Hooe of Alexandria, Oct. 10, 1843 (JJ)
John to Paulina Cazenove, May 26, 1831 (EH)
FOWLER, Daniel to Julia Ann Rawlings, June 3, 1830 (IR)
FOX, James to Catharine Piper, April 28, 1815 (ON)
Joseph to Mary Ann Carter both of Alexandria, Aug. 11, 1829 (WJ)
FOXWOOD, Daniel to Sarah Hill, July 25, 1811 (JM)
FRANCES, Matthew to Ann Durrington, June 10, 1804 (JM)
FRANCIS, Emmanuel to Julia A. Mansfield, Dec. 31, 1844 (WR)
Manuel V. of Island of Madaira to Martha J. Dreese of Alexandria, Jan. 28, 1841 (JJ)
FRANKLAND, Thomas to Nancy E. Horwell, Feb. 5, 1825 (WHW)
FRANKLIN, Benjamin to Catherine Parson, April 29, 1835 (EH)
FRAZER, Jeremiah to Sarah A. McDiller, June 6, 1843 (IR)
Wm. H. to Jane Ann Padgett, Nov. 21, 1844 (WR)
FRAZIER, George to Sarah Davis, April 17, 1814

FRAZIER (continued)
(WHW)

FREEMAN, Wm. to Elizabeth Bowser, Nov. 6, 1814 (See also: Bowzer) (WHW)

FRENCH, David M. of Virginia to Mary Eliza Smoot of Alexandria, Oct. 4, 1849 (JJ)

FRENELL, Isaac to Caroline Janson, Oct. 15, 1815 (WHW)

FRIGNETT, John to Elizabeth Haney, Aug. 9, 1815 (IR)

FRISKIN, Michael to Catherine Kirsh, Feb. 25, 1827 (WJ)

FUGITT, Martin to Phebe Wright, May 1, 1834 (CAD)

FULLER, Edward H. to Emely Thomas, Jan. 19, 1839 (EH)

FULLERTON, Peter to Rose Savery, Oct. 30, 1820 (JF)

FULMORE, John to Mary Ann Garlic, July 20, 1809 (JM)

FULTON, Alexander to Alice McAllan, Aug. 22, 1850 (EH)

FUREMAN, David to Elizabeth Hoakes, Oct. 3, 1822 (EH)

GAITHER, John to Margaret Carew, March 3, 1811 (FB)

GALT, James to Eve Resler, April 22, 1804 (WM)

GANES, Griffin to Elizabeth Parsons of Alexandria, July 27, 1827 (WJ)

GANT, Charles to Margaret Preston, Dec. 20, 1821 (Also: Gantt) (IR)

GANTT, Thomas to Pamelia

GANTT (continued)
Butler, Lic. May 14, 1836 (LFM)

GARDINER, John Charles to Indiana J. McClery, Aug. 19, 1851 (GAS)

GARDNER, William C. to Eliza F. Cazenove, May 16, 1816 (JM)

GARFORD, James to Mary Ann Kelly, Dec. 10, 1816 (ON)

GARNER, William to Margaret Simms, Sept. 12, 1809 (JM)

GARRISON, James to Elizabeth Kilham, May 22, 1817 (JMH)

GASCH, Frederick to Molley Catharly, October 7, 1804 (JM)

GASZ, John G. Gasz of Washington City, D. C. to Louise Hesse of Alexandria, D. C., Feb. 24, 1843 (JJ)

GATCHELL, John G. to Hannah Ann Davis, Oct. 19, 1840 (EH)

GATES, Thomas to Sally Risinger, July 15, 1816 (JMH)

GAWLER, Charles to Sarah Wilbar, Dec. 13, 1833 (CAD)

GEASLING, Wm. L. to Rebecca Jane Mills, May 28, 1843 (WR)

GIBBS, John H. to Sarah S. Williams, Nov. 5, 1817 (IR)

Walter to C. Curtis, Dec. 26, 1816 (ON)

GIBSON, John to Louisa Boyd, Jan. 5, 1831 (EH)

Samuel to Eleanor Thomp-

GIBSON (continued)
son, July 15, 1834 (EH)
Theodore to Jane Williams, Sept. 25, 1816 (IR)
GILBERT, Capt. to Sally Heble, July 31, 1815 (WHW)
John to Eliza Cary, April 10, 1813 (IR)
GILDEN, John to Joanna Gilbreth, Nov. 25, 1817 (Also: Gillwith) (JMH)
GILMAN, Ephraim to Ann Crawford, June 18, 1805 (DC)
GLANDERS, John to Fanny Myers, March 29, 1815 (JM)
GLASGOE, George W. to Hannah Ann Jacobs both of Alexandria, Nov. 4, 1830 (WJ)
GLISSART, Thomas J. to Ann Luckett, Sept 9, 1817 (Married in Fairfax County) (WHW)
GLOVER, William to Nancy Martin, April 12, 1814 (JM)
GLOVERMAN, Martin to Elizabeth Wasser, Oct. 8, 1803 (JM)
GODWIN, Peter F. to Dorcas Gotare, Aug. 23, 1813 (ON)
GOINGS, John to Catharine Evans, Lic. July 27, 1843 (IR)
GONSOLVES, Samuel to Mary Byrne, Feb. 14, 1811 (JM)
GOSS, Andrew to Sarah Pearson, June 5, 1804 (JM)
GOWEN, Joseph to Mary Sherron, July 17, 1803 (JM)
GRADY, Grigsby to Nancy

GRADY (continued)
Baggett, Feb. 24, 1801 (JM)
GRAEFF, Rev. J. E. to Marriah Morril, June 1, 1853 (EH)
GRAHAM, John C. of Alexandria to Mary Chatham of Alexandria, Oct. 19, 1843 (JJ)
GRANT, John W. to Susan Bowle (free coloured), Feb. 3, 1820 (WHW)
GRAY, James to Prescilla Weed, Sept. 12, 1801 (JM)
Levi to Anne Osburn, Feb. 22, 1814 (JM)
Wm. A. to Ann Busby, Aug. 16, 1809 (IR)
Wm. Jr. of Alexandria to Laura Dundas (coloured) of Alexandria, March 14, 1844 (JJ)
GRAYSON, Spece to Sarah Blunt, Oct. 30, 1811 (JM)
GREEN, Frederick to Catharine Cheverill, Feb. 15, 1812 (JM)
George to Catharine Patterson, March 8, 1802 (JM)
James to Esther H. Hucorn, Oct. 16, 1815 (JM)
Thomas to Susannah Lanham, Sept. 8, 1804 (JM)
GREENE, Thomas B. to Rebecca Hicky, April 24, 1809 (IR)
William to Emily Reynolds, Society of Friends at Woodlawn, Virginia, June 25, 1849 (QM)
GREENWOOD, Benjamin to Catherine Myers, Dec. 4, 1817 (WHW)
GREER, William to Susan Coleman, Sept. 4, 1821

GREER (continued)
(ON)
GREGORY, Douglas L. to Mary L. Mark, June 15, 1853 (EH)
Wm. to Margaret D. Bartleman, Dec. 3, 1822 (WA)
GREW, John of Boston, Massachusetts to Rebecca H. Fowle of Alexandria, May 27, 1835 (JJ)
GRIFFIN, John to Mary Simmons, Aug. 17, 1837 (SGR)
William to Letitia Lannon, April 3, 1804 (JM)
GRIFFITH, David to Mary Williams, Jan. 28, 1804 (WM)
John to Frances Ashton, May 18, 1844 (WR)
Kinsey to Phebe A. Mills, Aug. 1, 1844 (WR)
GRIGSBY, James to Nancy Freeman, Dec. 8, 1814 (WHW)
GRIMES, Thomas to Latitia Hepburn (coloured), Aug. 28, 1821 (ON)
William to Rhode Purkins, July 10, 1811 (IR)
GRISWELL, Lyman to Ann Taylor, June 24, 1830 (JL)
GROVES, Caleb to Nancy Davis, May 28, 1811 (IR)
GRUBB, John to Eliza Kelton, Sept. 19, 1815 (WHW)
GRYMES, Enoch to Mary A. Harrington, July 3, 1834 (CAD)
Robert to Precilla Gray, Nov. 24, 1803 (JM)
Thomas J. T. of King George County, Virginia, to Frances F. Irwin of Alexandria, May 12, 1852 (CBD)

GRYMES (continued)
Wm. of Alexandria to Jane Brooks of Alexandria, Nov. 5, 1846 (JJ)
GULY, Thomas C. to Mary Ann Cohen, Aug. 22, 1822 (See also: Tuley)
GUTHRIE, William to Eliza Couchman, July 29, 1814 (IR)
GUY, John to Winifred Bustle, Dec. 29, 1815 (IR)
GUYTON, George B. to Catherine O. McIntire, Oct. 22, 1835 (EH)
HADEN, Garret to Eleanor Wood, April 17, 1803 (JM)
HALL, Henry of Anne Arundel County, Maryland, to Ann Eliza Berry of Fairfax County, Virginia, June 7, 1827 (WJ)
Isaac to Frances Davis, Lic. Aug. 7, 1838 (IR)
James to Ann Eliza Cox both of Alexandria County, April 5, 1827 (WA)
James to Jane Gray (coloured) both of Alexandria, Nov. 13, 1834 (JJ)
John P. to Martha Jane Smith, Lic. Sept. 28, 1836 (LFM)
John to Jane Eliza Dogan, May 2, 1833 (IR)
Washington to Cecilla Dutchy (both colored), Feb. 12, 1812 (IR)
William to Penelope Graham, Oct. 22, 1818 (JM)
HALLBRIGHT, Joseph to Nancy Campbell, Jan. 19, 1804 (WM)
HALLOWOOD, Charles to Rody Bussell, Oct. 25, 1812 (JM)

HALLS, George to Bertha Furguson, June 16, 1812 (IR)

HAMILTON, Alfred to Hannah Ann Seaton (coloured), March 15, 1846 (JJ)

David to Ann Going, Sept. 11, 1801 (JM)

Prince to Ann Chinn, Oct. 18, 1841 (IR)

Wesley to Delia Page (coloured), Feb. 25, 1830 (JL)

HAMMERSLEY, Francis to Jane Rodgers, March 22, 1816 (JMH)

HAMMILL, Henry to Bridget Cullin, Oct. 11, 1852 (GW)

HAMMIT, John B. to Mary McIntire, May 7, 1829 (EH)

HAMMOCK, Benjamin to Susan Padett, Lic. May 8, 1839 (IR)

HAMMOND, James to Grace Hanson (coloured), Oct. 30, 1822 (ON)

HANCOCK, Andrew of Alexandria to Drucilla Smith of Alexandria, Apr. 5, 1836 (JJ)

John B. to Mary Hull, Sept. 4, 1816 (JMH)

HANDLESS, Moses to Nancy Grant (coloured), Nov. 16, 1815 (WHW)

HANEY, William to Delila Emerson, July 11, 1822 (EH)

HANNON, Walter N. to Ann Daily, Dec. 19, 1815 (ON)

William H. to Mary Hodgkin, Dec. 30, 1813 (JM)

HANSON, Mark to Catharine Townshend (coloured), May 20, 1818 (IR)

Mark to Elizabeth Clarke,

HANSON (continued) May 2, 1822 (EH)

HARDIN, Lauriston B. of Washington, D. C. to Anna M. H. Hooe of Alexandria, Feb. 16, 1836 (JJ)

HARDY, Patrick to Catharine Wheaton, April 16, 1822 (JF)

HARLEY, Enoch to Debby Dewain, Feb. 26, 1804 (JM)

HARMON, Allen C. to Margaret Ann Potter, Dec. 6, 1842 (FM)

Danl. to Mary E. Wood, Feb. 23, 1853 (WBE)

HARMOND, Aaron D. to Mary Pascoe both of Alexandria, May 6, 1823 (WA)

HARPER, Robert to Mary Ann Davis, May 17, 1809 (JM)

Washington to Ann Ellicott, March 15, 1826 (WA)

Wm. to Ann Grimsley, Feb. 1, 1823 (IR)

HARRIDEN, Andrew to Ann Dates, July 31, 1820 (WHW)

HARRIS, Anthony to Fanny Wood (both coloured), Oct. 31, 1816 (ON)

George W. of Alexandria to Eliza Williams of Alexandria, July 18, 1837 (JJ)

Mathias of Prince George's County, Maryland, to Mary Eliz. Mandell of Alexandria, Jan. 11, 1831 (WJ)

Nathan to Margaret W. Corcorn, July 10, 1823 (IR)

Samuel to Laura Budd, May 7, 1835 (EH)

Thomas A. to Imogen Porter, Aug. 12, 1851 (EH)

HARRIS (continued)

Walter to Julia Ann Vernon, April 28, 1829 (WJ)

William to Catharine Ross, Aug. 2, 1820 (LHC)

Rev. Wm. A. of Harrisburg, Pennsylvania, to Catherine A. Butcher of Alexandria, Oct. 11, 1838 (JJ)

HARRISON, Elias to Elizabeth Veitch, May 12, 1820 (JM)

George to Polly Snyder, Oct. 13, 1814 (JM)

George W. to Virginia Smith, Feb. 8, 1853 (WBE)

John D. to Elizabeth Carlin, Dec. 30, 1815 (JMH)

John to Mary Watkins, Sept. 28, 1820 (JM)

HARROWER, Hynaman to Eliza McDonald, Oct. 26, 1815 (JM)

HART, Edward to Eliza Zimmerman, April 2, 1825 (WHW)

John to Elizabeth Urie, Aug. 4, 1836 (WH)

HARTSHORNE, William to Susannah Shreve, June 30, 1803 (TM)

HATHERINGTON, James to Mary Ann B. Yearly, Feb. 24, 1821 (IR)

HATTON, William to Catharine Bruce (coloured), Dec. 31, 1841 (JWR)

HAWKINS, Benjamin to Nancy Willie, Jan. 28, 1801 (JM)

HAWLEY, Rev. William to Wilhelmina S. Potts, Aug. 25, 1818 (ON)

HEAD, Benjamin to Anna Limrick, July 6, 1806 (JM)

HEAD (continued)

Lewis to Sarah Reason, Dec. 5, 1806 (DC)

HEALING, Edward to Martha Dunn, Jan. 15, 1801 (JM)

HELM, Francis L. to Sarah B. McKenney, Sept. 16, 1816 (JM)

HENDERSON, James L. to Julia Ann Moore, Dec. 17, 1829 (James Louis Henderson) (JL)

Tarleton T. to Eliza Ann Hewes, March 29, 1827 (WA)

HENTON, Richard to Julia Ann Armstrong, Nov. 15, 1830 (IR)

HERBERT, Stephen to Eliz. Kirby, June 16, 1834 (CAD)

Wm. U. to Elizabeth Penn, Jan. 23, 1836 (BNB)

HERNDON, Richard N. to Elizabeth Jane Tyler, Oct. 28, 1852 (TDH)

HESTON, Samuel to Susan McKay, May 1, 1823 (IR)

HICKS, William to Chloe Ann Davis, Jan. 2, 1838 (SGR)

HICKSAN, James to Matilda Davis, Dec. 17, 1829 (JL)

HIGDON, John to Rebecca Reynolds, Feb. 21, 1816 (JMH)

Wm. J. of Alexandria to Julia Ann Allen of Alexandria, Feb. 24, 1842 (JJ)

HILL, Godardus to Rachael Logan, Dec. 12, 1809 (IR)

John to Eleanor Calender, Aug. 8, 1822 (JF)

Lawrence to Jane Berry, March 29, 1810 (JM)

HILL (continued)
Richard of Alexandria to Julia Ann Crupper of Alexandria, March 13, 1839 (JJ)
Robert to Elizabeth Curry, Sept. 21, 1841 (Also: Hills) (IR)
Samuel V. to Mary E. Basford, Feb. 3, 1835 (SM)
HILLARY, Washington of Prince George's County, Maryland, to Emeline Jenkins of Alexandria, Dec. 2, 1830 (WJ)
HILLIARD, Joseph to Sophia Lutz, Aug. 15, 1810 (IR)
HILTON, Samuel to Catharine Steel, Feb. 16, 1830 (JL)
HINES, Alfred to Maria Odleton, Aug. 11, 1830 (IR)
John to Isabella Gilbert, Oct. 4, 1820 (WA)
HINGSTON, Nicholas to Jane Evans, Aug. 25, 1825 (WHW)
HODGES, Benj. F. of Prince George's County, Maryland, to Elizabeth A. Claggett of Alexandria, Dec. 15, 1836 (JJ)
Benjamin T. of Prince George's County, Maryland, to Maria Daingerfield, of Alexandria, Oct. 1, 1840 (JJ)
Thomas P. to Mary Gates, Aug. 18, 1842 (FM)
HODGKIN, Robert to Clara Taylor, Sept. 10, 1817 (AG)
HODGKINS, James to Susanna Armstrong, July 14, 1810 (IR)
HOIT, Ruben to Cleary Flan-

HOIT (continued)
agen, Aug. 19, 1810 (JM)
HOOF, Powell to Elizabeth Kessner, March 5, 1816 (WHW)
HOOFF, Charles R. of Alexandria to Rebecca Janney of Alexandria, Sept. 29, 1851 (JJ)
J. Wallace of Alexandria to Jannete Brown of Alexandria, Feb. 17, 1853
HOPKINS, James A. to Matilda Allen, Dec. 21, 1841 (FM)
Wm. to Mary Brooks, Nov. 29, 1814 (WHW)
HORWELL, Charles to Ann Phenix, Sept. 23, 1801 (JM)
Edward C. to Frances E. Settle, Aug. 9, 1842 (FM)
Richard to Susan Sleigh, Sept. 10, 1817 (WHW)
HOUGH, Peyton to Harriet R. Mills, June 2, 1825 (SC)
HOUSTON, John M. of Philadelphia, Pennsylvania, to Mary Larmour of Alexandria, July 5, 1837 (JJ)
HOWARD, Beall Jr. to Elizabeth Roundsavell, 1817 (LHC)
John to Ann Maddox, June 9, 1820 (ON)
John to Ann Yearly, Dec. 25, 1834 (EH)
Samuel to Ann Abbott, May 26, 1823 (JF)
HOXTON, William W., United States Surgeon, United States Army to Eliz. L. Griffith of Alexandria, Nov. 17, 1835 (CBD)
HUBBARD, Jeremiah to Susan Ann M. Patterson,

HUBBARD (continued)
Dec. 22, 1825 (SC)
HUDGES, James to Nancy
Leary, Sept. 26, 1826 (EH)
HUFFMAN, Peter to Aminta
Mason, April 13, 1804
(WM)
HUGAL, George F. to Sarah
H. Carlin, Feb. 4, 1830
(Also: Hugle) (JL)
HUGHES, Benjamin to Har-
riett Price, Lic. July 18,
1837 (Also: Hannah Price)
(IR)
Thomas to Amelia Egling,
May 15, 1802 (JM)
HUGHS, Benj. to Elizabeth
Bell, Aug. 3, 1844 (WR)
HUMPHRIES, Carrel to
Catharine A. Glassgow,
June 17, 1830 (JL)
HUNT, Philip to Rebecca
Yost, Dec. 19, 1811 (JM)
HUNTER, Alexander to Lou-
ise A. A. Chapin, Feb. 2,
1815 (WHW)
Robert to Eunice Hurley,
April 18, 1810 (IR)
Robert to Mary Wood, March
3, 1818 (AG)
Robert W. to Elizabeth
Bryan, Aug. 21, 1817 (AG)
HUNTINGTON, William to
Elizabeth Smitherman,
Dec. 25, 1806 (JM)
HUNTLEY, George to Sarah
Pepper, June 13, 1802
(JM)
HURDLE, Edward James to
Ann Elizabeth Walker,
Dec. 7, 1841 (FM)
Jesse to Rebecca Duty, Feb.
22, 1816 (ON)
Levi to Lydia B. Jenkins
both of Alexandria, June 8,
1830 (WJ)

HURST, Richard to Isabella
Hepburn, Sept. 6, 1835
(EH)
HUTCHENS, B. F. to Sarah
Jarvins, Oct. 17, 1852
(WBE)
HUTTON, Isaac of Wash-
ington to Rebecca E.
Smith of Alexandria, Dec.
16, 1823 (WA)
IRVIN, James to Ann D.
Marshall both of Alex-
andria, Aug 5, 1828 (WJ)
ISACKS, Samuel to Edith
Powell, May 19, 1810 (IR)
ISH, Peter to Hariet Kirk,
Nov. 20, 1817 (AG)
JACKSON, Daniel to Ann
Waters, April 7, 1821
(WHW)
James to Sarah Gray, May 8,
1825 (WHW)
John to Jane A. Simms,
Nov. 10, 1814 (WHW)
John to Susan Madella, Aug.
25, 1853 (WBE)
Styles to Elizabeth Bontz,
Dec. 7, 1808 (IR)
Thomas to Ann Moore, Nov.
20, 1816 (ON)
William to Bridget Roberts,
June 9, 1815 (JM)
Wm. of Alexandria to Eliz-
abeth Guy, Jan. 13, 1842
(JJ)
JACOBS, Edward H. to Ann
Boyd, Jan. 21, 1809 (JM)
George to Sarah A. Childs,
Sept. 23, 1817 (AG)
John to Dorothy Sylvia, Dec.
23, 1817 (Also: Selvey)
(WHW)
Samuel to Hannah Morgan,
1826 (RK)
Thomas to Charlotte Dea-
gon, Dec. 22, 1829 (EH)

JACOBS (continued)

Thos. Jr. to Catharine Henrickson, Aug. 17, 1809 (IR)

JAMES, Henry to Susannah Taylor, Nov. 29, 1804 (JM)

JANNEY, Moses to Judith Laurence, Feb. 21, 1805 (JM)

Samuel H. to Elizabeth Mark, Jan. 10, 1831 (EH)

JARBOW, Andrew to Rachel Johnson (coloured), Nov. 4, 1830 (JL)

JAVINS, Armstead T. to Sabina Huntington, May 18, 1839 (IR)

Harrison to Elizabeth Philips, Lic. Aug. 18, 1844 (IR)

Richard to Virginia Walker, May 17, 1842 (FM)

Wm. to Roda Compton, Sept. 27, 1817 (JMH)

JEFFERY, John to Nancy Henderson, March 14, 1821 (LHC)

JEMMINY, John to Matilda Fiss, April 24, 1815 (WHW)

JENKINS, Wm. H. to Julia A. Javins, Sept. 12, 1833 (CAD)

JENNINGS, Horace to Leantha Dean, Lic. Sept. 21, 1836 (IR)

Matthias to Eugenia Jeffries, Feb. 1, 1849 (ERL)

JEWETT, Joseph H. to Tacy M. Janney at the house of Rich. H. Stabler in Alexandria, Feb. 21, 1850 (QM)

JILLETT, Jeptha to Eliz. Hills, Aug. 19, 1833 (CAD)

JOCHAIM, Henry C. to Lettice Harding, Nov. 22, 1810 (JM)

JOHNSON, Alexius to Eliz. Masters, Dec. 15, 1833 (CAD)

Aquilla to Hetty Carter of Alexandria, July 22, 1827 (WJ)

Samuel to Arminta King, June 13, 1804 (JM)

Theophilus to Polly Fowles, Dec. 30, 1820 (See also: Johnston) (LHC)

William C. of Bristol, Virginia, to Ann E. Washington of Fairfax County, Virginia, March 15, 1831 (WJ)

JOHNSTON, George to Linny Long, Jan. 2, 1818 (IR)

Hezakiah to Nancy Talbott, Nov. 5, 1809 (JM)

James to Caroline Cannon, Dec. 15, 1812 (IR)

Wm. P., M.D. of Savannah, Georgia, to Mary E. Hooe of Alexandria, Dec. 3, 1840 (JJ)

JONES, Abraham to Letty Shavers, July 7, 1831 (EH)

Francis B. to Harriett Wright both of Alexandria, Nov. 4, 1830 (WJ)

John to Catharine McKelvec, May 4, 1844 (WR)

Lewis to Mary Whitmore, July 23, 1816 (JM)

Wesley to Rozetta Baker, Lic. Sept. 21, 1837 (IR)

William to Celestial Campbell, Sept. 14, 1852 (GW)

William to Mary E. Hamilton, Aug. 8, 1841 (JWR)

JULIUS, Jonas to Milly Door (coloured), Jan. ?, 1816 (WHW)

KAIN, Robert E. to Julia A. Sparks, Aug. 19, 1835

23

KAIN (continued)
(BNB)
KEASER, Braxton of Alexandria to Eliza Keaser of Alexandria, D. C., May 15, 1844 (JJ)
KEATING, James R. to Thamer Pernal, Nov. 9, 1818 (ON)
William to Sarah Brown, May 31, 1837 (SGR)
KEENE, Newton to Nancy Dundas, May 23, 1811 (Nancy Hooe Dundas) (JM)
KEIFER, Chr. to Sarah Violett, Sept. 5, 1821 (LHC)
KEITH, Anderson D. to Catherine C. Keith, 1826 (RK)
James to Isabella McMahon, July 22, 1802 (JM)
KELL, Isaac Jr. to Mary Harrison, Dec. 30, 1841 (FM)
KELLY, John to Ellinor Heath, July 18, 1832 (IR)
KEMPFIELD, Isaac to Mary Ann Korne, Oct. 5, 1820 (ON)
KENDALL, Luvig to Endine Stepnay (coloured), May 20, 1841 (JWR)
KENNAN, Joseph to Mary Howard, Nov. 5, 1817 (JMH)
KENNEDY, John to Susanna Maria Kennedy, Feb. 1, 1826 (WA)
KENNER, George to Elizabeth Conner, Dec. 11, 1806 (DC)
KENT, John to Marthe Ballard, Jan. 28, 1802 (JM)
KIBBY, Alex. to B. McFarlane, Sept. 9, 1802 (JM)
KIDWELL, John to Martha Ann Lynn, Sept. 3, 1853

KIDWELL (continued)
(WBE)
KING, Benjamin to Elizabeth Dorcey, June 12, 1806 (JM)
Charles to Anna Sword, Nov. 11, 1827 (SC)
Isaac N. to Hannah C. Spear, July 6, 1820 (WHW)
James to Nancy Groves, June 14, 1815 (JMH)
John W. to Ann W. Childs, Nov. 4, 1830 (JL)
Patrick to Susanna Baggett, June 29, 1811 (IR)
Richard to Mary Davis, Oct. 5, 1820 (ON)
Robert to Margaret Susan McKnight, June 9, 1829 (EH)
Samuel to Elizabeth Gales, June 25, 1801 (JM)
KINGSTON, Thomas to Susan Hodgkins, Jan. 12, 1816 (JM)
KINSOLVING, Ovid A. of Harrison County, Virginia, to Julia H. Krauth of Alexandria, D. C., Nov. 6, 1845 (JJ)
KINZEY, Enoch to Mary Dorcey April 4, 1804 (WM)
KIRBY, Jesse to Rebecca Dudley, Lic. Aug. 15, 1843 (IR)
KIRK, Richard L. to Mary W. Farquhar at the house of Benj. Hallowell, Sept. 19, 1852 (QM)
Samuel to Mary McCue, July 27, 1809 (IR)
Samuel to Rebecca Fletcher, July 20, 1815 (IR)
KNOWEL, James to Ann Boothe, Aug. 26, 1824 (WA)

KNOWLES, John to Mary Ann Westcott, Oct. 12, 1815 (JM)

KOON, Richard to Ann Ratcliff, Dec. 7, 1817 (IR)

LABILLE, Louis J. C. to Mary O'Neale, Aug. 5, 1823 (JF)

LADD, William to Sophia Ann Stidolph, Oct. 19, 1801 (JM)

LAMAR, G. B. to Harriett Cazenove, July 11, 1839 (EH)

LAMBERT, George to Catharine Denneson, Oct. 30, 1811 (IR)

Joseph to Mary Bogan, Jan. 1, 1817 (IR)

LANDRES, Henry White to Maria Thompson, July 23, 1803 (JM)

LANDRESS, Henry W. to Nancy Davis, April 12, 1801 (JM)

LANHAM, Elisha to Mary Ann Jenkins, July 10, 1817 (AG)

John to Ann McFadden, Sept. 5, 1802 (JM)

John to Catharine Snell, Feb. 3, 1810 (JM)

John to Olphair Longdon, Oct. 22, 1801 (JM)

LARMOUR, Samuel B. to Susan Mandeville, Dec. 29, 1814 (WHW)

LATHRAM, Edward to Rachel Stephenson, Feb. 19, 1818 (See also: Latham) (WHW)

LATRUITE, William to Barbara More, April 9, 1821 (See also: Moore) (JM)

LAURENCE, George to Sarah Caderton, Jan. 19, 1804

LAURENCE (continued) (WM)

Joseph to Mickey Gaenolds, Jan. 13, 1814 (JM)

Wm. to Rebecca Marle, Feb. 3, 1803 (JM)

LAURIE, Rev. James to Elizabeth B. Hall, April 4, 1815 (JM)

LAWRENCE, James to Betsey Brin, Sept. 6, 1815 (JM)

LAWSON, John to Elizabeth May 24, 1821 (ON)

LEDDY, Hugh to Charlotte Summers, Aug. 19, 1822 (JF)

LEDERER, John Leonard to Frances M. Porcell, both of Alexandria, May 28, 1835 (JJ)

LEDUM, Isaac to Ann Godwin, April 23, 1822 (Also: Gooding) (ON)

LEE, Aaron to Polly Parker (coloured), May 3, 1815 (WHW)

Cassius Francis of Alexandria, D. C. to Ann Eliza Gardner of Alexandria, D. C., Apr. 15, 1846 (JJ)

Charles H. of Alexandria, D. C. To Elizabeth A. Dunbar of Alexandria, D. C. Nov. 7, 1844 (JJ)

Hancock to Mary Nicholson Jan. 22, 1818 (Fairfax County) (WHW)

John to Mary Chitterson, Nov. 24, 1825 (SC)

John to Sarah Ann Riley, Dec. 26, 1832 (IR)

Richard H. to Mary Green, April 15, 1816 (JM)

Sydney Smith of the United States Navy to Anna Maria

LEE (continued)
Mason of Fairfax County, Virginia, Feb. 5, 1835 (Robert E. Lee's brother) (CBD)

LEIBERMAN, Charles H. of Washington City to Louisa C. Betzold of Alexandria, Feb. 18, 1841 (JJ)

LEIMAIN, Wm. of Alexandria To Lucretia Allen of Alexandria, Dec. 24, 1840 (JJ)

LEONARD, Jacob to Sophia E. Faw, Nov. 3, 1814 (WHW)

LESLIE, Benjamin to Rebecca Kinsey, March 23, 1814 (JM)

Henry P. of the County of Norfolk, Virginia, to Helen Marion Gray of the County of Alexandria, Aug. 8, 1836 (ERL)

LEVERMAN, John to Elizabeth Devereux, August 15, 1801 (JM)

LEWIS, Ansel to Jane M. Campbell, Feb. 7, 1818 (JM)

Enoch M. to Julian M. Faw, Nov. 14, 1815 (WHW)

James B. of Jefferson County, Virginia, to Catherine Ann Hume of Alexandria, June 16, 1841 (JJ)

Joseph to Elizabeth Holton, Feb. 1823 (No day given) (JF)

Levey to Agnes Richardson, Feb. 10, 1831 (IR)

Reeve of Alexandria to Sarah Eliza McIntire of Alexandria, Apr. 6 1837 (JJ)

Robert A. to Eleanor Mattox, Feb. 9, 1815 (WHW)

LEWIS (continued)
Thomas to Nancy Evans, May 29, 1815 (JM)

William to Salome Way, Dec. 18, 1806 (JM)

LIGHTFOOT, George to Ann Sanford, Nov. 12, 1812 (JM)

John M. to Elizabeth Sandford, June 14, 1801 (JM)

LINDSAY, William to Mary Ketling, Nov. 13, 1817 (IR)

LINDSEY, James to Julia A. Walker, Sept. 10, 1844 (WR)

LINTON, George to Henrietta McKinney, Feb. 10, 1810 (JM)

William to Letitia Hartley, May 17, 1804 (JM)

LIPSCOM, W. to Phebe Adgate, Nov. 30, 1815 (WHW)

LITTLEFIELD, Theodore to Susanna Markley, Aug. 18, 1844 (WR)

LLOYD, John J. of Baltimore, Maryland, to Eliza Armistead Selden of Alexandria County, D. C., Oct. 16, 1845 (ERL)

LOCKAN, James Jr. to Mimay Simpson, Oct. 6, 1813 (JM)

LOGAN, Hugh M. to Elizabeth Currie, Oct. 15, 1815 (WHW)

John to Jane Fuller (coloured), Dec. 23, 1818 (WHW)

William to Elizabeth Williams, Nov. 1, 1821 (ON)

LOMAX, John to Elizabeth McClea, Dec. 14, 1803 (JM)

LONG, Seth to Sarah Harper,

LONG (continued)
Oct. 9, 1806 (JM)
LONGDEN, George C. to
Elizabeth Ann Scott, Sept.
7, 1813 (JM)
LONGDON, John A. to
Elizabeth Howard, Nov.
12, 1816 (ON)
LOVEJOY, John A. to Nancy
Halls, May 20, 1815 (IR)
LOVEL, Ezekiel to Mary Ann
Reyly, Dec. 30, 1830 (EH)
LOVELESS, Nance to Alley
Dove, Jan. 6, 1814 (ON)
LOWE, Thomas to Mary Ann
Bryan, March 1, 1820 (AG)
Thomas to Mary Cannon,
July 22, 1806 (JM)
LOWRIE, Rev. John C. to
Louisa A. Wilson, March
5, 1833 (EH)
LOWRY, James to Judith
Swann, Nov. 6, 1829 (IR)
LUSCABET, Jesse W. H. to
Jane E. Walker, May 17,
1852 (WBE)
LUTTZTO, George to Eliza-
beth Lee, Nov. 20, 1806
(DC)
LUVIG, William H. to Mary
E. McQueen (coloured),
June 3, 1841 (JWR)
LYLES, Dennis M. to Eliza
W. Seaton, Nov. 13, 1817
(WHW)
Henry to Mary Davis, Oct.
31, 1805 (JM)
James to Mary Ann Davis,
June 5, 1811 (IR)
John to Betsy Tridle, Jan. 8,
1818 (IR)
Thomas C. to Rebecca Sea-
ton, Jan. 12, 1814 (WHW)
William to Hannah Smith,
Nov. 16, 1830 (IR)
LYNCH, James to Catherine

LYNCH (continued)
Neale, Dec. 29, 1826 (SC)
Samuel J. to Elizabeth
Karkeek, July 11, 1822
(EH)
LYON, Andrew to Mary Mas-
sey, Feb. 26, 1805 (JM)
LYONS, John J. to Catharine
Tyler, Dec. 9, 1829 (IR)
Vincent to Eliza Semms,
July 23, 1820 (WHW)
M'CORMACK, Bernard to
Lucy Marbury, Oct. 27,
1801 (JM)
M'DOUGALL, Daniel to Mary
Talbot, Sept. 17, 1801
(JM)
M'GLENN, William to Rosa
Latham, July 22, 1817
(WHW)
M'KENZIE, Capt. to Cas-
sandra Smith, June 29,
1815 (WHW)
MACE, Wm. to Sarah E. Sit-
lar, Feb. 6, 1853 (WBE)
MACHINHEIMER, George L.
of Alexandria to Elizabeth
Page of Alexandria, Oct.
23, 1827 (WJ)
MacPHERSON, Col. to Julia
Chapin, Nov. 7, 1815
(WHW)
MAFFITT, Wm. to Harriet
Turberville, May 5, 1803
(JM)
MAHONY, John to Ann Un-
derwood, May 9, 1818 (ON)
MANDELL, John C. to Susan
Smedley, Dec. 29, 1835
(BNB)
MANKIN, Charles to Sarah J.
Legg, Aug. 15, 1850 (LR)
MANLY, Francis to Helen
Lewis, Dec. 30, 1841 (FM)
MARBLE, Henry to Betsy
Clark (coloured) July 26,

MARBLE (continued)
1816 (WHW)

MARBURY, John H. of Prince George's County, Maryland, to Eliza C. Fendall of Alexandria, Dec. 23, 1830 (WJ)

Leonard to Margaret Dyer, Dec. 22, 1831 (EH)

Leonard to Mary W. Hunter, Aug. 20, 1816 (JM)

MARKELL, Samuel of Alexandria, D. C. to Eliz. Churchman, Feb. 18, 1841 (JJ)

MARLE, David to E. H. Smith, Sept. 30, 1813 (JM)

MARRIOT, John to Jane Hurdleston, Aug. 6, 1844 (WR)

MARTIN, James to E. J. Johnson, Oct. 10, 1843 (WR)

John to Nancy Cook, May 21, 1806 (DC)

William to Mary Woodrow, Oct. 17, 1805 (JM)

MARVEL, David to Ann Grymes, March 3, 1803 (WM)

MASKEL, Joseph to Sarah Marston, Sept. 4, 1830 (EH)

MASKETT, Wm. A. to E. O'Neal, Dec. 12, 1843 (WR)

MASON, Benjamin to Mary Ann Stone, Sept. 1, 1804 (JM)

John to Jane Lithcoe, June 13, 1806 (JM)

MASSEY, Rudolph of Alexandria, D. C. to Ursula Daley of Alexandria, D. C., April 29, 1845 (JJ)

MASSIE, William J. B. of

MASSIE (continued)
New Orleans to Elizabeth G. Ashton of Alexandria, Aug. 19, 1835 (CBD)

MASSOLETTI, Vincent to Sarah M. Horwell, Oct. 27, 1818 (WHW)

MASTER, William to Elizabeth Johnson, Aug. 17, 1818 (IR)

MASTERS, Capt. John R. to Hannah M. Baird, Jan. 23, 1849 (EH)

MATTHEWS, Jabez to Sarah McPherson, Nov. 26, 1803 (JM)

James to Mildred Powell, Jan. 25, 1827 (SC)

MAXWELL, Geo. W. of Alexandria to Alvina V. Churchman of Alexandria, June 2, 1840 (JJ)

MAY, John to Sally Howard, Jan. 3, 1811 (FB)

MAYHOLE, James to Ann Ellis, March 5, 1801 (JM)

McBRIDE, Alexander to Susan Crandle, 1818 (LHC)

McCABE, Edward to Lucy Wood, April 22, 1813 (IR)

McCARTY, James to Betsy William, Oct. 17, 1833 (IR)

McCAUGHAN, Thomas to Mary Taylor, July 3, 1803 (JM)

McCAULY, William to Elizabeth Jones, Sept. 12, 1812 (IR)

McCLATELY, John P. to Rachel Ann Sewell of Alexandria, Sept. 13, 1852 (?D)

McCLEAN, Allen to Jane Turner, 1826 (RK)

McCOBB, John to Sarah

McCOBB (continued)
Weston, May 13, 1802 (JM)
Thomas F. of Washington County to Marion L. Berry of Alexandria, Sept. 21, 1841 (ERL)
McCREA, Peter to Mary Reynolds, March 27, 1803 (JM)
McDUMICK, James to Lydia Talbot, April 24, 1803 (JM)
McELHENNEY, William to Hannah Ingram, Feb. 22, 1814 (JM)
McFARLIN, George to Kitty Richards, Jan. 24, 1802 (JM)
McFLHANY, James of Loudon County to Elizabeth Johnston of Alexandria, Oct. 22, 1850 (CBD)
McGUIRE, Rev. Ed. C. to Judith Lewis, April 17, 1816 (WHW)
Thomas to Elizabeth Arnold, July 11, 1852 (?D)
McKAY, Benjamin to Ellenor Swann, July 27, 1815 (IR)
McKENZIE, James to Sarah E. Sanford, Sept. 22, 1829 (EH)
McKEWIN, Robert of Alexandria to Mary McKewin of Alexandria, May 16, 1850 (JJ)
McLANE, Isaac to Mary Turner, April 2, 1801 (JM)
McLEAN, Andrew to Ann Eliza Sellers, April 9, 1822 (EH)
Samuel to Susan W. Smoot, June 1, 1820 (WHW)
McNEIL, Patrick to Mariah Night, Dec. 2, 1809 (JM)

McNISH, Horatio to Susan O. Dean, March 12, 1821 (Also: Deane) (JM)
McPHERSON, Samuel W. H. of Charles County, Maryland, to Elizabeth C. Marbury of Alexandria, Feb. 14, 1843 (JJ)
McQUIN, John S. to Elizabeth M. Young, Oct. 28, 1850 (EH)
McWILLIAMS, Andrew to Nancy Wiseman, May 10, 1825 (WHW)
MEAD, Theodore to Catherine Ann Padgett, Dec. 14, 1841 (FM)
MEADS, Samuel to Ellenor McCutcheon, April 21, 1808 (IR)
MERCER, John Francis to Mary Swann June 25, 1818 (ON)
MERCY, Robert to Susannah Mertland, June 23, 1803 (JM)
MIDDLETON, David to Hannah Harris, June 24, 1830 (IR)
Henry O. to Nancy Tollson, Feb. 15, 1814 (WHW)
MILBURNE, Benedict of Alexandria to Thirza Coad of Alexandria, June 10, 1828 (WJ)
MILLAS, Benjamin to Mary Ross, April 26, 1825 (Also: Milles) (WA)
MILLER, Charles B. to Roberta E. Edmonds, Oct. 11, 1842 (FM)
Elisha J. to Bettie S. Ashby, June 1, 1853 (WBE)
Robert to Elizabeth Howard, Oct. 5, 1815 (JM)
Samuel to Catharine Smith,

29

MILLER (continued)
Oct. 20, 1853 (WBE)
MILLIKIN, Francis to Casa
Taylor, Sept. 5, 1815
(WHW)
MILLINGTON, Richard to
Peggy Thompson, April
22, 1813 (IR)
MILLS, James to Fidelia
Taylor, Feb. 9, 1815
(WHW)
Robert A. to Martha Russell,
Dec. 8, 1814 (WHW)
William Nelson to Ann
Leap, Feb. 26, 1806 (JM)
William to Lucinda Fugitt,
Aug. 26, 1818 (JM)
MINOR, Phillip H. to Sarah
W. Washington, May 9,
1816 (ON)
MITCHELL, Thomas to Lu-
cretia Brett, June 27, 1824
(WA)
William to Mary Lanham,
June 14, 1816 (IR)
MOFFIT, John to Matilda
Ann Vardin, Sept. 21, 1820
(See also: Moffett) (JM)
MONCH, Wm. to Catherine
Febegin both of Alex-
andria, March 6, 1853
MONROE, Thomas to Geor-
giana Kelton, April 22,
1826 (SC)
MOODY, John to Sarah Bai-
ley, Nov. 30, 1809 (IR)
MOORE, Alexander to Caro-
line Cottringer, June 7,
1822 (JF)
Wm. of Alexandria to Ann
Jones of Alexandria,
March 17, 1842 (JJ)
MORELAND, Hanson to Sa-
rah Atkins, Sept. 7, 1809
(JM)
MORGAN, Alexander to

MORGAN (continued)
Catharine Padgett, Aug.
14, 1821 (ON)
Hiram to Elizabeth Young,
Oct. 13, 1842 (See also:
Henry Morgan) (FM)
John to Barbara Myers both
of Alexandria, April 22,
1830 (WJ)
W. to Patty Ransom (col-
oured), May 4, 1815
(WHW)
William to Martha Johnson,
Sept. 4, 1817 (AG)
MORISON, Samuel to Mar-
garet McFarlin, Nov. 18,
1841 (FM)
MORRIS, Gouverneur of Mor-
risania, New York, to Pat-
sey Jefferson Cary of
Alexandria, Jan. 10, 1842
(JJ)
Henry to Maria Payne, Dec.
1, 1815 (WHW)
L. to Sarah Walker, Sept.
22, 1812 (JM)
MOSEBY, John to Sarah
Jenkins, June 3, 1807 (IR)
MOTHERSHEAD, Christopher
to Jane Keatly, Feb. 24,
1831 (JL)
Vincent L. to Mary Laskey,
Dec. 1, 1853 (WBE)
MUIR, John to Lydia Robin-
son, Nov. 16, 1830 (JL)
Wm. H. of Alexandria to
Eliza Ann Green, of
Alexandria, April 27, 1841
(JJ)
MULLIN, Lumsford to Mary
Mullin, Dec. 24, 1833
(CAD)
MURPHY, John to Joanna
Lawless, Oct. 2, 1852
(GW)
John to Margaret M. Man–

MURPHY (continued)
ning, March 14, 1811 (JM)
MURRAY, Edward to Hepzaba Goodwin, May 11, 1801 (JM)
Francis to Lucretia Cattison, Oct. 24, 1801 (JM)
Lemuel N. to Mary Correl, July 7, 1829 (JL)
Oliver to Lucretia Shermandino, Oct. 6, 1817 (WHW)
Thomas to Margaret McDonald, Dec. 12, 1816 (JM)
Thomas to Mary Pendall, Oct. 27, 1803 (JM)
MUSE, Elliott to Hannah Hunter, Feb. 10, 1814 (WHW)
Wm. to Mary Edmondson, March 31, 1825 (SC)
MYERS, George W. to Phoebe Heikling both of Alexandria, May 1, 1828 (Also: Henklin) (WJ)
John to Margaret Stevenson, 1817 (LHC)
Joseph G. to Susannah Ballinger, Oct. 16, 1826 (EH)
NALLS, George W. to Martha Brent, April 28, 1841 (IR)
NEALE, Aloyisius to Elizabeth L. A. Brandt, July 30, 1818 (JF)
NELSON, Geo. W. to Elizabeth Armstrong, Lic. Dec. 8, 1836 (LFM)
NEWTON, Albert G. of Alexandria County to Harriet Louisa Pratt of Alexandria County, May 18, 1843 (EK)
NICHING, Wm. to Rebecca Lucas (coloured), May 13, 1841 (JWR)
NICHOLAS, Zachariah to Jesica Baggott, Feb. 3,

NICHOLAS (continued)
1820 (JF)
NICHOLS, John to Martha Thomas (coloured), July 25, 1812 (WHW)
NICHOLSON, Henry to Ann Ballard, Oct. 27, 1803 (JM)
Joseph to Elizabeth Frank, May 15, 1803 (SA)
Thomas to Sarah Baker, Jan. 31, 1803 (SA)
NICKENS, John to Lucy Brown, Dec. 22, 1835 (BNB)
NICKOLSON, Henry to Margaret Hyneman, June 14, 1814 (JM)
NOLAND, Philip to Jane Foote (coloured), Dec. 31, 1818 (WHW)
NORRIS, James of Alexandria to Georgianna C. Gray of Alexandria, Oct. 26, 1841 (JJ)
James to Susanna Patrerell, Feb. 10, 1814 (WHW)
Joseph to Winnifred Dorsey, Dec. 17, 1801 (JM)
NORRISS, James to Lucy Longdon, Nov. 4, 1813 (JM)
NOYES, Robert to Mary G. Skinner, 1818 (LHC)
O'NEIL, Robert to Margaret Anderson, June I, 1809 (IR)
OGDON, Hezekiah to Mary Elizabeth Phillips, Lic. Sept. 14, 1837 (IR)
OGHTON, Anthony to Ellen Johnson (coloured), May 30, 1841 (JWR)
OSBURN, Dennis to Jane Howard, Nov. 12, 1818 (IR)
Lawson to Elizabeth Thom-

OSBURN (continued)
as, Nov. 16, 1815 (IR)
OSGOOD, Isaac to Jane Bean both of Alexandria, Feb. 6, 1820 (WA)
OSWALD, Henry to Martha Kelly, Feb. 16, 1804 (JM)
OWEN, James H. to Jane Hammond, August 14, 1811 (IR)
OWENS, Robert to Susan Windsor, May 18, 1852 (WBE)
PADGET, George R. to Rebecca Sheriff, Jan. 9, 1853 (WBE)
PADGETT, Geo. H. to Mary E. French, Dec. 11, 1851 (?D)
John to Ann Louisa Robinson, June 29, 1841 (JWR)
Joseph to Mary Ann Jefferson, June 10, 1830 (JL)
William to Sarah Padgett, Aug. 20, 1822 (EH)
PARISH, Charles J. to Mary Jane Thompson, June 23, 1852 (?D)
PARK, Alexander to Harriett G. Reed, Aug. 1, 1833 (CAD)
PARKER, Jesse to Sarah Green (coloured), Oct. 2, 1817 (WHW)
John to Mary Hill, Oct. 27, 1805 (JM)
Samuel to Ann Watson, Sept. 18, 1820 (LHC)
PARKS, George to Sarah Church, Dec. 15, 1813 (JM)
PARSONS, John to Ann M. Askin, Dec. 18, 1822 (ON)
Tho. to Sarah Ann Baker, Jan. 28, 1829 (IR)
Walter to Sarah Williams,

PARSONS (continued)
August 27, 1811 (JM)
Wm. to Margaretta B. Thomas, July 6, 1815 (IR)
PASCOE, Frederick to Eliza Douglass, April 10, 1830 (EH)
John L. to Ann Rebecca Shirly, April 24, 1831 (JL)
William to Sarah Ann Johnston, April 10, 1833 (EH)
PATERSON, James D. to Joanna Kincaid, Jan. 20, 1818 (JM)
PATTERSON, Joseph to Elizabeth Kune, May 22, 1803 (JM)
Wm. to Sally Simpson, March 25, 1828 (SC)
PATTON, John to Dorcas Green, Jan. 17, 1822 (ON)
PAUL, Zechariah to Elizabeth Bowling, July 21, 1810 (JM)
PAYNE, Larkin to Nancy Payne, Oct. 12, 1816 (JMH)
London to Sarah Boots, Nov. 10, 1815 (JMH)
Os... L. of Washington D.C. to Mary Alton Jewett of Fairfax County, Virginia, May 5, 1831 (WJ)
PEACHY, William S. of James City, Virginia, to Virginia B. Daingerfield of Alexandria, D. C., Oct. 9, 1843 (JJ)
PELTON, Enoch to Sarah M. Patterson, Dec. 23, 1802 (JM)
PEMBROKE, Thomas to Desdemonia West (coloured), Aug. 15, 1815 (WHW)

PERKINS, Francis to Ann Smith, May 25, 1803 (JM)

PERRY, Alexander to Henrietta Solers both of Alexandria, Sept. 4, 1823 (Also: Sollers) (WA)

PEVERELL, Isaac of Alexandria to Mary E. Craven of Alexandria, May 16, 1850 (JJ)

PEYTON, Thomas West to Sophia Matilda Dundas, Feb. 26, 1811 (JM)

PHILIPS, James to Eliza Avery, Jan. 24, 1816 (IR)

John to Lucy Hillman, Oct. 11, 1817 (AG)

William to Kitura Ball, Dec. 20, 1815 (IR)

PICKERING, Levi to Sarah Norris, Dec. 29, 1812 (IR)

PICKETT, Albert G. to Elizabeth Harris, Jan. 19, 1837 (WH)

PIERCE, Thomas to Elizabeth Mandley, Sept. 3, 1812 (JM)

PIERSIN, Thomas W. to Rose McGlennin, Jan. 10, 1822 (JF)

PILES, Christian to Sarah Brooks, May 26, 1817 (AG)

Lewis to Ann Harriss, April 28, 1803 (JM)

PILTER, James to Sarah Duff, May 19, 1808 (IR)

PIPER, James to Catharine Bontz, Aug. 11, 1807 (IR)

PIPSICO, Franklin to Lucy Ann Chapman, Dec. 21, 1843 (EK)

PLANT, James to Alice M. Bowie, Sept. 1, 1825 (WHW)

PLEASANTS, Rev. Chas. E. of St. Andrews, Wil-

PLEASANTS (continued) mington, Delaware, to Caroline Wattles of Alexandria, Jan. 7, 1836 (JJ)

PLUMB, Joseph to Elizabeth Marie, August 1, 1803 (JM)

PLUMMER, Charles P. to Eliza Dougherty, 1817 (LHC)

Samuel to Lucy Talbot, July 22, 1817 (WHW)

POLLOCK, George to Elizabeth Shropshire, Sept. 3, 1804 (DC)

POMELY, John to Fanny Grinnage, March 22, 1827 (SC)

POMERY, John F. of Alexandria to Margaret Churchman of Alexandria, May 9, 1839 (JJ)

POPHAM, John to Mary Ann Thompson, April 14, 1818 (ON)

PORTER, Denton S. of Washington City to Priscilla C. Norfolk of Alexandria County, June 10, 1845 (JJ)

John to Rosanna Speaks, Aug. 1, 1801 (WM)

POSEY, Henry to Elizabeth King, May 20, 1812 (JM)

James to Cecelia Lee (coloured), April 23, 1822 (ON)

POSTEN, John to Ann Major, Feb. 18, 1830 (JL)

POSTON, Francis E. to Amelia Day, Oct. 7, 1816 (JM)

POTTER, Rheuben to Fanny Chadwell, Feb. 12, 1801 (JM)

POWELL, Alfred to Ann Far,

POWELL (continued)
April 29, 1820 (IR)

PREBLE, Edward Dearing of Portland, Maine to Sophia Elizabeth Wattles of Alexandria, Virginia, Nov. 11, 1833 (JJ)

PRICE, David to Margaret Crook, August 1, 1810 (IR)

Ellis L. of Alexandria to Judith P. Butts of Alexandria, May 18, 1837 (JJ)

PRING, Henry to Mary Ann Grimes, June 7, 1820 (ON)

PRITCHARD, Stephen to Sarah Ballenger, April 3, 1818 (Bond dated April 23) (JM)

PROCTOR, John J. to Rosetta L. Taylor at Mrs. Tatspaugh's, July 10, 1834 (AW)

PUPPO, Daniel C. to Elizabeth Stroman, September 6, 1803 (JM)

QUEST, John W. of Fairfax County, Virginia, to Jane Wescott of Alexandria, April 2, 1828 (WJ)

QUINN, Wm. to Louisa Whittington, April 19, 1823 (IR)

RAND, Saml. F. of Portland, Maine to Sarah Jane Smith of Alexandria, Mar. 15, 1849 (JJ)

RANDALL, Theophelus to Ann Clifford, Feb. 22, 1816 (IR)

RATCLIFFE, Richard to Ann Damaine, March 31, 1825 (WA)

RAWLINGS, John T. to Jane Brookes, Jan. 19, 1811 (JM)

REED, Ellis to Betsy Cree-

REED (continued)
dy, Dec. 10, 1817 (JMH)

Frank to Polly Johnson, June 7, 1827 (SC)

Sandford to Ann Feilder Patton, June 20, 1816 (IR)

Thomas to Mary Sexton, June 1, 1809 (IR)

William to Catharine Hutcheson , Oct. 24, 1805 (DC)

REILLY, William to Sabina Kent, Dec. 20, 1803 (JM)

REXTER, Ludwell Jr. to Rachel Satterwhite, July 8, 1829 (JL)

REYNOLDS, John to Elizabeth Simpson, Sept. 24, 1803 (JM)

John to Mary Lee, Sept. 27, 1809 (JM)

William to Margaret McAllister, Feb. 15, 1821 (JM)

Wm. to Phoebe Veitch, Dec. 28, 1831 (JL)

RHODES, Augustus C. of Baltimore to Virginia C. Hewitt of Alexandria, Nov. 17, 1852 (JJ)

RICE, George to Hannah O'Conner, Jan. 21, 1812 (IR)

RICHARDS, John Jr., M.D. of Alexandria to Laura Peyton, April 19, 1841 (JJ)

John to Rebecca Carlin, Sept. 20, 1815 (JMH)

RICHARDSON, Judson to Milley Richards, July 18, 1811 (JM)

RICHEY, William to Ann Maria May both of Alexandria, Feb. 19, 1828 (WJ)

RICHTER, John to Mary Etser, May 23, 1802 (JM)

RICKS, George to Ellenor

34

RICKS (continued)
Johnson, June 22, 1816 (JMH)
RIGGS, Elisha to Alice Lawrason, Sept. 17, 1812 (WHW)
Romulus to Mary Anne Lawrason, May 29, 1810 (FB)
RISTORO, James S. of Alexandria to Mary E. Whitmore of Alexandria, Jan. 13, 1853 (JJ)
ROACH, John to Monica Drury, June 14, 1801 (JM)
ROBBINS, Isaac to Mary D. Howell, Sept. 3, 1803 (HJ)
ROBINSON, Edward to Jane A. Kenner, Jan. 28, 1817 (WHW)
Richard to Susan J. Crupper, Oct. 10, 1844 (WR)
ROBY, Joseph to Margaret Simpson, Aug. 15, 1822 (Also: Robey) (EH)
ROCK, Richard to Margaret Spunaugle, Dec. 10, 1812 (JM)
ROGERS, William to Elizabeth Allison, Oct. 15, 1818 (IR)
ROSE, Henry B. to Ann R. Dunbar, Nov. 3, 1825 (EH)
Henry S. to Jane Shaw, Dec. 26, 1826 (EH)
ROSS, Samuel to Sarah Hamilton, March 9, 1816 (IR)
ROTCH, George to Susan McBride, Feb. 9, 1825 (SC)
John to Melinda Rotch, May 21, 1819 (JF)
RUDD, James to Belinda Wood at Mrs. McCloud's, Oct. 9, 1834 (AW)
Richard A. to Elizabeth

RUDD (continued)
Ward, July 26, 1821 (IR)
RUNKLES, David to Eliza Gould, March 24, 1824 (WA)
RUSHMAN, William to Harriet Clarke, Lic. Oct. 14, 1836 (LFM)
RUSSELL, John B. F. to Cornelia Peyton, Feb. 28, 1828 (both of Alexandria) (WJ)
William to Rhody Clark, Jan. 15, 1809 (JM)
William W. to Virginia Fletcher of Alexandria, Oct. 15, 1850 (CBD)
Rev. Wm. C., Rector of St. Andrews in Wilmington, Delaware, to Margaret A.B. Brown of Alexandria, D. C., Dec. 1, 1835 (JJ)
RUSTICK, Thomas to Eliza. Peirce, June 4, 1803 (JM)
RYE, Jesse to Jane V. Asker, July 30, 1828 (IR)
SAMPSON, Henry to Sarah F. Berry, Oct. 29, 1853 (WBE)
SANDERSON, Samuel to Sarah Day, both of Alexandria, Jan. 21, 1836 (JJ)
SANFORD, Manly Whiting to Deborah Mitchell both of Delaware, (No date given) (WA)
SANGER, Stephen S. to Mary Lowe, June 13, 1833 (CAD)
SAX, Joseph to Lucy Yost, May 28, 1820 (ON)
SAYRES, John J. of Jefferson County, Virginia, to Matidae Roberts of Alexandria, Dec. 17, 1829 (See also: Sayrs) (WJ)

SCOTT, Charles to Elizabeth Beadle, Sept. 23, 1806 (JM)

Horatio to Caroline Koones, June 1, 1815 (WHW)

James to Mary Adgete, Nov. 26, 1801 (JM)

Robert to Mary Ann Lewis, Sept. 23, 1818 (WHW)

S. E. to Maria Mandeville, July 17, 1817 (WHW)

Thomas to Mary Chafline, July 10, 1810 (JM)

Thomas to Sarah A. Davis, June 24, 1852 (WBE)

SEAMAN, John L. to Martha Cooke, Nov. 7, 1818 (JM)

SEPPLES, Sam. S. of Alexandria to Elizabeth Duffey of Alexandria, Oct. 8, 1851 (JJ)

SERGEANT, John to Peggy Moody, Dec. 16, 1810 (FB)

SERVOIRE, William to Mary Ramsey (coloured), April 19, 1822 (ON)

SHAKESPEARE, William to Susannah Price, July 27, 1801 (WM)

SHAME, James to Louisa Frey, Dec. 26, 1839 (EH)

SHEDD, Wm. P. to Cath. M. Simms, May 20, 1834 (CAD)

SHEPARD, William B. to Charlotti Busti Cazenove, Oct. 7, 1834 (EH)

SHERIFF, John A. to Mary C. D. Padget, Oct. 19, 1852 (WBE)

Joshua to Mary Locker, Feb. 19, 1811 (JM)

Samuel to Susannah Locker, Jan. 8, 1812 (JM)

SHERWOOD, George Lewis to Jane M. Davis, Dec. 29,

SHERWOOD (continued) 1842 (FM)

Jesse to Sarah Brooke, Dec. 5, 1844 (WR)

Lewellen to Polly Robinson, June 4, 1815 (JM)

SHIELDS, John to Nancy Ward, August 12, 1811 (IR)

Thomas to Elizabeth Stevens, April 28, 1810 (IR)

Thomas to Mary Ann Gee, April 2, 1807 (DC)

SHREVE, Benjamin to Sarah Kitely, Jan. 14, 1802 (JM)

SHROLD, James S. to Ann R. Cannon, Jan. 3, 1842 (FM)

SHUCK, Frederick to Elizabeth Bogan, March 14, 1805 (JM)

SIDES, Geo. W. of Baltimore, Maryland, to Jane E. Hudgens of Alexandria, June 2, 1850 (JJ)

SILICK, James to Mary Ann Nicholson, Feb. 19, 1840 (EH)

SIMMONS, Cyrus to Mary E. Edward, Aug. 2, 1832 (IR)

SIMMS, James to Betsey Lightfoot, Jan. 9, 1803 (JM)

John to Elizabeth Petitt, Lic. June 16,1836 (IR)

SIMPSON, Alfred to Susanna Cash, Dec. 3, 1817 (AG)

Gilbert to Susannah Zimmerman, Feb. 3, 1803 (JM)

Harrison to Sarah Randell, May 23, 1816 (See also: Hanson Simpson) (IR)

Peter W. to Mary Mohler, Feb. 26, 1852 (EH)

William to Elizabeth Davis, Jan 8, 1816 (IR)

36

SIPPLE, Samuel to Mary Ann
Hookes, April 24, 1822
(EH)
SKIDMORE, Jesse to Sarah
Boyd, Oct. 18, 1815 (JMH)
SKINNER, Burditt to Mar-
garet Cheshier, March 20,
1816 (IR)
Wm. A. to Aletha Moan,
March 3, 1816 (ON)
SLATER, John to Mary E.
longdon at Rev. Webster's
residence, June 17, 1834
(AW)
SLEIGH, Isaac to Maria
Bowie, April 29, 1819 (JM)
SLIMMER, Daniel to Ellinor
Williams, March 10, 1810
(IR)
SLOAN, James to Harriott
Throop, Sept. 9, 1809 (IR)
SLY, John L. to Susanne Cur-
tain, June 22, 1801 (JM)
SMALL, Noah to Lucretia
Jackson, 1818 (LHC)
SMITH, Charles to Elizabeth
Loyd, Dec. 25, 1814 (JM)
Charles to Mary H. Bowie,
1818 (LHC)
Daniel to Amanda F. Bull
(coloured), Nov. 15, 1842
(FM)
Daniel to Betsy Stithley,
Oct. 29, 1801 (JM)
George W. to Mary Norris,
Oct. 3, 1843 (WR)
Isaac to Mary Welsh, Feb.
26, 1806 (JM)
John A. W. of Fauquier
County, Virginia, to Julia
Ann Macpherson of Alex-
andria, Virginia, Oct. 18,
1827 (WJ)
John F. to Martha Kent,
June 20, 1811 (JM)
John Thomas to Sarah Ann

SMITH (continued)
Grimes, 1826 (RK)
John to Louisa Jenkins,
June 5, 1825 (EH)
Julius to Mary Ann Ten-
nison, Sept. 11, 1816 (JM)
Madison to Matilda Delphy,
Nov. 10, 1817 (JMH)
Robert to Ann Watson, Feb.
19, 1801 (JM)
Samuel P. to Maria Wood,
Dec. 1, 1825 (WHW)
Thomas to Mary C. Deane,
Nov. 26, 1818 (JM)
Thomas W. of Alexandria,
D. C. to Ellen Wattles of
Alexandria, Nov. 12, 1840
(JJ)
William C. R. to Mary Mor-
gan, July 27, 1805 (JM)
William to Sarah McKee,
July 19, 1822 (EH)
Wm. to Sarah Morgan, July
19, 1802 (JM)
SMOOT, George A. to
Elizabeth Bland, Aug. 22,
1817 (AG)
James E. to Phoebe C.
Lowe both of Alexandria,
March 13, 1828 (WJ)
SMYTH, William of Henrico
County, Virginia, to Mary
M. Hewes of Alexandria,
Nov. 27, 1833 (JJ)
SNOWDEN, Samuel to Ann
Longdon, Jan. 7, 1802
(WM)
SOMERS, Joseph R. of Fair-
fax County, Virginia, to
Mary C. Atkinson of Alex-
andria County, Sept. 26,
1837 (ERL)
SOTHORON, Wm. Bruce of
St. Mary's Co., Maryland,
to Ann White of Alex-
andria, March 5, 1835 (JJ)

SOUTHARD, James to Sarah West, Jan. 22, 1833 (IR)

Wm. to Sarah Beatly, Dec. 26, 1820 (LHC)

SPENCER, James to Dorothy Bladen, August 10, 1817 (WHW)

SPRAGUE, Joshuah to Susannah Lee, Sept. 2, 1804 (JM)

STABLER, Francis to Cornelia Miller at the house of R. H. Miller, Sept. 4, 1850 (QM)

STACKPOLE, Wm. of Cumberland County, Maine, to Caroline Gerry of Alexandria, D. C., Dec. 28, 1841 (JJ)

STANDSFORD, John to Mary Louisa House both of Alexandria, Sept. 29, 1852 (JJ)

STANLY, George to Mary Chisel, April 19, 1804 (JM)

STAUNTON, Richard to Harriet Perry, Sept. 26, 1811 (JM)

STEED, Robert E. of Norfolk, Virginia, to Julia Lowe of Alexandria, May 31, 1829 (WJ)

STEEL, Jonathan H. to Julia Ann Adams both of Alexandria, Feb. 27, 1823 (WA)

STEPHESON, George G. to Elizabeth Piles, March 31, 1828 (WJ)

STEPNEY, John W. to Margaret E. Harris, Oct. 19, 1852 (WBE)

STERRETT, James to Polly Mills, Oct. 9, 1803 (JM)

STEUART, William B. to

STEUART (continued) Catharine Reed, May 2, 1815 (JM)

STEVENS, Thomas to Mary S. Deming, Oct. 21, 1835 (BNB)

STEVENSON, John to Rebecca Silence, Dec. 23, 1828 (IR)

Robert to Mary Young, 1817 (LHC)

STEWART, Charles F. to Ann Lucretia Deneala, April 27, 1820 (ON)

James M. to Elizabeth Tretcher, April 23, 1812 (JM)

John A. to Eliza Dunlap, Nov. 9, 1824 (WA)

Wm. to Delia Downes, July 30, 1821 (LHC)

STORK, Richard B. to Hannah J. White, Oct. 24, 1833 (CAD)

STRICKLAND, Daniel to Susannah Tracy, Sept. 11, 1803 (JM)

STRINGFELLOW, Horace Jr. of Petersburg to Mary M. Greene, July 16, 1849 (JJ)

STRNIDER, George to Phoebe E. Bailes, June 27, 1852 (WBE)

STUART, William to Sarah Forrest, May 18, 1827 (WJ)

Wm. Y. to Ann Maria Hodgkins, both of Alexandria, Nov. 26, 1829 (WJ)

STUERTEN, Morris to Betsy Mayhall, July 11, 1822 (Also: Steuter) (EH)

SUMMERS, Thomas to Rachel Hooper, Sept. 2, 1802 (JM)

SUPTON, Daniel S. to Sarah Lambert, June 8, 1813 (IR)

SUTTON, John to Patience Purdie, May 20, 1816 (JM)
William to Elizabeth Moore, March 3, 1801 (JM)
SWALLOW, John to Delila Penn both of Alexandria County, July 9, 1843 (EK)
SWANN, John to Ann Bellford, April 21, 1803 (JM)
Thomas to Mary Drewry, Dec. 28, 1819 (JF)
Wm. T. to Frances Alexander, July 12, 1810 (FB)
SWAYNE, George to Mary Violet, Oct. 4, 1817 (AG)
SWIFT, William R. to Mary D. Harper, Aug. 1, 1815 (JM)
SWILER, Joseph to Elizabeth McFadden, Jan. 6, 1806 (JM)
SYDEBOTTAM, Wilfred to Ardry Grady, Dec. 10, 1816 (IR)
SYKE, Peter to Isabella McFadden, Nov. 2, 1809 (JM)
TALBOTT, Alexander to Rachel Walker, Lic. Sept. 28, 1836 (IR)
TATE, Benjamin to Nelly Smallwood, August 11, 1803 (JM)
Josiah to Patsy Simms (coloured), March 8, 1815 (WHW)
William E. to Mary Brown, Lic. March 16, 1842 (IR)
TATSAPAUGH, Henry to Margaret Gates, Jan. 7, 1819 (JF)
TATTERSHALL, Thomas to Nancy Boyd, Dec. 2, 1803 (JM)
TAYLOR, Charles of Alexandria to Zoretta Tats-

TAYLOR (continued)
apaugh of Alexandria, Dec. 23, 1830 (WJ)
Charles S. of Jefferson County, Virginia, to Harriet B. Fowle of Alexandria, D. C., May 15, 1845 (JJ)
Even W. to Rebecca Lawrence, Feb. 16, 1813 (WHW)
George to Mary Eaton, June 25, 1801 (JM)
John to Catharine Mitchel, June 10, 1841 (JWR)
Joseph to Elizabeth Jacobs, Sept. 15, 1825 (EH)
Joshua to Cornelia Harris both of Alexandria County, May 18, 1827 (WA)
Thomas to Eliza Dogan, Lic. March 15, 1837 (IR)
Thomas to Sarah Shuck, Oct. 28, 1802 (JM)
William to Ann Lucinda Poston, March 5, 1818 (AG)
William to Sally Simpson, March 3, 1802 (JM)
TEMPLE, William to Catharine Lowber, Aug. 4, 1852 (JHR)
TENNISON, Samuel to Catherine Mankins, Jan. 14, 1802 (WM)
TEUTE, Nicholas to Betsy Neale, June 5, 1817 (See also: Turk) (AG)
THOMAS, George J. to Maria Harper, Sept. 16, 1839 (EH)
William H. to Cordelia Ellen Beitels, Aug. 9, 1842 (Not Veitch) (FM)
William to Mary Hitton, April 25, 1815 (JM)

THOMAS (continued)
Wm. of Alexandria to Jane Holt of Alexandria, Jan. 16, 1842 (JJ)
THOMPSON, Douglas to Eliza Cranston, Jan. 30, 1821 (ON)
George to Rebecca Gardner, Sept. 12, 1803 (JM)
John to Jenny Manly, Nov. 2, 1803 (JM)
John to Matty Davis, August 15, 1802 (JM)
Richard to Sophia Williams, Jan. 5, 1811 (IR)
Samuel to Emeline Slacum, Oct. 30, 1821 (St. John's Church in Washington) (ON)
Woodward to Frances Baggett, July 23, 1811 (IR)
THORNTON, Nicholas to Susanna L. Carne, Feb. 29, 1816 (ON)
THROOP, Thomas to Mary Ann Mankin, Feb. 2, 1826 (SC)
THULER, Jacob to Elizabeth Boyd, Nov. 28, 1808 (IR)
TIBBET, Walter to Ann M. Hunter, Feb. 22, 1827 (SC)
TIGNELL, Magor to Louise Wood, June 12, 1806 (JM)
TIPPETT, Jonathan to Catherine Tucker, Sept. 6, 1834 (SM)
TOLLSON, Francis to Sarah Middleton, Sept. 18, 1817 (Married in Maryland) (WHW)
TOWERS, Thomas to Elizabeth Chatham, Jan. 30, 1806 (JM)
TOWNSHEND, John P. of Suffolk County, Massachusetts, to Laura Dun-

TOWNSHEND (continued)
bar of Alexandria, D.C., July 21, 1842 (JJ)
Samuel H. to Catharine Lumsdon, Jan. 28, 1823 (IR)
TRACY, Thomas D. to Sarah May, Aug. 14, 1817 (IR)
TRAMMELL, George W. to Sarah Southard, Lic. May 15, 1836 (IR)
TRAVIS, John to Milly Knight, Lic. May 9, 1844 (IR)
Robert to Nancy Williams, Aug. 20, 1820 (IR)
TRIPLETT, Charles H. to Esther Ann Dunlap, Feb. 7, 1833 (EH)
George W. to Jane R. Dale, Nov. 21, 1839 (EH)
TROTTER, Mark to Violet Jenkins, March 29, 1824 (WA)
TUCKER, Wm. to Ann Skidmore, Dec. 1, 1833 (CAD)
TURNER, John R. of Charles County, Maryland, to Mary H. Hall of Alexandria, D. C., Feb. 4, 1845 (JJ)
John to Mary Reily, July 25, 1811 (JM)
TUTTON, John to Ann Williams, September 4, 1803 (JM)
TYLER, Henry to Mary Ann Willis, Dec. 5, 1817 (IR)
UHLER, Peter G. to Martha Ann Veitch, Sept. 22, 1842 (FM)
UPTON, Charles H. of Penobscot County, Maine, to Martha Ellen Page, May 18, 1836 (JJ)
VAIS, Anthony to S. Stuart, March 26, 1816 (ON)

VANSANT, James to Elizabeth L. Abercrombie, Oct. 31, 1816 (JMH)

VAUGHN, David to Sally Frazier, April 19, 1814 (ON)

VERMILLIN, Benj. to Mary A. E. Horseman, Dec. 11, 1851 (?D)

VIECHARIA, Frederick to Rosa Pearson, Sept. 18, 1823 (JF)

VIOLETT, John to Catharine Gray, Jan. 2, 1809 (IR)

VOWELL, Ebenezer to Eliza Orme, Nov. 12, 1813 (JM)

John Cripps to Mary Jacqueline Taylor, Dec. 7, 1810 (JM)

Thomas to Elizabeth Mills, May 26, 1842 (FM)

WADDELL, John of the Parish of Natchitoches, Louisiana, to Lucia C. Porter of Alexandria, Aug. 25, 1835 (CBD)

WADDY, Thomas to Eliza Walker, May 13, 1841 (FM)

WADE, George to Sarah Williams, Jan. 13, 1801 (JM)

Robert to C. Jane Cook, June 30, 1841 (IR)

Robert to Elizabeth Smallwood, Jan. 17, 1811 (SB)

WAIGLEY, George to Ann Murray, May 28, 1830 (JL)

WALDEN, Thomas to Kitty Stentsman, Oct. 27, 1803 (JM)

WALKER, James to Elizabeth Wilson, July 31, 1810 (JM)

James to Kitty Wise, Nov. 11, 1813 (JM)

John to Sarah Smith, April

WALKER (continued) 25, 1822 (ON)

Levin to Margaret Williams, Jan. 30, 1806 (JM)

Samuel to Rana Lloyd, May 14, 1852 (WBE)

WALKOM, Jonathan P. to Elizabeth Rowe, Nov. 15, 1820 (ON)

WALLACE, Richard to Elizabeth Hurst, June 2, 1831 (IR)

Richard to Peggy Ballinger, Jan. 15, 1801 (JM)

Richard to Sarah Griffith, June 26, 1816 (JM)

Thomas to Tobitha Glanders, Jan. 19, 1804 (WM)

Wm. J. of New York to Caroline J. Hooff of Alexandria, June 12, 1851 (JJ)

WALLACK, Richard to Nancy Simms, March 2, 1813 (WHW)

WANNALL, Thomas to Mary Roberts, June 24, 1816 (JMH)

WARD, Enoch to Mary Ann Evans, Lic. Jan. 25, 1842 (IR)

James to Hepsey Swallow, Aug. 3, 1815 (IR)

James to Lucy Coates, March 20, 1821 (LHC)

John W. to Henrietta Carlin, May 22, 1834 (CAD)

Jonathan to Sarah Bealle, Jan. 15, 1818 (AG)

Lewis to Eleanor Lambkin, Jan. 21, 1830 (EH)

Thomas to Ann Young, Dec. 23, 1809 (IR)

William to Louisa D. Cook, Lic. March 3, 1842 (IR)

WARREN, Erasmus to Julia A. Worthington, Aug. 26,

WARREN (continued)
1852 (WBE)
John to Phebe London (coloured), July 7, 1842 (FM)
WASHINGTON, Wm. H. to Rebecca W. Cracroft, July 21, 1814 (ON)
WATERHOUSE, Elias B. to Alice Cartwright, 1818 (LHC)
WATERS, Benjamin G. to Lucy J. Berkley, Jan. 17, 1843 (FM)
WATKINS, Robert to Eliza Tate , Sept. 14, 1809 (free blacks) (JM)
Thomas to Mary Williams, Dec. 12, 1812 (JM)
William to Elizabeth Benter, July 29, 1841 (FM)
WATSON, John to Caroline E. Keffer, Jan. 9, 1830 (IR)
Thomas to Chloe Wattles, Dec. 24, 1803 (WW)
William to Elizabeth Uhler, Nov. 20, 1806 (JM)
WAUGH, Albert P. to Rachael Atwell, Sept. 19, 1821 (IR)
WAY, Frederick to Elizabeth Shortell, Nov. 27, 1806 (DC)
WEBB, Lewis W. of Norfolk to Mary R. Jamiesson of Alexandria, Oct. 9, 1850 (CBD)
WEBSTER, Adam L. to Sarah H. Hand, Nov. 3, 1810 (JM)
Armstead to Lydia Murray (coloured), Jan. 2, 1822 (ON)
John B. to Sarah Latham, June 22, 1817 (WHW)
WEIR, Philip H. to Mary

WEIR (continued)
Jane Cole (coloured), Oct. 16, 1851 (JJ)
WELLS, James M. to Ann Waygly, Aug. 16, 1838 (SGR)
William to Sarah Hawkins, May 21, 1811 (IR)
WENSCHA, Martin to Elizabeth Kelly, May 21, 1801 (JM)
WEST, Francis to Clara Jackson (coloured), Dec. 23, 1815 (WHW)
James to Sarah Dudley, Dec. 27, 1827 (SC)
Martin to Catharine Burger, Oct. 27 1831 (IR)
WHALE, James C. to Elizabeth Bluffield, Feb. 17, 1816 (JM)
WHALEY, David L. to Jennet Darne (Married at the residence of Allen Scott of Alexandria County), Oct. 14, 1834 (AW)
James to Harriott Gooding, Feb. 16, 1812 (JM)
WHEAT, John J. of Alex. to Emily E. Dixion of Alexandria, Nov. 1, 1842 (JJ)
William to Molly Fagins, June 7, 1804 (JM)
WHEELER, Jebez to Louisa M. B. Meade, March 6, 1836 (BNB)
Samuel to Jane Summers, July 24, 1817 (IR)
Samuel to Sarah Parsons, Dec. 19, 1803 (WM)
Samuel to Winifred Winkfield, August 16, 1805 (JM)
Thomas to Catharine Lucas, Sept. 16, 1816 (JMH)

WHITE, Raisin to Faith Coles (coloured), Nov. 30, 1815 (WHW)

Samuel B. to Ann Hutchinson, Nov. 11, 1815 (JMH)

WHITING, Fabius to Louisa T. Yeaton, Dec. 3, 1821 (ON)

Thacker to Martha Ganett, Lic. June 20, 1836 (LFM)

WHITTINGTON, Thomas to Margaret C. Dearborn, Dec. 29, 1825 (WA)

WHITTLE, Thomas to Mary Buckland, Dec. 5, 1815 (WHW)

WHORSON, William of Washington County to Margaret McCarty of Alexandria, July 29, 1830 (WJ)

WILCOX, Anthony to Phebe Lacock, April 23, 1811 (IR)

WILEY, Ephraim to Phillis Hessen, July 22, 1802 (JM)

Hugh G. to Mary Wright, Feb. 6, 1816 (JMH)

Littleton to Margaret Deakins, June 30, 1803 (JM)

WILLIAM, John to Sarah Perry, July 9, 1816 (JM)

WILLIAMS, Daniel to Maria Derrick (coloured), Apr, 6, 1848 (JJ)

Henry to Elizabeth Boyer, Oct. 30, 1806 (JM)

Hiram O. to Matilda Simms, Dec. 21, 1820 (ON)

John to Catherine Goldsmith, Dec. 23, 1804 (JM)

John to Elizabeth Baggott, Jan. 21, 1804 (WM)

Joseph to Elizabeth Knight, June 3, 1822 (ON)

Joseph to Priscilla Darnell,

WILLIAMS (continued) Jan. 26, 1830 (JL)

Presley to Nelly Robinson, Dec. 15, 1803 (WW)

Thomas to Ann Wilkins, Aug. 23, 1818 (JF)

WILLIAMSON, Philip D. of Virginia to Mary M. Vowell of Alexandria, Jan. 9, 1823 (WA)

WILLS, John C. of Virginia to Catherine Duffey of Alexandria, Dec. 9, 1847 (Possibly: Wells) (JJ)

John to Ailsey Thomas, March 12, 1816 (IR)

WILSON, Jacob H. to Elizabeth B. Hills, Nov. 23, 1831 (EH)

James Wilson to Alice Fletcher, May 29, 1811 (IR)

Nathaniel H. to Elizabeth Mouldz, July 24, 1801 (WM)

Oliver to Mary Heineman, March 29, 1810 (JM)

Richard to Fanny B. B. Coffee, April 18, 1812 (IR)

Thomas to Mary Cruse, May 5, 1815 (ON)

William Jr. to Ann Carson, Aug. 19, 1806 (JM)

William to Catharine Glover, April 16, 1820 (ON)

William to Flora E. Morgan (coloured), Nov. 4, 1841 (FM)

WINDSOR, Robert N. to Sarah Ann H. Shepherd, Dec. 18, 1809 (IR)

William to Susanna Small, March 11, 1802 (JM)

WINGARTY, William to Rachel Kitely March 1, 1801 (JM)

WINTER, Gabriel to Sarah Ann Peyton, March 17, 1818 (WHW)

WISE, George Carr to Mary Ann Fulton, July 23, 1801 (JM)

George P. to Sarah Ann Newton, March 12, 1829 (EH)

George to Elizabeth Miller, Jan. 13, 1814 (WHW)

George to Margaret Green, April 10, 1816 (JM)

WITHERS, Addison L. to Frances T. Buckey, May 19, 1829 (JL)

WOLFE, Thomas to Mary Ann Paton, May 14, 1816 (See also: Patten) (ON)

WOOD, John to Elizabeth Fig, Dec. 8, 1801 (JM)

John to Elizabeth Myers, March 21, 1810 (IR)

John to Jemima Hall, Dec. 31, 1811 (JM)

Richard to Catherine Bagget, May 3, 1810 (JM)

Thomas W. to Ellen F. Backir, May 8, 1853 (WBE)

William to Susan Key Bond, Oct. 22, 1818 (WHW)

William W. to Eleanor Denon, Feb. 19, 1801 (JM)

WOODARD, Joseph to Catharine Oliver, Nov. 10, 1816 (JMH)

WORTHINGTON, Isaac to Catharine Rease, Jan. 27, 1821 (ON)

WRIGHT, George to Charlotte Copper, Nov. 12, 1815 (WHW)

Harrison D. to Charlotte Douglass, Jan. 10, 1839 (EH)

Thomas A. to Mary Craw-

WRIGHT (continued) ford, Sept. 30, 1835 (BNB)

Wm. to Elizabeth Conner, April 9, 1803 (JM)

YEARLY, Nathaniel to Nancy Boothe, Aug. 3, 1820 (WHW)

YOUNG, John W. to Susanna Price, Sept. 1852 (?D)

William to Ellen Sullivan June 9, 1815 (JMH)

ZIMMERMAN, Adam to Sarah Simpson, Dec. 18, 1817 (JMH)

George to Ann Simpson, Aug. 24, 1806 (JM)

Jacob to Emily Frederick both of Alexandria, July 8, 1829 (WJ)

Jacob to Jane Smith, March 22, 1810 (JM)

44

MARRIAGE BONDS

ABERCROMBIE, Robert & Susan Wood, Jan. 25, 1820 - bdsm: Robert Abercrombie, John Wood

ACKER, John N. & Sarah E. Bisby, May 24, 1848 - bdsm: John N. Acker, Aquilla Emmerson

ADAM, John & Mary Dunlap, Feb. 20, 1816 - bdsm: John Adam, William Ramsay

ADAMS, Abijah & Margaretta H. Wherry, June 12, 1821 - bdsm: Abijah Adams, Andrew H. Adams

Francis & Mary R. Newton, Dec. 20, 1814 - bdsm: Francis Adams, William Newton

George R. & Mary A. Bontz, Jan. 20, 1836 - bdsm: George R. Adams, Jacob Bontz

James & Catharine Bruner, Feb. 24, 1802 - bdsm: James Adams, John Bruner

John & Mary Hayes, July 28, 1803 - bdsm: John Adams, Andrew Hayes

John A. & Ellen B. Simons, April 30, 1834 - bdsm: John A. Adams, Richard B. Mitchell

ADAMS (continued)
John G. & E. F. Bradley, Sept. 9, 1840 - bdsm: John G. Adams, H. Bradley

Leonard & Catharine Spunaugle, June 16, 1812 - bdsm: Leonard Adams, Hugh W. Deneale

Leonard & Nancy Davis, March 4, 1802 - bdsm: Leonard Adams, John Davis

Leonard C. & Margaret E. Ball, Jan. 17, 1833 - bdsm: Leonard C. Adams, John Ball

Samuel R. & Theresa Veitch, Oct. 21, 1845 - bdsm: Samuel R. Adams, W. C. Yeaton

ALABY, James & Verlinda Webb, Sept. 4, 1827 - bdsm: James Alaby, Samuel Smith

ALEXANDER, Amos & Elizabeth Wroe, Jan. 10, 1805 - bdsm: Amos Alexander, John Bonsall

Austin & Eleanor Sherwood, Dec. 24, 1816 - bdsm: Austin Alexander, Joseph Jenkins

Lawrence G. & Eliza McLean, June 14, 1824 - bdsm: Lawrence G. Alex-

45

ALEXANDER (continued)
ander, Robert Barry

Walter L. & Catharine Dade, Feb. 3, 1804 - bdsm: Walter L. Alexander, Baldwin Dade

ALLBRITTAN, John & Mary Scott, Nov. 14, 1839 - bdsm: John Allbrittan, William G. Violett

ALLBRITTON, Edward & Louisa Gowings, July 1, 1841 - bdsm: Edward Allbritton, John Allbritton

ALLEN, David & Sarah Jordon, May 25, 1836 - bdsm: David Allen, Thompson Jordon

Edwin J. & Mary C. Harris, license issued Dec. 12, 1850 - bdsm:

Elijah & Maria Ingraham, Oct. 5, 1840 - bdsm: Elijah Allen, Richard Berry

Ignatius & Eliza Posey, Jan. 22, 1823 - bdsm: Ignatius Allen, Ezikiel Jones

Ignatius & Eliza Posey, Jan. 22, 1822 - (Married by Rev. O. Norris)

James & Lucretia Murray (widow), Jan. 2, 1828 - bdsm: James Allan, Elizah Spernaugle

William & Anna Donaldson, March 11, 1803 - bdsm: William Allen, Andrew Donaldson

ALLISON, Amos & Ann Geiger, March 29, 1803 - bdsm: Amos Allison, Benjamin Shreve

Bryant & Mary Ann Barr, April 9, 1801 - bdsm: Bryant Allison, Jesse Scott

ALLISON (continued)
Daniel & Mary Stewart, Dec. 31, 1821 - bdsm: Daniel Allison, John Fant

Elias & Nancy Kent, Feb. 15, 1803 - bdsm: Elias Allison, James Awbrey

James & Elizabeth Childs, Dec. 5, 1814 - bdsm: James Allison, John Childs

John & Nancy Darnes, Dec. 26, 1815 - bdsm: John Allison, Simon Darnes

Thomas D. & Nancy Ellis, Dec. 26, 1844 - bdsm: Thomas D. Allison, Willaim Swann

William & Matilda Penn, July 15, 1837 - bdsm: William Allison, Henry Patterson

ALTERFREH, Peter & Margaret Bartlett, Sept. 26, 1805 - bdsm: Peter Alterfreh, Thomas Smith

ANDERSON, James & Nancy Davis, Jan. 12, 1836 - bdsm: James Anderson, Reuben Johnston, Jr.

James & Nelly Weylie, Sept. 2 , 1802 - bdsm: James Anderson, Ephraim Weylie

John & Eleanor Dunlaney, Dec. 15, 1810 - bdsm: John Anderson, Owen Sullivan

Robert & Mary Black, June 3, 1837 - bdsm: Robert Anderson, Robert Jamieson

Samuel & Amelia Syphax, Dec. 27, 1848 - bdsm: Samuel Anderson, Robert Henry

ANDERSON (continued)
Thomas (slave) & Louisa Evans (a free black), May 16, 1844 - bdsm: Thomas Anderson, John Davis

ANDOL, Bernard & Eleanor Stone, Aug. 27, 1801 - bdsm: Bernard Andol, William Stone

ANDREWS, Elijah & Ann Wheatley, March 1, 1821 - bdsm: Elijah Andrews, James Hill

Jacob & Polly Baxter, April 7, 1810 - bdsm: Jacob Andrews, Henley Nelson

Joshua & Harriot Potts, July 3, 1822 - bdsm: Joshua Andrews, Isaac Buckingham

ANSART, Felix & Martha L. Brown, Nov. ? 1816 - bdsm: Felix Ansart, John M. Tyler

ANTRIM, Parnell & Sarah Manley June 28, 1802 - bdsm: Parnell Antrim, E. Wiley

APPICH, Gottlieb & Barbara Stuppar, Aug. 7, 1832 - bdsm: Gottlieb Appich, Frederick Betzold

ARMSTRONG, James L. & Mary Jane Smith, March 9, 1829 - bdsm: James L. Armstrong, Samuel Smith

John & Susan Caywood, July 28, 1807 - bdsm: John Armstrong, Henry Carrell

John T. & Catharine Tennison, Dec. 19, 1827 - bdsm: John T. Armstrong, Samuel Tennison

Samuel & Lucy Mullen, Aug. 24, 1837 - bdsm: Samuel Armstrong, Wm. Mullen

ARMSTRONG (continued)
William & Mary Hopkins, Aug. 15, 1845 - bdsm: William Armstrong, John J. Armstrong

ARNOLD, Alexander & Mary Ann Fugatt, Sept. 6, 1837 - bdsm: Alexander Arnold, Gustavus Fugitt

Alexander & Mary Herbert, June 30, 1846 - bdsm: Alexander Arnold, Wm. Arnold

Garrett & Elizabeth Chisam, Dec. 24, 1803 - bdsm: Garrett Arnold, Benjamin Glover

Harrison H. B. & Mary J. A. Brooke, daughter of John H. Brooke, June 5, 1850 - bdsm: Harrison H. B. Arnold, John H. Brooke

James & Sarah Lindsay, Sept. 17, 1827 - bdsm: James Arnold, Fielder Jewell

John & Ann Eliza Mitchell, Sept. 2, 1846 - bdsm: John Arnold, Judson Mitchell

John & Susan Hall, Aug. 30, 1837 - bdsm: John Arnold, John J. Practor

William & Ann Stephenson, Sept. 4, 1816 - bdsm: William Arnold, Wesley Carlin

William & Jane Rhodes, Sept. 27, 1837 - bdsm: William Arnold, John J. Proctor

ARTHUR, Samuel & Catharine Prescott, Dec. 3, 1817 - bdsm: Samuel Arthur, William Prescott

ARUNDELL, John & Catharine Boyd, July 23, 1818 -

ARUNDELL (continued)
bdsm: John Arundell, Enoch Pelton

ASHBOURN, John & Sarah Brown, Dec. 30, 1826 – bdsm: John Ashbourn, Samuel Smith

ASHFORD, Francis P. & Paulina Jones, June 29 1849 – bdsm: Francis P. Ashford, John R. Dale

George & Susanna Compton, Dec. 23, 1806 – bdsm: George Ashford, Lewis Simpson

John & Nancy Davis, March 5, 1849 – bdsm: John Ashford, Ludwell H. Davis

ASHTON, Thomas & Elizabeth Wallace, Nov. 17, 1836 – bdsm: Thomas Ashton, Sarah Wallace

William & Fanny Johnston, July 5, 1842 – bdsm: William Ashton, Simeon Tate

ATCHESON, Gustavius & Elizabeth Coby, Jan. 13, 1810 – bdsm: Gustavius Atcheson, William Coby

ATKINSON, Guy & Albina Birch, April 6, 1803 – bdsm: Guy Atkinson, William Birch

Richard & Ruth Ann Atkinson, Nov. 14, 1842 – bdsm: Richard Atkinson, James Atkinson

ATWELL, Joseph & Nancy Davis, April 11, 1822 – bdsm: Joseph Atwell, Richard H. King

Manly & Rebecca S. Berry, June 12, 1834 – bdsm: Manly Atwell, William M. Morrison

Richard & Elizabeth Meads,

ATWELL (continued)
May 30, 1811 – bdsm: Richard Atwell, Benjamin Baden

Samuel & Harriet S. Adams (daughter of Leonard Adams), Dec. 30, 1828 – bdsm: Samuel Atwell, Leonard Adams

William & Julia Ann Dorsey, July 14, 1828 – bdsm: William Atwell, William Deneale

William & Mary Jane Higdon, May 3, 1837 – bdsm: William Atwell, Edward C. Horwell

William & Susan Rotch, Nov. 24, 1829 – bdsm: William Atwell, John M. Monroe

AUBINOE, Summerset & Jane Cliford, Sept. 3, 1829 – bdsm: Summerset Aubinoe, Horatio Day

AUDLEY, Thomas & Catharine Javins, March 18, 1816 – bdsm: Thomas Audley, William Javins

AUSTIN, William & Prescilla Kidwell, July 14, 1813 – bdsm: William Austin, James M. Kidwell

AVERY, Philip & Sarah Slatford, Dec. 7, 1809 – bdsm: Philip Avery, George William Slatford

Thomas & Margaret Walker, daughter of John S. Walker, Sept. 4, 1850 – bdsm: Thomas Avery, John S. Walker

Wesley & Mary Jane Ball, Dec. 18, 1834 – bdsm: Wesley Avery, John Ball

BADDIN, Sainttobin & Mary

BADDIN (continued)
Ann Ball, Jan. 6, 1804 -
bdsm: Sainttobin Baddin,
Bazil Ball

BAGGETT, Alexander & Ann
Chatham, May 12, 1803 -
bdsm: Alexander Baggett,
Charles Pascoe

Charles & Elizabeth Bag-
gett, March 29, 1804 -
bdsm: Charles Baggett,
James Davidson

Samuel & Elizabeth Keating,
Sept. 22, 1813 - bdsm:
Samuel Baggett, Henry
Tatsepaugh

Thomas & Nancy Henry,
Dec. 2, 1842 - bdsm:
Thomas Baggett, Jeremiah
Frank

Townsend & Catherine Bal-
lenger, Oct. 24, 1831 -
bdsm: Townsend Baggett,
John Baggett (guardian of
Catherine Ballenger)

William & Elizabeth Brown,
July 28, 1825 - bdsm:
William Baggett, David
Cadis

BAGGOTT, John & Mary
Mattochs, May 12, 1804 -
bdsm: John Baggott,
Alexander Baggott

John H. & Margaret T.
Semms, May 28, 1835 -
bdsm: John H. Baggott,
George H. Semms

John T. & Ann Virginia
Nevett, June 28, 1843 -
bdsm: John T. Baggott,
James C. Nevett

BAILEY, Carr Jr. & Catha-
rine A. Hunger, April 18,
1807 - bdsm: Carr Bailey,
Jr., James R. M. Lowe

William & Lucy S. Baily,

BAILEY (continued)
Feb. 20, 1843 - bdsm:
William Bailey, John H.
Bailey

BAILISS, Thomas & Ellen
Cook (daughter of David
Cook), Nov. 27, 1828 -
bdsm: Thomas Bailiss,
David Cook

BAKER, Carrol & Mary
Chiles, Feb. 27, 1817 -
bdsm: Carrol Baker, John
H. Manley

Daniel & Sarah Goodrich,
Feb. 7, 1804 - bdsm:
Daniel Baker, James
Baker

Michael & Jane Dixon, Feb.
6, 1826 - bdsm: Michael
Baker, John Manery

Samuel & Susan Gladdin,
May 30, 1815 - bdsm:
Samuel Baker, Thomas
Gray

Zachariah & Elizabeth
Green, July 30, 1805 -
bdsm: Zachariah Baker,
Thomas Birch

BALDWIN, George & Jane
Hayes, July 24 1801 -
bdsm: Wm. Pickard,
George Baldwin

BALENGER, Valentine &
Frances Harre, June 3,
1809 - bdsm: Valentine
Balenger, William Violett

BALL, Allen & Ann Wiley,
Dec. 22, 1801 - bdsm: Al-
len Ball, George Wiley

Andrew A. & Jane A. Taylor,
Nov. 19, 1842 - bdsm:
Andrew A. Ball, Reason P.
Taylor

Erasmus & Sarah Weiley,
Oct. 24, 1805 - bdsm:
Erasmus Ball, James An-

BALL (continued)
derson
John & Mary Tolson, July 7,
1837 - bdsm: John Ball,
Wm. Thomas
Robert & Ann Thrift, June 9,
1803 - bdsm: Robert Ball,
George Minor, Jr.
Spencer & Eliza Luke, Feb.
25, 1814 - bdsm: Spencer
Ball, Jobez Rooker
Thomas & Jane Mackelroy,
Dec. 23, 1815 - bdsm:
Thomas Ball, Patrick King
William & Ann Brockett,
Jan. 2, 1836 - bdsm: Wil-
liam Ball, Alexander
Moore
BALLARD, Edward J. &
Eliza Ann Smith, July 12,
1832 - bdsm: Edward J.
Ballard, Samuel Smith
Richard & Sarah Hudson,
March 6, 1804 - bdsm:
Richard Ballard, William
Schakespear (Also: Shake-
speare)
BALLENGER, James & Ann
Stephenson, Nov. 14, 1816
- bdsm: James Ballenger,
John Crump
BANK, Hugh & Rhoda Hol-
lowood, Jan, 2, 1817 -
bdsm: Hugh Bank, George
Kincaid
BANKS, Gerald & Elizabeth
Grimes, May 24, 1832 -
bdsm: Gerald Banks,
Thomas Brocchus
BARBER, Peter & Patty
Kennedy, Aug. 12, 1811 -
bdsm: Peter Barber, Chris-
tian Christophe
BARECROFT, Titus & Maria
Percy, May 6, 1820 -
bdsm: Titus Barecroft,

BARECROFT (continued)
Charles McKnight
BARKER, Rezin & Julia Mor-
ris, July 20, 1815 - bdsm:
Rezin Barker, James Mor-
ris
BARNES, Henry & Margaret
Powell, Nov. 26, 1822 -
bdsm: Henry Barnes,
Sandford Anderson
Jesse & Susannah Green,
January 8, 1803 - bdsm:
Jesse Barnes, Thomas
Green
BARNETT, George & Mary
Ann Cranston, March 15,
1810 - bdsm: George Bar-
rett, John Crauston
William & Elizabeth Par-
sons, May 9, 1829 - bdsm:
William Barnett, David
Caddis
BARON, James & Sarah Da-
vis, Nov. 1, 1821 - bdsm:
James Baron, George
Wright
BARRETT, Isaac & Lucy
Burgess, Aug. 4, 1803 -
bdsm: Isaac Barrett, Wm.
Burgess
BARRY, David & Mary Ann
Foster, Oct. 3, 1834 -
bdsm: David Barry, John
Hurst
James & Ann Davis, March
14, 1811 - bdsm: James
Barry, Edward Parry
Richard & Patty Marshall,
June 2,1835 - bdsm:
Richard Barry, Reuben
Johnston, Jr.
Robert & Amelia Ramsay,
Oct. 20, 1824 - bdsm:
Robert Barry, Joseph H.
Hampson
Robert & Eliza H. O'Reiley,

BARRY (continued)
Dec. 29, 1823 - bdsm: Robert Barry, Alexander Simmes

William & Mary Cook, widow of Wm. Cook, May 20, 1803 - bdsm: William Barry, Ann Forgerson

BARTLE, Samuel & Susan Rhodes, March 24, 1814 - bdsm: Samuel Bartle, Anthony Rhodes

Wm. H. & Ann Davis, Feb. 17, 1842 - bdsm: Wm. H. Bartle, George Bartle

BARTLETT, Henry & Mrs. Lethe Clarke, Oct. 21, 1848 - bdsm: Henry Bartlett, Joseph Weeks

Peyton C. & Isabella F. Lyles, Dec. 21, 1850 - bdsm:

BARTON, George Goodall & Eliza Mary Gird, June 5, 1843 - bdsm: George Goodall Barton, Benjamin Barton

BASFORD, Jacob & Sarah Patterson, March 21, 1822 - bdsm: Jacob Basford, Thomas Whittington

BASSETT, William H. & Eleanor O'Neille, Jan. 18, 1822 - bdsm: William H. Bassett, Charles B. K. Douglass

BATES, Edgar H. & Elizabeth Bontz, Dec. 19, 1839 - bdsm: Edgar H. Bates, George R. Adams

BAUGH, Lewis K. & Eliza Ann Beedle, Oct. 30, 1817 - bdsm: Lewis K. Baugh, Charles Scott

BAVERS, Thomas & Delila Davis, Nov. 21, 1815 -

BAVERS (continued)
bdsm: Thomas Bavers, John Buttes

BAYLISS, Daniel & Sarah Swann, May 25, 1833 - bdsm: Daniel Bayliss, John Jackson

George & Mary Stodder, Feb. 12, 1849 - bdsm: George Bayliss, Edward Sauls

BAYLY, William T. & Harriett Short, May 30, 1844 - bdsm: William T. Bayly, George Mouldy

BAYNE, John & Sally Pelty, July 10, 1823 - bdsm: John Bayne, Elisha Simmons

BEACH, James & Jane Runnells, Dec. 8, 1848 - bdsm: James Beach, Samuel Lewis

James & Theodocia Harrison, Dec. 16, 1830 - bdsm: James Beach, Thomas M. Gopom

James H. Harriet Taylor, April 25, 1850 - bdsm: James H. Beach, Samuel Beach

Solomon & Mary E. Harris, license issued Feb. 5, 1851 - bdsm:

BEALE, Henry & Matilda Baggett, Sept. 11, 1843 - bdsm: Henry Beale, John H. Baily

Richard & Sally Nelson, May 26, 1810 - bdsm: Richard Beale, George Kenner

BEALL, Benjamin Lloyd of Washington County, D.C. & Elizabeth Taylor of Fairfax County, Jan. 1, 1825 - bdsm:

Gideon & Ann F. Weston,

BEALL (continued)

May 9, 1825 - bdsm: Gideon Beall, John McCobb

John & Mary McKerven, May 23, 1812 - bdsm: John Beall, James Armitage

BEAN, Benjamin & Matilda Lee Hughnely, Aug. 18, 1823 - bdsm: Benjamin Bean, Horace Field

Henry H. & Matilda Talbot, Dec. 5, 1833 - bdsm: Henry H. Bean, John Corse

BEARCROFT, Dominick & Sarah Watson, Dec. 20, 1811 - bdsm: Dominick Bearcroft, Thomas Watson

BEARD, George & Elizabeth Berry, Sept. 12, 1818 - bdsm: George Beard, Bayne S. Berry

BEATTY, Robert M. & Mary Ann Barton, daughter of Richard C. Barton, March 21, 1848 - bdsm: Robert M. Beatty, Richard C. Barton

BECKLEY, Archibald & Lavinia Burns, July 11, 1826 - bdsm: Archibald Beckley, Francis Norris

John & Sophia Whiting, May 2, 1828 - bdsm: John Beckley, Gustavus Gibson (See also: Whitney)

John A. & Mary Jackson, Jan. 16, 1845 - bdsm: John A. Beckley, William Williamson

William & Ann Watson, Nov. 7, 1827 - bdsm: William Beckley, Gustavus Gibson

BEECH, James & Elizabeth Hutson, June 8, 1825 -

BEECH (continued)

bdsm: James Beech, Peter Daviss

Thomas & Cordelia Smith, Oct. 1, 1812 - bdsm: Thomas Beech, Hugh W. Deneale

BEHIER, Peter & Ann King, April 14, 1806 - bdsm: Peter Behier, Dixon Brittingham

BEIYER, Henry & A. Louisa Arbinoe, June 24, 1850 - bdsm: Henry Beiyer, W. P. Collinsworth

BELFOUR, James & Ann Banks, June 1, 1802 - bdsm: James Belfour, John Edwards

BELL, Alexander & Susanna Evans, Dec. 23, 1830 - bdsm: Alexander Bell, James Birch

George & Sally Waugh, Aug. 17, 1820 - bdsm: George Bell, William Waugh

George W. J. & Ann M. Stull, June 6, 1850 - bdsm: George W. J. Bell, William Bawler

James & _____ Woolles, Nov. 18, 1802 - bdsm: James Bell, William Woolles

Robert & Brittania Harle, Nov. 11, 1802 - bdsm: Robert Bell, Ann Harle

Robert & Jane L. Hamilton, June 29, 1837 - bdsm: Robert Bell, Philip Hamilton

William & Maria Hines, Widow, July 28, 1836 - bdsm: William Bell, George Johnson

Wm. & Maria Furley, Nov.

BELL (continued)
15, 1836 - bdsm: Wm.
Bell, Reuben Johnston, Jr.
BELT, Alfred Campbell of
Loudoun County, Virginia,
& Rebecca Mills, Oct. 16,
1850 - bdsm:
BENHAM, Joseph S. & Mary
Louisa Slacum, June 17,
1829 - bdsm: Joseph S.
Benham, W. A. Slacum
BENNET, Washington &
Maria Dennison, Dec. 4,
1830 - bdsm: Washington
Bennet, Thomas Dennison
BENNETT, James H. &
Lawrence Hooff, Sr., Sept.
4, 1823 - bdsm: James H.
Bennett & Lawrence Hooff,
Sr.
John & Anne Perry, August
30, 1804 - bdsm: John
Bennett, John Parsons
Joseph Turner & Elizabeth
Mann, Dec. 22, 1802 -
bdsm: Jospeh Turner Ben-
nett, Robert Roberts
Mordecai & Milly McCarty,
Oct. 16, 1817 - bdsm:
Mordecai Bennett, John
Duffy
Walter & Mary Fumpuson?,
Aug. 9, 1827 - bdsm: Wal-
ter Bennett, William
Evans
BENNOT, Francis & Eliza-
beth Stewart, Feb. 28.
1818 - bdsm: Francis
Bennot, Henry 8rame
BENSON, James & Elizabeth
Dorsey, Jan. 22, 1828 -
bdsm: James Benson,
Edmund Hewett
BENTER, George H. & Mary
Jane Summers, March 20,
1846 - bdsm: George H.

BENTER (continued)
Benter, John W. Padgett
Wesley & Ann Bontz, Dec.
12, 1816 - bdsm: Wesley
Benter, George Varnell
BENTLEY, Robert & Kitty
Longden, Oct. 9, 1817 -
bdsm: Robert Bentley,
James Galt
BENTON, James M. & Mar-
garet A. Harrison, Oct. 25,
1848 - bdsm: James M.
Benton, John D. Harrison
Samuel & Elizabeth Vowell,
July 8, 1805 - bdsm:
Samuel Benton, Charles
Mankins
BERNARD, John & Sarah
Dove, May 30, 1807 -
bdsm: John Bernard, Wil-
liam O'Conner
BERRY, Charles C. & Eliz-
abeth Campbell, Jan. 4,
1842 - bdsm: Charles C.
Berry, William Campbell
George & Elizabeth Cole,
March 8, 1820 - bdsm:
George Berry, William
Salomons
George & Mary Ann Gossen,
Jan. 3, 1842 - bdsm:
George Berry, John T. Bal-
lenger
John E. & Rachael Wells
Harper, Sept. 5, 1811 -
bdsm: John E. Berry,
Samuel Lindsay
John E. & Virginia Harper,
Feb. 5, 1846 - bdsm: John
E. Berry, W.C. Yeaton
Reuben & Jane Pollard, June
4, 1836 - bdsm: Reuben
Berry, Josiah Rutter
Thomas & Elizabeth Sil-
mone, Sept. 18, 1827 -
bdsm: Thomas Berry,

BERRY (continued)
Elizabeth Silmone
William & Lucinda Fox, July 15, 1830 – bdsm: William Berry, William Survay
BIGGS, James & Nancy Talbutt, Feb. 4, 1804 – bdsm: James Biggs, John White
James & Rebecca Talbott, Dec. 20, 1801 – bdsm: James Biggs, Josiah Talbott
BIGSLEY, Peter & Sarah Ball, Oct. 4, 1838 – bdsm: Peter Bigsley, Lewis Campbell
BINES, David & Margaret M. Cannon, Oct. 23, 1817 – bdsm: David Bines, Madison Smith
BINNS, Charles W. D. & Marianna T. S. Alexander, Jan. 27, 1825 – bdsm: Charles W. D. Binns, A. G. Waterman
BIRCH, Caleb & Mary Bowling, Sept. 4, 1806 – bdsm: Caleb Birch, Joseph Bowling
Isaac & Elizabeth Walker, Sept. 6, 1815 – bdsm: Isaac Birch, Elijah Chenault
James & Aletha Buchanan, Feb. 4, 1823 – bdsm: James Birch, James Slatford
Joseph & Sarah Posey, Jan. 22, 1818 – bdsm: Joseph Birch, Elijah Chenault
Samuel & Carey Richards, March 9, 1815 – bdsm: Samuel Birch, Archibald J. Taylor
BIRD, John & Rebecca

BIRD (continued)
Clearpole, Aug. 20, 1811 – bdsm: John Bird, Edmund Edmonds
Thomas & Mary King, July 8, 1824 – bdsm: Thomas Bird, John M. Clark
BIRKY, Joseph & Mary Major (daughter of John Major), July 5, 1833 – bdsm: Joseph Birky, John Major
BISHOP, John S. & Armanda M. Horwell, April 23, 1829 – bdsm: John S. Bishop, George Price
BLACK, James & Helen Talbot, August 3, 1831 – bdsm: James Black, John Dunlap
BLACKFORD, Henry & Sarah Parsons, March 27, 1815 – bdsm: Henry Blackford, John Butler
BLACKLOCK, Dennis R. & Sarah A. Swann, March 4, 1850 – bdsm: Dennis R. Blacklock, George Washington
Nicholas & Eliza J. Ramsay, Dec. 9, 1813 – bdsm: Nicholas Blacklock, Jesse T. Ramsay
Robert J. & Ann M. Ramsay, April 16, 1816 – bdsm: Robert J. Blacklock, Benjamin C. Ashton
BLACKWELL, Lewis & Milly Bennett, July 19, 1834 – bdsm: Lewis Blackwell, Reuben Johnston, Jr.
BLADEN, Thomas Jr. & Ann Carolin, Sept. 4, 1811 – bdsm: Thomas Bladen, John Suter
William L. & Catharine Daniel, Oct. 27, 1810 –

BLADEN (continued)
bdsm: William L. Bladen, Thomas Daniel
BLAKE, William & Nancy Keene, Oct. 6, 1842 - bdsm: William Blake, Edmund J. Lee
BLAKENEY, John & Jane Spriggs, Dec. 24, 1803 - bdsm: John Blakeney, Samuel Summers
BLANCHARD, Jason & Ann J. Jinkinns, Jan. 12, 1822 - bdsm: Jason Blanchard, Francis Somes
BLAYLOCK, Richard & Statia Ann Bryan, Nov. 17, 1847 - bdsm: Richard Blaylock, John H. Watkins
BLINCOE, William & Maria Longdon, Sept. 19, 1840 - bdsm: William Blincoe, Wm. P. Thomas
BLOZHAM, James & Catharine Dunnington, March 17, 1803 - bdsm: James Bloxham, William Fletcher
BLUE, John & Catherine Evans, March 27, 1806 - bdsm: John Blue, John Underwood
BLUME, Joseph H. & Elizabeth Lyles, Sept. 15, 1823 - bdsm: Joseph H. Blume, Alexander Clarke
BODKIN, Washington L. & Catherine A. Harper, Dec. 13, 1837 - bdsm: Washington L. Bodkin, John Laurence
BOGUE, Francis S. & Elizabeth Boyd, March 4, 1830 - bdsm: Francis S. Bogue, Isaac H. Robbins (guardian of Elizabeth Boyd)
BOLIVER, Elias & Elizabeth

BOLIVER (continued)
Miller, May 24, 1810 - bdsm: Elias Boliver, George Deneale
BOMBON, Dennis & Rachael Lyles (free people of color), Dec. 17, 1838 - bdsm: Dennis Bombon, Henry Gibson
BOND, William & Nancy Taylor, Sept. 3, 1807 - bdsm: William Bond, William Taylor
BONIS, Joseph C. & Eletia Hubball, Sept. 22, 1830 - bdsm: Joseph C. Bonis, William A. Williams
BONTS, George & Mary Benter, June 25, 1818 - bdsm: George Bonts, William Benter
BONTZ, Jacob & Mary Carlin, June 5, 1811 - bdsm: Jacob Bontz, Charles Mankin
Jacob & Sarah Carlin, March 11, 1818 - bdsm: Jacob Bontz, John Y. Smith
John & Elizabeth House, March 28, 1816 - bdsm: John Bontz, David House
BOOKMAN, Peter & Rosanna Nevitt, May 1, 1815 - bdsm: Peter Bookman, Charles McShane
BOOTH, William & Ann Crys, Oct. 25, 1828 - bdsm: William Booth, James Nowell
BOOTHE, William & Christiana Lowe, Sept. 20, 1843 - bdsm: William Boothe, Ellis Price
BOSS, Abraham & Ann D. Hickey, Oct. 15, 1816 - bdsm: Abraham Boss, Ann

BOSS (continued)
D. Hickey
BOSTICK, George & Eleanor
Wilson, Aug. 13, 1812 –
bdsm: George Bostick,
George G. Sisson
BOSTON, Joshua & Ann
Thrift of Alexandria Coun-
ty, March 14, 1805 –
bdsm: Joshua Boston,
Wm. Answorth
Samuel E. & Julia Ann
Love, Feb. 29, 1828 –
bdsm: Samuel E. Boston,
Elizabeth Love
BOURNE, Daniel & Rebecca
Burk, Oct. 10, 1805 –
bdsm: Daniel Bourne, Ben-
jamin King
William & Margaret Neale,
Oct. 13, 1836 – bdsm:
William Bourne, William
Gardner
BOUSH, Nathaniel & Jane
Chatham, July 3, 1839 –
bdsm: Nathaniel Boush,
Henry Chatham
BOWEN, Strother H. & Mary
E. M. Peak, June 22, 1843
– bdsm: Strother H.
Bowen, John Lawsan
BOWLER, John & Frances
Leary, Feb. 6, 1822 –
bdsm: John Bowler,
Andrew Leary (Married
Feb. 10, 1822 by Rev. O.
Norris)
BOWLES, Richard & Betsey
Piper, Feb. 27, 1822 –
bdsm: Richard Bowles,
William Harris
Richard & Betsy Mankins,
April 22, 1840 – bdsm:
Richard Bowles, Henry
Brown
Thomas & Susan Sales, June

BOWLES (continued)
9, 1813 – bdsm: Thomas
Bowles, Richard Thomp-
son
William & Phillis (alias
Ann Henry) (both mulat-
toes), May 26, 1823 –
bdsm: William Bowles,
Henry Morris
BOWLING, Ambrose G. &
Margaret James, July 29,
1809 – bdsm: Ambrose G.
Bowling, John Potten
George & Elizabeth Veitch,
Feb. 22, 1805 – bdsm:
George Bowling, James
Hall
John & Franky Griffin, Feb.
11, 1818 – bdsm: John
Bowling, Richard Wallace
Robert & Jane Christie
Neille, Nov. 28, 1816 –
bdsm: Robert Bowling,
John Neille (See also:
Neal)
BOWMAN, Leonard & Mary
Talbott, Jan. 2, 1841 –
bdsm: Leonard Bowman,
Richard Reeder
BOYD, James P. & Louisa
Hipkins, Aug. 31, 1839 –
bdsm: James P. Boyd,
Lewis Hipkins
John & Delilah Slater, June
15, 1836 – bdsm: John
Boyd, William Violett
John & Jane Watkins, July
5, 1809 – bdsm: John
Boyd, James Popler
John & Mary Kirk, June 30,
1810 – bdsm: John Boyd,
Samuel Kirk
Reuben S. & Elizabeth
Moore, Oct. 1, 1835 –
bdsm: Reuben S. Boyd,
Daniel Minor

BOYD (continued)
Robert & Betsey Bayley, Nov. 20, 1810 - bdsm: Robert Boyd, Samuel Kirk
Robert B. & Ann O. Murray, Jan. 16, 1841 - bdsm: Robert B. Boyd, Henry Mansfield
BOYER, Elias & Ann Bruce, August 15, 1803 - bdsm: Elias Boyer, Jeremiah Satterwhite
George & Frances Ward, July 7, 1846 - bdsm: George Boyer, John Boyer
Henry & Mary Yardley, Feb. 10, 1836 - bdsm: Henry Boyer, Meredith Edmonds
John & Martha Ann Reynolds, Nov. 9, 1812 - bdsm: John Boyer, William Moore
Joseph & Ann Kirk, Jan. 21, 1840 - bdsm: Joseph Boyer, George Davis
BOYLE, John & Julia Ann Hudson, Feb. 24, 1830 - bdsm: John Boyle, William Lipscomb
BRADDOCK, Thomas S. & Margaret Ann Dogan, June 23, 1842 - bdsm: Thomas S. Braddock, Timothy Mountford
BRADLEY, Christopher Columbus & Ann Eliza Ball, Sept. 20, 1837 - bdsm: Christopher Columbus Bradley, George Snyder
Gabriel & Eliza Taylor, Aug. 1, 1822 - bdsm: Gabriel Bradley, Laughlin Masterson
Harrison & Elishaba Harris Huguely, April 23, 1816 - bdsm: Harrison Bradley,

BRADLEY (continued)
Horace Field
John Henry & Jane Douglass Miller, licence issued Oct. 17, 1850 - bdsm:
BRADY, John S. & Susan Brown, Jan. 22, 1828 - bdsm: John S. Brady, William Davis
Thomas & Sally McBrocklin, Dec. 1, 1802 - bdsm: Thomas Brady, Charles Pascoe
BRAMEL, William W. & Mary H. Jones, Sept. 19, 1827 - bdsm: William W. Bramel, John W. Barker
BRANDT, Richard H. & Ann Caroline Smoot, Jan. 7, 1828 - bdsm: Richard H. Brandt, William Page
BRANNON, William & Joicey Forrest, July 24, 1833 - bdsm: William Brannon, John Clare
BRANTHWAITE, William & Elizabeth Curry, August 14, 1802 - bdsm: William Branthwaite, David Jenkins
BRAWNER, Henry & Elizabeth Anness, June 24, 1815 - bdsm: Henry Brawner, Presley Haynie
Henry & Kitty McRea, June 8, 1815 - bdsm: Henry Brawner, James Wilson
Wm. H. & Mary C. Speake, Sept. 14, 1840 - bdsm: Wm. H. Brawner, John J. Sayre
BREAST, James A. & Eliza Talbott, Nov. 29, 1826 - bdsm: James A. Breast, Horatio Day
BRENNER, John & ___

BRENNER (continued)
Drum?, Feb. 6, 1838 –
bdsm: John Brenner, John
Higdon
BRENT, Elton & Jane Gray-
son, Oct. 7, 1837 - bdsm:
Elton Brent, Alfred Gray
Henry & Elizabeth Blue,
Dec. 26, 1818 – bdsm:
Henry Brent, John Blue
BREST, Clement & Margaret
Flood, Feb. 12, 1827 –
bdsm: Clement Brest,
Thomas Dewy
BRIANT, Reuben & Elizabeth
Stone, Dec. 10, 1840 –
bdsm: Reuben Briant, John
Briant
BRICK, Samuel & Ann
Cleaveland, Sept. 30, 1822
- bdsm: Samuel Brick,
Beale Howard
BRIGHT, John & Frances
Deeton March 9. 1818 –
bdsm: John Bright,
Frances Deeton
John & Nancy Young, Dec.
20, 1823 - bdsm: John
Bright, Nancy Young
BRIGHTMAN, Joseph & Mary
Schearman, July 23, 1805
- bdsm: Joseph Bright-
man, Dixon Brittingham
BRISCOE, Warner W. & Jane
H. Slacum, Nov. 16, 1825
- bdsm: Warner W. Bris-
coe, Albert Fairfax
BRISON, John & Mary
McKinney, April 17, 1818
- bdsm: John Brison,
Thomas Williams
BRITTINGHAM, James &
Polly Browne, June 30,
1803 – bdsm: James Brit-
tingham, Robert Brown
BROAD, Michael & Jane

BROAD (continued)
Martin, Jan. 14, 1804 –
bdsm: Michael Broad,
Charles Pascoe
Thomas & Mary May, Dec.
26, 1820 - bdsm: Thomas
Broad, Thomas Murray
BRAODWATER, William E.
& Margaret Darne, Nov.
22, 1816 - bdsm: William
E. Broadwater, Simon
Darne
BROCCHUS, Thomas & Ra-
chael Ashton, Nov. 5, 1801
- bdsm: Thomas Broc-
chus, Daniel C. Tupp
BROCKETT, Robert Jr. &
Elizabeth Longdon, Dec.
14, 1815 - bdsm: Robert
Brockett, Jr., John A.
Longdon
Walter & Elizabeth Byrne,
Nov. 18, 1815 - bdsm:
Walter Brockett, David
Dick
BRODBECK, Jacob & Mary
Ann Appich, Sept. 19, 1844
- bdsm: Jacob Brodbeck,
David Appich
BRODERS, James & Eliza-
beth Curtain, Jan. 29, 1814
- bdsm: James Broders,
Susannah Sly
Joseph & Eliza Stoops, Sept.
14, 1824 - bdsm: Joseph
Broders, Jesse Smith
BROGDON, George & Sarah
Solomon (free blacks)
Aug. 24, 1809 - George
Brogdon, George Russell
BROOKE, John Henry & Jane
Ann Nash, Sept. 15, 1829 –
bdsm: John Henry Brooke,
Richard A. Brown
Thomas & Sarah Coffin,
Sept. 2, 1809 - bdsm:

BROOKE (continued)
Thomas Brooke, John Crevell
BROOKS, David & Mary Jones, Sept. 12, 1829 – bdsm: David Brooks, George Millon (See also: Brookes)
Frederick & Phebe Ann Tyler (both colored), Sept. 18, 1850 – bdsm:
George & Ann O. Fugitt, May 29, 1849 – bdsm: George Brooks, George Wise
George & Elizabeth Kirby, Sept. 13, 1821 – bdsm: George Brooks, John Kirby
James & Sarah Johnston, Aug. 27, 1817 – bdsm: James Brooks, James Arshcome
John & Esther Jane Fowle, April 22, 1846 – bdsm: John Brooks, John B. Daingerfield
John T. & Sarah T. Dangerfield, Jan. 12, 1830 – bdsm: John T. Brooks, Edward Daingerfield
Wm. H. & Mary Ann Elizabeth Parsons, Nov. 29, 1850 – license issued; permission given by John Parsons, her father
BROUAUGH, Cary & Ann G. Jacob, Jan. 27, 1814 – bdsm: Cary Brouaugh, H. Miller
BROUGH, Heppel & Betsy Lunt, Feb. 4, 1804 – bdsm: Heppel Brough, Joseph Cowan
BROWERS, John & Maria Mahauny, March 9, 1820 – bdsm: John Browers,

BROWERS (continued)
James King (Also: Mahanny)
BROWN, Alexander & Mary Jane Billingsly (free persons of colour), Nov. 25, 1841 – bdsm: Alexander Brown, Daniel Ford
Charles & Charlotte Wheeler, June 8, 1809 – bdsm: Charles Brown, Thomas Leeder
Edmond L. & Catharine B. Bayne, July 12, 1825 – bdsm: Edmond L. Brown, Leonard Adams
George & Elizabeth Holly, Oct. 20, 1834 – bdsm: George Brown, Nimrod H. Nowland
Henry (freeman of colour) & Sarah Ann Piper, June 25, 1813 – bdsm: Henry Brown, James Evans
James & Lucy Whiting, Oct. 2, 1829 – bdsm: James Brown, William Thomas
James & Susan Martin, Nov. 14, 1817 – bdsm: James Brown, John Chauncey
John & Margaret Coates, Aug. 12, 1812 – bdsm: John Brown, James Young
John & Maria Leathrum, August 25, 1823 – bdsm: John Brown, John Hill
John & Martha Bowlin, June 3, 1816 – bdsm: John Brown, Charles Drew (See also: Bolen)
John D. & Mary G. Gretter, Oct. 22, 1811 – bdsm: John D. Brown, Robert Harrison
John S. & Lewellin A. Harding, April 5, 1842 – bdsm:

BROWN (continued)
John S. Brown, E.R. Violett
Samuel & Robert Smith, March 14, 1811 - bdsm: Samuel Brown, Robert Smith
Theodore of Jefferson County, Kentucky, & Sally Bryan of Alexandria County, July 3, 1852 (license) -- bdsm:
BRUCE, Aaron & Nancy Smith, August 31, 1815 -- bdsm: Aaron Bruce, Thomas Sandford
Charles & Rachael Brown, Jan. 15, 1845 - bdsm: Charles Bruce, Robert Turley
Robert & Eliza Carpenter, Dec. 20, 1838 - bdsm: Robert Bruce, Daniel Bruce
BRYAN, George & Caroline Pattison, Jan. 18, 1848 - bdsm: George Bryan, J. Louis Kinzer
James D. & Martha Arnold, May 18, 1850 - bdsm: James D. Bryan, William Jenkins
John & Ann Boyer, Dec. 15, 1846 - bdsm: John Bryan, James Quaid
John L. & Hariet Noland, Sept. 1, 1830 - bdsm: John L. Bryan, John S. Humphries
Robert & Paulina Lloyd, June 30, 1846 -- bdsm: Robert Bryan, George H. Smith
BUCHANNON, Robert E. & Elizabeth M. Padgett, Nov. 20, 1834 - bdsm:

BUCHANNON (continued)
Robert E. Buchannon, John A. Rudd
BUCKINGHAM, Edmund F. & Andenetta Jackson Anna Allmassi Gertrude Scott, Sept. 23, 1844 - bdsm: Edmund F. Buckingham, Mathew W. Galt
Isaac & Mary Brown, July 15, 1821 - bdsm: Isaac Buckingham, Philip P. Johnston (Married July 15, 1821 by Rev. O. Norris)
BUCKLER, James & Mary Gillbreth, Aug. 27, 1812 -- bdsm: James Buckler, John Gillbreth
BUCKLEY, John D. & Margaret Legg, Aug. 25, 1817 - bdsm: John D. Buckley, Samuel Catts
BULL, George A. & Rebecca A. Jourdan, May 25, 1815 - bdsm: George A. Bull, Benoni Wheat
BUNOUF, John & Elizabeth Keach, Sept. 14, 1815 - bdsm: John Bunouf, Thomas Potts (See also: Bunuff)
BURCHELL, Edward & Ann Bates, Feb. 20, 1821 - bdsm: Edward Burchell, Charles Scott
BURFORD, John A. & Hannah Dyson, Feb. 23, 1804 - bdsm: John A. Burford, Thomas Crandell
John Atkins & Mary Smith, Oct. 9, 1802 - bdsm: John Atkins Burford, Mary Smith
BURK, Henry & Frances Ann Anderson, Dec. 15, 1842 - bdsm: Henry Burk, Wil-

BURK (continued)
liam Anderson

BURKE, Delany & Sarah Jane Berry, Oct. 30, 1850 - bdsm:

T. M. & Marie C. Andrews, parental consent given Nov. 8, 1852 - Witnesses: J. W. Harper, S. F. Harper

BURKS, Richard S. & Mary Ann McDennick, Feb. 18, 1830 - bdsm: Richard S. Burks, William McDennick

BURNS, Thomas & Elizabeth Lathram, April 15, 1831 - bdsm: Thomas Burns, John Fizall

BURRAG, Thomas & Hannah Simms, May 20, 1834 - bdsm: Thomas Burrag, N. J. Croggon

BURROWS, John & Jane Payne, April 27, 1824 - bdsm: John Burrows, Levi Pickering

BURRUS, Robert & Sophia Brown, Oct. 16, 1830 - bdsm: Robert Burrus, William S. Ricketts

BURSON, Stephen & Rebecca Myers, Jan. 14, 1822 - bdsm: Stephen T. Burson, Elijah Walter (Married Jan. 14, 1822 by Rev. O. Norris)

BURTON, Thomas W. & Caroline M. Buckers, Dec. 23, 1828 - bdsm: Thomas W. Burton, John Buckers

BURWICK, James & Margaret Adams, daughter of Benj. Adams, June 16, 1834 - bdsm: James Burwick, Benj. Adams

BUSH, George W. & Emma

BUSH (continued)
N. Danforth, Sept. 10, 1850 - bdsm: George W. Bush, Edward Betts; J. N. Danford father of Emma N. Danforth

BUSHBY, James & Margaret Boyer, daughter of John Boyer, June 11, 1838 - bdsm: James Bushby, John Boyer

William & Lucinda E. Delphy, Sept. 30, 1851 - bdsm:

BUSSELL, William & Rhody Clark, April 15, 1809 - bdsm: William Bussell, James Keith

BUTLER, Abraham & Mary G. Dulany, Sept. 6, 1821 - bdsm: Abraham Butler, Edward Murphy

David & Selia Harris, Dec. 2, 1823 - bdsm: David Butler, Davis Bowie

Edward & Elizabeth Watkins, Nov. 26, 1810 - bdsm: Edward Butler, John Watkins

Harry & Nelly Hoy, March 1, 1827 - bdsm: Harry Butler, Isaiah Taite

Horatio & Lucy Forrester, Dec. 24, 1807 - bdsm: Horatio Butler, Daniel Wells

James & Flora Johnson, Oct. 5, 1839 - bdsm: James Butler, Reuben Johnston, Jr.

Robert & Elizabeth Julius, Nov. 5, 1840 - bdsm: Robert Butler

BUTTS, Augustus & Catharine Tatterson, July 5, 1817 - bdsm: Augustus

BUTTS (continued)
Butts, Alexander Tatterson
L. Washington & Mary Elizabeth Wells, Dec. 12, 1844 - bdsm: L. Washington Butts, Francis M. Walker

CABLE, George & Polly Stott, June 16, 1810 -- bdsm: George Cable, William Hilton

CADDIS, David & Sarah Henderson, July 5, 1820 - bdsm: David Caddis, Davis Bowie (Celebrated July 5, 1820 by Rev. O. Norris)
Henry & Adeline Heath, Dec. 2, 1828 - bdsm: Henry Caddis, Charles M. Wright

CADEN, James & Ellen White, May 17, 1820 - bdsm: James Caden, William A. Williams

CAIN, John & Lucy Hamilton, Nov. 15, 1817 - bdsm: John Cain, James Brown

CAIRNS, Wm. D. & Mary C. Deneale, April 29, 1826 - bdsm: William D. Cairns, Wm. Byrd Page (See also: Carnes)

CALDWELL, Josiah F. & Maria Magruder, Nov. 20, 1815 - bdsm: Josiah F. Caldwell

CALLAWAY, C. M. K. & Martha M. Holtzman, July 12, 1850 - bdsm: C. M. K. Callaway, Samuel Clements

CALLENDER, Bartholemew & Ellinder Latham, Nov. 13, 1806 - bdsm: Bartholemew Callender, William Latham

CALLIT, Joseph & Ann Day, June 4, 1816 - bdsm: Joseph Callit, Owen Sullivan

CALVIN, George & Nancy Ann Crany, April 4, 1837 - bdsm: George Calvin, Reubin Johnston, Jr.

CAMBLE, Lewis & Milly Julius, Nov. 24, 1843 - bdsm: Lewis Camble

CAMERON, James & Susan Fendley, Oct. 4, 1832 -- bdsm: James Cameron, Noblet Lindsay

CAMPBELL, James & Kitty Cahall, Dec. 24, 1805 - bdsm: James Campbell, Hugh West Deneale
James & Melvina A. Wilson, Nov. 25, 1828 - bdsm: James Campbell, Robert J. T. Wilson
Samuel L. & Mary A. E. Satterwhite, April 26, 1832 -- bdsm: Samuel L. Campbell, Wm. H. Shirley
St. George T. & Sarah E. Mason, Nov. 17, 1841 - bdsm: St. George T. Campbell, Richard Bache
William & Elizabeth Smedley, July 27, 1818 - bdsm: William Campbell, Robert Abercrombie
William T. of Charles County, Maryland, & Mary Ann Banque, July 14, 1845 - bdsm: Wm. T. Campbell, Hugh Banque
Wm. R. & Julia Ann Zimmerman, March 9, 1840 - bdsm: Wm. R. Campbell, Wm. H. Zimmerman

CANNON, John Newton & Ann Wattles, June 5, 1802

CANNON (continued)
- bdsm: John Newton Cannon, George Singleton
Joseph & Amie Brown, Dec. 18, 1817 - bdsm: Joseph Cannon, David Bowie
Washington & Ann Simmes, May 28, 1822 - bdsm: Washington Cannon, John Simmes
CARDWELL, David A. & Rebecca M. Drinker, Aug. 1, 1839 - bdsm: David A. Cardwell, Benj. S. Kinsey
CAREW, Thomas & Margaret Korn, Oct. 1, 1806 - bdsm: Thomas Carew, John Korn
CARLAN, James & Litia Skydmore, Nov. 21, 1821 - bdsm: James Carlan, John Skydmore
CARLIN, Geo. W. & Elizabeth Harris, April 20, 1810 - bdsm: Geo. W. Carlin, John Boyer
James F. & Martha J. Wheat, Nov. 10, 1845 - bdsm: James F. Carlin, John A. Dixion
CARLISLE, Christopher & Ann Mandeville, May 22, 1811 - bdsm: Christopher Carlisle, Joseph Mandeville
CARLOS, Francis & Mary DeWarren, April 10, 1805 - bdsm: Francis Carlos, John Frignett
CARNE, Richard L. & Cecelia Shakes, July 1, 1821 - bdsm: Richard L. Carne, Robert L. White
CAROLIN, Westley & Catharine Richards, July 5, 1811 - bdsm: Westley Carolin, Thomas Donald-

CAROLIN (continued)
son
CARPENTER, Randall & Sophia Williams, May 28, 1816 - bdsm: Randall Carpenter, James Dudley
CARRINGTON, Ely & Alesanna Kell, Aug. 31, 1815 - bdsm: Ely Carrington, Isaac Kell
CARROLL, James & Mary Ann Hutson, Aug. 9, 1824 - bdsm: James Carroll, Levin Tucker
Sinclair & Ann Alexander, May 12, 1802 - bdsm: Sinclair Carroll, Robert Alexander
Thomas L. & Mildred Thompson, March 23, 1841 - bdsm: Thomas L. Carroll, James Thompson
CARSON, George & Margaret G. Lewis, Jan. 8, 1835 - bdsm: George Carson, George Hutchison
John & Elizabeth Jerome, May 19, 1809 - bdsm: John Carson, John Wood
John B. & Margaret Ann Gonsolve, Aug. 29, 1843 - bdsm: William W. Triplett, Patrick Gallagher
Samuel & Jane Hamilton, Nov. 28, 1806 - bdsm: Samuel Carson, Thomas Cruse
CARTER, Ellzey & Elizabeth Howard, Jan. 16, 1828 - bdsm: Ellzey Carter, Libren Carter
Libren & Nancy Howard, June 26, 1826 - bdsm: Libren Carter, Nathaniel Yearly
Richard & Sarah Armitage,

CARTER (continued)
July 30, 1836 - bdsm: Richard Carter, James P. Coleman

Richard H. & Susanna Dogan, daughter of Betsey Duval, Dec. 16, 1847 - bdsm: Richard H. Carter, James E. Piper

Robert & Sarah Taylor, Jan. 25, 1834 - bdsm: Robert Carter, Edward Evans

CARTWRIGHT, Jonathan & Eliza S. Dade, Aug. 15, 1833 - bdsm: Jonathan Cartwright, John Bryan

CARUSI, Nathaniel & Jane Hollywood, Nov. 16, 1830 - bdsm: Nathaniel Carusi, John Adam, guardian of Jane Hollywood

CASEY, Daniel & Mary O'Daye, license issued May 2, 1851 - bdsm:

CASH, Joseph & Sarah Javins, Jan. 2, 1804 - bdsm: Joseph Cash, John Javins

CATLETT, George W. & Margarett Murray, July 8, 1823 - bdsm: George W. Catlett, Walter L. Darrell

CATTERTON, Thomas Ward & Linnay Finnik, Feb. 23, 1804 - bdsm: Thomas Ward Catterton, John Catterton

CATTS, Samuel & Elizabeth Legge, Dec. 27, 1815 - bdsm: Samuel Catts, Cornelius Stokey

CAWOOD, Benjamin & Anna Ferguson, Nov. 12, 1814 - bdsm: Benjamin Cawood, Samuel Armstrong

Benjamin H. & Mary Ann Magee, July 8, 1829 -

CAWOOD (continued)
bdsm: Benjamin H. Cawood, Moses O. B. Cawood

Daniel & Mary McAfee, March 14, 1816 - bdsm: Daniel Cawood, Mark Butts

Grafton & Sally R. Madden, Feb. 24, 1824 - bdsm: Grafton Cawood, Robert Barry

Moses F. A. & Elizabeth Underwood, Oct. 23, 1835 - bdsm: Moses F. A. Cawood, William Thomas

Moses F. A. & Susan G. Spilman, Oct. 9, 1841 - bdsm: Moses F. A. Cawood, Robert Taylor

Moses O. B. & Delilah Robertson, Jan. 13, 1818 - bdsm: Moses O. B. Cawood, James Hetherington

CHAMBERLAIN, Lincoln & Mary Harris, Nov. 2, 1822 - bdsm: Lincoln Chamberlain, Joseph harris

Luther & Jane S. Adam, Jan. 18, 1825 - bdsm: Luther Chamberlain, John Adam

Wm. G. & Margaret W. Musgrove, Dec. 9, 1843 - bdsm: Wm. G. Chamberlain, Thomas Parsons

CHANCE, John & (widow) Mary Paget, March 14, 1814 - bdsm: John Chance, Patrick Granville

CHAPIN, Charles & Mary Ann Martha Wise, Dec. 3, 1827 - bdsm: Charles Chapin, George Wise

CHAPMAN, Charles T. & Margaret S. Gadsby, Oct. 12, 1807 - bdsm: Charles

64

CHAPMAN (continued)
T. Chapman, John Gadsby
Jeremiah & Maria Grymes,
March 31, 1831 - bdsm:
Jeremiah Chapman, Maria
Grymes
CHARLES, John & Elizabeth
Angel, Oct. 10, 1833 -
bdsm: John Charles, Abra-
ham E. Potts
John & Sarah Williams,
Dec. 3, 1839 - bdsm: John
Charles, Jas. Carroll
CHASE, Peter & Eleanor
Smallwood, April 9, 1803 -
bdsm: Peter Chase, Wil-
liam Skidmore
CHICHESTER, Daniel M. &
Louisa Kidwell, July 6,
1840 - bdsm: Daniel M.
Chichester, Patsy Chi-
chester
CHICK, William M. & Ann
Smith, April 9, 1816 -
bdsm: William M. Chick,
E. Linsley
CHILDS, David & Mary Mit-
tchum, Jan. 22, 1806 -
bdsm: David Childs, John
Turner
William & Rebecca Allison,
March 7, 1815 - bdsm:
William Childs, James
Allison
CHINN, Charles & Mary J.
Chapman, daughter of
George Chapman, Nov. 2,
1847 - bdsm: Charles
Chinn, George Chapman
CHIPLEY, Samuel & Sarah
M. Bayliss, July 4, 1833 -
bdsm: James Chipley, Al-
fred Price
CHISELDINE, Washington &
Mary Ann Clapdore, Dec.
19, 1833 - bdsm: Wash-

CHISELDINE (continued)
ington Chiseldine, Lewis
Fuier
CHISSON, Lewis & Ann
Freeman, Oct. 3, 1801 -
bdsm: Louis Chisson,
Wm. Freeman
CHRISMAN, John & Eliza-
beth Barr, Nov. 24, 1804 -
bdsm: John Chrisman,
Hugh Barr
CHRISMOND, Robert M. &
Jane E. Barger, license
issued July 1, 1851 -
bdsm:
CHRISTOPHE, Christian &
Harriot Cox, April 16, 1811
- bdsm: Christian Chris-
tophe, James Armitage
CHURCH, Gilbert & Sarah
Hayes, March 11, 1807 -
bdsm: Gilbert Church,
Andrew Hayes
Henry & Margaret McCol-
lester, May 5, 1802 -
bdsm: Henry Church, Peter
Wise
John & Mary Harrington,
Dec. 19, 1833 - bdsm:
John Church, David Jarvis
(Also: Hethrington)
CLAGETT, Darius & Ann
Louisa Thompson, Jan.
18, 1818 - bdsm: Darius
Clagett, Jonah Thompson
& B. W. Clagett
James A. & Mary Francis
Minor, Sept. 12, 1844 -
bdsm: James A. Clagett,
Mary F. Minor
Richard H. & Sarah Ramsay,
Nov. 11, 1823 - bdsm:
Richard H. Clagett, Colin
Auld
Thomas & Eliza Courts,
both of Prince George's

CLAGETT (continued)
County, Maryland, Aug. 31, 1824 - bdsm:
William H. & Mary Harrison, April 1, 1845 - bdsm: William H. Clagett, Washington C. Page
William W. & Ann Page, June 14, 1815 - bdsm: William W. Clagett, Charles Page
CLAPDOR, John Michael & Ann Vernon, April 6, 1802 - bdsm: John Michael Clapdor, Jesse Crosby
CLAPDORE, Jacob L. & Louisa Boswell, Jan. 9, 1837 - bdsm: Jacob L. Clapdore, Moses F. A. Cawood
Jacob L. & Mary Jane Brent, May 8, 1848 - bdsm: Jacob L. Clapsdore, Thomas Craven
John M. & Elizabeth A. Frederick, Dec. 29, 1833 - bdsm: John M. Clapdore, Jacob Zimmerman
CLARK, Edward & Catherine Emerson, Oct. 20, 1837 - bdsm: Edward Clark, John Kidwell
Edward & Maria Fletcher, April 8, 1844 - bdsm: Edward Clark, Peyton Clark
Elias & Catherine Mitchell, Jan. 6, 1825 - bdsm: Elias Clark, Davis Bowie (See also: Clarke)
Isaac & Mary Smith, Oct. 9, 1815 - bdsm: Isaac Clark, William N. Chick
James C. & Hannah E. Taylor, Oct. 17, 1842 - bdsm: James C. Clark, Franklin Taylor

CLARK (continued)
John & Wilhemina Smith, Jan. 14, 1841 - bdsm: John Clark, Charles Hawkins
John M. & Nancy King, Nov. 2, 1815 - bdsm: John M. Clark, Charles King
Nathaniel & Sarah Handless, Nov. 10, 1842 - bdsm: Nathaniel Clark, Wm. Hines
Robert C. & Hestor Elleanor Gibson, Sept. 26, 1844 - bdsm: Robert C. CLark, Henry Gibson
Rufus W. & Eliza Walton, June 13, 1843 - bdsm: Rufus W. Clark, Robert Jamieson
CLARKE, Henry & Sarah A. Sherfield, June 25, 1834 - bdsm: Henry Clarke, Stephen Milburn
Horatio D. & Nancy Williams, Aug. 21, 1821 - bdsm: Horatio D. Clarke, Bazil Williams (Married Aug. 21, 1821 by Rev. O. Norris)
John P. & Ann Moulden, Aug. 27, 1840 - bdsm: John P. Clarke, Richard H. Wheeler
Peyton & Emmeline Mullen, May 21, 1836 - bdsm: Peyton Clarke, Abner Humphries (Also: Emeline Mullen)
Peyton & Mary Williams, Oct. 9, 1849 - bdsm: Peyton Clarke, Benjamin H. Berry
Thompson & Billezid Essex, Feb. 2, 1816 - bdsm: Thompson Clarke

CLARKSON, Edward & Elizabeth H. Green, Nov. 27, 1827 - bdsm: Edward Clarkson, William Call

CLARRIDGE, James H. & Mary A. Padgett, Sept. 7, 1842 - bdsm: James H. Carridge, James Padgett (Also: Padget)

CLEARY, William & Hannah A. McClean, May 31, 1831 - bdsm: William Cleary, Chas. E. Dade

CLEMENTS, Henry & Elizabeth Jones, August 16, 1817 - bdsm: Henry Clements, Moses Jones

Robert H. & Alice L. Ramsay, July 19, 1825 - bdsm: Robert H. Clements, Thomas Munroe

William & Sarah Booth, June 2, 1802 - bdsm: William Clements, William Smith

CLEVELAND, William & Mary J. Howard, Jan. 21, 1846 - bdsm: William Cleveland, Mary Jane Howard

CLIFFORD, Nehemiah & Nancy Nelson, August 21, 1805 - bdsm: Nehemiah Clifford, William Mitchell

CLOWES, Thomas J. & Martha McCormick, Sept. 3, 1839 - bdsm: Thomas J. Clowes, James M. Eaches

COATS, Frederick & Sally Adams, Nov. 2, 1842 - bdsm: Frederick Coats, John Coats

COCKRANN, Geo. H. & Elisabeth Duffy, Feb. 21, 1834 - bdsm: Geo. H. Cockrann, William Duffy

COCKRELL, Martin & Mary Stonemets, Jan. 1, 1805 - bdsm: Martin Cockrell, Amos Alexander

COCKSON, Charles & Mary Gulatt, Aug. 29, 1822 - bdsm: Charles Cockson, William Gulatt

COFFER, George (of Charles County, Maryland) & Sarah Posey, Feb. 17, 1825 - bdsm: George Coffer, Ignatius Allen

COFFIN, Daniel & Sarah Findly, Dec. 17, 1801 - bdsm: Daniel Coffin, John Duffy

John & Elizabeth Bennett, June 5, 1802 - bdsm: John Coffin, Daniel Haley

COGAN, Anthony & Maria Rooe, April 7, 1823 - bdsm: Anthony Cogan, Philip Dogan

COHAGAN, John & Elizabeth Bowie, May 24, 1813 - bdsm: John Cohagan, William Veitch

COHEN, William & Catharine Cary, April 29, 1801 - bdsm: Samuel Smith, Wm. Cohen

COLE, Hezekiah & Helen Jones, Dec. 25, 1823 - bdsm: Hezekiah Cole, James D. Bryan

James & Elizabeth Morgan (both coloured), April 4, 1811 - bdsm: James Cole, Thomas Morgan

James & Elizabeth Parsons, Nov. 14, 1822 - bdsm: James Cole, Thomas Parson (Married Nov. 14, 1822 by Rev. O. Norris)

James & Lucy Boyle, Dec.

COLE (continued)
4, 1826 - bdsm: James Cole, Sally Tyson
James & Mary Ann Credit, Nov. 28, 1844 - bdsm: James Cole, Carroll Rodgers
John & Mary Ann Wood, Jan. 12, 1840 - bdsm: John Cole, Joseph Stone
Thomas & Tryphasa Hand, Nov. 6, 1806 - bdsm: Thomas Cole, John A. Stewart
William & Mary Ann Baker (formerly Nutt), Jan. 13, 1842 - bdsm: William Cole and Isaac Jackson
COLEGATE, Edward & Ann E. Laws, Aug. 14, 1823 - bdsm: Edward Colegate, William Lyle
COLEMAN, George & Elizabeth Marsteller, Sept. 25, 1806 - bdsm: George Coleman, Robert Anderson
James P. & Caroline Carolin, May 14, 1832 - bdsm: James P. Coleman, Hugh Carolin
COLLINS, Thomas & Ellen Lindsay, May 10, 1830 - bdsm: Thomas Collins, William Pomery
William A. & Sarah Slatford, June 11, 1802 - bdsm: William A. Collins, George Slatford
COLLINSWORTH, A. D. & Mary Tennison, Sept. 13, 1827 - bdsm: A. D. Collinsworth, Levi Hurdle (Also: Collingsworth)
COLONE, Vincent & Catharine Donaldson, March 17, 1810 - bdsm: Vincent

COLONE (continued)
Colone, John H. Manley
COLSTON, Joseph & Nancy Anderson, May 3, 1806 - bdsm: Joseph Colston, Dommick Bearcroft
COLUMBAL, Carlo & Elisa Rixter, Nov. 2, 1820 - bdsm: Charles Columbus, Mary Rixter (See also: Charles Columbus)
COLVERT, Henry & Eleanor Willis, Aug. 6, 1821 - bdsm: Henry Colvert & Robert Willis (Also: Calvert)
COLYER, John & Elizabeth Mullen, April 15, 1833 - bdsm: John Colyer, John Clare
COMPTON, Ludwell & Adeline Smith, Aug. 26, 1831 - bdsm: Ludwell Compton, Cyrus Compton
CONN, Philip & Ann Smith, July 13, 1809 - bdsm: Philip Conn, John Bogan
CONWAY, Andrew J. & Mary Ann VanZant, April 27, 1840 - bdsm: Andrew J. Conway, Andrew J. Fleming
Richard & Margaret Ashton, Nov. 8, 1806 - bdsm: Richard Conway, William Herbert
Robert & Margaret Sweet, May 22, 1809 - bdsm: Robert Conway, Andrew Jamieson
COOK, Henry & Hortensia H. Mark, July 29, 1841 - bdsm: Henry Cook, Elias Harrison
Joseph & Anna Baggot, July 10, 1827 - bdsm: Joseph

COOK (continued)
Cook, Henry Gilbreth
Lemuel A. & Emeline Gosser, Sept. 21, 1846 - bdsm: Lemuel A. Cook, Chas. F. Cox
Leonoard & Elizabeth Suter, May 25, 1825 - bdsm: Leonard Cook, Henry A. Webster
Lewis & Lydia Bayley, Nov. 30, 1809 - bdsm: Lewis Cook, Elizabeth Bayley, Daniel Crump
William & Mary King, Nov. 16, 1809 - bdsm: William Cook, Thomas M. Davis
COOKE, Joseph & Jane Gilbreth, Dec. 19, 1810 - bdsm: Joseph Cooke, John Gilbreth
COOLY, Azariah & Susan Taylor, April 5, 1828 - bdsm: Azariah Cooly, Alexander Tatterson
COOPER, Joseph & Ann Morris, April 5, 1821 - bdsm: Joseph Cooper, Ignatius Murray
William & Sally Dover, Dec. 9, 1830 - bdsm: William Cooper, Gus. Gibson
CORDERY, Henry & Elizabeth Green, Dec. 7, 1813 - bdsm: Henry Cordery, David Koones
CORE, Daniel & Mary Lambert, Aug. 5, 1815 - bdsm: Daniel Core, Daniel L. Lupton
CORSE, John & Julia G. Talbot, Nov. 11, 1813 - bdsm: John Corse, Jacob Douglass
CORWIN, Stephen & Julia Hopewell, June 26, 1806 -

CORWIN (continued)
bdsm: Stephen Corwin, William F. Gird
CORWINE, William R. & Sabrina Bartlett, May 18, 1840 - bdsm: William R. Corwine, Edward C. Horwell
COSGROVE, John & Mary Calico, Jan. 22, 1844 - bdsm: John Cosgrove, Mathew Mankin
COULSON, Anthony D. & Priscilla Merrick, April 2, 1835 - bdsm: Anthony D. Coulson, Reuben Johnson, Jr.
COULTER, Henry & Martha McCutchens, June 4, 1806 - bdsm: Jenry Colter, Frederick Shuck
COVERT, John & Elizabeth Dorcey, Aug. 22, 1807 - bdsm: John Covert, George Hill
COWING, Robert & Sophia Ann Biggs, June 22, 1829 - bdsm: Robert Cowing, Hugh Banks
COWMON, John P. & Mary Ann Edmonson, April 29, 1817 - bdsm: John P. Cowmon
COX, Cornelius & Caroline Jacobs, Nov. 10, 1842 - bdsm: Cornelius Cox, Wm. H. McKnight
William & Mary Curtis, May 8, 1811 - bdsm: William Cox, Thomas Flood
COXEN, Nathaniel & Catharine Gullatt, Oct. 18, 1821 - bdsm: Nathaniel Coxen, William Guatt
William & Matilda Badkin, Feb. 8, 1845 - bdsm: Wil-

COXEN (continued)
liam Coxen, James W. Ak-
tinson

COYLE, Randolph & Jane J.
Moore, Dec. 11, 1837 –
bdsm: Randolph Coyle,
Alexander Moore

CRABTREE, Eleazer &
Elizabeth Beleher Aug. 22,
1817 – bdsm: Eleazer
Crabtree, John B. Ham-
matt

CRAIK, George Washington
& Maria D. Tucker, Oct. 3,
1805 – bdsm: George
Washington Craik, John
Tucker

CRAM, Samuel & Mary
Hickman, Jan. I, 1812 –
bdsm: Samuel Cram,
Joseph G. Jewett

CRANDELL, Philip & Catha-
rine A. McKnight, March
I7, 1834 – bdsm: Philip
Crandell, Charles Mc-
Knight

CRANDLE, James of Wash-
ington County & Priscilla
Hascum, April 11, 1821 –
bdsm: James Crandle,
Lewis W. Plum of Alex-
andria

Thomas & Maria Moxley,
Jan. 10, 1810 – bdsm:
Thomas Crandle, John
Boyer

Thomas & Sarah Strait, Jan.
16, 1802 - bdsm: Thomas
Crandle, William Spears

CRANSTON, Samuel & Sarah
Varnell, Oct. 1, 1822 –
bdsm: Samuel Cranston,
John Cranston

CRAWFORD, William &
Elizabeth Higdon, Nov. 12,
1822 – bdsm: William

CRAWFORD (continued)
Crawford, Timothy Mc-
Carty

CREASE, John Hipsley &
Jane Newton, Oct. 20,
1813 – bdsm: John Hipsley
Crease, Augustine Newton

CREDIT, (Harry) Henry &
Ann Cole, April 26, 1820 –
bdsm: Henry Credit,
James Dudley (Married
April 27, 1820 by Oliver
Norris)

John & Sarah Ann Carter,
Dec. 11, 1844 – bdsm:
John Credit, James Cole

CREIGHTON, John T. &
Mary Carlin, May 25, 1837
– bdsm: John T. Creigh-
ton, Daniel Minor

Thomas B. & Roberta
English, May 20, 1846 –
bdsm: Thomas B. Creigh-
ton, George O. Dixion

CREMITT, Ebenezer & Mary
Ann Stewart, July 28, 1801
– bdsm: Ebenezer Cremitt,
Thomas Mahony

CREMPSEY, John Thomas &
Selina R. Johnston, Oct.
28, 1848 – bdsm: John
Thomas Crempsey, John
A. Field

CROCKETT, James & Cath-
arine A. Webster, license
given April 28, 1852 –
bdsm: none given

CROFT, Airhart & Lucinda
Bailess, Jan. 1, 1836 –
bdsm: Airhart Croft,
Thomas Baggett

CROGGON, Charles S. &
Mary Hillyard, May 28,
1830 – bdsm: Charles S.
Croggon, Griffin Carter
(See also: Craggins)

CRONMILLER, Samuel & Elizabeth Martin, May 20, 1830 – bdsm: Samuel Cronmiller, James Simms

CROOK, Thomas & Polly Philips, June 9, 1818 – bdsm: Thomas Crook, Polly Philips

Walter & Jane Ann Price, Oct. 4, 1837 – bdsm: Walter Crook, David Price

CROOKE, Bernard H. & Susan H. Windsor, Sept. 25, 1839 – bdsm: Bernard H. Crooke, Robert N. Windsor

CROSBY, Lewis & Sarah Ann Russell, May 17, 1809 – bdsm: Lewis Crosby, Jacob Hokes

CROSON, Ira & Mary E. Poor, daughter of Charles Poor, May 16, 1849 – bdsm: Ira Croson, William W. Rock

CROSS, Samuel & Milly Ann Jones, Jan. 18, 1806 – bdsm: Samuel Cross, Thomas Clark

Walter & Jane Nash, July Z8, 1821 – bdsm: Walter Cross, Wilfred Sidebottoms

CROWDER, Thomas L. & Elleanor P. L. Franklin, June 15, 1841 – bdsm: Thomas L. Crowder, Richard Donalson

CRUMP, Daniel & Elizabeth Skidmore, Nov. 23, 1811 – bdsm: Daniel Crump, John Skidmore

James T. & Ann Elizabeth Summers, Dec. 9, 1846 – bdsm: James T. Crump, Aquilla Emerson

Thornton & Teresa Butler,

CRUMP (continued)
Sept. 22, 1826 – bdsm: Thornton Crump, Gustavus Gibson

CULBERT, James & Grace Dixon, Oct. 1, 1810 – bdsm: James Culbert, Richard Hokes

CULLINS, James & Nancy Carter, Nov. 13, 1822 – bdsm: James Cullins, Carter Cullins

CUMMINGS, George M. & Elizabeth Jane Turner, April 16. 1824 – bdsm: George M. Cummings, Wm. McCliff

CUNNINGHAM, Robert & Elizabeth Shepherd, Nov. 1, 1837 – bdsm: Robert Cunningham, Elijah Taylor

William & Ann Fitzgerald, May 13, 1812 – bdsm: William Cunningham, Anthony Rhodes

CUPID, Robert & Louisa Savoy, daughter of Wm. Savoy, May 29, 1848 – bdsm: Robert Cupid, William Savoy (free blacks)

CURBY, Thomas & Susan Best, August 10, 1820 – bdsm: Thomas Curby, John B. Gorman

CURRY, Anthony & Nelly Mittchell, August 13, 1804 – bdsm: Anthony Curry, Isaac Howard

Thomas & Mary Ann Barnett, Oct. 2, 1817 – bdsm: Thomas Curry, John Crauston

CURSINE, Bartholomew & Peggy Carlin, July 18, 1807 – bdsm: Bartholomew Cursine, Lewis Simpson

71

CURTIS, Zachariah & Permelia W. Boyier, Jan. 6, 1850 - bdsm: Zachariah Curtis, Hezekiah Patton

CUSTIS, George Washington Parke & Mary Lee Fitzhugh, July 7, 1804 - bdsm: George Washington Parke Custis, William Fitzhugh

Isham & Nancy Smith, March 1, 1816 - bdsm: Isham Custis, Evan Williams

CUTSHAW, George W. & Martha Jane Moxley, Oct. 3, 1831 - bdsm: George W. Cutshaw, Benjamin Moxley

DADE, Charles S. & Jane Adam, May 22, 1809 - bdsm: Charles S. Dade, John Adam

Francis & Harriot Shepherd, Dec. 2, 1811 - bdsm: Francis Dade, James Shepherd

Langhome & Eliza Scott, July 18, 1816 - bdsm: Langhome Dade, James S. Scott

DAILY, Richard B. & Ann E. Beane, Aug. 16, 1826 - bdsm: Richard B. Daily, John W. Cook

DAINGERFIELD, Henry & Rosalie A. Taylor, Nov. 1, 1838 - bdsm: Henry Daingerfield, Robert J. Taylor

John B. & Rebecca H. Grew, June 29,1841 - bdsm: John B. Daingerfield, George D. Fowle

DALTON, Daniel & Margaret Emmitt, June 10, 1801 - bdsm: Daniel Dalton, Josiah Emmitt

DANGERFIELD, Edward & Margaret B. Vowell, Oct. 20, 1831 - bdsm: Edward Daingerfield, Vernon Dorsey

DANIEL, William & Julianna Berry, Nov. 13, 1815 - bdsm: William Daniel, Thomas Berry

DANIELS, James & Matilda Bayliss, Jan. 1, 1831 - bdsm: James Daniels, William Bayliss

Thomas & Catharine S. Berry, June 30, 1810 - bdsm: Thomas Daniels, Laurence Lacey

DANRIDGE, William & Dolly Bell, Sept. 17, 1840 - bdsm: William Danridge, John Harriss

DARLEY, Thomas & Chloe Kidwell, Feb. 19, 1807 - bdsm: Thomas Darley, Elijah Kidwell

William & Mary Mills, Sept. 11, 1845 - bdsm: William Darley, John Thompson

DARLY, Charles & Sarah A. Cook, March 23, 1850 - bdsm: Charles Darly, William Kelley

DARNALL, Henry & Letty Grayson, May 17, 1815 - bdsm: Henry Darnall, George Russell

DARNALL, John & Rhodey Taylor, August 16, 1810 - bdsm: John Darnall, William King

DARNELL, Henry Jr. & Sophia Chin, Nov. 13, 1834 - bdsm: Henry Darnell, Jr., David Cunny

DARRE, Frederick & Mary Ann Sherwood, license

DARRE (continued)
issued June 30, 1851 –
bdsm:
DASHIELL, Thomas B. &
Mary W. McCobb, March
27, 1825 – bdsm: Thomas
B. Dashiell, H. M. Steiner
DAUGHERTY, Arthur & Re-
becca Smith, June 27,
1801 – bdsm: Arthur Dau-
gherty, John Duffy (Also:
Dougherty)
DAVENPORT, Samuel B. &
Mary Ophelia Hunt, May
15, 1841 – bdsm: Samuel
B. Davenort, John Gemeny
DAVEY, Thomas & Susan
Abercrombie, Feb. 11,
1833 – bdsm: Thomas
Davey, John Wood
DAVIDSON, Bazil & Eliza
Hunter, July 8, 1807 –
bdsm: Bazil H. Davidson,
John Hunter
Francis R. & Jane Wel-
borne, March 21, 1831 –
bdsm: Francis R. David-
son, Charles H. Triplett
James & Nancy Kirby, Sept.
29, 1804 – bdsm: James
Davidson, Robert Brockett
John C. & Mary Ann Rock,
April 27, 1837 – bdsm:
John C. Davidson, Mat-
thew O'Brien
DAVIS, Benjamin & Mary
Turner, Sept. 23, 1812 –
bdsm: Benjamin Davis,
James Baron
Cornelius & Maria Stanton,
Dec. 30, 1813 – bdsm:
Cornelius Davis, John H.
Stanton
Cornelius & Polly Bolling,
April 12, 1821 – bdsm:
Cornelius Davis, Richard

DAVIS (continued)
Wallace
Daniel & Louisa Carter,
Dec. 13,1830 – bdsm:
Daniel Davis, Wm. P.
Green
Daniel & Nancy Grimes,
April 13, 1802 – bdsm:
Daniel Davis, Zachariah
Penn, Thomas Copper
Edward & Frances Davis,
Oct. 12, 1826 – bdsm: Ed-
ward Davis, John Jordon
Edward & Mary Ann Gibson,
June 18, 1829 – bdsm:
Edward Davis, Obediah
Moss
Elias & Mary Creble, Nov.
19, 1810 – bdsm: Elias
Davis, Daniel Wright
Francis C. & Louisa Ashrod,
daughter of William Ash-
ford, Dec. 4, 1849 – bdsm:
Francis C. Davis, Eman-
uel G. Compton
Geo. E. & Elizabeth A.
Ward, Dec. 2, 1834 –
bdsm: Geo. E. Davis, Wil-
liam Hutchins
George & Hannah Ann Allen,
May 27, 1840 – bdsm:
George Davis, Henry Wil-
liams
Gideon & Maria W. Rhodes,
Feb. 20, 1821 – bdsm:
Gideon Davis, John L.
Gardener
Henry & Elizabeth Shirley,
Nov. 10, 1834 – bdsm:
Henry Davis, Horatio Day
Henry & Mary Ann Beckley,
Sept. 9, 1831 – bdsm:
Henry Davis, Jesse Be-
ckley
Henry W. & Constance T.
Gardner, Oct. 29, 1845 –

DAVIS (continued)
bdsm: Henry W. Davis, Wm. G. Cazenove

James & Bridget Gray, Nov. 4, 1831 - bdsm: James Davis, Robert Kelly

James & Martha Weaver, May 19, 1846 - bdsm: James Davis, Lewis S. Davis

James & Susan E. Morris, Dec. 16, 1833 - bdsm: James Davis, Robert E. Brickhannon

John & Elizabeth Throop, July 11, 1820 - bdsm: John Davis, Alexander Anderson

John & Louisa Cole, Sept. 21, 1843 - bdsm: John Davis, William Cole

John & Matilda Kiteley, June 19, 1818 - bdsm: John Davis, Susanna Kightley (Also Kightley)

John & Sally Taylor, June 18, 1803 - bdsm: John Davis

John & Sally Wright, March 20, 1816 - bdsm: John Davis, James Stephenson

John & Sarah Crandell, Aug. 1, 1801 - bdsm: Thomas Fry, John Davis

Kidwallader & Betsey Wright, March 15, 1825 - celebrated 16 March

Kidwallader & Betsey Wright, March 15, 1817 - bdsm: Kidwallader Davis, Thomas Potts

Moses & Elizabeth Henson, Aug. 28, 1827 - bdsm: Moses Davis, David Evans (See also: Heisson)

Noah & Mary Young, July

DAVIS (continued)
10, 1823 - bdsm: Noah Davis, John Bryce

Peter & Jane Williams, July 1, 1824 - bdsm: Peter Davis, Reuben Reuxberry

Richard & Margaret Coleman, Dec. 26, 1842 - bdsm: Richard Davis, James D. Kerr

Robert W. & Elizabeth Ann Ford, Feb. 13, 1833 - bdsm: Robert W. Davis, Jonathan Field

Thomas & Sarah Ann Charlotte Markell, Sept. 11, 1828 - bdsm: Thomas Davis, George Markell

Washington & Lucinda Pipsico, Sept. 13, 1821 - bdsm: Washington Davis, John Pipsico (Married Sept. 13, 1821 by Rev. O. Norris)

William & Catharine Cone, June 1, 1830 - bdsm: William Davis, George Price (See also: Coxe)

William & Jane E. Violett, Sept. 28, 1830 - bdsm: William Davis, Wm. B. English

William & Nancy Davis, March 15, 1825 - bdsm: William Davis, Benjamin Moxley

William & Susanna E. Tyler, daughter of Thompson Tyler, Aug. 13, 1849 - bdsm: William Davis, Thompson Tyler

DAVY, Davy & Betsy Bowling, Aug. 21, 1806 - bdsm: Davy Davy, James Gullatt

DAWSON, Philemon & Nancy Ord, May 12, 1818 - bdsm:

DAWSON (continued)
Philemon Dawson, Benjamin Posey
DAY, Baldwin & Lucretia Guthrie, Jan. 19, 1828 - bdsm: Baldwin Day, Jacob Douglass
Benjamin of Clavert County, Maryland, & Elizabeth Mary Cooke, Sept. 11, 1821 - bdsm: Benjamin Day, James Clare of Alexandria
Hanson & Peggy Tarleton, Oct. 17, 1822 - bdsm: Hanson Day, Matthew Manley (See also: Peggy Fullerton)
Horatio & Martha Dunnington, May 17, 1815 - bdsm: Horatio Day, John Overman
DEAKINS, Francis W. & Jane Cook, April 16, 1835 - bdsm: Francis W. Deakins, Wm. D. Nutt
William F. & Elizabeth Nutt, May 29, 1832 - bdsm: William D. Nutt, Traverse D. Herndore
DEAN, William & Mary A. Wyer, May 31, 1836 - bdsm: William Dean, Joseph B. Ladd
DEARBORN, Charles & Elizabeth Markley, April 22, 1830 - bdsm: Charles Dearborn, Thomas E. Jacobs
George W. & Mary L. Markley, Sept. 9, 1835 - bdsm: George W. Dearborn, George W. Harris
Simon & Christiana Ward, Oct. 16, 1838 - bdsm: Simon Dearborn, James

DEARBORN (continued)
Shackelford
DEATLEY, James C. & Marietta Price, daughter of Wm. Price, Aug 8, 1850 - bdsm: James C. Deatley, William Price
DEATON, George & Ann E. Thompson, April 29, 1833 - bdsm: George Deaton, Woodward Thompson
DeCOURCY, William H. & Eliza B. Rozier, Oct. 3, 1815 - bdsm: William H. Decourcy, Edmund Fitzhugh
DEEBLE, Edward & Margaret McClish, June 11, 1816 - bdsm: Edward Deedble, Samuel Barbley (Also: McCleish)
DEGGE, Robert & Rebecca Evans, July 19, 1814 - bdsm: Robert Degge, Ephraim Evans
DeKRAFFT, F. C. & Harriot Scott, Feb. 13, 1812 - bdsm: F. C. DeKrafft, Alexander Perry
DELLEWAY, John W. & Nancy Barnett, Jan. 28, 1818 - bdsm: John W. Delleway, Francis Dormans
DELPHEY, Bartholomew & Mary Cravall, Sept. 2, 1817 - bdsm: Bartholomew Delphey, Richard Delphey
DEMAINE, John & Elizabeth Benton, Nov. 12, 1833 - bdsm: John Demaine, James Guy
William & Elizabeth Mankin, Dec. 22, 1840 - bdsm: William Demaine, Wm. Mankin

DEMAINE (continued)
William & Sarah Hamack, July 4, 1834 - bdsm: William Demaine, John Clare

DEMENT, Richard & Violetta Shannon, Nov. 17, 1814 - bdsm: Richard Dement, John K. Smith

DEMPSEY, James & Esther W. Sanford, Nov. 15, 1841 - bdsm: James Dempsey, James P. Smith

DENNEY, John P. & Lucinda C. Crandell, June 28, 1830 - bdsm: John P. Denney, John L. Alfred

DENNIS, James U. & Jane Cecilia Hooe, Oct. 8, 1846 - bdsm: James U. Dennis, George D. Fowle

Littleton & Anne Carolin Fowle, Oct. 9, 1843 - bdsm: Littleton Dennis, Henry Allen Taylor

DERICK, Townshend & Julia Fitzgerald, both free blacks, July 20, 1836 - bdsm: Townshend Derick, Isaac Trunnel

DERRICK, William & Margaret Franklin (both coloured), license issued Feb. 28, 1851 - bdsm:

DESHIELDS, Joseph Jr. & Sarah A. E. G. Monroe, March 24, 1825 - bdsm: Joseph Deshields, Jr., Newton Keene

DETERLY, Michael & Mary Coones, March 29, 1804 - bdsm: Michael Deterly, Peter Tastepaugh

DEVAUGHN, Daniel & Rebecca Sly, Jan. 1, 1833 - bdsm: Daniel Devaughn, Edward Bayliss

DEVAUGHN (continued)
John & Catharine Workman, May 8, 1816 - bdsm: John Devaughn, Degina Workman

John & Nancy Cady, March 20, 1816 - bdsm: John DeVaughn, Samuel Hattersley

Thomas & Nancy Harper, Nov. 13, 1823 - bdsm: Thomas Devaugh, William Harper

William & Mary Churchman, June 29, 1815 - bdsm: William Devaughn, Frederick Churchman

DEVERS, Lancelot & Ann Sutherland, May 31, 1832 - bdsm: Lancelot Devers, Samuel Beach

DICK, David & Molly Atwell, Feb. 22, 1823 - bdsm: David Dick, Obediah Kesley

David & Sarah Ann Posey, September 18, 1810 - bdsm: David Dick, Randolph Logan

Joseph & Catharine Pipsico, July 3, 1817 - bdsm: Joseph Dick, John Pipsico

DICKS, Thomas & Elisa Powers, Dec. 26, 1836 - bdsm: Thomas Dicks, John T. Ballenger

DIEZ, Adam & Eva C. Fredericksen, April 13, 1820 - bdsm: Adam Diez, Louis Beeler

DIFFENDAFFER, John & Barbary Wilkes, Jan. 17, 1816 - bdsm: John Diffendaffer, William Frazer

DIGGS, John B. & Sarah Jane Patterson, March 24, 1834

DIGGS (continued)
- bdsm: John B. Diggs, James D. Bryan
DIXION, John A. & Fanny Chatham, daughter of Henry Chatham, Nov. 16, 1847 - bdsm: John A. Dixion, George O. Dixion
DIXON, David & Celia Fitzgerald (free black), March 11, 1835 - bdsm: David Dixon, Charles Ross
John & Elizabeth Pitten, June 23, 1836 - bdsm: John Dixon, John H. Gibson
John & Henrietta Dixon, Jan. 5, 1836 - bdsm: John Dixion, George Jarboe
John & Jane Davis, Jan. 2, 1806 - bdsm: John Dixon, William Hanson
John & Mary Jerro, April 13, 1805 - bdsm: John Dixon, John Wood
John & Sarah White, June 17, 1806 - bdsm: John Dixon, Richard Dinmore
Turner & Mary Jane Paton, June 22, 1832 - bdsm: Turner Dixon, Charles McKnight (Mary Jane Paton, ward of Charles McKnight)
DOANE, Daniel & Semphonica Huguely, Nov. 30, 1850 - bdsm: father, Geo. F. Huguely
DOBIE, William & Ann Jefferson, June 25, 1817 - bdsm: William Dobie, John Shackelford
DODGE, William & Sally E. Mason, Sept. 2, 1844 - bdsm: William Dodge, Hunter H. Minor

DOE, Josiah H. & Mary R. Butler, May 13, 1818 - bdsm: Josiah H. Doe, Sarah Butler
DOERR, Conrad & Elizabeth Reynolds, June 18, 1814 - bdsm: Conrad Doerr, John Seeten
DOGAN, John & Jane Fuller, Nov. 3, 1818 - bdsm: John Dogan, James S. Scott
John & Lucinda Butler, Sept. 14, 1842 - bdsm: John Dogan, Philip Dogan
DOLEMAN, Austin & Elizabeth Marmaduke, Oct. 4, 1838 - bdsm: Austin Doleman, William Reeves
William & Matilda Nicholls, Dec. 31, 1834 - bdsm: William Doleman, John Clare
DONALDSON, James & Jane F. Skidmore, Sept. 18, 1839 - bdsm: James Donaldson, William Skidmore
Robert & Elizabeth Birch, Jan. 4, 1815 - bdsm: Thomas Donaldson, James Birch, Robert Donaldson
Thomas G. & Elenor Southern, May 8, 1843 - bdsm: Thomas G. Donaldson, Benjamin F. Shreve
William & Hannah Donaldson, Jan. 1, 1817 - bdsm: William Donaldson, Benjamin Donaldson
DOOLEY, John & Sarah D. McNamara, Aug. 24, 1836 - bdsm: John Dooley, John J. Dooley
DORSEY, Edward & Ann Lee, July 23, 1834 - bdsm: Edward Dorsey, Philip Lee

DORSEY (continued)
Edward & Martha Lee, Nov. 29, 1832 - bdsm: Edward Dorsey, Philip Lee
Edward J. & Ann Ross, Oct. 7, 1823 - bdsm: Edward J. Dorsey, John Ross
Thomas J. & Jane P. Robbins, Dec. 22, 1829 - bdsm: Thomas J. Dorsey, Benjamin Waters
DORCEY, Biscoe L. & Eliza Goods, June 11, 1811 - bdsm: Biscoe Dorcey, Eliza Goods
DORSETT, Fielder & Ann A. McRea, June 19, 1817 - bdsm: Fielder Dorsett, Henry Brawner
DOUGAN, Philip & Kitty Botts, Feb. 20, 1823 - bdsm: Philip Dougan, Andrew Bell
DOUGHTERTY, Daniel & Jane M. Summers, Dec. 15, 1818 - bdsm: David Dougherty, William Summers
DOUGLASS, George P. & Harriet B. Chapman, license issued Nov. 14, 1850 - bdsm:
DOUGLASS, Jacob & Mary Ann Guthrie, Dec. 19, 1816 - bdsm: Jacob Douglass, Thomas Smith
James & Eliza Kincaid, Nov. 17, 1812 - bdsm: James Douglass, George Carson
James & Jane S. Blue, Sept. 6, 1827 - bdsm: James Douglass, John J. Blue
James & Margaret Fleming, Oct. 25, 1825 - bdsm: James Douglass, John

DOUGLASS (continued)
Douglass
Richard L. & Maria Blacklock, Dec. 31, 1816 - bdsm: Richard L. Douglass, Augustine Newton
DOVE, Joseph & Lucinda Hale, June 23, 1810 - bdsm: Joseph Dove, William Dove
DOVER, Samuel & Sarah Moore, June 3, 1824 - bdsm: Samuel Dover, David Jarbour
DOWNEY, Thomas & Mary Grimes, license issued May 28, 1851 - bdsm:
DOWDALL, Colin & Margaret Stokeley, April 23, 1804 - bdsm: Colin Dowdall, George Dagan
DOWELL, Jeremiah & Ellen Violett, Dec. 14, 1815 - bdsm: Jeremiah Dowell, Elijah Wood
DOWNS, Ignatius & Eliza Chrise, Sept. 19, 1818 - bdsm: Ignatius Downs, Silas Elliott
DREES, Nicholas & Hersey Ward, Dec. 16, 1814 - bdsm: Nicholas Drees, Josiah Ward
DREW, Charles & Polly Hubble, Dec. 7, 1804 - bdsm: Charles Drew, Samuel H. Davis
DROWN, John & Sally Higdon, Dec. 30, 1805 - bdsm: John Drown, John Higdon
Thomas & Ebbey Goods, Nov. 29, 1806 - bdsm: Thomas Drown, Frederick Treidle

DROWNS, John T. & Delilah Thompson, May 26, 1835 – bdsm: John T. Drowns, David Watkins

DUDLEY, B. F. & Mary F. Vernon, Sept. 24, 1846 – bdsm: John W. Jefferson, Benjamin F. Dudley

James & Margaret A. Shields, Feb. 21, 1831 – bdsm: James Dudley, George R. Adams

John & Elizabeth Ward, Feb. 15, 1821 – bdsm: John Dudley, William Moore

John & Rebecca Greenwood, Dec. 25, 1823 – bdsm: John Dudley, John Greenwood

Joseph & Mary D. Simmes, Feb. 2, 1828 – bdsm: Joseph Dudley, William Simmes

William & Nancy Credit, Nov. 6, 1826 – bdsm: William Dudley, James Cole

William & Sarah Bowling, August 13, 1817 – bdsm: William Dudley, Ann Bowling

DUFFEY, George H. & Sarah Catharine Steele, July 1, 1845 – George H. Duffey, H. N. Steele

DUGAN, William & Betsey Marvel, July 30, 1829 – bdsm: William Dugan, Philip Dugan

DULANY, Bladen & Mary W. Carter, ward of Thomas Turner of Fauquier County, June 17, 1823 – bdsm:

Richard Henry & Rebecca Ann Dulany, ward of John A. Carter, Oct. 7, 1847 –

DULANY (continued) bdsm: Richard Henry Dulany, John A. Carter

William & Mary G. Towers, June 4, 1810 – bdsm: Wm. Dulany, Dorcas Henderson

DUNBAR, Peter & Ann R. Cracroft, June 27, 1816 – bdsm: Peter Dunbar, William Washington

DUNCAN, Robert & Hannah Bennett, Dec. 17, 1801 – bdsm: Robert Duncan, Richard Bennett

Samuel & Elizabeth Price, August 10, 1833 – bdsm: Samuel Duncan, Somerset Aubenor

Samuel J. & Ann Jane Coats, Sept. 8, 1829 – bdsm: Samuel J. Duncan, Daniel Coats

DUNN, James & Penelope Cayton, Oct. 19, 1810 – bdsm: James Dunn, John Dogan

DUVAL, Jefferson & Elizabeth Dogans, Aug. 17, 1842 – bdsm: Jefferson Duval, Philip Dogans

DuVALL, Edmund B. & Caroline D. Lansdale, Oct. 28, 1846 – bdsm: Edmund B. DuVall, M. E. Ewing

John P. & Ann E. Davis, Jan. 1, 1840 – bdsm: John P. Duvall, William L. Reise

John P. & Ann F. Tebbs, Dec. 20, 1815 – married the same day by Rev. Norris

DYE, Henry & Mary Ann Taylor, July 26, 1835 – bdsm: Henry Dye, Rezin Taylor

DYE (continued)

Reubin & Elizabeth Turner, July 14, 1804 - bdsm: Reubin Dye, Samuel Wroe

DYER, Amos & Margaret Parsons, Dec. 21, 1843 - bdsm: Amos Dyer, Theo. Norris

Anthony & Sarah Grayson, May 7, 1833 - bdsm: Anthony Dyer, Joseph B. Blunt

Francis & Margaret Hunter, March 18, 1813 - bdsm: Francis Dyer, Robert Hunter

James & Elizabeth Rollins, April 22, 1824 - bdsm: James Dyer, James H. Carlin

John F. & Rosalie Higginson Davis, Nov. 21, 1844 - bdsm: John F. Dyer, Leonard Marbury

Thomas & Margaret Grumble, May 10, 1842 - bdsm: Thomas Dyer, William Worthington

Walter & Deborah Dyer, June 21, 1815 - bdsm: Walter Dyer, Daniel Thompson

William & Mary Skinner (daughter of John Skinner), March 17, 1831 - bdsm: William Dyer & John Skinner

DYKES, Andrew & Ann Lutz, Oct. 30, 1816 - bdsm: Andrew Dykes, William Cowen

EARLE, Samuel & Margaret Way, Jan. 4, 1813 - bdsm: Samuel Earle, Daniel Stoner

EARP, Simon & Milly Scott,

EARP (continued)
Nov. 2, 1802 - bdsm: Simon Earp, William Payne

EASTON, Tildon & Rebecca C. Cook, July 30, 1834 - bdsm: Tildon Easton, Rebecca H. Cook

EATON, Burnaham & Mary Brook, March 21, 1844 - bdsm: Burnaham Eaton, John H. Ball

ECHLE, Charles & Charlotte Perry, May 19, 1818 - bdsm: Charles E. Echle, William Williams

EDD, John Thomas & Mary Ann Webster, April 23, 1842 - bdsm: John Thomas Walker, John Williams

EDELEN, Samuel & Sally C. Hamilton, July 21, 1817 - bdsm: Samuel Edelen, Alexander Hamilton

Thomas J. & Jane E. Wood, July 28, 1846 - bdsm: Thomas J. Edelen, Thomas H. Payne

EDELIN, Edward & Sarah Moore, Jan. 6, 1802 - bdsm: Edward Edelin, James Murray

Robert & Marion W. Summers, Dec. 12, 1843 - bdsm: Robert Edelin, John Summers

EISSERMAN, Jacob & Anna Shoemaker, Sept. 22, 1807 - bdsm: Jacob Eisserman, John Wood

ELLERY, Christopher Jr. & Hannah Kinsey, Feb. 20, 1836 - bdsm: Christopher Ellery, Jr., Zenas Kinsey

ELLIOT, Reason & Rebecca Padgett, April 9, 1844 -

ELLIOT (continued)
bdsm: Reason Elliot, James H. Robinson
ELLIOTT, John & Amelia Mills, Dec. 19, 1812 – bdsm: John Elliott, Samuel Baggett
John & Julia Ann Avery, Feb. 1, 1834 – bdsm: John Elliott, James Avery (guardian of both parties)
Silas & Ann Bradley, Sept. 2, 1812 – bdsm: Silas Elliott, Richard Rock
ELLIS, James H. & Virginia Boyer, April 16, 1846 – bdsm: James H. Ellis, John Boyer
John W. & Sarah G. Ching, April 2, 1829 – bdsm: John W. Ellis, Eldridge R. Veitch
Joseph & Sarah Emerson, May 18, 1812 – bdsm: Joseph Ellis, Aquilla Emerson
Samuel T. & Laura Balis, Oct. 30, 1849 – bdsm: Samuel T. Ellis, Samuel Sanford
EMBERSON, Richard D. & Catharine Williams, Nov. 14, 1815 – bdsm: Richard D. Emberson, Alexander Williams
EMERSON, Aquila & Drury Coade, Nov. 25, 1818 – bdsm: Aquila Emerson, John S. Emerson
Aquila & Nancy McCarty, March 14, 1833 – bdsm: Aquila Emerson, William C. Rives
George W. & Endocia C. Suter, Jan. 19, 1842 – bdsm: George W. Emer-

EMERSON (continued)
son, Sarah Thomas
Harrison & Jane Watson, Jan. 6, 1820 – bdsm: Harrison Emerson, James Galt
Harrison A. & Fanny Deblaun, Jan. 13, 1831 – bdsm: Harrison A. Emerson, John P. Emerson (Also: Deblauce)
John L. & Catharine Ball, May 23, 1822 – bdsm: John L. Emerson, John Ball
John L. & Sarah Ann Coade, Dec. 23, 1818 – bdsm: John L. Emerson, John Simpson
John P. & Harriet A. Dearborn, Feb. 16, 1831 – bdsm: John P. Emerson, Simon Dearborn
William D. & Ellen Dowell, June 20, 1825 – bdsm: William D. Emerson, Christian Keefer
EMMERSON, William R. & Isabella V. Dailey, ward of John Lawson, May 8, 1848 – bdsm: William R. Emmerson, John Lawson (See also: Daly)
ENDICOTT, Samuel & Polly Call, Sept. 30, 1805 – bdsm: Samuel Endicott, Thomas Howland
ENGLISH, David & Mary Slade, Dec. 3, 1816 – bdsm: David English, Charles Slade
William B. & Juliet G. Violett, Feb. 7, 1828 – bdsm: William B. English, James H. Anderson
ENNIS, James & Sarah Self,

ENNIS (continued)
July 28, 1850 -- bdsm: James Ennis, Nathaniel Beacham

ENTWISLE, Isaac & Ann Ryan, Jan. 13, 1806 - bdsm: Isaac Entwisle, Robert Nash

ERVINE, David & Sarah Lanham, August 6, 1806 - bdsm: David Ervine, William Neale

ESHON, George & Liddia Blakeney, Aug. 2, 1801 - bdsm: George Eshon, Joseph Farmer

ESTEY, John & Elizabeth Ann Cawood, Feb. 8, 1825 - bdsm: John Estey, Singleton S. Walker

EVANS, Edward & Letitia Waugh, April 7, 1834 - bdsm: Edward Evans and William Clagett

Ephraim & Jane L. Wadsworth, June 23, 1823 - bdsm: Ephraim Evans, Charles B. R. Douglas

Henry Wayne & Elizabeth Ann Reid, Oct. 6, 1831 - bdsm: Henry Wayne Evans, William Barnes

James & Helen Evans, Jan. 23, 1839 - bdsm: James Evans, George Semmes

John & Elizabeth Derment, March 28, 1809 - bdsm: John Evans, John Parker

Robert & Harriet Randell, April 19, 1811 - bdsm: Robert Evans, Theophilus Randell

Robert & Jane Sears, Nov. 28. 1818 - bdsm: Robert Evans, George Crook

Samuel & Elizabeth Shute,

EVANS (continued)
Oct. 24,1837 - bdsm: Samuel Evans, Henry Brent (See also: Shule)

Samuel & Mary Ann Henderson, April 7, 1831 - bdsm: Samuel Evans, Ann Jeffery

Thomas & Mary Humphrey, May 18, 1812 - bdsm: Thomas Evans, Asa Crockett

William & Betsey Thompson, Oct. 15, 1807 - bdsm: William Evans, John Smith

William & Louisa Braddack, July 23, 1840 - bdsm: William Evans, James Derreck

William S. & Adaline Kinsey, July 12, 1835 - bdsm: William S. Evans, Zenus Kinsey

Zeagle & Elizabeth Lebrey, May 9, 1839 - bdsm: Zeagle Evans, George Guy

EVELETH, Ebenezer & Mary W. Butts, April 27, 1832 - bdsm: Ebenezer Eveleth, Mark Butts, Jr.

James & Harriotte McKenzie, Jan. 7, 1845 - bdsm: James Eveleth, Lewis McKenzie

John & Julia Carolin, June 23, 1831 - bdsm: John Eveleth, Hugh Carolin

EWART, Horatio & Cloanna Dudley, July 11, 1803 - bdsm: Horatio Ewart, John Johns

EWELL, Charles & Bridget Borrowdale, Feb. 18, 1812 -- bdsm: Charles Ewell, Charles Page

Charles of Prince William

EWELL (continued)
County, Virginia, & Maria
D. Craik of Alexandria
County, Sept. 29, 1818 –
bdsm: Charles Ewell,
John Tucker; celebrated
Oct. 1, 1818 by Rev.
Oliver Norris
FADLEY, James & Ann Rob-
inson, May 24, 1832 –
bdsm: James Fadley,
Moses O. B. Cawood
FAGAN, John & Elizabeth
Wiley, June 23, 1829 –
bdsm: John Fagan, James
Beach
FAIRBROTHERS, John &
Elizabeth Ends, May 30,
1805 – bdsm: John Fair-
brothers, Bennett Reary
FAIRFAX, John A. & Mar-
garet Dorsey, licence
issued Oct. 22, 1850 –
bdsm:
FALCONER, Alexander &
Ann Maria Spilman, May
27, 1845 – bdsm: Alex-
ander Falconer, William
C. Spilman
FANNING, Wm. H. & Wil-
helmina Lucas, July 22,
1846 – bdsm: Wm. H.
Fanning, David Appich
FANT, John & Elizabeth
Shreve, Oct. 25, 1815 –
bdsm: John Fant, Andrew
Rounsavell
FARDY, Patrick & Catharine
Wheaton, April 13, 1822 –
bdsm: Patrick Fardy,
Thomas Smith
FAREALL, Jason & Nancy
Crowe, Jan. 15, 1811 –
bdsm: Jason Fareall, Eb-
bsworth Bayne, Henry
Bayne, Jas. Laurason

FARLAN, Patrick M. & Mary
Kily, (no date) 1852 –
bdsm:
FARMER, Edward & Ann E.
Drake, Aug. 14, 1850 –
bdsm: Edward Farmer,
Sarah Hall
FARRALL, Grafton & Sarah
Green, May 7, 1823 –
bdsm: Grafton Farrall,
William Green
FAW, Abraham & Sarah
Moody, April 19, 1806 –
bdsm: Abraham Faw, Wil-
liam Reily
FAWCETT, William & Su-
san Stabler, April 4, 1837
– bdsm: Willis Fawcett,
John Leadbeater
FELL, Christopher & Ger-
trude Smallridge Aug. 27,
1818 – bdsm: Christopher
Fell, Gertrude Smallridge
FENDALL, Philip R. & Eliz-
abeth Mary Young, March
29, 1827 – bdsm: Philip R.
Fendall, Elizabeth Young
Townshend D. & Eliza
Eaches, Jan. 15, 1849 –
bdsm: Townshend D. Fen-
dall, Turner W. Ashby
FERGUSON, Isaac & Eliza
Self, Sept. 21, 1841 –
bdsm: Isaac Ferguson,
Stephen Mothersed
John W. & Martha Ann
Simpson, orphan of Hanson
Simpson, date? – bdsm:
John W. Ferguson, Benj.
H. Berry
FIELD, Horatio & Elizabeth
Boyer, Nov. 3, 1804 –
bdsm: Horatio Field, Ar-
chibald McClish
Oliver & Jane Dixon, Aug. 9,
1826 – bdsm: Oliver

FIELD (continued)
Fields, John Dixon
Stephen & Catharine L. Howard, July 11, 1828 – bdsm: Stephen Field, Beale Howard
Stephen & Mary Ann Whittington, June 14, 1821 – bdsm: Stephen Field, Thomas Whittington
FIELDS, William & Mary Weaver, Nov. 22, 1838 – bdsm: William Fields, William Reeves
FINDLEY, James & Ruth Devaughn, June 2, 1825 – bdsm:
FINNICUM, John & Mary Jane Glaster, Jan. 31, 1836 – bdsm: John Finnicum, James N. Glaster
FISHER, Michael & Catherine Hirsh, Feb. 23, 1832 – bdsm: Michael Fisher, Conrad Hirsh
Robert & Martha Patterson, Feb. 26, 1840 – bdsm: Robert Fisher, John B. Diggs
FITCH, Oscar & Grace Demain, Oct. 21, 1833 – bdsm: Oscar Fitch, Julius Swain (Demaine)
FitzGERALD, James & Mary Ann Robinson, Aug. 21, 1833 – bdsm: James Fitzgerald, Alfred Hines
FitzHUGH, John T. & Rachael D. McCobb, Feb. 2, 1828 – bdsm: John T. Fitzhugh, Josiah H. Davis
Norman R. & Mary Ann Vowell, April 8, 1823 – bdsm: Norman R. Fitzhugh, John Dunlap
William G. & A. P. Jones,

FitzHUGH (continued)
Oct. 10, 1839 – bdsm: William G. Fitzhugh, Thomas H. Jones
William W. & Jane Haley, Nov. 9, 1815 – bdsm: William W. Fitzhugh, Dearborn Doe
FLANNERY, Michael & Rebecca Turner, April 26, 1806 – bdsm: Michael Flannery, George Deneale
FLEMING, Moses & Mary Elizabeth Hancock, March 28, 1839 – bdsm: Moses Fleming, John B. Hancock
Thornton & Sally Cohagan, Jan. 8, 1806 – bdsm: Thornton Fleming, John Cohagan
FLETCHER, Charles & Marie Taylor, Aug. 21, 1828 – bdsm: Charles Fletcher, Ignatius Murray
Edward C. & Ann C. Wilson, May 18, 1836 – bdsm: Edward C. Fletcher, George W. D. Ramsay
FLEURY, John Rudolph & Sarah Elizabeth Kincaid, July 21, 1825 – bdsm: John Rudolph Fleury, Louis Beeler
FOARD, Daniel & Louisa Hatton, Jan. 24, 1843 – bdsm: Daniel Foard, Israel Marcel
FOLEY, Beverly R. & Margaret Nowland, April 3, 1838 – bdsm: Beverly R. Foley, George H. Markell
FONT, David G. & Mary G. Windsor, Jan. 16, 1849 – bdsm: David G. Font, Wm. B. Richards, Jr.
FOOTE, Frederick & Cath-

FOOTE (continued)
arine R. Ramsay, Oct. 20,
1825 - bdsm: Frederick
Foote, Colin Auld
Frederick & Verlinda Ash-
ton, May 14, 1838 - bdsm:
Frederick Foote, John W.
Massie
FORBES, John L. & Mary
Elizabeth Semmes, May
13, 1840 - bdsm: John L.
Forbes, Thomas Semmes
FORCE, Peter & Hannah
Evans, Dec. 31, 1817 -
bdsm: Peter Force, Jonah
Isabell
FORD, West & Prescilla
Bell, Aug. 14, 1812 -
bdsm: West Ford, Henry
Bell
West & Sally Bearcroft,
April 12, 1832 - bdsm:
West Ford, George Murray
William & Daniel Henrietta
Bruce, Sept. 3, 1840 -
bdsm: William Ford,
Daniel Bruce
William & Eunice Arrington,
Sept. 30, 1818 - bdsm:
William Ford, Jesse Shin-
cer
FORDHAM, Wm. & Mary
Ann Kiteley, March 12,
1823 - bdsm: Wm. Ford-
ham, John Davis
FOREMAN, David & Eliz-
abeth Hokes, Oct. 3, 1822
- bdsm: David Foreman,
William D. Miller
FORREST, David M. of
Washington County, D. C.
& Mary Clagett of Fairfax
County, Virginia, Jan. 29,
1820 - celebrated Feb. 1,
1820 by Rev. Oliver Norris
FORTNEY, Richard & Eliz-

FORTNEY (continued)
abeth Philips, July 31,
1823 - bdsm: Richard
Fortney, William McClish
(Married July 31, 1823 by
Rev. O. Norris)
FORTUNE, Ashbell R. &
Mary A. Hills, Aug. 19,
1833 - bdsm: Ashbell R.
Fortune, Lewis Hipkins
James & Mary Lane, July 8,
1830 - bdsm: Bartholemew
Rotchford, James Fortune
FOSTER, James W. B. &
Ann Berry, Nov. 9, 1835 -
bdsm: James B. W. Fos-
ter, William Shinn
John S. & Mary Francis,
May 23, 1816 - bdsm:
John S. Foster, Thomas
Potts
FOWLE, George D. & Sarah
Ellen Hooe, Oct. 9, 1843 -
bdsm: George D. Fowle,
Henry Allan Taylor
John & Pauline Cazenove,
May 26, 1831 - bdsm:
John Fowle, Will. C.
Gardner
William & Hetty D. Tayler,
April 30, 1807 - bdsm:
William Fowle, Noblet
Herbert
William H. & Eliza T.
Hooe, August 13, 1831 -
bdsm: William H. Fowle,
Robert Washington
FOWLER, Daniel & Julia
Ann Rawling, June 3, 1830
- bdsm: Daniel Fowler,
John Rawling
FOX, A. L. Fitzwilliam &
Elisabeth C. Blacklock,
Nov. 28, 1839 - A. L.
Fitzwilliam Fox, G.W. D.
Ramsay

FOX (continued)

James & Catharine Piper,
April 28, 1815 - bdsm:
James Fox, Jacob Zim-
merman

Joseph & Mary Ann Carter,
Aug. 10, 1829 - bdsm:
Joseph Fox, Aquilla John-
son

William & Eleanor Sum-
mers, June 25, 1805 -
bdsm: William Fox,
George Summers

FOXWOOD, Daniel & Sarah
Hill, July 25, 1811 -
bdsm: Daniel Foxwood,
Thomas Scott

FOY, Patrick & Mocky Shif-
field, Dec. 15, 1831 -
bdsm: Patrick Foy, James
Hill

FRANCIS, Emanuel & Julia
Ann Mansfield, Dec. 30,
1844 - bdsm: Emanuel
Francis, John T. Ballenger

John G. & Jane Hays, May
9, 1807 - bdsm: John G.
Francis, Andrew Hays

Manuel V. & Martha Jane
Dreese, Jan. 27, 1841 -
bdsm: Manuel V. Francis,
Robert Green

Matthew & Ann Durrington,
June 9, 1804 - bdsm: Mat-
thew Francis, Owne Sul-
livan

Matthew & Sarah Irwin,
March 9, 1811 - bdsm:
Matthew Francis, John
Avermon

FRANK, Andrew J. & Ann
Humphries, Oct. 26, 1837
- bdsm: Andrew J. Frank,
John S. Humphries

Ephraim & Ellen Lindsay,
May 26, 1831 - bdsm:

FRANK (continued)

Ephraim Frank, Wm. C.
Spillman

Jeremiah & Mary Eliza
Owens, Aug. 11, 1842 -
bdsm: Jeremiah Frank,
Samuel Lewis

FRANKLAND, Henry W. &
Sarah Longdon, July 12,
1838 - bdsm: Henry W.
Frankland, James P. Mid-
dleton

FRANKLIN, Benjamin &
Cathrine Parson, April 27,
1835 - bdsm: Benjamin
Franklin, Walter Hawx-
hurst

Francis & Mary O'Neal,
Aug. 22, 1843 - bdsm:
Francis Franklin, Joseph
Furguson

Lemuel P. & Rebecca Pick-
ens, Aug. 6, 1837 - bdsm:
Lemuel P. Franklin,
Robert Lowry

FRAZER, George & Sally
Davis, April 16, 1814 -
bdsm: George Frazer,
Henry Frazer

James & Mary A. Campbell,
June 11, 1832 - bdsm:
James Frazer, John T.
White

Jeremiah & Ann McDeller,
June 6, 1843 - bdsm:
Jeremiah Frazier, John
Ross (Also: McDiller)

FRAZIER, Jeremiah & Lucy
Kinsey, July 16, 1807 -
bdsm: Jeremiah Frazier,
George Russell

William Henry & Jane Ann
Baggett, Nov. 21, 1844 -
bdsm: William Henry
Frazier, James T. Ball
(See also: Jane Ann

FRAZIER (continued)
Padgett)

FREMAN, William & Elizabeth Bowzer, Nov. 15, 1814 - bdsm: William Freman, John Tatspaugh (Elizabeth Bowzer's guardian) Also: (Bowser)

FRENCH, David M. & Mary E. Smoot, daughter of George H. Smoot, Oct. 1, 1849 - bdsm: David M. French, George H. Smoot

FRENEAU, Philip & Milly Rye, July 31, 1803 - bdsm: Philip Freneau, George Deneale

FRENNELL, Isaac & Carline Jenson, Oct. 15, 1815 - bdsm: Isaac Frennell, Samuel Hattersley

FRIGNETT, John & Elizabeth Haney, Aug. 9, 1815 - bdsm: John Frignett, Samuel Isaacs

FUGATE, William & Mary Thomas, Aug. 2, 1822 - bdsm: William Fugate, William Mills

FUGETT, James & Susan Javins, May 15, 1821 - bdsm: James Fugett, Dennis Javins (Also: Feugit)

FUGITT, George T. & Mary A. E. Cawood, daughter of Moses F. A. Cawood, Dec. 27, 1849 - bdsm: George T. Fugitt, Moses F. A. Cawood

Martin & Phebe Wright, May 1, 1834 - bdsm: Martin Fugitt, Thomas Wallace

Thomas M. & Mary E. Howard, May 28, 1836 - bdsm: Thomas M. Fugitt, John Moffitt

FULLER, Edward H. & Emily Thomas, Feb. 19, 1839 - bdsm: Edward H. Fuller, George J. Thomas

FULLERTON, Peter & Rose Savery, Oct. 30, 1820 - bdsm: Peter Fullerton, John Fruling

FULMORE, John & Mary Ann Garlic, June 1, 1809 - bdsm: John Fulmore, Samuel Cooper

FULTON, Alexander & Alice McAllan, Aug. 22, 1850 - bdsm: Alexander Fulton, B. H. Berry

GAHAN, Nicholas & Jane Carson, Nov. 17, 1836 - bdsm: Nicholas Gahan, James Carson

GAITHER, John & Margaret Carew, March 2, 1811 - bdsm: John Gaither, Jacob Gregg

GALLIGHER, Patrick & Mercer A. Berry, Aug. 10, 1842 - bdsm: Patrick Galligher, John Taylor

GALT, James & Eve Resler, April 28, 1804 - bdsm: James Galt, Jacob Gregg

GANES, Griffin & Elizabeth Parsons, July 27, 1827 - bdsm: Griffin Ganes, John Rose

GANTT, Basil E. & Maria W. Paine, orphan of Horace Payne, April 6, 1850 - bdsm: Basil E. Gantt, Alexander H. Terrett

Charles & Margaret Preston, Dec. 20, 1821 - bdsm: Charles Gantt, Elisha Kitchen, William B. Sears

Thomas & Pamelia Butler, May 14, 1836 - bdsm:

GANTT (continued)
Thomas Gantt, Nilson Bentley
William H. & Elizabeth C. Hunter, July 12, 1832 – bdsm: William H. Gantt, Spencer M. Ball
GARDNER, William C. & Eliza F. Cazenove, May 15, 1816 – bdsm: William C. Garder, Anthony C. Cazenove
GARFORD, James & Mary Ann Kelly, Dec. 10, 1816 – bdsm: James Garford, James Caton
GARNER, William & Margaret Simms, Sept. 11, 1809 – bdsm: William Garner, Abel Willis
GARRELL, James & Elizabeth Cowing, Dec. 15, 1830 – bdsm: James Garrell, John H. Gibbs
GARRISON, James & Elizabeth Kilham, May 22, 1817 – bdsm: James Garrison, Thomas L. Martin
GASCH, Frederick & Molly Catherly, Oct. 5, 1804 – bdsm: Frederick Gasch, Peter Tatspaugh
GASZ, John G. & Louisa Heisse, Feb. 24, 1843 – bdsm: John G. Gasz, Frederick Fisher
GATCHILL, William & Hannah Ann Davis, Oct. 19, 1840 – bdsm: William Gatchill, Josiah H. Davis
GATES, Thomas & Francis Ann Penn, Sept. 24, 1846 – bdsm: Thomas Gates, Walter L. Penn
Thomas & Sally Risinger, July 15, 1816 – bdsm:

GATES (continued)
Thomas Gates, John Devaughn
GAWLER, Charles & Sarah Wilbar, Dec. 12, 1833 – bdsm: Charles Gawler, Isaac George
GEASLIN, Wm. L. & Rebecca Jane Mills, May 26, 1843 – bdsm: Wm. L. Geaslin, John Padgett
GEFFERS, William J. G. & Nancy Lindsay, July 6, 1843 – bdsm: WIlliam J. G. Geffers, Jacob Curtis
GEMENY, Richard H. & Margaret M. Kesley, Aug. 29, 1846 – bdsm: Richard H. Gemeny, John A. Dixion
GENNEY, John & Matilda Figg, June 24, 1816 – bdsm: John Genney, John B. Dixon
GEORGE, Martin & Catharine Kline, May 12, 1807 – bdsm: Martin George, Gabriel Kline
GIBBS, John H. & Mary Ann Tatsapaugh, Jan. 24, 1826 – bdsm: John H. Gibbs, John Tatsapaugh
John H. & Sarah S. Williams, Nov. 5, 1817 – bdsm: John H. Gibbs, Alexander Williams
Walter & Charlotte Curtis, Dec. 26, 1816 – bdsm: Walter Gibbs, Joseph Spear
GIBSON, George & Ellen Brown, May 13, 1837 – bdsm: George Gibson, Daniel Gibson
John & Louisa Boyd, Jan. 6, 1831 – bdsm: John Gibson, Gus Gibson

GIBSON (continued)
John S. & Mary A. Hunter,
March 11, 1835 - bdsm:
John S. Gibson, Thomas
Wright
Samuel & Eleanor Thomp-
son, July 14, 1834 - bdsm:
Samuel Gibson, Robert
Nash
Theodore & Jane Williams,
Sept. 25, 1816 - bdsm:
Theodore Gibson, Alex-
ander Williams
William & Ann Flemming,
Dec. 25, 1821 - bdsm:
William Gibson, John Har-
ris
GILBERT, John & Eliza
Cary, April 10, 1813 -
bdsm: John Gilbert, Wil-
liam Bond
Joseph R. & Sarah T. Hebb,
July 31, 1816 - bdsm:
Joseph R. Gilbert, Mark
Butts, Theo. Sandford
GILBREATH, Henry & Ann
Coans, June 15, 1831 -
bdsm: Henry Gilbreath,
John West
GILDEN, John & Joanna
Gillwith, Nov. 25, 1817 -
bdsm: John Gilden, Thom-
as W. Pearson (Also:
Gilbreth)
GILLICK, Thomas & Sarah
G. Mason, Oct. 29, 1807 -
bdsm: Thomas Gillick,
Alexander Dunbar
GILLIS, James M. & Re-
becca S. Roberts, Dec. 4,
1837 - bdsm: James M.
Gillis, Thomas Semmes
GILMAN, Ephraim & Ann
Crawford, June 18, 1805 -
bdsm: Ephraim Gilman,
John Dixon, guardian of

GILMAN (continued)
Ann Crawford
GIRD, John & Sarah Kenady,
Sept. 25, 1810 - bdsm:
John Gird, Richard Walsh
GLANDERS, John & Fanny
Myers, March 29, 1815 -
bdsm: John Glanders,
Lewis Boswell
GLASCOCK, Charles & Mar-
garret Dorrety, June 28,
1844 - bdsm: Charles
Glascock, Henry E. Holt
GLASSGOW, Geo. W. &
Hannah Ann Jacobs, Nov.
3, 1830 - bdsm: Geo. W.
Glassgow, Wm. B. Price
(See also: Glasgoe)
Milton & Emily A. Atwell,
Oct. 16, 1848 - bdsm: Mil-
ton Glassgow, Charles D.
Rudd
GLENN, Robert & Elizabeth
Holton, Feb. 15, 1823 -
bdsm: Robert Glenn,
Joseph Lewin
Robert & Elizabeth Jour-
doun, July 5, 1817 - bdsm:
Robert Glenn, L. Master-
son
GLOVER, Joseph & Jane
Roxbury, May 2, 1840 -
bdsm: Joseph Glover,
Joseph Glover
William & Nancy Martin,
April 11, 1814 - bdsm:
William Glover, John
Evans
GLOVERMAN, Martin &
Elizabeth Wasser Oct. 8,
1803 - bdsm: Martin Glov-
erman, John Duffy
GLUYAS, Geo. K. & Helen
Ann M. Boothe, Aug. 9,
1836 - bdsm: Geo. K.
Gluyas, Ellicott Hewes

GODDARD, William & Eleanor Violette, May 5, 1815 – bdsm:

Wm. & Eleanor Violett, May 5, 1809 – bdsm: William Goddard, John Bogan

GOERS, John Albertus & Margaret O'Connell, June 26, 1833 – bdsm: John Albertus Goers, David Appich

GOINGS, Calvert & Jane Duff, Oct. 28. 1830 – bdsm: Calvert Goings, James Duff

John & Catharine Evans, July 27, 1843 – bdsm: John Goings, Loyd Douglas

John & Susan Duff, Oct. 8, 1828 – bdsm: John Goings, James Duff

GONSOLVE, Samuel & Mary Byrne, Feb. 14, 1811 – bdsm: Samuel Gonsolve, Elijah Chenault

GOODWIN, James K. & Rebecca Ann Ustick, Jan. 22, 1834 – bdsm: James K. Goodwin, Stephen G. Ustick

Peter & Dorcus Gotare, Aug. 23, 1813 – bdsm: Peter Goodwin, Loughlin Masterson

GORDON, George F. & Hannah Chard, Feb. 27, 1822 – bdsm: George F. Gordon, John Webb

GORRELL, James & Lucinda Franks, March 25, 1824 – bdsm: James Gorrell, Joseph M. Clark

GOSS, Andrew & Sarah Pearson, June 4, 1804 – bdsm: Andrew Goss, James

GOSS (continued) Young

GOULD, John & Eliza Rumney, Feb. 14, 1824 – bdsm: John Gould, John Foucard

GOWEN, Joseph & Mary Sherron, July 14, 1803 – bdsm: Joseph Gowen, Henry Oswald

GRACE, John & Teresa Ann Spence, Jan. 21, 1832 – bdsm: John Grace, John Humphreys

GRAEFF, John Jr. & Ann Brook, Sept. 29. 1818 – bdsm:

GRAHAM, Charles & Elizabeth Reefe, Sept. 22, 1831 – bdsm: Charles Graham, John McNamara

John & Cecilia Freeman, Jan. 1, 181S – bdsm: John Graham

John C. & Mary Chatham, Oct. 19, 1843 – bdsm: John C. Graham, Mary Chatham

John Jr. & Sarah Hattersley, May 21, 1814 – bdsm: John Graham, George Gordon

GRANT, John (coloured) & Ann Harris (coloured), Sept. 17, 1844 – bdsm: John Grant, William Morrison

John W. & Susan Bowles, Feb. 2, 1820 – bdsm: John W. Grant, George Parker

GRAY, Alfred & Maria Rowe, Feb. 13, 1840 – bdsm: Alfred Gray, William Hatton

Bazil H. & Jane Ross, July 3, 1835 – bdsm: Bazil H.

GRAY (continued)
Gray, Emmit Kain
George W. & Dianna Gladden, Jan. 10, 1826 – bdsm: George W. Gray, John T. Evans
James & Priscilla Weeden, Sept. 12, 1801 – bdsm: James Gray, Henry Weeden
John H. & Ann N. Franks, orphan of Robert Franks, July 13, 1847 – bdsm: John H. Gray, James E. Mankin
Levi & Anne Osburn, Feb. 22, 1814 – bdsm: Levi Gray, John Cunningham
Robert & Mildred Ann Nicholas, Nov. 27, 1828 – bdsm: Robert Gray, William Mastin
William & Emily Cole, Jan. 20, 1839 – bdsm: William Gray, John Simpkins
William A. & Ann Busby, Aug. 10, 1809 – bdsm: William A. Gray, Edward Lloyd
Wm. Jr. & Laura Dundass (Also: Dundas) (free coloured persons), March 14, 1844 – bdsm: William Gray, Jr., William Gray
GRAYSON, Bernard & Sally Day, Oct. 19, 1837 – bdsm: Bernard Grayson, Thomas Holland
Spence & Sarah Blunt, Oct. 30, 1811 – bdsm: Spence Grayson, Daniel Somers
GREEN, Baszille & Maria Hicks, May 14, 1845 – bdsm: Baszille Green, James Javins
Edward & Ann Carson, Dec.

GREEN (continued)
20, 1827 – bdsm: Edward Green, James Carson
Edward & Henrietta M. Brewer, Jan. 5, 1837 – bdsm: Edward Green, Alexander Moore
Frederick & Catharine Cheverill, Feb. 15, 1812 – bdsm: Frederick Green, Richard H. Lee
George & Catherine Patterson, March 8, 1802 – bdsm: George Green, William Patterson
James & Esther H. Hucorn, Oct. 16, 1815 – bdsm: James Green, Nicholas Drews
James & Jane Muir, Nov. 21, 1825 – bdsm: James Green, Stephen Shinn
Thomas & Susannah Lanham, Sept. 7, 1804 – bdsm: Thomas Green, John Duff
Thomas B. & Rebecca Hickey, April 21, 1809 – bdsm: Thomas B. Green, George Hair
William P. & Hopewell Gunther Farlton, April 26, 1828 – bdsm: William P. Green, John F. Green
GREENOLDS, John & Mary Allen, April 27, 1807 – bdsm: John Greenolds, William Harper Griffin
GREENWELL, Cornelius & Eliza G. Southard, April 9, 1830 – bdsm: Cornelius Greenwell, William Southard
GREENWOOD, Benjamin & Catharine Myers, Dec. 3, 1817 – bdsm: Benjamin

GREENWOOD (continued)
Greenwood, Mary Myers
James & Ann Eliza Wade,
Dec. 27, 1833 - bdsm:
James Greenwood, Zeph-
eniah S. Wade
James & Mary Ann Casey,
Dec. 8, 1836 - bdsm:
James Greenwood, John
Frizzell
GREER, William & Susan
Coleman, Sept. 4, 1821 -
bdsm: William Greer,
George W. Slacum
GREGORY, William & Mar-
garet D. Bartleman, Dec.
2, 1822 - bdsm: William
Gregory, William Bartle-
man
William & Mary D. Long,
March 5, 1838 - bdsm:
William Gregory, Robert
Jamieson
GREW, John & Rebecca H.
Fowle, May 26, 1835 -
bdsm: John Grew, Thomas
Semmes
GRIFFIN, John & Mary Sim-
mons, Aug. 17, 1837 -
bdsm: John Griffin
Robert & Sarah Sayres, Oct.
23, 1832 - bdsm: Robert
Griffin, Samuel J. Stapples
William & Letitia Lannum,
April 3, 1804 - bdsm: Wil-
liam Griffin, John Lannum
GRIFFITH, David & Mary
Williams, Jan. 28, 1804 -
bdsm: David Griffith,
Alexander Williams
John & Frances Ashton, May
18, 1844 - bdsm: John
Griffith, Jacob Wilson
Kinsey & Phebe Ann Mills,
August 1, 1844 - bdsm:
Kinsey Griffith, Richard

GRIFFITH (continued)
Rotchford
Kinzey & Mary Ann McLeod,
March 20, 1832 - bdsm:
Kinzey Griffith, John Mof-
fett
GRIGG, Joseph & Caroline
Solomon, March 5, 1828 -
bdsm: Joseph Grigg,
Thomas Davy
GRIGSBY, James & Nancy
Freeman, Nov. 7, 1814 -
bdsm: James Grigsby,
John Livingston
GRIMES, Joseph & Margaret
Barnes, Sept. 30, 1830 -
bdsm: Joseph Grimes,
James P. Coleman
Nicholas & Mary Payne,
widow of the late George
Payne deceased, Jan. 13,
1803 - bdsm: Nicholas
Grimes, Sylvester Grimes
Thomas & Latitia Hepburn,
Aug. 21, 1821 - bdsm:
Thomas Grimes, Jonah
Isabell (Married Aug. 28,
1821 by Rev. O. Norris)
William & Rhode Purkins
July 10, 1811 - bdsm:
William Grimes, John
Workman
GRIMSHAW, Thomas & On-
nar Radden, July 7, 1804 -
bdsm: Thomas Grimshaw,
James Flood
GRISWALD, Lyman & Ann
Taylor, June 22, 1830 -
bdsm: Lyman Griswald,
Robert Hodskins
GRIZZELL, John & Maria
Latham, July 29, 1836 -
bdsm: John Grizzell,
Thomas Burns
GROVER, Stinson & Eliz-
abeth E. Hanson, May 30,

GROVER (continued)
1842 - bdsm: Stinson Grover, John H. Morris
GROVES, Caleb & Nancy Davis, May 28, 1811 - bdsm: Caleb Groves, Henry Davis
GRUBB, John & Eliza M. Kilton, Sept. 19, 1816 - bdsm: John Grubb, W. H. Rice
John S. & Emily Pratt, Jan. 22, 1848 - bdsm: John S. Grubb, Benjamin Berry
GRUBER, John & Elizabeth Tyler, May 11, 1825 - bdsm: John Gruber, Henry Tyler
GRYMES, Edward & Mary Sinclair, March 29, 1802 - bdsm: Edward Grymes, Thomas Sinclair
Enoch & Mary Ann Harrington, July 3, 1834 - bdsm: Enoch Grymes, Moses O. B. Cawood
Robert & Precilla Gray, Nov. 21, 1803 - bdsm: Robert Grymes, Hezekiah Gray
Wm. & Jane Brooks, Nov. 5, 1846 - bdsm: Wm. Grimes, Barthol Delphy
GUNNELL, William P. & Martha A. Lindsay, Jan. 22, 1851 - bdsm:
GUTHRIDGE, John of Alexandria County & Elizabeth Shannon, Oct. 23, 1805 - bdsm: John Guthridge, Robert Walker
GUTHRIE, William & Eliza Couchman, July 29, 1814 - bdsm: Wm. Guthrie, Letticia Couchman
GUY, James & Adeline Benton, Jan. 6, 1831 - bdsm:

GUY (continued)
James Guy, Adeline Benton
John & Winifred Bustle, Dec. 29, 1815 - bdsm: John Guy, Samuel Isaacs
John W. & Elizabeth Ann Cortin, March 14, 1839 - bdsm: John W. Guy, John T. Creighton
GUYTON, Geo. B. & Catherine O. McIntyre, Oct. 22, 1835 - bdsm: Geo. B. Guyton, John Dooly (See also: Gwyton)
HACKETT, Dennis & Amy Bell, Nov. 20, 1846 - bdsm: Dennis Hackett, Nathaniel Oden
HADEN, Garret & Eleanor Wood, April 15, 1803 - bdsm: Garret Haden, John Greenwood
HALE, Benjamin & Judith White, August 18, 1804 - bdsm: Benjamin Hale, Alexander Smith
H. D. & Francis L. D. Yates, Jan. 29, 1822 - bdsm: Henry D. Hale, Alexander Hunter
HALL, Ephraim W. & Louisa H. Ball, May 29, 1849 - bdsm: Ephraim W. Hall, C. C. Bradley
Isaac & Frances Davis, Aug. 7, 1838 - bdsm: Isaac Hall, Henry Calvert
Jacob & Delia Hall, Dec. 25, 1813 - bdsm: Jacob Hall, Zebediah Hall
James & Ann Eliza Coax, April 5, 1827 - bdsm: James Hall, William B. Coax (See also: Cox)
James & Jane Gray, Nov.

HALL (continued)
10, 1834 - bdsm: James Hall, Reuben Johnston, Jr.
John & Jane Eliza Dogan, May 2, 1833 - bdsm: John Hall, Philip Dogan
John P. & Martha J. Smith, Sept. 28, 1836 - bdsm: John P. Hall, Charles Hawkins
Richard & Ellen M. Reynolds, July 21, 1830 - bdsm: Richard Hall, Henry Hobbs
Thomas & Nancy Lee, July 30, 1831 - bdsm: Thomas Hall, Mathew Manly
Washington & Ceilla Dutchy, Feb. 13, 1812 - bdsm: Washington Hall, Leonard Dutchy
William & Mary Ann Greenwood, daughter of Mary Ann Greenwood, May 3, 1849 - bdsm: William Hall, Mary Ann Greenwood
William & Penelope Graham, Oct. 22, 1818 - bdsm: William Hall, George Russell
HALLBRIGHT, Joseph & Nancy Campbell, Jan. 19, 1804 - bdsm: Joseph Hallbright, Henry Oswald
HALLIS, Spencer & Sarah Grant, July 28, 1813 - bdsm: Spencer Hallis, George Russell
HALLOWOOD, Charles & Rody Bussell, Oct. 24, 1812 - bdsm: Charles Hallowood, William Patterson
HAMILTON, Alfred & Hannah A. Seaton, (Negroes), no date 1846; married Mar. 15, 1846 - bdsm: Daniel

HAMILTON (continued)
Gibson, George Seaton
David & Ann Going, Sept. 11, 1801 - bdsm: David Hamilton, Charles Thompson
Prince & Ann Chin, Oct. 18, 1841 - bdsm: Prince Hamilton, Samuel Reeler
Wesley & Delilah Page, Feb. 24, 1830 - bdsm: Wesley Hamilton, Jeremiah W. Satterwhite
HAMMERSLEY, Francis & Jane Rodgers, March 22, 1816 - bdsm: Francis Hammersley, Benjamin Rodgers
HAMMETT, John B. Jr. & Mary M'Intyre, May 6, 1828 - bdsm: John B. Hammett, John B. Hammett, Jr. (See also: Hammitt)
Robert & Ann T. Nicholas, June 29, 1841 - bdsm: Robert Hammett, Zachariah Nicholas
HAMMOCK, Benjamin & Susan Piddit, May 8, 1839 - bdsm: Benjamin Hammock
HAMMOND, J. Pinkney & Ann Catharine Page, daughter of Washington G. Page, Dec. 7, 1847 - bdsm: J. Pinkney Hammond, Benj. H. Berry
James & Grace Hanson, Oct. 30, 1822 - bdsm: James Hammond, Mark Hanson
John & Sarah Frazier, July 5, 1837 - bdsm: John Hammond, Geo. W. Carlin
HAMPTON, Roderick & Emily Gibson, Feb. 20, 1834 - bdsm: Roderick Hamp-

HAMPTON (continued)
ton, Jas. Gibson

HANCOCK, Andrew & Drucilla Smith, April 5, 1836 - bdsm: Andrew Hancock, John W. Smith

John B. & Mary Hull, Sept. 4, 1816 - bdsm: John B. Hancock, Benjamin Baden

HANDLESS, Moses & Nancy Grant, Nov. 13, 1815 - bdsm: Moses Handless, George Russell

HANDLIS, Robert & Harriet Middleton, Sept. 3, 1838 - bdsm: Robert Handlis, William Mankins

HANES, London & Polly Morgan, Dec. 20, 1804 - bdsm: London Hanes, James Evans

HANEY, Charles & Ann Laws, Aug. 20, 1830 - bdsm: Charles Haney, Ann Laws

HANEY, Robert & Jane Cheshire, Nov. 25, 1802 - bdsm: Robert Haney, Thomas L. Griffin

William & Delila Emerson, July 11, 1822 - bdsm: William Haney, Aquilla Emerson

HANNON, Walter W. & Ann Dailey, Dec. 19, 1816 - bdsm: Walter W. Hannon, Edward Dailey

Walter W. & Julia Longdon, Sept. 12, 1832 - bdsm: Walter W. Hannon, James Harris

William H. & Mary Hodgkin, Dec. 30, 1813 - bdsm: William H. Hannon, Ephraim Gilman

HANSON, Mark & Catharine

HANSON (continued)
Townshend, May 20, 1818 - bdsm: Mark Hanson, George Ellis

Mark & Elizabeth Clarke, May 2, 1822 - bdsm: Mark Hanson, Josiah Tate & Gustavus Gibson

HARDIN, Lauriston B. & Anna M. H. Hooe, Feb. 16, 1836 - bdsm: Lauriston B. Hardin, Bernard Hooe

HARDING, George M. & Alice Smedley, Dec. 8, 1824 - bdsm: George M. Harding, Edward Pittman

Richard & Lucretia Catterton, Feb. 16, 1805 - bdsm: Richard Harding, John Catterton

HARGRAVES, John T. & Charlotte E. Rose, Oct. 18, 1832 - bdsm: Rev. John T. Hargraves, Wm. Wright

HARLEY, Enoch & Debby Duvaun, Feb. 23, 1804 - bdsm: Enoch Harley, Lewis Simpson

HARLY, George & Eleanor Higs, March 10, 1830 - bdsm: George Harly, John Conggin

HARMON, Allen C. & Margaret Ann Potter, Dec. 5, 1842 - bdsm: Allen C. Harmon, Thomas Dorsey

HARMOND, Aaron D. & Mary Pascoe, May 5, 1823 - bdsm: Aaron D. Harmond, Charles Pascoe

HARPER, John & Mary Ann Broadback, June 20, 1829 - bdsm: John Harper, Nancy Harper

John & Sarah Davis, June 5,

HARPER (continued)
1805 – bdsm: John Harper, William Harper
Robert & Mary Ann Davis, May 17, 1809 – bdsm: Robert Harper, Alexander Lethgon
Samuel B. & Julia R. Harper, Oct. 11, 1831 – bdsm: Samuel B. Harper, William A. Harper
Washington T. & Ann Ellicott, March 14, 1827 – bdsm: Washington T. Harper, William Page
William & Ann Grimsley, Feb. 1, 1823 – bdsm: William Harper, James Mankins
William W. & Isabella Fleming, Oct. 22, 1845 – bdsm: William W. Harper, W. C. Yeaton
HARRIDEN, Andrew & Ann Dates, July 31, 1820 – bdsm: Andrew Harriden, Levi Pickering
HARRIS, Anthony & Fanny Wood, Oct. 31, 1816 – bdsm: Anthony Harris, Jonathan Chambers
George W. & Eliza Williams, July 17, 1837 – bdsm: George W. Harris, Townshend Fendall
Hugh & Nancy William, Dec. 13, 1802 – bdsm: Hugh Harris, William Brooks
John & Lucretia Miles, March 25, 1831 – bdsm: John Harris, Abraham Miles
John & Zenobia Lee, Feb. 2, 1822 – bdsm: John Harris, Thomas Bush

HARRIS (continued)
Joseph & Rebecca Ward, Jan. 10, 1824 – bdsm: Joseph Harris, Andrew Hancock
Joseph & Winnifred Dorsey, Dec. 16, 1801 – bdsm: Joseph Harris & Hugh West
Maulias & Mary E. Mandell, Jan. 10, 1831 – bdsm: Maulias Harris, John C. Mandell (Also: Matthias Harris)
Morgan & Elizabeth Lawson, March 19, 1836 – bdsm: Morgan Harris, Thomas Baggett
Nathan & Margaret W. Corcorn, July 10, 1823 – bdsm: Nathan Harris, Henry H. Webster
Nathan & Mary Clagett, Nov. 2, 1829 – bdsm: Nathan Harris, Samuel Hawkins
Samuel & Laura W. Budd, May 6, 1835 – bdsm: Samuel Harris, Charles Ross
Walter & Julia Ann Vernon, April 27, 1829 – bdsm: Walter Harris, Philip B. Vernon
William & Catharine Ross, Aug. 2, 1820 – bdsm: William Harris, George Russel
William & Catharine Thompson, Dec. 4, 1817 – bdsm: William Harris, Robert Butler
William & Nancy Stridmore, May 8, 1809 – bdsm: William Harris, Gerrard Stridmore
William E. & Mary Javins,

HARRIS (continued)
daughter of Thomas Javins, Dec. 2, 1847 - bdsm: William E. Harris, William Walker

Wm. A. & Catharine A. Butcher, Oct. 10, 1838 - bdsm: Wm. A. Harris, Jonathan Butcher

HARRISON, Benjamin & Lucy Branham (former slave of G. W. P. Custis), June 24, 1830 - bdsm: Benjamin Harrison, William H. Dangerfield

Elias & Elizabeth Veitch, May 13, 1820 - bdsm: Elias Harrison, Edmund J. Lee, Jr.

George & Polly Snyder, Oct. 1, 1814 - bdsm: George Harrison, William Hicks, Jr.

Hugh T. & Elisa C. Thompson, June 3, 1834 - bdsm: Hugh T. Harrison, Jonah P. Thompson

John D. & Elizabeth Carlin, Dec. 30, 1815 - bdsm: John D. Harrison, John Skidmore

Thomas & Elizabeth Crandell, Feb. 14, 1827 - bdsm: Thomas Harrison, Anthony Rhodes

Timothy P. & Ann R. Maddock, June 4, 1813 - bdsm: Timothy P. Harrison, Matthew Robinson

William & Ann Goodrick, Sept. 25, 1805 - bdsm: Wm. Harrison, Jeremiah Sommoks

HARRISS, James & Lucy Longden, Nov. 4, 1813 - bdsm: James Harriss,

HARRISS (continued)
Ralph Longden

HARROWER, Hyram & Eliza McDonald, Oct. 24, 1815 - bdsm: Hyram Harrower, Andrew Rounsavell

HART, Edwart & Eliza Zimmerman, April 2. 1825 - bdsm: Edward Hart, Thomas A. Hawke

John & Mrs. Elizabeth Urie, Aug. 4, 1836 - bdsm: John Hart, James P. Middleton

HARTLEY, George & Sarah Pepper, June 12, 1802 - bdsm: George Hartley, Edward Keating

HASKINS, James & Jane E. Tennison, June 4, 1835 - bdsm: James Haskins, John T. Armstrong

HASON, John & Lucy Thomas, July 3, 1815 - bdsm: John Hason, John Duff

HATCHER, Thomas & Ann Elizabeth Pollard, Sept. 16, 1845 - bdsm: Thomas Hatcher, William Pollard

HATHERINGTON, James & Maria Ann B. Yearly, Feb. 24, 1821 - bdsm: James Hatherington, Bernard Mager

HATTON, Wm. & Catharine Bruce, Dec. 25, 1841 - bdsm: Wm. Hatton, John Lee

HAWKINS, Charles & Lucinda Somers, Nov. 11, 1831 - bdsm: Charles Hawkins, Thomas Jacobs, Sr.

Robert & Ann Switzer, Feb. 14, 1823 - bdsm: Robert Hawkins, Elias P. Legg

HAWLEY, William & Wil-

HAWLEY (continued)
helmina D. Potts, Aug. 25, 1818 - bdsm: William Hawley, William Herbert, Jr.

HAWLING, Joseph L. & Martha D. Johnston, May 6, 1844 - bdsm: Joseph L. Hawling, Reuben Johnston

HAYMAN, James & Agnes Bloxham, Feb. 23, 1832 - bdsm: James Hayman, Henry McMachen

HAYNES, John & Mary Barber, Jan. 13, 1810 - bdsm: John Haynes, Henry Bayne, guardian of Mary Barber

HAYNIE, Henry & Margaret King, licence issued Oct. 22, 1850 - bdsm:

HEAD, Benjamin & Anna Limrick, July 5, 1806 - bdsm: Benjamin Head, Thomas Mezarvey

Lewis & Sarah Reason, Dec. 5, 1806 - bdsm: Lewis Head, William Johnson

HEATHERLY, Nathan & Rebecca Cooke, Dec. 17, 1803 - bdsm: Nathan Heatherly, Patrick Curry

HEDLEY, John P. & Mary Ann Merchant, May 8, 1843 - bdsm: John P. Hedley, Thomas Merchant

HEFERAN, John & Mary Kelly, license issued March 8,1851 - bdsm:

HEIMANN, Martin & Mary Brook, Feb. 15, 1842 - bdsm: J. W. Aubinoe, Christian Brooks

HEIS, William & Elizabeth Miller, May 7, 1803 - bdsm: William Heis, John

HEIS (continued)
Berrey

HELM, Francis L. & Sarah B. McKinney, Sept. 16, 1816 - bdsm: Francis L. Helm, John McKenney

HELMS, Strother M. & Mary Ann Vasse, Dec. 15, 1812 - bdsm: Strother M. Helms, Ambrose Vasse

HEMMICK, William H. & Caroline R. Tatsapaugh, daughter of John Tatsapaugh, Aug. 21, 1848 - bdsm: William H. Hemmick, John Tatsapaugh

HENDERSON, Archibald & Anna Maria Cazenove, Oct. 14, 1823 - bdsm: Archibald Henderson, William G. Gardner

James L. & Julia Ann Moore, Dec. 15, 1829 - bdsm: James L. Henderson, Wilkinson Williams

Peter & Elizabeth Curry, Aug. 26, 1829 - bdsm: Peter Henderson, Alexander P. Austin

Tarleton T. & Eliza Ann Hewes, March 29 1827 - bdsm: Tarleton T. Henderson, James P. Coleman

Willis & Catharine Sanford, July 3, 1823 - bdsm: Willis Henderson, William Coan

HENRY, Charles S. & Sophia Lee, Oct. 3, 1833 - bdsm: Charles S. Henry, John Harris

Edward H. & Lucinda Scott, Jan. 28, 1846 - bdsm: Edward H. Henry, William Wright

Isaac & Maibrey Underwood,

HENRY (continued)
August 5, 1811 - bdsm: Isaac Henry, John B. Hill
John & Elizabeth Williamson, May 3, 1816 - bdsm: John Henry, Robert Hodgkin
John & Emelia Gates, May 1, 1809 - bdsm: John Henry, Owen Sullivan
Thomas (free black) & Maria Chase, Jan. 24, 1831 - bdsm: Thomas Henry, Gus Gibson
HENTON, Richard & Julia Ann Armstrong, Nov. 15, 1830 - bdsm: Richard Henton, Carroll Bacon
HENYAN, Nathaniel & Emily Evans (daughter of James Evans), Jan. 19, 1829 - bdsm: Nathaniel Henyan, James Evans
HEPBURN, Anderson & Lucy Washington, March 3, 1831 - bdsm: Anderson Hepburn, Margaret Garner
HERBERT, William Jr. & Maria H. Dulany, Dec. 21, 1814 - bdsm:
Wm. Uriah & Elizabeth Penn, Jan. 23, 1836 - bdsm: Wm. Uriah Herbert, Walter Penn
HESTON, Samuel & Susan McKay, May 1, 1823 - bdsm: Samuel Heston, Zenas Kinsey
HEUITT, John C. & Ellen C. Lindsay, Jan. 5, 1845 - bdsm: John C. Heuitt, John Masterson
HEWHART, Levin & Sally Tyler, June 20, 1835 - bdsm: Levin Hewhart, John Palmer

HEWITT, Edmund & Sarah Dorsey, Sept. 27, 1821 - bdsm: Mial Dorsey, Edmund Hewitt
HEWS, Benjamin & Elizabeth Bell, Aug. 2, 1844 - bdsm: Benjamin Hews, George W. Walker (See also: Hughs)
HICKEY, Daniel & Susanna Goods, Dec. 26, 1814 - bdsm: Daniel Hickey, Thomas Jarvis (guardian of Susanna Goods)
HICKS, William & Jenny Parker, Feb. 5, 1825 - bdsm: William Hicks, John Grant
HICKSON, James & Matilda Davis, Dec. 17, 1829 - bdsm: James Hickson, Richard W. Davis
HIENTS, Mordecai & Elizabeth Mason, June 11, 1804 - bdsm: Mordecai Hient, John Hill
HIGDON, John & Rebeckah Reynolds, Feb. 21, 1816 - bdsm: John Higdon, John Shackleford
John F. S. & Marg. E. Banque, May 8, 1845 - bdsm: John F. S. Higdon, Francis Wills
John H. & Mary Ann Pickering, Dec. 13, 1848 - bdsm: John H. Higdon, Henry Cryss
William & Julia Ann Allan, Feb. 23, 1842 - bdsm: William Higdon, Ignatius Allan (See also: Allen)
HIGGINS, William & Eleanor Bradshaw, July 6, 1807 - bdsm: William Higgins, Davis & James Bowie

HILL, George Jr. & Martha Cooley, Jan. 16, 1834 - bdsm: George Hill, George Hill, Jr.

Godardus & Rachael Logan, Dec. 12, 1809 - bdsm: Godardus Hill, John Wood

James & Eleanor Tenneson, Jan. 11, 1817 - bdsm: James Hill, George Kincaid

John & Eleanor Calender, Aug. 8, 1822 - bdsm: John Hill, Eleanor Calender

John B. & Mary Underwood, Nov. 25, 1807 - bdsm: John B. Hill, Bolitha Laws

Joseph & Caroline Barker, March 22, 1827 - bdsm: Joseph Hill, Harry Darnell

Lawrence & Jane Perry, March 29, 1810 - bdsm: Lawrence Hill, Alexander Perry

Richard & Julia Ann Crupper, March 13, 1839 - bdsm: Richard Hill, Robert Crupper

Robert & Jane Johnson, Nov. 7, 1832 - bdsm: Robert Hill, Isaac Fox

Samuel V. & Mary E. Basford, Feb. 3, 1835 - bdsm: Samuel V. Hill, George Snyder

HILLARY, Washington & Emeline Jenkins, Nov. 25, 1830 - bdsm: Washington Hillary, Uriah Jenkins

HILLIARD, Joseph & Sophia Lutz, August 15, 1810 - bdsm: Joseph Hilliard, William Cohen

HILLS, Josiah B. & Mercy A. Wilson, May 24, 1832 - bdsm: Josiah B. Hills,

HILLS (continued)
Jacob H. Wilson

Robert & Elizabeth Currie (free persons of colour), Sept. 21, 1841 - bdsm: Robert Hills, John Nelson (See also: Hill)

Thomas E. & Elizabeth Lanphier, June 11, 1833 - bdsm: Thomas E. Hills, Richard H. Stanton

HILTON, Samuel & Cath. Steele, Feb. 16, 1830 - bdsm: Samuel Hilton, Horatio N. Steel

HIMINDENER, C. D. & Ann Churchman, Jan. 7, 1829 - bdsm: C. D. Himindener, William Deneale

HINES, Alfred & Maria Odleton, Aug. 11, 1830 - bdsm: Alfred Hines, Benjamin Cawood

John & Isabella Gilbert, Oct. 4, 1820 - bdsm: John Hines, Samuel Armstrong

HINGSTON, Nicholas & Jane Evans, Aug. 25, 1825 - bdsm: Nicholas Hingston, Daniel Minor

HIPKINS, Lewis & Jane E. Morgan, Feb. 25, 1842 - bdsm: R. F. Prettyman, Wm. Morgan

Lewis & Mary Carne, Aug. 15, 1809 - bdsm: Lewis Hipkins, Wm. Carne

HIXSON, James & Mary King, license granted Aug. 4, 1852 - bdsm:

HOBART, Nathaniel & Anna H. Potts, April 17, 1813 - bdsm: Nathaniel Hobart, Thomas Semmes

HOBB, Henry & Sarah Runnells, June 18, 1823 -

HOBB (continued)
bdsm: Henry Hobb, George W. Catlett
HODGES, Benjamin T. & Elizabeth A. Clagett, Dec. 15, 1836 - bdsm: Benjamin T. Hodges, Upton Ball
Benjamin T. & Maria Dangerfield, Oct. 1, 1840 - bdsm: Benjamin T. Hodges, Richard L. Ogle
Thomas F. & Mary A. Gates, Aug. 18, 1842 - bdsm: Thomas F. Hodges, James Hutcheson
HODGKIN, Robert & Clary Taylor, Sept. 10, 1817 - bdsm: Robert Hodgkin, John Horner
Robert & Elizabeth Frazer, June 28, 1831 - bdsm: Robert Hodgkin, Harrison Bradley
HODGKINS, Daniel & Alley Scott, Aug. 8, 1813 - bdsm: Daniel Hodgkins, Townshend Ball
James & Susanna Armstrong, July 14, 1810 - bdsm: James Hodgkins, Benjamin Caywood
John & Mary Shepherd, July 5, 1843 - bdsm: John Hodgkins, John H. Taylor
HOGE, William & Rachel E. Janney, March 12, 1850 - bdsm: William Hoge, Washington T. Harper
HOIT, Reuben & Cleary Flannagin, August 17, 1810 - bdsm: Reuben Hoit, Samuel Simmonds
HOKES, George & Ann Street, June 7, 1805 - bdsm: George Hokes, Daniel

HOKES (continued)
Street
HOLLIDAY, William L. & Ann McCleren, Nov. 22, 1802 - bdsm: William L. Holliday, William Glassford
HOLT, George & Jane Eliza Adams, April 12, 1838 - bdsm: George Holt, Isaac Wood
Henry E. & Ann H. Flowers, January 12, 1846 - bdsm: Henry E. Holt, James Quaid
HOOE, Howsand L. & Ann O'Neil, June 9, 1831 - bdsm: Howsand L. Hooe, Ferdinand O'Neil
HOPKINS, James A. & Matilda Allen, Dec. 21, 1841 - bdsm: James A. Hopkins, Reuben Gerry
John & Cornelia Lee, Oct. 16, 1806 - bdsm: John Hopkins, Wm. Hodgson
William & Mary Brooks, Nov. 29, 1814 - bdsm: William Hopkins, James Mansfield
HOPWOOD, Thomas & Catharine Latham, Sept. 16, 1843 - bdsm: Thomas Hopwood, Enoch Ward
HORSEMAN, Elijah & Betsy Edmonds, ward of Owen Leddy, Aug. 2, 1832 - bdsm: Elijah Horseman, Owen Leddy
HORTON, Cossom & Lucy Rye, Sept. 27, 1805 - bdsm: Cossom Horton, Robert Smith
HORWELL, Charles & Ann Phenix, Sept. 23, 1801 - bdsm: Charles Horwell,

HORWELL (continued)
Robert Abercrumbie
Edward C. & Frances E. Settle, Aug. 9, 1842 – bdsm: Edward C. Horwell, Henry Mansfield
Richard & Susan Sleigh, Sept. 17, 1817 – bdsm: Richard Horwell, William Sleigh
HOUGH, Peyton & Harriet R. Mills, May 31, 1825 – bdsm: Peyton Hough, Charles B. R. Douglass
HOUSTON, John M. & Mary Larmour, July 5, 1837 – bdsm: John M. Houston, Samuel B. Larmour
HOWARD, Beal & Ann L. Howard, July 1, 1822 – bdsm: Beal Howard, Ann Howard
Beal Jr. & Elizabeth Rounsavell, Jan. 22, 1817 – bdsm: Beal Howard, Jr., Andrew Rounsavell
James & Eugenia Howard, Aug. 24, 1837 – bdsm: James Howard, Thomas Fugett
John & Ann Maddox, June 9, 1820 – bdsm: John Maddox, Joseph Sax
John & Ann Maddox, June 9, 1820 – (Married June 9, 1820 by Rev. O. Norris)
John & Ann Yearly, Dec. 25, 1834 – bdsm: John Howard, William Benter
John & Elizabeth Finch, Nov. 5, 1840 – bdsm: G. Y. Howard, Peter Brenner
Samuel & Ann Abbott, May 24, 1825 – bdsm: Samuel Howard, William B. Stuart
HOWISON, William G. & Sa-

HOWISON (continued)
rah E. Birch, May 7, 1833 – bdsm: William G. Howison, James Birch
HOXTON, William W. & Elisa L. Griffith, Nov. 17, 1835 – bdsm: William W. Hoxton, Thomas Semmes
HUBBARD, Jeremiah & Susan Ann Maria Patterson, Dec. 21, 1825 – bdsm: Jeremiah Hubbard, William Patterson
HUDDLESTON, John E. & Mary Ann Smith, Aug. 20, 1835 – bdsm: John E. Huddleston, Joseph Smith, guardian of Mary Ann Smith
HUDGES, James & Nancy Leavy, Sept. 26, 1826 – bdsm: James Hudges, Michael Gardner
HUFFMAN, Peter & Aminta Mason, April 13, 1804 – bdsm: Peter Hoffman, William Bayless
HUGHES, Benjamin & Hannah Price, July 18, 1837 – bdsm: Benjamin Hughes, Christopher Motherson
George G. & Elizabeth Piles, March 31, 1829 – bdsm: George G. Hughes, George Millan
John & Ann M. Marston, Sept. 21, 1824 – bdsm: John Hughes, John Mason
John & Lydia I. Smedley, July 2, 1823 – bdsm: John Hughes, C. B. R. Douglass
John & Sarah Harding, March 26, 1806 – bdsm: John Hughes, Elijah Shay
Thomas & Amelia Egling, May 15, 1802 – bdsm:

HUGHES (continued)
Thomas Hughes, David Mankins
HUGHS, Richard & Betty Davis, Jan. 14, 1817 - bdsm: Richard Hughs, George Brogdon
HUGLE, Geo. F. & Sarah H. Carlin, Feb. 4, 1830 - bdsm: Geo. F. Hugle, Levi Hurdle
HULL, Robert & Hannah Ann Janney, May 29, 1832 - bdsm: Robert Hull, R. S. Hopkins
William & Ann Colston, April 24, 1812 - bdsm: William Hull, Isaac Payne
HULLS, George & Bertha Ferguson, June 14, 1812 - bdsm: George Hulls, Benjamin Cawood
George & Fanny Armstrong, March 1st, 1805 - bdsm: George Hull, James Flood
HUMPHREYS, Correl & Cath. A. Glassgow, June 17, 1830 - bdsm: Correl Humphreys, James McDaniel
Richard L. & Mary Reese, Dec. 19, 1805 - bdsm: Richard L. Humphreys, Jacob Shuck
HUMPHRIES, Abner & Lucy Ann Dillon, July 18, 1838 - bdsm: Abner Humphries, James Wallace
George & Eliza Brooks, Nov. 24, 1837 - bdsm: George Humphries, Alfred Lee
George & Kitty Barnes, Oct. 11, 1844 - bdsm: George Humprhies, John Lee
William & Susan Stevenson, Sept. 25, 1832 - bdsm:

HUMPHRIES (continued)
William Humphries, Samuel Church (guardian of Susan Stevenson)
HUNT, Philip & Rebecca Yost, Dec. 19, 1811 - bdsm: Philip Hunt, William Simpson
William & Helen Rudd, daughter of Richard A. Rudd, Oct. 17, 1849 - bdsm: William Hunt, Henry Pollard
HUNTER, Alexander & Louisa Ann Adilaide Chapman, Feb. 2, 1815 - bdsm: Alexander Hunter, John D. Simms (guardian of Laura Chapman)
Peter & Julia Ann Deneale, June 9, 1830 - bdsm: Peter Hunter, Hector Leary
Robert & Eunice Harley, April 18, 1810 - bdsm: Robert Hunter, William L. Webster
Robert & Mary C. Wood, March 3, 1818 - bdsm: Robert Hunter, Benjamin Wood
Robert W. & Elizabeth Bryan, Aug. 21, 1817 - bdsm: Robert W. Hunter, Bazil H. Davidson
William & Mary Ann Harrison Smith, March 6, 1822 - bdsm: William Hunter, Benjamin Bowie
HUNTINGTON, William & Elizabeth Smitherman, Dec. 24, 1806 - bdsm: William Huntington, James Grimsley
HURDLE, Edward James & Ann E. Walker, Dec. 4, 1841 - bdsm: Edward

103

HURDLE (continued)
James Hurdle, Geo. W.
Walker
Jesse & Rebeccah Duty,
Feb. 21, 1816 - bdsm:
Jesse Hurdle, Anthony
Frazier
Levi & Lydia B. Jenkins,
June 8, 1830 - bdsm: Levi
Hurdle, Uriah Jenkins
HURLEY, George & Hopey
Sutherland, Sept. 30, 1815
- bdsm: George Hurley,
William W. Fitzhugh
Maurice & Ann M. O'Neale,
Jan. 7, 1830 - bdsm:
Maurice Hurley, John Tat-
sapaugh
HURST, Richard & Isabella
Hepburn, Sept. 5, 1835 -
bdsm: Richard Hurst,
Alexander Hepburn
HUSBAND, John J. & Ann
Eliza Capron, July 3, 1849
- bdsm: John J. Husband,
J. R. Ludlow
HUSSEY, Andrew & Maria A.
Rhodes, June 28, 1828 -
bdsm: Andrew S. Hussey,
Anthony Rhodes
HUTCHINS, William & Mary
Austin, Jan. 15, 1824 -
bdsm: William Hutchins,
John Boyer
HUTCHINSON, Thompson &
Rachael Lawson, Feb. 3,
1816 - bdsm: Thompson
Hutchinson, Thompson
Clarke
HUTCHISON, Alexander &
Maria Janney, Jan. 6, 1825
- bdsm: Alexander Hut-
chison, Phineas Janney
James & Margaret A. Par-
mer, Dec. 22, 1842 -
bdsm: James Hutcheson,

HUTCHISON (continued)
Elias Mothersead
HUTTON, Isaac G. & R. E.
Smith, Dec. 15, 1823 -
bdsm: Isaac G. Hutton,
Rebecca E. Smith
HYDE, Thomas V. & Con-
stantia Boyd, Oct. 8, 1839
- bdsm: Thomas V. Hyde,
Isaac H. Robbins
IMMOHR, Frederick & Re-
becca Jones, Nov. 27,
1813 - bdsm: Frederick
Immohr, Robert Allison
IRELAND, Richard & Matilda
E. Dickens, July 13, 1846
- bdsm: Richard Ireland,
Middleton Elwood Dickens
IRVIN, Davis & Sarah Ann
Nalby, June 27, 1835 -
bdsm: Davis Irvin, James
Alexander
IRWIN, James & Ann D.
Marshall, Aug. 4, 1828 -
bdsm: James Irwin, John
M. Johnson
Wm. H. & Ann B. Paton,
Oct. 7, 1839 - bdsm: Wm.
H. Irwin, Peter E. Hoffman
ISAACS, Samuel & Sarah
Keefer, Aug. 9, 1847 -
bdsm: Samuel Isaacs,
Thomas Whittington
ISACKS, Samuel & Edith
Powell, May 19, 1810 -
bdsm: Samuel Isacks,
Robert Erskin
ISH, Peter & Harriot Kirk,
Nov. 20, 1817 - bdsm:
Peter Ish, William Kirk
JACKSON, Archibald & Nelly
Gorden, Sept. 13, 1824 -
bdsm: Archibald Jackson,
Mark Hanson
Daniel & Ann Waters, April
7, 1821 - bdsm: Daniel

JACKSON (continued)

Jackson, John Channcey Frederick A. & Mary E. Martin, July 29, 1847 - bdsm: Frederick A. Jackson, John M. Magor

Isaac & Letty Jones (free coloured persons), March 7, 1844 - bdsm: Isaac Jackson, William Cole

James & Mary Turner, May 2, 1811 - bdsm: James Jackson, William Godard

James & Sarah Gray, May 7, 1825 - bdsm: James Jackson, John G. Gray

John & Amelia Jane Watson Simms, Nov. 10, 1814 - bdsm: John D. Summers, John Jackson

John & Lucretia Hill, July 23, 1805 - bdsm: John Jackson, George Hill

John & Mary F. Alexander (both coloured), license issued June 20, 1851 - bdsm:

John & Mary M. Fairbush, Feb. 18, 1833 - bdsm: John Jackson, John Simpkins

Nathaniel & Lucy Harris, Nov. 4, 1847 - bdsm: Nathaniel Jackson, Charles Edward Guss

Thomas & Ann Caverly Moore, Nov. 14, 1816 - bdsm: Thomas Jackson, James Rector Magruder Lowe

Thomas & Janney Loggins, June 27, 1811 - bdsm: Thomas Jackson, George Russell

William & Bridget Roberts, June 8, 1815 - bdsm: Wil-

JACKSON (continued)

liam Jackson, Zachariah Mann

William & Elizabeth Guy, Jan. 13, 1842 - bdsm: William Jackson, John Marston

William & Nancy Gray, Nov. 20, 1806 - bdsm: William Jackson, Robert Bell

JACOBS, Alfred & Elizabeth Lindsay, license issued Dec. 24, 1850 - bdsm:

George & Sarah A. Chiles, Sept. 22, 1817 - bdsm: George Jacobs, James Allison

John & Dorothy Selvey, Dec. 22, 1817 - bdsm: John Jacobs, John Evans

Lemuel & Emeline Mansfield, May 21, 1845 - bdsm: Lemuel Jacobs, Henry Mansfield

Samuel & Hannah Morgan, Jan. 2, 1826 - bdsm: Samuel Jacobs, William Morgan

Thomas & Catharine Henrickson, Aug. 17, 1809 - bdsm: Thomas Jacobs, David Price

Thomas & Charlotte Deagan, Dec. 21, 1829 - bdsm: Thomas Jacobs, James VanZant

Thomas E. & Sarah A. Markley, Jan. 11, 1832 - bdsm: Thomas E. Jacobs, Charles H. Dearborn

JAMES, Henry & Susannah Taylor, Nov. 28, 1804 - bdsm: Henry James, William Reed

JAMIESON, Andrew & Eliza V. Douglass, daughter of

JAMIESON (continued)
John Douglass, Nov. 2, 1849 - bdsm: Andrew Jamieson, John Douglass

John & Maria Groverman, Feb. 17, 1836 - bdsm: John Jamieson, G. W. D. Ramsay

Robert & Catharine Porter Sanford, Nov. 2, 1824 - bdsm: Robert Jamieson, Thomas Sandford

JANNEY, Moses & Judith Laurence, Feb. 19, 1805 - bdsm: Moses Janney, John Corse

Samuel H. & Elizabeth Mark, Jan. 20, 1830 - bdsm: Samuel H. Janney, Frederick Wilson

JARBOUR, Andrew & Rachal Johnson, Nov. 4, 1830 - bdsm: Benj. S. Kinsey, John B. Hampson

JASPER, Israel & Winifred Day, August 9, 1811 - bdsm: Israel Jasper, George Russell

JAVINS, Harrison & Elizabeth Phillips, Aug. 18, 1843 - bdsm: Harrison Javins, William Phillips (See also: Philips)

John & Victorina Smith, April 29, 1833 - bdsm: John Javins, James D. Bryan

Richard & Virginia Walker, May 14, 1842 - bdsm: Richard Javins, Geo. Wiley

William & Rhoda Compton, Sept. 27 1817 - bdsm: William Javins, Dennis Javins

JAY, Jabez & Ann Brewer,

JAY (continued)
Dec. 26, 1843 - bdsm: Jabez Jay, William Powell

JEFFERSON, Clayton & Eliza Marr, daughter of Matthew Marr, Dec. 30, 1847 - bdsm: Clayton Jefferson, Joseph B. Harbin

Samuel & Rebecca Wallace, orphan of Aaron Wallace, Aug. 31, 1848 - bdsm: Samuel Jefferson, William Campbell

JEFFERY, John & Nancy Henderson, March 14, 1821 - bdsm: John Jeffery, Davis Bowie

JEFFREY, Samuel & Sarah Mahony, Feb. 17, 1803 - bdsm: Samuel Jeffrey, George Woolls

JENKINS, Wm. H. & Julia A. Javins, Sept. 11, 1833 - bdsm: William H. Jenkins, Thompson Javins

JENNINGS, Matthias & Eugenia Jeffries (free mulattoes), Feb. 1, 1849 - bdsm: Matthias Jennings, Samuel Skidmore

Paul & Desdemona Brooks, (coloured) June 12, 1849 - bdsm: Paul Jennings, Richard H. Gibson

JEWETT, Aaron & Eliza Mark, July 11, 1814 - bdsm: Aaron Jewett, Samuel Mark

JILLETT, Jeptha & Elizabeth J. Hills, Aug. 19, 1833 - bdsm: Jeptha Jillett, Lewis Hipkins

JOACHIM, Henry C. & Lettice Harding, Nov. 21, 1810 - bdsm: Henry C.

JOACHIM (continued)

Joachim, Bettice Harding

JOHNS, John & Catharine McKelvin, May 4, 1844 - bdsm: John Johns, Elizabeth McKelvin (See also: John Jones, McKelvec)

Thomas & Anna Maria V. Seaton, Sept. 5, 1821 - bdsm: Thomas Johns, Nathaniel S. Wise

JOHNSON, Alexious & Elizabeth Masters, Dec. 12, 1833 - bdsm: Alexious Johnson, William Drake

Aquilla & Hetty Carter, July 22, 1827 - bdsm: Aquilla Johnson, James Brooks

Dennis & Patty Ferguson, May 27, 1830 - bdsm: Dennis Johnson, William Gibson

James & Caroline Cannon, Dec. 15, 1812 - bdsm: James Johnson, William Williams

John & Elizabeth Taylor, Nov. 29, 1848 - bdsm: John Johnson, John A. Keys

John & Margaret Hodgskins, March 7, 1807 - bdsm: John Johnson, Benjamin Head

Noble H. & Mary Ann Morgan, April 27, 1830 - bdsm: Noble H. Johnson, William Morgan

Richard & Ann Maria Smith, Jan. 16, 1833 - bdsm: Richard Johnson, William N. Ward

Richard & M. A. Haney (free coloured persons), no date 1846 - bdsm: (Mary Ann Haney)

JOHNSON (continued)

Robert & Elizabeth Moore, June 9, 1820 - bdsm: Robert Johnson, George Grayson

Robert W. & Anna Harris, orphan of John Harris, May 25, 1848 - bdsm: Robert W. Johnson, Edwin T. Allen

Samuel & Aminta King, June 13, 1804 - bdsm: Samuel Johnson, Thomas Arthur

Thomas & Martha Williams, April 2, 1846 - bdsm: Thomas Johnson, Lewis Sherwood (Thomas Johnson was the guardian of Martha Williams)

Wm. & Eliza Black, March 11, 1844 - bdsm: William Johnson, Samuel K. Shay

JOHNSTON, Clement & Susannah Patton, Jan. 1, 1812 - bdsm: Clement Johnston, Hezekiah Johnston

George & Linny Long, Jan. 2, 1818 - bdsm: George Johnston, William Long

Hezakiah & Nancy Talbott, Nov. 5, 1809 - bdsm: Hezakiah Johnston, Kyrle Allen

James W. & Rachael Dobbin, Feb. 6, 1817 - bdsm: James W. Johnston, Henry Drain

John & Nancy Mills, March 20, 1815 - bdsm: John Johnston, James Millan

Reuben Jr. & Mary C. LeGrand, June 29, 1840 - bdsm: Reuben Johnston, Jr., Cassius F. Lee

Richard & Eleanor Freeman,

JOHNSTON (continued)
May 18, 1826 - bdsm: Richard Johnston, John S. Emerson

Samuel & Ann Sexton, Oct. 3, 1809 - bdsm: Samuel Johnston, Vincent Taylor

Theophilus & Polly Fowles, Dec. 30, 1820 - bdsm: Theophilus Johnston, James Hill

W. C. & Louisa Hantzmon, Nov. 18, 1843 - bdsm: W. C. Johnston, Henry Hantz-mon

William & Betsey Hurse, Dec. 23, 1847 - bdsm: William Johnston, John Johnston

William P. & Mary Elizabeth Hooe, Dec. 3, 1840 - bdsm: William P. Johnston, Bernard Hooe

JOLSON, William & Ellen Pindred (Perdred), Sept. 29, 1838 - bdsm: William Jolson, William Gulatt

JONES, Abraham & Letty Shavers, July 2, 1831 - bdsm: Abraham Jones, Theopolus Randall

Benjamin & Susan Giesta, Oct. 27, 1827 - bdsm: Benjamin Jones, Gustavus Gibson

Charles & Ann Elizabeth Brown, Dec. 14, 1838 - bdsm: Charles Jones, Thacker Jones

Edward & Jane Nicholson, June 7, 1838 - bdsm: Edward Jones, William R. Beers

Ezekiel & Maria Allen, Jan. 6, 1824 - bdsm: Ezekiel Jones, Hanson Day

JONES (continued)
Francis B. & Harriet Wright, Nov. 4, 1830 - bdsm: Francis B. Jones, Charles M. Wright

Frederick & Maria Ann Turley, Jan. 16, 1845 - bdsm: Frederick Jones, Robert Turley

George & Martha Lavender, April 27, 1824 - bdsm: George Jones, John O. Young

George of Prince George's County, Maryland, & Sally Bryan of the same county, Jan. 20, 1824 - bdsm: Aquila Beall, B. Harwood

Henry A. & Eliza Shortell, Dec. 8, 1828 - bdsm: Henry A. Jones, Alexander Brown

John & Eliza Pitcher (free black), Nov. 19,1834 - bdsm: John Jones, John Beckley

John & Mary Brown, Sept. 28, 1839 - bdsm: John Jones, Walter L. Penn

Joseph & Debrah Welsh, Nov. 16, 1822 - (Marriage celebrated by Rev. O. Norris)

Lewis & Mary Whitmore, July 20, 1816 - bdsm: Lewis Jones, Levin Morris

Thacker & Martha Ganett, June 20, 1836 - bdsm: Thacker Jones, John A. Beckley (See also: Thacker Whiting)

Wesley & Rosetta Baker, Sept. 21, 1837 - bdsm: Wesley Jones, Peter Hewett

William & Mary Ellen Ham-

JONES (continued)
ilton, Aug. 7, 1841 - bdsm: William Jones, Wesley Hamilton

William & Rebecca Hitler, Sept. 18, 1802 - bdsm: William Jones, John Dixon

JORDAN, John L. & Sarah J. Bowdon, Sept. 21, 1850 - bdsm: John L. Jordan, Hiram Morgan

JULIUS, Jonas & Milly Dover, Jan. 2, 1816 - bdsm: Jonas Julius, William Syphax

Thomas & Betsy Dover, June 7, 1820 - bdsm: Thomas Julius, George Russell

KAIN, Robert E. & Julia A. Sparks, Aug. 19, 1835 - bdsm: Robert E. Kain, George Hutchinson

KEASER, Braxton & Eliza Keaser, May 15, 1844 - bdsm: Braxton Keaser, Samuel G. Brann

KEATING, George W. & Sarah Jones, Nov. 13 1834 - bdsm: George W. Keating, Richard Davis

James R. & Thamer Pernel, Nov. 9, 1818 - bdsm: James R. Keating, William A. Harris

KEENE, Newton & Nancy Moore Dundas, May 22, 1811 - bdsm: Newton Keene

KEIFER, Christopher & Sarah Violett, Sept. 5, 1821 - bdsm: Christopher Keifer, Albert P. Waugh

KEITH, Anderson D. & Catharine C. Keith, Nov. 2,

KEITH (continued)
1826 - bdsm: Anderson D. Keith, Thomas R. Keith

James & Isabella McMahan, July 22, 1802 - bdsm: James Keith, John Turner

KELL, Isaac Jr. & Mary Harrison, Dec. 27, 1841 - bdsm: Isaac Kell, Edwin R. Violett

Nathaniel & Susannah Hipkins, June 27, 1838 - bdsm: Nathaniel Kell, R. F. Prettyman, Lewis Hipkins

KELLAM, Thomas & Mary Mauncey, Oct. 18, 1802 - bdsm: Thomas Kellam, Robert Gray

KELLY, John & Eleanor Heath, July 18, 1832 - bdsm: John Kelly, William Heath

Patrick & Elizabeth Latham, Nov. 7, 1811 - bdsm: Patrick Kelly, Joseph Guthrow

Wm. & Martha E. Elliot, March 30, 1841 - bdsm: Wm. Kelly, John Jacobs

KEMPFIELD, Isaac & Mary Ann S. Korn, Oct. 5, 1820 - bdsm: Isaac Kempfield, Greenbary Gaither (Marriage celebrated same day bY Rev. O. Norris)

KENDALL, Lewis & Emeline Stepney, May 19, 1841 - bdsm: Lewis Kendall, David Easton

KENNARD, Joseph & Mary Howard, Nov. 5, 1817 - bdsm: Joseph Kennard, John Howard

KENNEDY, John & Susanna Maria Kennedy, Feb. 1,

KENNEDY (continued)
1826 - bdsm: John Kennedy, Jas. Douglas
KENNER, George & Elizabeth Conner, Dec. 11, 1806 - bdsm: George Kenner, Charles Mankin
George & Emeline Mills, Jan. 12, 1839 - bdsm: George Kenner, William Mills
Jacob & Louisa Walderstaffer, March 12, 1803 - bdsm: Jacob Kenner, Simon Stedecorn
KENT, John & Martha Ballard, Jan. 27, 1802 - bdsm: John Kent, William Ballard
Thomas H. & Ann Maria Peyton, May 10, 1813 - bdsm: Thomas H. Kent, Francis Peyton
William & Elizabeth Ross, August 28, 1805 - bdsm: Wm. Kent, Edward McDearmot
KERR, David & Eleanor Gallahan, Nov. 18, 1815 - bdsm: David Kerr, Samuel Gallahan
James D. & Lucretia McClean, Sept. 22, 1823 - bdsm: James D. Kerr, Charles B. R. Douglass
KIBBEY, William B. & Sarah A. Rinker, April 7, 1825 - bdsm: William B. Kibbey, Zenas Kinsey
KIBBY, Alexander & Benny McFarlain, Sept. 9, 1802 - bdsm: Alexander Kibby, George McFarlen
KIDD, William & Margaret Watkins, ward of Geo. Padgett, Oct. 14, 1839 -

KIDD (continued)
bdsm: William Kidd, George Padgett
KIDWELL, Iverton & Pricey Auston, Nov. 12, 1832 - bdsm: Iverton Kidwell, Patrick Foy
John H. & Elizabeth Dorsey, June 14, 1832 - bdsm: John H. Kidwell, Julius G. Swayne
KINE, Obadiah & Elizabeth Hunt, Sept. 12, 1827 - bdsm: Obadiah Kine, John McFarlane
KING, Benjamin & Elizabeth Dorsey, June 9, 1806 - bdsm: Benjamin King, Joseph Reinber
Benjamin & Mildred Matthews, June 18, 1833 - bdsm: Benjamin King, Henry Warner
Benjamin & Virginia Price, May 17, 1837 - bdsm: Benjamin King, Thompson F. Mason
Charles & Anna Sword, Nov. 10, 1827 - bdsm: Charles King, John M. Clarke
Isaac N. & Hannah C. Spear, July 6, 1820 - bdsm: Isaac N. King, Edward Murphy
James & Ally Mahoney, Sept. 4, 1817 - bdsm: James King, John Sutton
James & Nancy Groves, June 14, 1815 - bdsm: James King, Reuben Johnson
John W. & Ann W. Childs, Nov. 1, 1830 - bdsm: John W. King, Samuel K. Shay
Patrick & Susanna Baggett, June 29, 1811 - bdsm: Patrick King, Thomas

110

KING (continued)
Steel
Richard & Mary Davis, Oct. 5, 1820 – bdsm: Richard King, Richard Rudd (Celebrated same day by Rev. O. Norris)
Robert & Margaret S. McKnight, June 9, 1829 – bdsm: Robert King, William H. McKnight
Samuel & Elizabeth Gates, June 13, 1801 – bdsm: Thomas Gates, Samuel King
KINGSTON, Thomas & Susan Hodgkins, Jan. 11, 1817 – bdsm: Thomas Kingston, Samuel Bartle
KINSALOW, Fowell & Mary Fannall, Aug. 29, 1837 – bdsm: Fowell Kinsalow, Matthew Magher
KINSLEY, Patrick & Susan Latham, June 10, 1833 – bdsm: Patrick Kinsley, Thomas Burns
KINSOLVING, Ovid A. & Julia H. Krauth, Nov. 5, 1845 – bdsm: Ovid A. Kinsolving, Henry C. Lay
KINZER, J. Louis & Margaret G. Wise, daughter of George Wise, Dec. 4, 1849 – bdsm: J. Louis Kinzer, William H. Semmes
KINZEY, Enos & Mary Dorcey, April 4, 1804 – bdsm: Enos Kinzey, Lewis Wilson Plum
KIRBY, Jesse & Rebecca Dudley, Aug. 14, 1843 – bdsm: Jesse Kirby, John Philips
John B. & Mary Eleanor Shakes, daughter of John

KIRBY (continued)
Shakes, marriage license issued Dec. 30, 1850 – bdsm:
KIRK, George E. & Rebecca Jane Devaughn, Jan. 8, 1844 – bdsm: George E. Kirk, William Devaughn
Harrison & Margaret Devaughn, Dec. 21, 1842 – bdsm: Harrison Kirk, Samuel H. Devaughn
Samuel & Mary MCcue, July 27, 1809 – bdsm: Samuel Kirk
Samuel & Rebecca Fletcher, July 20, 1815 – bdsm: Samuel Kirk, George Rice
KLIPSTEIN, William B. M.D. & Mary Ann Taylor, married by Rev. G. B. Dana, July 21, 1851 –
KNIGHT, Ferdinand & Elizabeth Johnson, parental consent given Nov. 25, 1851 – mother: Rebecca Ellen Williams; wit: John Woolen, John Bryan
KNOWEL, James (or Nowell) & Ann Boothe, Aug. 26, 1824 – bdsm: James Knowel, Jacob Gray
KNOWLES, John & Mary Ann Westcott, Oct. 12, 1815 – bdsm: John Knowles, Hermon Gurney
KOON, Richard & Ann Ratcliff, Dec. 7, 1817 – bdsm: Richard Koon, Ignatius Ratcliff
KOONES, Charles & Rebecca W. Leonard, Jan. 2, 1822 – bdsm: Charles Koones, Benjamin Wood
LABILLE, Louis J. C. & Mary T. O'Neale, August

LABILLE (continued)
5, 1823 – bdsm: Julius J.
C. Labille, Thomas Steel

LACEY, William & Elizabeth Davis, Sept. 22, 1817 – bdsm: William Lacey, Thomas Wallace

LADD, Charles H. & Susan L. Fowle, Nov. 4, 1839 – bdsm: Charles H. Ladd, Thomas H. Ludl...

John B. & Harriet V. Nicoll, Nov. 13, 1824 – bdsm: John B. Ladd, Harris Nicoll

Wm. & Sophia Ann Stidolph, Oct. 19, 1801 – bdsm: William Ladd, John Cunningham

LAKEMAN, John D. & Mary Ann Atwell, Oct. 2, 1844 – bdsm: John D. Lakeman, William J. Sibley

LAMAR, G. B. & Harriett Cazanove, July 10, 1839 – bdsm: Octavious A. Cazenove, William C. Gardner

LAMB, George & Jane Aubray, Nov. 26, 1818 – bdsm: George Lamb, John Boyd

LAMBARD, Benjamin H. & Harriet Lanham, Dec. 29, 1823 – bdsm: Benjamin H. Lambard, Bryant Johnson

LAMBERT, Benjamin H. & Adeline Bond Wheat, May 15, 1828 – bdsm: Benjamin H. Lambert, Frederick A. Krones

George & Catharine Dennison, Oct. 30, 1811 – bdsm: George Lambert, Robert Smith

Joseph & Mary Bogan, Jan. 1, 1817 – bdsm: Joseph

LAMBERT (continued)
Lambert, Jacob Farr

LAMBETH, William M. & George Anna Slacum, Aug. 6, 1839 – bdsm: William M. Lambeth, Bernard Hooe

LAMBOY, Sampson & Letty Cole, May 5, 1813 – bdsm: Sampson Lamboy, James Martin

LAMOINE, John & Elizabeth Vassy, July 20, 1809 – bdsm: John Lamoine, Peter Vassy, Alexander Perry

LAMON, Archibald & Charlotte M. Rapley, Aug. 30, 1832 – bdsm: Archibald H. Lamon, Lewis Hooff

LANCASTER, George B. & Virginia Bartle, daughter of Samuel Bartle, July 12, 1849 – bdsm: George B. Lancaster, Samuel Bartle

LANDRES, Henry White & Mariah Thompson, widow of John Thompson, July 22, 1803 – bdsm: Henry White Landres, Nancy Bradley

LANDRESS, Henry W. & Nancy Davis, April 11, 1801 – bdsm: Henry W. Landress, Daniel Bradly

LANE, Alexander & Nancy Steel, Feb. 17, 1820 – bdsm: Alexander Lane, Thomas Steel

William & Frances Ann Handless, Oct. 31, 1832 – bdsm: William Lane, Susanna Handless

LANHAM, Elisha & Mary Ann Jenkins, July 10, 1817 – bdsm: Elisha Lanham, Leonard Cook

LANHAM (continued)
John & Ann McFadden, Sept. 4, 1802 – bdsm: John Lanham, John Thompson
John & Catharine Snell, Feb. 2, 1810 – bdsm: John Lanham, Elias Lanham
John & Olfehair Longdon, Oct. 22, 1801 – bdsm: John Lanham, Walter Longdon
LANPHIER, John & Ann G. Martin, Dec. 23, 1830 – bdsm: John Lanphier, Thomas L. Martin
William Jr. & Elizabeth B. McDongall, Dec. 6, 1832 – bdsm: William Lanphier, Jr., John Corse
LARMOUR, Samuel B. & Susan Mandeville Dec. 29, 1814 – bdsm: Samuel Larmour, Joseph Mandeville
LASKEY, John T. & Mary Walker, June 7, 1848 – bdsm: John T. Laskey, John S. Walker
LATHAM, Edward & Rachael Stephenson, Feb. 19, 1818 – bdsm: Edward Latham, James Ballenger
Rowland & Elizabeth Hart, March 1, 1806 – bdsm: Rowland Latham, John Gooding
LATHROP, Jedediah H. & Marianna Bryan, Sept. 26, 1843 – bdsm: Jedediah H. Lathrop, John Withers
LATRUITE, John P. & Barbara Moore, April 9, 1821 – bdsm: John P. Latruit, Benjamin Wood
LAURENCE, George A. & Sarah Caderton, Jan. 9, 1804 – bdsm: George A.

LAURENCE (continued)
Laurence, John Caderton
John & Catharine January, Jan. 29, 1807 – bdsm: John Laurence, Thomas Mazarvey
Robert & Arrianna Jett, Jan. 7, 1836 – bdsm: Robert Laurence, Vincent Williams
William & Mary E. Wyley, July 9, 1840 – bdsm: William Laurence, Thomas Wyley
William & Rebecca Marle, Jan. 31, 1803 – bdsm: William Laurence, Joseph Plumb
LAW, Edward & Mary Berry, April 1, 1818 – married by Rev. Oliver Norris
James O. & Louisa Douglass, Jan. 21, 1836 – bdsm: James O. Law, Jacob Douglass
LAWRENCE, James & Betsey Brin, Sept. 6, 1815 – bdsm: James Lawrence, Presley Barker
Joseph & Mockey Grinnolds, Jan. 13, 1813 – bdsm: Joseph Lawrence, John Lawrence
William & Mary McCoy, Sept. 20, 1811 – bdsm: William Lawrence, Jacob Andrews
LAWS, Joshua Compton & Elizabeth Lyle, May 15, 1806 – bdsm: Joshua Compton Laws, William Peek
LAWSON, John & Elizabeth McKay, May 24, 1821 – bdsm: John Lawson, George Shaw (Married May

LAWSON (continued)
24, 1821 by Rev. O. Norris)
John & Rebecca Loyd, May
7,1846 - bdsm: John Law-
son, John Bryan
Stephen & Elizabeth Trust-
ler, Dec. 9, 1815 - bdsm:
Stephen Lawson, William
Simpson
LAYDEN, Michael & Hanora
Day, parental permission
given Sept. 13, 1851 -
bdsm:
LEDDY, Hugh & Charlotte
Summers, August 19, 1822
- bdsm: Hugh Leddy,
Laughlin Masterson
LEDERER, John Leonard &
Francis M. Porcell, May
21, 1835 - bdsm: John
Leonard Lederer, David
Appich
LEDUM, Isaac & Ann Good-
ing, April 23, 1822 -
bdsm: Isaac Ledum,
Samuel Howard
LEE, Aaron & Polly Parker,
May 31, 1815 - bdsm:
Aaron Lee, Benjamin
Branson
Cassius F. & Ann Eliza
Gardner, April 15, 1846 -
bdsm: Cassius F. Lee,
Richard Henry Lee
Charles Henry & Elizabeth
A. Dunbar, Nov. 6, 1844 -
bdsm: Charles Henry Lee,
Christopher Neale
Henry & Rebecca Kane,
Sept. 10, 1846 - bdsm:
Henry Lee, Theo. Meade
John & Ann Dogan, Nov. 19,
1840 - bdsm: Wm. Dogan,
John Dogan
John & Mary Chitterson,
Nov. 24, 1825 - bdsm:

LEE (continued)
John Lee, George Hicks
John & Sarah A. Riley, Dec.
26, 1832 - bdsm: John
Lee, Phillip Lee
John W. & Cornelia Ann
Bruce, May 25, 1843 -
bdsm: John W. Lee,
James Patterson
Luke & Sylvia Rogers (free
Negroes), Oct. 27, 1845 -
bdsm: Luke Lee, Dennis
Hackett
Richard H. & Mary Green,
April 15, 1817 - bdsm:
Richard H. Lee, John F.
Green
Robert E. & Mary A. R. Cus-
tis, June 21, 1831 - bdsm:
George W. P. Custis, Sid-
ney S. Lee (Marriage of
Robert E. Lee, later
General and Commander of
the Confederate Army of
Northern Virginia to Mar-
tha Washington's great-
granddaughter, Mary Ann
Randolph Custis)
Sidney S. & Anna M. Mason,
Feb. 3, 1835 - bdsm: Sid-
ney S. Lee, Charles C.
Turner (Robert E. Lee's
brother)
William & Mary Brown,
June 4, 1807 - bdsm: Wil-
liam Lee, John Dixon
LEGG, Elias P. & Catharine
Risener, Aug. 26,1823 -
bdsm: Elias P. Legg,
Francis Peyton
LEMEN, Nicholas & Catha-
rine Ann Minor, Oct. 3,
1846 - bdsm: Nicholas
Lemen, Wm. Minor
LENOX, George & Mary Ri-
ley, March 18, 1802 -

114

LENOX (continued)
bdsm: George Lenox, John
Duffy
LEONARD, Jacob & Eliza
Faw, Nov. 3, 1814 - bdsm:
Jacob Leonard, A. E. T.
Rhodes
LESLE, John Mark & Rosalie
C. Patton, Jan. 16, 1838 -
bdsm: John M. Lesle,
James W. Lesle
LESLIE, Benjamin & Re-
becca Kinsey, March 22,
1814 - bdsm: Benjamin
Leslie, Ezra Lunt
Henry P. & Helen M. Gray,
Aug. 6, 1836 - bdsm:
Henry P. Leslie, George
W. Gray
LEVERING, Aaron & Mary
Miller Lawrason, April 10,
1801 - bdsm: Aaron Lever-
ing, James Lawrason
Aaron Righton & Nancy Bul-
eher Laurason, Sept. 3,
1807 - bdsm: Aaron Righ-
ton Levering, James Lau-
rason
Septimus & Eliza Weston,
June 15, 1805 - bdsm:
Septimus Leveri, Eliza
Weston, John A. Stewart
LEWIS, Ansel & Jane M.
Campbell, Jan. 3, 1818 -
bdsm: Ansel Lewis, Wal-
ter Ross
Francis & Martha Bennett,
Sept. 4, 1809 - bdsm:
Francis Lewis, Dozier
Bennett
James & Slave Margaret,
Nov. 17, 1827 - bdsm:
James Lewis, Edward
McLaughen
James B. & C. Ann Hume,
June 15, 1841 - bdsm:

LEWIS (continued)
James B. Lewis, John
Butcher
John & Emeline Butler, July
26, 1833 - bdsm: John
Lewis, William Ferguson
Levey & Agnes Richardson,
Feb. 10, 1831 - bdsm:
Levey Lewis, Augusta
Gibson
Reeve & Sarah Eliza McIn-
tire, April 6, 1837 - bdsm:
Reeve Lewis, Josiah B.
Hills
Robert A. & Eleanor A. Mat-
tox, Feb. 9, 1815 - bdsm:
Robert A. Lewis, Bathurst
Dangerfield
Thomas & Nancy Evans,
May 26, 1815 - bdsm:
Thomas Lewis, John
Evans
William & Salome Way
(born 29 May 1784 in York,
Pennsylvania), Dec. 10,
1806 - bdsm: William
Lewis, John Smith
Wm. H. & M. E. McQueen,
June 2, 1841 - bdsm: Wm.
H. Lewis, Robert Butler
LIBBY, Isaac & Sally Kil-
lium, April 21, 1805 -
bdsm: Isaac Libby, Lou-
doun Smelling
LIEBERMANN, Charles Hen-
ry & Louisa Catharine
Betzold, Feb. 12, 1841 -
bdsm: Charles Henry Lie-
bermann, Daric Betzold
LIEVERMAN, John Chris-
topher & Elizabeth De-
vereux, Aug. 15, 1801 -
bdsm: John Christopher
Lieverman, Thomas
Frankland
LIGHTFOOT, George & Ann

LIGHTFOOT (continued)
Sanford, Nov. 10, 1812 –
bdsm: George Lightfoot,
Lewis Coles
John A. & Elizabeth Sand-
ford, June 13, 1801 –
bdsm: John M. Lightfoot,
Wm. Lightfoot
LIMRICK, John & Nancy
Adams, July 5, 1802 –
bdsm: John Limrick,
Thomas Simms
LINDSAY, George & Matilda
Sewell, Jan. 8, 1839 –
bdsm: George Lindsay,
John Simpkins
John & Mary Keating, Dec.
29, 1829 – bdsm: John
Lindsay, J. N. Keating
Noble & Eleanor Jones,
March 7, 1811 – bdsm:
Noble Lindsay, Henry
Frazier
William & Mary Ketling,
Nov. 13, 1817 – bdsm:
William Lindsay, John B.
Hill
LINDSEY, James & Julia
Ann Walker, Sept. 10,
1844 – bdsm: James Lind-
sey, John Walker
LINTER, William & Latitia
Hartly, May 17, 1804 –
bdsm: William Linter,
William Stoops
LINTON, George & Henrietta
McKinney, Feb. 10, 1810 –
bdsm: George Linton, Hen-
rietta McKinney
LIPSCOMB, William L. &
Phoebe Adgate, Nov. 27,
1815 – bdsm: William L.
Lipscomb, Robert F.
Degge
LITTLEFIELD, Theodore &
Susannah Markly, Aug. 17,

LITTLEFIELD (continued)
1844 – bdsm: Theodore
Littlefield, John T. White
LLOYD, James W. & Jane
Ann Pettit, Dec. 21, 1846
– bdsm: James W. Lloyd,
John Pettit
John & Ann Hennrietta Lee
of Shelburne Parish, Lou-
doun County, Virginia,
Nov. 1, 1820 – bdsm:
John J. & Eliza. A. Selden,
Oct. 15, 1845 – bdsm:
John J. Lloyd, Wm. C.
Yeaton
John Thomas & Mary A.
Wells, Feb. 8, 1850 –
bdsm: John Thomas
Lloyd, Wm. Henry Wells
LOCKAR, James Jr. & Mi-
may Simpson Oct. 6. 1813
– bdsm: James Lockar,
John Palmer
LOCKE, John & Rosalie
Hewitt, Oct. 11, 1841 –
bdsm: John Locke, Robert
H. Butcher
LOGAN, Hugh M. & Eliz-
abeth Curry, Oct. 23, 1816
– bdsm: Hugh M. Logan,
James Curry
William & Elizabeth Wil-
liams, Nov. 1, 1821 –
bdsm: William Logan,
John Picking (Married
Nov. 1, 1821 by Rev. O.
Norris)
LOGIE, David & Mahalan
Cowhen, May 3, 1838 –
bdsm: David Logie,
Stephen Field
LOMAX, John & Elizabeth
McClea, Dec. 14, 1803 –
bdsm: John Lomax, Henry
Oswald
LONDOUN, Peter & Phebe

LONDOUN (continued)
Marsh, Feb. 28, 1824 –
bdsm: Peter Londoun,
Francis Hoy
LONG, James H. & Catharine
V. Atwell, June 19, 1845 –
bdsm: James H. Long,
Charles P. Shaw
Seth & Sarah Harper, Oct. 8,
1806 – bdsm: Seth Long,
William Harper
William & Susannah Ste-
wart, Oct. 29, 1807 –
bdsm: William Long,
Charles McKnight
LONGDON, George C. &
Elizabeth Ann Scott, Sept.
7, 1813 – bdsm: George C.
Longden, Charles Scott
John A. & Elizabeth Howard,
Nov. 12, 1816 – bdsm:
John A. Longdon, Beale
Howard
LORBAHAYE, Peter & Eliz-
abeth Watson, May 11,
1812 – bdsm: Peter Lor-
bahaye, Elizabeth Watson
LOUDOUN, Frederick & Nan-
cy Johnson, April 4, 1827
– bdsm: Frederick Lon-
doun, George Loudoun
LOVEJOY, John A. & Nancy
Halls, May 20, 1815 –
bdsm: John A. Lovejoy,
John Crawford
LOVELESS, Nace & Alley
Dove, Jan. 6, 1814 –
bdsm: Nace Loveless,
James Taffe
LOW, Rev. Samuel & Mar-
garet P. M. Lawyer, Sept.
2, 1818 – married in Nor-
folk, Virginia
LOWE, David A. & Jane A.
Blacklock, Sept. 28, 1835
– bdsm: David A. Lowe,

LOWE (continued)
Robert T. Ramsay
Enoch M. & Juliana Marie
Faw, Nov. 13, 1815 –
bdsm: Enoch M. Lowe
John F. M. & Sophia E.
Leonard, Sept. 28. 1830 –
bdsm: John F. M. Lowe,
Frederick A. Koones
Thomas & Mary Ann Bryan,
March 1, 1820 – bdsm:
Thomas Lowe, Bernard
Bryan
Thomas & Mary Cannon,
July 22, 1806 – bdsm:
Thomas Lowe, Elihu
Smith
William & Elizabeth W.
Korn, June 26, 1817 –
bdsm: William Lowe,
John Korn
LOWELL, Ezekiel & Mary
Ann Reyly, Dec. 25, 1830
– bdsm: Ezeikiel Lowell,
Thomas Pierce
LOWERY, John & Mary Lark
Heiskell, Dec. 22, 1802 –
bdsm: John Lowery, John
Hooff
LOWRIE, John C. & Louisa
A. Wilson, March 4, 1833
– bdsm: John C. Lowrie,
Elias Harrison
LOWRY, James & Adeline
Wilkinson, July 22, 1843 –
bdsm: James Lowry,
James Griffin
James & Judith Swann, Nov.
6, 1829 – bdsm: James
Lowry, Stanfield Jones
LUCAS, John R. & Stacey
Robey, June 20, 1811 –
bdsm: John R. Lucas,
John Halley
LUGENBEEL, J. W. & Mar-
tha Alice Abercrombie,

LUGENBEEL (continued)
July 28, 1846 – bdsm: J. W. Lugenbeel, Thomas Davy
John W. & Mary Frances Simpson, April 20, 1846 – bdsm: John W. Lugenbeel, Henry L. Simpson
LUITON, William & Mary Saunders, March 25, 1806 – bdsm: William Luiton, George Singleton
LUNT, Samuel & Martha Harrison, Oct. 6, 1836 – bdsm: Samuel Lunt, Reuben Johnston, Jr.
LUTTZ, George & Elizabeth Lee, Nov. 20, 1806 – bdsm: George Luttz, William Wiggins
LYLE, Edward M. & Jane M. W. Davis, May 7, 1845 – bdsm: Edward M. Lyle, Henry W. Davis
LYLES, Dennis M. & Eliza Wise Seaton, Nov. 13, 1817 – bdsm: Dennis M. Lyles, John Lindsay
Henry & Mary Davis, Oct. 31, 1805 – bdsm: Henry Lyles, Benjamin Davis
James & Mary Ann Davis, May 31, 1811 – bdsm: James Lyles, William Davis
John & Betsey Tridle, Jan. 8, 1818 – bdsm: John Lyles, Beal Howard
Thomas & Isabella Deeton, Dec. 20, 1825 – bdsm: Thomas Lyles, Christopher Deeton
Thomas C. & Rebecca Seaton, Jan. 17, 1814 – bdsm: Thomas C. Lyles, James H. Dulany

LYLES (continued)
Wm. & Hannah Smith, Nov. 16, 1830 – bdsm: Wm. Lyles, Alfred Hynes
LYNCH, Barton & Dolly Wheeler, Jan. 10, 1814 – bdsm: Barton Lynch, Dolly Wheeler
James & Catharine Neale, Dec. 27, 1826 – bdsm: James Lynch, Levi Pickering
Samuel James & Elizabeth Karkeek, July 11, 1822 – bdsm: Samuel James Lynch, William Gluyas
LYON, Andrew & Mary Massey, Feb. 26, 1805 – bdsm: Andrew Lyon, Thomas Mathaney
LYONS, John & Louisa Anderson, Jan. 5, 1824 – bdsm: John Lyons, Charles B. R. Douglass
John S. & Catharine Tyler, Dec. 9, 1829 – bdsm: John S. Lyons, Henry Tyler
Vincent & Eliza Semms, July 22, 1820 – bdsm: Vincent Lyons, Thomas K. Dement
M'GLUE, John B. & Sarah Ann Bradley, Dec. 28, 1837 – bdsm: John B. M'Glue, Harrison Bradley
MACKENHEIMER, George L. & Eliza Page, Oct. 23, 1827 – bdsm: George L. Mackenheimer, Washington C. Page
MACKEY, Richard & Salley Lindsay, Dec. 9, 1809 – bdsm: Richard Mackey, William Patterson
MAFFITT, William & Harriot Turberville, May 3,

MAFFITT (continued)
1803 - bdsm: William Maffitt, James Muir
MAHONEY, Clement Barton & Mary Harrison, Dec. 31, 1813 - bdsm: Clement Barton Mahoney, Joseph Oard
John & Ann Underwood, May 9, 1818 - bdsm: John Mahoney, Joseph Fearson
MAJOR, James J. & Elizabeth Crook, Feb. 19, 1834 - bdsm: James J. Major, Wm. B. Richards
John Jr. & Margaret A. H. Johnston, March 21, 1832 - bdsm: John Major, Jr., John Johnston
MANDELL, John & Mary Abercrombie, Oct. 10, 1804 - bdsm: John Mandell, Robert Abercrombie
John C. & Susan Smedley, Dec. 29, 1835 - bdsm: John C. Mandell, Benoni Wheat
MANDLEY, Joseph & Elizabeth Waters, July 10, 1817 - bdsm: Joseph Mandley, William Morgan
MANKIN, Charles & Sarah J. Legg, August 15, 1850 - bdsm: Charles Mankin, William G. Legg
MANLEY, Matthew & Letty Tucker, Feb. 4, 1815 - bdsm: Matthew Manley, Loughton Masterson
MANLY, Francis & Helen Lewis, Dec. 27, 1841 - bdsm: Francis Manly, John L. Smith
George D. & Sarah A. Reardon, Sept. 4, 1832 - bdsm: George D. Manly, Charles

MANLY (continued)
M. Wright
MARBLE, Henry & Betsey Clarke, July 26, 1816 - bdsm: Henry Marble
MARBURY, John H. & Eliza C. Fendall, Dec. 7, 1830 - bdsm: John H. Marbury, Benj. T. Fendall
Leonard & Margaret Dyer, Dec. 22, 1831 - bdsm: Leonard Marbury, Robert W. Hunter
Leonard & Mary W. Hunter, Aug. 14, 1816 - bdsm: Leonard Marbury, John Hunter
William & Susan F. Fendall, May 16, 1826 - bdsm: William Marbury, Benjamin T. Fendall
Wm. H. & Anna E. Baird, Nov. 6, 1845 - bdsm: Wm. H. Marbury, Thomas E. Baird
MARKELL, George & Mary Ann Rain, Dec. 17, 1839 - bdsm: George Markell, Samuel Duncan
George C. & Elizabeth Shroder, May 1, 1826 - bdsm: George C. Markell, Hugh Stewart
Samuel W. & Elizabeth Churchman, Feb. 18, 1841 - bdsm: Samuel W. Markell, John Churchman
MARKLY, William & Harriet Allison, Jan. 23, 1840 - bdsm: William Markly, Richard Hill
MARKY, John & Mary White, Sept. 19, 1812 - bdsm: John Marky, Richard Rock
MARLE, David & Elizabeth Harriot Smith, Sept. 30,

MARLE (continued)
1813 - bdsm: David Marle, John Smith
MARMADUKE, Daniel & Lucinda R. McNeal, Dec. 5, 1848 - bdsm: Daniel Marmaduke, George H. Bryant
MARRIOTT, John W. & Jane Huddleton, Aug. 6, 1844 - bdsm: John W. Marriott, Edward Short (See also: Hurdleston, Marriot)
MARSHALL, Alexander G. & Maria Rose Taylor, Dec. 6, 1827 - bdsm: Alexander G. Marshall, John M. Johnson
MARSTON, William & Fanny Brooks, Feb. 1, 1834 - bdsm: William Marston, James Allen
William & Lucinda Coats, Aug. 26, 1824 - bdsm: William Marston, James Coates
MARTIN, David & Sarah Wells Harper, June 22, 1824 - bdsm: David Martin, Edward Green
Jacob L. & Julia Smither, May 7, 1827 - bdsm: Jacob L. Martin, Benjamin S. Kinsey
James & Elizabeth Jane Johnson, Oct. 10, 1843 - bdsm: James Martin, William Powell
John & Mary E. Brown, Sept. 15, 1834 - bdsm: John Martin, Richard H. Clagett
John & Nancy Cooke, May 21, 1806 - bdsm: John Martin, Walker Turner
Thomas L. & Harriet Lamphier, Oct. 18, 1814 - bdsm: Thomas L. Martin,

MARTIN (continued)
Robert G. Lamphier
William & Mary Woodrow, Oct. 17, 1805 - bdsm: Wm. Martin, Charles Pascoe
MARVEL, David & Ann Grymes, March 3, 1803 - bdsm: David Marvel, Mrs. Grymes
MASKETT, Wm. A. & Elizabeth O'Neale, Dec. 12, 1843 - bdsm: Wm. A. Maskett, Joseph Smith
MASON, Alexander H. & Jane A. Smith, Sept. 22, 1831 - bdsm: Alexander H. Mason, Jane A. Smith
Benjamin & Mary Ann Stone, Sept. 1, 1804 - bdsm: Benjamin Mason, William Stone
Edgar & Eugenia Fairfax, June 10, 1829 - bdsm: Edgar Mason, William E. Thompson
George of Hollin Hall & Sally E. Mason, July 25, 1846 - bdsm: G. Mason, R. C. Mason
John & Jane Brown, Jan. 14, 1822 - bdsm: John Mason, George Pipsicoe
John & Jane Lithcoe, June 13, 1806 - bdsm: John Mason, Jane Lithcoe
John & Nancy Aldery, Dec. 9, 1813 - bdsm: John Mason, Alexander Dunbar
Josiah & Cloe Gladen, Aug. 15, 1818 - bdsm: Josiah Mason, Richard Wood
MASSEY, Robert & Mary Norris, July 21, 1813 - bdsm: Robert Massey, Mark Norris

MASSEY (continued)
Rudolph & Ursula Daley, April 28, 1845 - bdsm: Rudolph Massey, John Lawson
William D. & Mary E. Kinsey, Oct. 28, 1841 - bdsm: William D. Massey, Ben. S. Kinsey
MASSIE, William B. & Elizabeth G. Ashton, Aug. 18, 1835 - bdsm: William B. Massie, John W. Massie
MASSOLETTI, Vincent & Sarah M. Horwell, Oct. 26, 1818 - bdsm: Vincent Massoletti, Richard Horwell
MASTER, William & Elizabeth Johnson, Aug. 17, 1818 - bdsm: William Master, William Johnson
MASTERS, John R. & Hannah Minthorn Baird, daughter of Thomas E. Baird, Jan. 23, 1849 - bdsm: John R. Masters, Thomas E. Baird
MASTERSON, Langhlin & Mary Ann Somers, Oct. 3, 1812 - bdsm: Langhlin Masterson, Peter Walsh
MATHIESON, Albert & Elizabeth Ballenger, Feb. 22, 1834 - bdsm: Albert Mathieson, James Williams
MATTHEWS, Jabez & Sarah McPherson, Nov. 28, 1803 - bdsm: Jabez Matthews, Peter Johns
James & Midred Powell, Jan. 25, 1827 - bdsm: James Matthews, Oliver Fields
MATTINGLEY, John E. & Catherine Buckey, Oct. 13, 1836 - bdsm: John E.

MATTINGLEY (continued)
Mattingley, John Buckey
MAXWELL, George W. & Albina V. Churchman, June 1, 1840 - bdsm: George W. Maxwell, John Churchman
MAY, Henry K. & Maria Rose Cracroft, May 8, 1805 - bdsm: Henry K. May, Henry Rose
John & Sally Howard, Jan. 3, 1811 - bdsm: John May, Samuel Howard
MAYNARD, James A. & Navine Geminy, daughter of John Geminy, Dec. 1, 1834 - bdsm: James A. Maynard, John Geminy
MAZINGO, John & Sarah Piles, Jan. 24, 1829 - bdsm: John Mazingo, George Millan
McBRIDGE, Alexander & Susan Crandle, April 21, 1818 - bdsm: Alexander McBride, Anthony Rhodes
McCABE, Edward & Lucy Wood, April 22, 1813 - bdsm: Edward McCabe, Loughin Masterson
McCARTY, James & Betsey Williams, Oct. 17, 1833 - bdsm: James McCarty, Isaac Kell
John & Mary McNamara, Feb. 3, 1831 - bdsm: John McCarty, John Kennedy
Joseph & Pender Ware, Sept. 27, 1816 - bdsm: Joseph McCarty, McKenzie Ware
Michael & Sarah Hingerts, Sept. 3, 1831 - bdsm: Wm. Ford (guardian of Sarah Hingerts), Michael

McCARTY (continued)
McCarty
McCAUGHAN, Thomas &
Mary Taylor, July 2, 1803
- bdsm: Thomas Mc-
Caughan, Mial Dorsey
McCAULEY, James & Nancy
Fair, license given May
22, 1852 - bdsm:
William & Elizabeth Jones,
Sept. 12, 1812 - bdsm:
William McCauley, Ri-
chard Rock
McCLATCHE, John F. & Ra-
chel Ann Sewell, Sept. 13,
1852 - Witnesses: Joseph
Sewell, Richard Sewell,
George Young
McCLEAN, Allen & Jane
Turner, Dec. 8, 1826 -
bdsm: Allen McClean,
Patrick Turner
Andrew B. & Ann Eliza Sel-
lers, April 8, 1822 - bdsm:
Andrew B. McClean, Sam-
uel Bartle
Joseph & Elizabeth Reardon,
Dec. 18, 1815 - bdsm:
Joseph McClean, William
Mansfield
Richard & Eliza Fulton,
June 9, 1823 - bdsm:
Richard McClean, John
Simpson
Samuel & Susana W. Smoot,
May 31, 1820 - bdsm:
Samuel McClean, James
Lawrason
McCLELLAN, A. & Mrs.
Mary Houston, May 25,
1844 - bdsm: Abraham
McClellan (Abraham),
George Washington Harris
McCLISH, William & Susan
Othram, Sept. 6, 1823 -
bdsm: William McClish,

McCLISH (continued)
Bryant Johnson
McCOBB, John & Sarah Wes-
ton, April 11, 1802 -
bdsm: John McCobb,
Robert Cooper
Thomas F. & D. Marian L.
Berry, Sept. 20, 1841 -
bdsm: Thomas F.
McCobb, Nathan E. Berry
McCORKLE, Joseph P. &
Julia E. Corse, Nov. 15,
1842 - bdsm: Joseph P.
McCorkle, Montgomery D.
Corse
McCORMACK, Bernard &
Ann Murphy, Oct. 27, 1801
- bdsm: Bernard McCor-
mack, Jeremiah Kelly
McCORMICK, Samuel J. &
Maria C. Newton, Dec. 3,
1845 - bdsm: Samuel J.
McCormick, James D.
Kerry, Jr.
Thomas M. & Jane Bell Har-
rison, April 20, 1842 -
bdsm: Thomas M. McCor-
mick, Elias Harrison
McCUBBIN, Edward & Susan
Jefferson, August 29, 1831
- bdsm: Edward McCub-
bin, Benjamin Jefferson
McCUE, Peter & Mary Rey-
nolds, March 26, 1803 -
bdsm: Peter McCue, Wil-
liam Reynolds
McCULLEN, Patrick & Al-
their Lanham, Jan. 17,
1804 - bdsm: Patrick
McCullen, Walter Longdon
McCUTCHEON, Patrick &
Lucy Keaton, Nov. 25,
1807 - bdsm: Patrick
McCutcheon, John Lanham
McDANIEL, Wm. & Mary
Ann Wilkins, June 2, 1831

McDANIEL (continued)
- bdsm: Wm. McDaniel, Thomas Williams

McDEVITT, John & Ann Kiggins, license issued July 2, 1851 - bdsm:

McDONALD, John & Anna King, Feb. 25, 1807 - bdsm: John McDonald, William King

John of Frederick County, Virginia, & Maria A. Perry of Alexandria County, Feb. 25, 1825 - bdsm:

McDOUGALL, Daniel & Mary Talbott, Sept. 17, 1801 - bdsm: Daniel McDougall, Robert Anderson

McDUNNICK, James & Lydia Talbut, April 12, 1803 - bdsm: James McDunnick, Charles Stevens

McELHENNEY, William & Hannah Ingram, Feb. 22, 1814 - bdsm: William McElhenney, Joseph Nevell

McEVOY, Joseph & Mary Ann Flanagan, Nov. 6, 1831 - bdsm: Joseph McEvoy, Michael McCarthy

McFARLEN, George & Kitty Richards, Jan. 23, 1802 - bdsm: George McFarlin, George Jones

McFARLIN, Ignatius & Mary Gowen, Nov. 17, 1804 - bdsm: Ignatius McFarlin, Joseph Gowen

McGEE, Peter & Maria Wood, April 14, 1829 - bdsm: Peter McGee, John Wood

McGLENNER, William & Rosa Latham, July 21,

McGLENNER (continued)
1817 - bdsm: William McGlenner, William Latham

McGUIRE, William P. & Mary Ann Foster, license issued June 10, 1851 - bdsm:

McHANY, James & Elizabeth Johnston, Oct. 22, 1850 - bdsm:

McKATHERINE, Dongall & Nancy Stephenson, July 7, 1831 - bdsm: Dongall McKatherine, John Stephenson

McKAY, Benjamin & Eleanor Swann, July 27, 1815 - bdsm: Benjamin McKay, James Young

McKENZIE, Alexander & Betsey Barton, Feb. 5, 1828 - bdsm: Alexander McKenzie, Robert Anderson

James Jr. & Sarah E. Sanford, Sept. 21, 1829 - bdsm: James McKenzie, Jr., Joseph L. Sanford

Kenneth & Cassandra Smith, Oct. 29, 1815 - bdsm: Kenneth McKenzie, Edward Fletcher

McKEOWN, Alexander & Mary Gavin, July 21, 1827 - bdsm: Alexander McKeown, Michael McCarty

McKEWIN, James M. & Nancy McKewin, May 15, 1850 - bdsm: James M. McKewin, Robert McKewin

McKNIGHT, Wm. H. & Margaret Jacobs, June 22, 1832 - bdsm: Wm. H. McKnight, Presley Jacobs

McLAIN, Isaac & Mary Turner, April 2, 1801 - bdsm: Walker Turner, Isaac McLain

McNAUGHTEN, George (McNoton) & Mary Lannegan, Oct. 20, 1832 - bdsm: George McNaughten, Peter McNaughten

McNEIL, Patrick & Mariah Night, Oct. 31, 1809 - bdsm: Patrick McNeil, William Huston

Richard & Margaret Oakley, August 30, 1803 - bdsm: Richard McNeil, John Duffy

McNISH, Horatio & Susan Deane, March 20, 1821 - bdsm: Horatio McNish, Thomas Smith

McPHERSON, Robert Hector & Julia Anna Chapin, Nov. 6, 1815 - bdsm: Robert Hector McPherson, Gustavus Brown

Samuel W. H. & Elizabeth C. Marbury, Feb. 13, 1843 - bdsm: Samuel W. H. McPherson, William Henry Marbury

McQUEEN, William & Susan Goldsbury, Oct. 18, 1817 - bdsm: William McQueen, Robert Bonner

McQUIRE, James C. & Marg. Deakins, Aug. 10, 1836 - bdsm: James C. McQuire, James P. Middleton

McRODDY, John & Mary Shields, Sept. 4, 1828 - bdsm: John McRoddy, Lawrence Waugh

McVEIGH, William N. & Janes S. Chamberlain, March 5, 1832 - bdsm:

McVEIGH (continued) William N. McVeigh, William Dean

McWILLIAMS, Andrew & Nancy Wiseman, May 10, 1825 - bdsm: Andrew McWilliams, Richard W. Davis

MEADE, Edwin T. & Catharine Ann Padgett, Dec. 12, 1841 - bdsm: Edwin Theodore Meade, John G. Padgett (Also: Theodore Meade)

William Alexander & Mary Elizabeth Hutchins, Nov. 9, 1842 - bdsm: William Alexander Meade, Theodore Meade

MEDELLA, Richard & Ann Craig, (free coloured), Nov. 21, 1849 - bdsm: Richard Medella, Richard Garrett

MEEK, Joseph H. & Elizabeth S. Wright, Aug. 31, 1817 - bdsm: Joseph H. Meek, Owen Sullivan

MELLEN, George & Elizabeth Piles, January 12, 1803 - bdsm: George Mellen, Peter Piles

MELLINGTON, Richard & Peggy Thompson, April 22, 1813 - bdsm: Richard Mellington, John Phillips

MERCER, John & Mary Swann, June 25, 1818 - bdsm:

MERCHANT, John & Margaret King, Sept. 12, 1811 - bdsm: John Merchant, William Crook

MERCY, Robert & Susannah Mertland, June 23, 1803 - bdsm: Robert Mercy, Wil-

MERCY (continued)
liam Kirkpatrick

MERIMON, John & Mary Brown, March 1, 1811 - bdsm: John Merimon, James Bullock

MERRYMAN, Horatio R. & Sarah Ann C. Meade, Feb. 7, 1832 - bdsm: Horatio R. Merryman, Theodore Meade

MIDDLETON, Alfred & Celia Brown (free persons of colour), Sept. 27, 1841 - bdsm: Alfred Middleton, James Day

David & Hannah Harris, June 24, 1830 - bdsm: David Middleton, Samuel Wheeler

MILBURN, Stephen & Elizabeth Ann Maddox, March 19, 1838 - bdsm: Stephen Milburn, Moses F. A. Cawood (Also: Millburn)

MILBURNE, Benedict C. & Therza Coad, June 9, 1828 - bdsm: Benedict C. Milburne, Aquilla Emerson

MILLAN, George & Mrs. Anna Piles (widow), Dec. 19, 1827 - bdsm: George Millan, Charles McKnight

MILLER, Charles B. & Roberta E. Edmonds, Oct. 10, 1842 - bdsm: Meredith M. Edmunds, Charles B. Miller

Robert & Elizabeth Howard, Oct. 5, 1815 - bdsm: Robert Miller, John Dixon

Robert & Margaret Daugherty, Oct. 23, 1802 - bdsm: Robert Miller, William Byrne

MILLES, Benjamin C. &

MILLES (continued)
Mary Ross, April 26, 1825 - bdsm: Benjanin Milles, John Ross

MILLIS, Archibald & Ann Eliza Parson, Feb. 9, 1832 - bdsm: Archibald Millis, James Hill

MILLS, James & Fedela Taylor, Feb. 9, 1815 - bdsm: James Mills, George Simms

Robert A. & Martha Russell, Dec. 6, 1814 - bdsm: Robert A. Mills, James Bloxham

Thomas M. & Mary J. Stephens, Feb. 20, 1845 - bdsm: Thomas M. Mills, John J. King

William & Eliza Cohen, May 30, 1850 - bdsm: William Mills, Isaac Buckingham

William & Jane B. Green, Jan. 4, 1840 - bdsm: William Mills, Jr., John F. Green

William & Lucinda Fugitt, Aug. 26, 1818 - bdsm: William Mills, Daniel K. Penn

William & Virginia Fulton, Dec. 13, 1828 - bdsm: William Mills, John T. Reardon

William N. & Ann Leap, Feb. 21, 1806 - bdsm: William Nelson Mills, Jacob Leap

MINCHTREE, John & Catherine Hellrigel, April 9, 1807 - bdsm: John Minchtree, George Hellrigel

MINIX, John P. & Catharine C. Newton, Nov. 3, 1814 -

MINIX (continued)
bdsm: John P. Minix, William C. Newton
MINOR, Anthony & Sally Harrison, July 14, 1825 – bdsm: Anthony Minor, Richard Bolds
Philip H. & Sarah Washington, May 9, 1816 – bdsm:
Smith & Mary Somers, Nov. 13, 1817 – bdsm: Smith Minor, Simon Somers
MITCHELL, George & Elizabeth Spinks, May 16, 1822 – bdsm: George Mitchell, James Walker
George & Harriet G. Howison, May 31, 1825 – bdsm: George Mitchell, Isaac Kell
James & Hope Shurmindine, April 29, 1813 – bdsm: James Mitchell, James Shurmindine
Joseph W. & John Rawlings, June 23, 1832 – bdsm: Joseph W. Mitchell, John Rawlings
Judson & Margaret A. McBride, July 6, 1842 – bdsm: Judson Mitchell, John H. Watkins
Thomas & Lucretia Breart, June 26, 1824 – bdsm: Thomas Mitchell, Robert Banks
William & Margaret Murphey, Aug. 30, 1847 – bdsm: John Howard, Benjamin H. Berry
William & Mary Lanham, June 14, 1816 – bdsm: William Mitchell, William Patterson
MOFFETT, John & Matilda

MOFFETT (continued)
Ann Vardin, Sept. 20, 1820 – bdsm: John Moffett, Robert Moffett
MOLIN, George & Margaret Jurno, Nov. 27, 1818 – bdsm: George Molin, James Murray
MONCURE, Thomas G. & Clarissa B. Hooe, Feb. 6, 1823 – bdsm: Thomas G. Moncure, Bernard Hooe, Jr. (Married Feb. 6, 1823 by Rev. O. Norris)
MONROE, James Harry & Maria E. Berkley, July 21, 1840 – bdsm: James Harry Monroe
John H. & Elizabeth Harrison, Feb. 10, 1846 – bdsm: John H. Monroe, John T. Creighton
John M. & Susannah Tresler, Aug. 19, 1835 – bdsm: John M. Monroe, Cyrus Compton
Thomas & Georgeanna Kelton, April 22, 1826 – bdsm: Thomas Monroe, Thomas H. Howland
MOODY, James & Edmonia Matthews, Dec. 30, 1846 – bdsm: James Moody, James House
John & Sarah Bayley, Nov. 30, 1809 – bdsm: John Moody, Elizabeth Bayley, Daniel Crump
MOORE, Alexander & Ann M. West, April 2, 1811 – bdsm: Alexander Moore, Hugh W. Deneale
Alexander & Caroline Cottringer, June 4, 1822 – bdsm: Alexander Moore, Bladen Dulany

MOORE (continued)
Richard L. & Ann Clements, Aug. 26, 1824 - bdsm: Richard L. Moore, Thomas S. Troop
William & Ann Jones, March 17, 1842 - bdsm: William Moore, Ezekiel Jones
MOPANG, John & Betsy Neill, March 20, 1826 - bdsm: John Mopang, Hanson Day
MORELAND, Hanson & Sarah Atkins, Sept. 7, 1809 - bdsm: Hanson Moreland, John Dyor
MORGAN, Alexander & Catharine Padgett, Aug. 14, 1821 - bdsm: Alexander Morgan, Charles Padgett (Married Aug. 14, 1821 by Rev. O. Norris)
Henry & Elizabeth Young, Oct. 13, 1842 - bdsm: Henry Morgan, William S. Greenwood
Henry & Julia Carolina Bontz, July 1, 1846 - bdsm: Henry Morgan, John Bontz
Jacob & Ann Harris Thompson, Feb. 19, 1812 - bdsm: Jacob Morgan, Jonah Thompson
John & Barbara Myers, April 22, 1830 - bdsm: John Morgan, William Morgan (Benj. Greenwood guardian of Barbara Myers)
William & Martha Johnston, Sept. 4, 1817 - bdsm: William Morgan, Samuel Wheeler
William & Patty Ransom, May 4, 1815 - bdsm: Wil-

MORGAN (continued)
liam Morgan, Patty Ransom
MORRIS, Henry & Maria Payne, Nov. 3, 1816 - bdsm: Henry Morris, George Russell
Levin & Sarah Walker, Sept. 22, 1812 - bdsm: Levin Morris, Francis Walker
MORRISON, Samuel & Margaret McFarlane, Nov. 17, 1841 - bdsm: Thomas King, John McFarlane (Also: McFarlin)
MORSE, Orlando S. & Catharine Reed, Feb. 19, 1834 - bdsm: Orlando S. Morse, John Rumney
MORSELL, Samuel T. G. & Susan A. Bradley, daughter of Harrison Bradley, Jan. 1, 1849 - bdsm: Samuel T. G. Morsell, Harrison Bradley
MORTIMER, George W. & Julia A. K. Price, July 12, 1823 - bdsm: George W. Mortimer, Jeremiah Price
MOSEBY, John & Sarah Jenkins, June 3, 1807 - bdsm: John Moseby, Richard Marshall
MOSS, Thomas & Alcinda Fleming, March 25, 1840 - bdsm: Thomas Moss, William Padgett
MOTHERSAID, E. J. & Maria Chilton, Dec. 18, 1828 - bdsm: E. J. Mothersaid, Samuel Sutton
MOTHERSHEAD, Christopher & Jane Kitty, Feb. 24, 1831 - bdsm: Christopher Mothershead, William Cole (Also: Keatly)

MOTHERSHEAD (continued)

Vincent L. & Mary Ann Hudson, Oct. 28, 1850 - Married by John L. Pascoe Oct. 28, 1850

MOULDEN, James & Mary Wiles, Nov. 29, 1836 - bdsm: James Moulden, Hugh Wiley

MOULDER, Edward & Matilda Wiley, Oct. 7, 1840 - bdsm: Edward Moulder, Hugh Wiley

MOULDING, Thomas & Elizabeth A. Posey, Jan. 19, 1832 - bdsm: Thomas Moudling, Gilbert Simpson

MOUNT, Thomas & Sally Smith, Sept. 21, 1809 - bdsm: Thomas Mount, Joseph Smith

MOXLEY, Daniel & Elizabeth Hare, Jan. 26, 1813 - bdsm: Daniel Moxley, Bernard Bryan

George & Becky Johnson, Sept. 15, 1807 - bdsm: George Moxley, Enoch Garrett

MUDD, Aloysius & Ann Mitchell, April 26, 1825 - bdsm: Aloysius Mudd, Thomas Whittington

MUIR, John & Lydia Robinson, Nov. 15, 1830 - bdsm: John Muir, Robert Brockett (guardian of Lydia Robinson)

William H. & Eliza Ann Green, April 26, 1841 - bdsm: William H. Muir, James Green

MULLEN, Lumsford & Mary Mullen, Dec. 24, 1833 - bdsm: Lumsford Mullen, John Clare

MULLEN (continued)

Robert & Catharine Russell, Aug. 11, 1845 - bdsm: Robert Mullen, Samuel Mullen

Simon & Charlotte Brent, Oct. 23, 1832 - bdsm: Simon Mullen, Reuben Johnston, Jr.

MURPHY, Edward & Elizabeth Towers, Jan. 10, 1822 - bdsm: Edward Murphy, Joseph T. Hollowell

John & Margaret M. Manning, March 13, 1811 - bdsm: John Murphy, Edward Redmonde

Thomas & Harriet Miller, parental consent given by Zetisha Miller on Dec. 4, 1852 - bdsm:

MURRAY, Edward & Hebziba Goodwin, May 11, 1801 - bdsm: Samuel Goodwin, Edward Murray

George & Susan Noland, April 1, 1830 - bdsm: George Murray, William Nolan

Ignatius & Eleanor Morris, Oct. 24, 1807 - bdsm: Ignatius Murray, James Shurmindine

James & Eliza Street, Jan. 26, 1813 - bdsm: James Murray, Daniel Street, Elijah Jewell

James & Eliza Watkins, Feb. 4, 1825 - bdsm: James Murray, Alfred Hines

John & Milly Pearson, April 7, 1806 - bdsm: John Murray, John Pearson

Lemuel N. & Mary Carrol, July 2, 1829 - bdsm:

MURRAY (continued)
Lemuel M. Murray, William McMechen
Oliver C. & Lucretia Shurmindine (Shermoudyne), Oct. 4, 1817 - bdsm: Oliver C. Murray, James Shurmoudyne
Patrick C. & Jane Massey, May 23, 1832 - bdsm: Patrick C. Murray, George Keating
Ralph & Amanda Stanton, May 1, 1838 - bdsm: Ralph Murray, Perry E. Brocchus
Robert L. & Sarah Tidings, April 10, 1846 - bdsm: Robert L. Murray, Wm. Padgett, Jr.
Thomas & Margaret McDonald, Dec. 12, 1816 - bdsm: Thomas Murray, James McDonald
Thomas & Mary Pendal, Oct. 27, 1803 - bdsm: Thomas Murray, James Murray
William & Frances Powell, June 28, 1832 - bdsm: William Murray, William Grimsley
MUSE, William & Mary Edmondson, March 30, 1825 - bdsm: William Muse, Robert P. Marshall
MUTTER, John & Lucinda Gilliez, Dec. 24, 1807 - bdsm: John Mutter, Landon Carter
MYERS, George W. & Phoebe Henklin, April 30, 1828 - bdsm: George W. Myers, James Entwisle
John & Margaret Stevenson, April 21, 1817 - bdsm:

MYERS (continued)
John Myers, James Kelly
Joseph T. & Susannah Ballenger, Oct. 14, 1826 - bdsm: Joseph T. Myers, Stephen Pritchard (See also: Ballinger)
NAILOR, Thomas & Sarah A. Parsons, April 7, 1832 - bdsm: Thomas Nailor, William McDennick
NALLS, George W. & Martha Brent, April 28, 1841 - bdsm: George W. Nalls, Henry Brent
James W. T. H. & Mary Jefferson, Feb. 11, 1839 - bdsm: James W. T. H. Nalls, Henry Jefferson
Martin G. & Harriet E. Bailey, Oct. 8, 1846 - bdsm: Martin G. Nalls, Edwin T. Allen
NEALE, Aloysius & Elizabeth L. A Brandt, July 30, 1818 - bdsm: Aloysius Neal, Thomas L. Griffin
George & Sarah Ann Disney, April 21, 1836 - bdsm: George Neal
NELSON, Geo. W. & Elizabeth Armstrong, Dec. 8, 1836 - bdsm: George W. Nelson, William G. Violett
George W. & Jane E. Crease, May 12, 1834 - bdsm: George W. Nelson, Thomas Smith
Sampson & Ann Carnes, June 26, 1812 - bdsm: Sampson Nelson, Ann Carnes
Thomas & Chloe McAttee, Dec. 24, 1802 - bdsm: Thomas Nelson, Samuel

NELSON (continued)
McAttee
NEVIT, Thomas & Catharine Maro, July 14, 1812 - bdsm: Thomas Nevit, Andrew Leary
NEVITT, James C. & Olivia Keating, Aug. 29, 1846 - bdsm: James C. Nevitt, Samuel O. Baggett.
Joseph & Ann Baggett, May 11, 1812 - bdsm: Joseph Nevitt, Presley Barker
NEWMAN, Morris & Eleanor Wheeler, March 16, 1805 - bdsm: Morris Newman, John B. Carroll
NEWTON, Albert G. & Harriet Louise Pratt, May 18, 1843 - bdsm: Albert G. Newton, William Pratt
Charles A. & Sarah A. Minor, Aug. 12, 1833 - bdsm: Charles A. Newton, William Minor
NICHENS, William & Rebecca Lucas, May 13, 1841 - bdsm: William Nichens, Frederick Brooks (See also: Nichings)
NICHOLAS, Zachariah & J. Baggott, Feb. 3, 1820 - bdsm: Zachariah Nicholson, William Kensey
NICHOLLS, John & Martha Thomas, July 25, 1812 - bdsm: John Nicholls, David Easton
NICHOLSON, Henry & Ann Ballard, Oct. 27, 1803 - bdsm: Henry Nicholson, Joseph Mandeville, Jr.
Henry & Margaret Hyneman, June 14, 1814 - bdsm: Henry Nicholson, Jacob Hyneman

NICHOLSON (continued)
Joseph & Elizabeth Frank, May 9, 1803 - bdsm: Joseph Nicholson, Isaac Green
Thomas & Sarah Baker, Jan. 21, 1803 - bdsm: Thomas Nicholson, Elisha Baker
NICKENS, John & Lucy Brown, Dec. 22, 1835 - bdsm: John Nickens, Daniel Smith
NIGHTINGALE, James & Mary Currey, Jan. 3, 1832 - bdsm: James Nightingale, William Thomas
John & Isabelle Herse, Dec. 19. 1837 - bdsm: John Nightingale, John Southerd
NOLAND, Nimrod & Catharine Latham, April 23, 1835 - bdsm: Nimrod Noland, George Brown
William & Elizabeth Roxbury, Dec. 6, 1832 - bdsm: William Noland, James Fadley
NOMIS, David & Martha Alexander, license granted July 3, 1845 - bdsm:
NORRIS, James & Georgianna C. Gray, Oct. 26, 1841 - bdsm: James Norris, John T. Johnson
James & Susanna Patrerell, Feb. 8, 1814 - bdsm: James Norris, Charles Pascoe
John & Emeline Zimmerman, April 24, 1830 - bdsm: John Norris, George Zimmerman
Oliver & Sarah Fairfax Herbert, May 31, 1813 - bdsm: Oliver Norris, William Herbert, Sr.

NORTON, Hamilton M. & Hannah Waite, Oct. 10, 1826 – bdsm: Hamilton M. Norton, Matthew Waite

NOWELL, William H. & Sarah Allen, April 10th, 1838 – bdsm: William H. Nowell, James Allen

NOWLAND, Alfred & Julia Bennett, Nov. 15, 1837 – bdsm: Alfred Nowland, Lewis Blackwell

Charles W. & Susan C. Skinner, Dec. 24, 1844 – bdsm: Charles W. Nowland, John King

Piercen & Jane M. Taylor, license issued March 6, 1851 – bdsm: father, George F. Taylor

Theophilus & Margaret Skinner, April 23, 1812, – bdsm: Theophilus Nowland, William Nowland

NOYES, Robert & Mary G. Skinner, Dec. 7, 1818 – bdsm: Robert Noyes, Gshraim Gilman

NUTT, James & Mima Deakens, Sept. 30, 1802 – bdsm: James Nutt, Leonard Cooke

O'BRIEN, Matthew & Hannah C. Harrison, Jan. 28, 1841 – bdsm: Matthew O'Brien, James P. Middleton

O'GALLAGHER, James & Julia Ann Maria Lyles, Jan. 12, 1825 – bdsm: James O'Gallagher, Joseph Boyer

O'NEAL, Robert & Margaret Anderson, June 1, 1809 – bdsm: Robert O'Neal, Henry Marshall

OAKLEY, Thomas J. & Mar-

OAKLEY (continued) garet J. Taylor, daughter of Joseph Taylor, Aug. 2, 1849 – bdsm: Thomas J. Oakley, Joseph Taylor

ODEN, Nathaniel & Ann Laws (free people of color), Sept. 3, 1839 – Nathaniel Oden, Bernard Hooe

OGDEN, Andrew J. & Martha Ann Evans, April 20, 1841 – bdsm: Andrew J. Ogden, James D. Bryan

Hezekiah & Mary Elizabeth Philips, Sept. 14, 1837 – bdsm: Hezekia Ogden, John J. Blue (Also: Phillips)

OGLETON, Antnony & Ellen Johnson, May 29, 1841 – bdsm: Anthony Ogleton, Henry Gibson

ORISON, Albert W. & Elizabeth Javens, Oct. 2, 1839 – bdsm: Albert W. Orison, Walter L. Penn

OSBORN, Dennis & Jane Howard, Nov. 20, 1818 – bdsm: Dennis Osborn, Richard Rock

OSBURN, Lawson & Elizabeth Thomas, Nov. 16, 1815 – bdsm: Lawson Osburn, James Thomas

OSGOOD, Isaac & Jane B. Bean, Feb. 5, 1823 – Isaac Osgood, George Swain

OSWALD, Henry & Martha Kelly, Feb. 16, 1804 – bdsm: Henry Oswald, John Lomax

OWEN, James H. & Jane Hammond, Aug. 14, 1811 – bdsm: James H. Owen, Frederick Way

PADGETT, John & Ann Louisa Robinson, June 28, 1841 - bdsm: John Padgett, John W. Robinson

John W. & Libby Ann Graham, March 11, 1844 - bdsm: John W. Padgett, John Graham

Joseph & Mary Ann Jefferson, June 9, 1830 - bdsm: Joseph Padgett, John Richardson

William & Sarah Padgett, Aug. 19, 1822 - bdsm: William Padgett, Alexander Morgan

William F. & Harriet E. Powell, Dec. 9, 1845 - bdsm: William F. Padgett, Samuel Isaac, guardian of Harriet E. Powell

PAGE, Washington & Elizabeth Ann Clagett, Oct. 21, 1824 - bdsm: Washington Page, Horatio Clagett

William & Mary Ramsay, Oct. 23, 1828 - bdsm: William Page, Colin Auld

PARADISE, John & Elizabeth Smoot, May 31, 1810 - bdsm: John Paradise, Nehemiah Carson

PARK, Alexander & Harriett G. Reed, July 31, 1833 - bdsm: Alexander Park, John M. Farlane

PARKER, Jesse & Sarah Green, Oct. 13, 1817 - bdsm: Jesse Parker, Henry Marvel

John & Mary Hill, Oct. 26, 1805 - bdsm: John Parker, Jesse Barnes

John & Mary Simkin, Sept. 29, 1831 - bdsm: John

PARKER (continued)
Parker, Elias Mashersead

Samuel & Anna Watson, Sept. 18, 1820 - bdsm: Samuel Parker, William Waugh

Selby & Sarah Ann Ward, April 2, 1829 - bdsm: Selby Parker, Peter Brenner

William H. & Mary Augusta Hipkins, April 11, 1832 - bdsm: William H. Parker, Lewis Hipkins

PARKS, George & Sarah Church, Dec. 16, 1813 - bdsm: George Parks, John Thompson

PARSON, Thomas & Maria Musgrove, Oct. 6, 1838 - bdsm: Thomas Parsons, Philip B. Vernon

PARSONS, John & Ann M. Askin, Dec. 18, 1822 - bdsm: John Parsons, Alfred Arrington (Married by Rev. O. Norris)

John & Elizabeth Brooks, Aug. 7, 1848 - bdsm: John Parsons, John W. Sherwood

John & Elizabeth Swoden, June 1, 1831 - bdsm: John Parsons, George Waigly

Thomas & Sarah Ann Baker, Jan. 28, 1829 - bdsm: Thomas Parsons, Carrol Baker

Walter & Sarah Williams, Aug. 27, 1811 - bdsm: Walter Parsons, Aquilla Emerson

William & Margaretta B. Thomas, July 6, 1815 - bdsm: William Parsons, Thomas Thomas, John

PARSONS (continued)
Parsons
PASCOE, Frederick & Eliza
Douglass, April 9, 1830 –
bdsm: Frederick Pascoe,
Christian Himerdenger
John L. & Ann R. Shirley,
April 27, 1831 – bdsm:
John L. Pascoe, Charles
McKnight
William & Sarah A. John-
son, April 8, 1833 – bdsm:
William Pascoe, George
Johnson
PASQUALL, Peter & Eliza-
beth Laferty, Oct. 21, 1804
– bdsm: Peter Pasquall,
Garret Headon
PASQUELL, Peter & Re-
becca Churchman, Dec. 5,
1807 – bdsm: Peter Pas-
quell, Frederick Church-
man
PATRICK, William & Phil-
icia Burns (free coloured
persons), Feb. 29, 1844 –
bdsm: William Patrick,
James O. C. Hoskins
PATTERSON, Henry & Mary
Jane Mankins, Sept. 4,
1837 – bdsm: Henry Pat-
terson, William Allison
James & Kilaney Field,
April 11, 1831 – bdsm:
James Patterson, Jonathan
Field
John W. & Maria F. Whit-
ing, Jan. 14, 1837 – bdsm:
John W. Patterson,
Thomas J. Noland
Joseph & Elizabeth Kune,
May 21, 1803 – bdsm:
Joseph Patterson, James
Nightingale
William & Sally Simpson,
March 25, 1828 – bdsm:

PATTERSON (continued)
William Patterson, Jer-
emiah Hibbard
PATTON, Hezekiah & Mar-
garet E. Bushby, Feb. 10,
1845 – bdsm: Hezekiah
Patton, John L. Boyer
John & Dorcas Green, Jan.
17, 1822 – bdsm: John
Patton, Samuel McGee
(Married Jan. 17, 1822 by
Rev. O. Norris)
Robert & Ann Clifton
Reeder, Sept. 2, 1805 –
bdsm: Robert Patton,
James Patton
PAUL, Zachariah & Eliza-
beth Bowling, July 21,
1810 – bdsm: Zachariah
Paul, Robert Moore
PAYNE, Inmane & Marian
Massie, Jan. 30, 1845 –
bdsm: Inmane Payne,
Robert H. Miller
John & Elizabeth Kennedy,
Aug. 2, 1847 – bdsm: John
Payne, S. M. Wilkins
John & Martha Ann Rollins,
Nov. 9, 1811 – bdsm: John
Payne, Alexander Dunbar
John Jr. & Lucretia Janney,
Oct. 23, 1823 – bdsm:
John Payne, Thomas Jan-
ney
Larkin & Nancy Payne, Oct.
12, 1816 – bdsm: Larkin
Payne, James Evans
London & Sarah Booth, Nov.
10, 1815 – bdsm: London
Payne, John Hayson
Thomas & Mary Jane
Devaugh, Sept. 25, 1839 –
bdsm: Thomas Payne,
Samuel H. Devaughn
William & Rebecca Sim-
mons, daughter of Samuel

PAYNE (continued)
Simmons, May 30, 1836 -
bdsm: William Payne,
Samuel Simmons
PEACHY, William G. & Virginia B. Daingerfield, Oct.
9, 1843 - bdsm: William
G. Peachy, Boyd Smith
PEARCE, Gideon & Julia
Dick, Feb. 20, 1805 -
bdsm: Gideon Pierce,
Elisha Cullen Dick
PEASLEY, Ithrean & Jane
Ellender Weaver, May 3,
1816 - bdsm: Ithrean
Peasley, Samuel Armstrong
PELTON, Enoch & Sarah
Matilda Patterson, Dec.
23, 1802 - bdsm: Enoch
Pelton, William Patterson
PEMBROOK, Thomas &
Desdemona West, Aug.
12, 1816 - bdsm: Thomas
Pembrook, Samuel Mark
PENN, John Thomas & Henrietta Evans, June 27,
1831 - bdsm: John
Thomas Penn, George L.
Lynton
Walter L. & Mary Elizabeth
Durr, June 2, 1842 - bdsm:
Walter L. Penn, Charles
F. Wilson
PERKINS, Francis & Ann
Smith, May 25, 1803 -
bdsm: Francis Perkins,
James Smith
PERLEY, James & Elizabeth
Cook, Dec. 4, 1828 -
bdsm: James Perley, William McMechen
PERRY, Alexander & Henrietta Sollers, Sept. 4,
1823 - bdsm: Alexander
Perry, Henry A. Webster

PERRY (continued)
Alfred & Sarah Fox, Sept.
25, 1828 - bdsm: Alfred
Perry, Jemina Harrison
James & Nancy Marvell,
Dec. 26, 1805 - bdsm:
James Perry, George Williams Wyatt
John & Sarah Avery, Feb.
13, 1822 - bdsm: John
Perry, Richard Wood
William H. & Mary F. Madden, Sept. 15, 1807 -
bdsm: William H. Perry,
Dwight Metcalf
PETTIT, William & Mary
Ann Munay (possibly
Murray), Sept. 3, 1840 -
bdsm: William Pettit,
James M. Watkins
PETTY, Eli & Mary Jane
Boyd, Jan. 2, 1839 -
bdsm: Eli Petty, Jacob
Zimmerman
PEVERELL, Isaac & Mary
C. Craven, May 15, 1850 -
bdsm: Isaac Peverell,
John Craven
PEYTON, Thomas West &
Sophia Matilda Dundas,
Feb. 26, 1811 - bdsm:
Thomas West Peyton,
John Dundas
Wm. H. & Sarah Ann Clark,
Oct. 7, 1845 - bdsm: Wm.
H. Peyton, James E.
Mankin
PHILIPS, George & Ann
Maria Moods, Nov. 14,
1839 - bdsm: George
Philips, John Tippett
John & Lucy Hillman, Oct.
11, 1817 - bdsm: John
Philips, John Elliot
John T. & Jane Eliza
Greenwood, April 25, 1846

PHILIPS (continued)
- bdsm: John T. Philips,
John Greenwood
William & Kitura Ball, Dec.
20, 1815 - bdsm: William
Philips, James Ball
William & Rebecca Boyd,
Sept. 23, 1812 - bdsm:
William Philips, John
Nelson
PHILLIPS, Cornelius & Sarah
A. Grinells, license issued
Nov. 29, 1850 - bdsm:
James & Eliza Avery, Jan.
24, 1816 - bdsm: James
Phillips, James Avery
(Also: Philips)
John & Catharine Evans,
Dec. 22, 1814 - bdsm:
John Blue, John Phillips
PICKERING, Levi & Sarah
Norris, Dec. 24, 1812 -
bdsm: Levi Pickering,
Thomas Scott
PICKETT, Albert G. & Eliz-
abeth Harris, Jan. 18, 1837
- bdsm: Albert G. Pickett,
Joseph Harris
PIERCE, Thomas & Eliza-
beth Mandley, Sept. 3,
1812 - bdsm: Thomas
Pierce, Alexander Dunbar
PIERCEN, Thomas W. &
Rose McGlennin, Jan. 10,
1822 - bdsm: Thomas W.
Piercen, George Webster
PILES, Christian & Sarah
Brook, May 26, 1817 -
bdsm: Christian Piles,
William Hopkins
Jacob & Jane Jones, Nov. 4,
1831 - bdsm: Jacob Piles,
George Mellen
Lewis & Anne Harriss, April
27, 1803 - bdsm: Lewis
Piles, James Harriss

PILES (continued)
Lewis & Elizabeth Lomax,
April 8, 1802 - bdsm:
Lewis Piles, Stephen
Lomax
Lewis J. & Eliza Bishop,
Oct. 9, 1827 - bdsm:
Lewis J. Piles, Elizah
Taylor
Walter & Sinthy Redman,
Sept. 11, 1838 - bdsm:
Walter Piles, William
Sherwood
PIPER, James & Catharine
Bontz, Aug. 11, 1807 -
bdsm: James Piper, Jacob
Bontz
PIPSICO, Franklin & Lucy A.
Chapman, Dec. 19, 1843 -
bdsm: Franlin Pipsico,
Henry Pipsico
PLANT, James & Alice A.
M. Bowie, Aug. 29, 1825 -
bdsm: James Plant, John
Cohagen
PLEASANTS, Rev. Charles
E. & Caroline Wattles,
Jan. 6, 1836 - bdsm: Rev.
Charles E. Pleasants,
Nathaniel Wattles
PLUMB, Joseph & Elizabeth
Marle, August 1, 1803 -
bdsm: Joseph Plumb,
Joseph Marle
PLUMMER, Burrill T. & Ann
Cornelia Cross, June 12,
1843 - bdsm: Burrill T.
Plummer, Reid Cross
Charles H. & Eliza Dou-
gherty, Oct. 14, 1817 -
bdsm: Charles H. Plum-
mer, John Mark, Jr.
PLUNKETT, James & Jane
Carlin, March 16, 1812 -
bdsm: James Plunkett,
Jane Carlin

135

POLLARD, Henry & Marian Rudd, daughter of Richard A. Rudd, Jan. 16, 1850 - bdsm: Henry Pollard, Charles D. Rudd

POLLOCK, George & Elizabeth Schropshire, Sept. 3, 1804 - bdsm: George Pollock, Robert Laurason

POMELY, John & Fanny Grinnage, March 22, 1827 - bdsm: John Pomely, Robert H. Bell

POMEROY, Francis D. & Nancy Garrett, Feb. 24, 1807 - bdsm: Francis Dade Pomeroy, William Carroll

POMERY, John & Milly Marrow (Free black), Oct. 19, 1807 - bdsm: John Pomery, Marbury Hanson

John T. & Margaret J. Churchman, May 8, 1839 - bdsm: John T. Pomery, John Churchman

Walter & Jane Baggott, Dec. 31, 1829 - bdsm: Wm. Pomery, Walter Pomery

POOR, William A. & Sarah Perry, widow of James Perry, Jan. 9, 1849 - bdsm: William A. Poor, William Rushman

POORER, Pompy & Lucy Clarke (both coloured), Dec. 11, 1810 - Pompy Poorer

POPHAM, John & Mary Ann Thompson, April 14, 1818 - bdsm: John Popham, Jonah Thompson

POPLAR, James & Sarah Wheeler, Nov. 14, 1804 - bdsm: James Poplar, Thomas Locke

PORTER, Denton S. of Washington, D. C. & Priscilla C. Norfolk, June 10, 1845 - bdsm: Denton S. Porter, John Lauson

John & Rosanna Speaks, Aug. 1, 1801 - bdsm: John Porter, Bennett Ralay

POSEY, Henry & Elizabeth King, May 20, 1812 - bdsm: Henry Posey, Reubin Bowie

James & Cecilia Lee, April 23, 1822 - bdsm: James Posey, Lewis Lee

James S. & Bethia Skinner, April 2, 1846 - bdsm: James S. Posey, William R. Worthan

William & Mary Lawson, April 2, 1846 - bdsm: William Posey, Stephen Kent

POSS, John Philip & Harnett Brown, May 4, 1840 - bdsm: John Wilson, Levi Hurdle

POSTON, Francis E. & Amelia Day, Oct. 7, 1817 - bdsm: Francis E. Poston, Joseph Poston

John & Ann Major, Feb. 17. 1830 - bdsm: John Poston, Jonathan Field

POWELL, Alfred & Ann Far, April 29, 1820 - bdsm: Alfred Boswell, Frances Ballenger

Charles L. & Selina Lloyd, Oct. 26, 1830 - bdsm: Charles L. Powell, John Lloyd

William & Cornelia Cornwell, April 15, 1822 - bdsm: William Powell, Isaac Trunnel

POWER, John & Ann Cruse,

POWER (continued)

Dec. 11, 1812 – bdsm: John Power, Thomas Cruse

PREBLE, Edward D. & Sophia Elizabeth Wattles (daughter of Nathaniel Wattles), Nov. 15, 1833 – bdsm: Edward D. Preble, Nathaniel Wattles

PRESTON, Thomas & Eleanor Philips, Dec. 27, 1804 – bdsm: Thomas Preston, Thomas L. Griffin

PRETTYMAN, Robert & Margaret Virginia Morgan, July 22, 1842 – William Morgan, Henry Morgan

PREVOST, Henry M. & Sophia Hough, Oct. 31, 1842 – bdsm: Henry M. Prevost, Edward S. Hough

PRICE, Charles S. & Mary A. T. Dearborn, June 26, 1837 – bdsm: Charles S. Price, Ellis L. Price

David & Margaret Crooke, August 1, 1810 – bdsm: David Price, Bernard Crooke

Ellis L. & Judith P. Butts, May 18, 1837 – bdsm: Charles Price, Ellis L. Price

William & Ann Clarke, April 17, 1834 – bdsm: William Price, J. C. Bryan

William & Sarah May, March 10, 1825 – bdsm: William Price, Francis B. May

PRINCE, John & Sarah Dennistown, Feb. 2, 1805 – bdsm: John Prince, John Boyer

PRING, Henry & Mary Ann

PRING (continued)

Grimes, June 7, 1820 – bdsm: Henry Pring, John Rawlings (Marriage celebrated June 7, 1820 by O. Norris)

PRITCHARD, Stephen & Sarah Ballenger, April 23, 1818 – bdsm: Stephen Pritchard, Levi Pickering

PROCTOR, John J. & Rosetta L. Taylor, July 10, 1834 – bdsm: John J. Proctor, James C. Goods

PUKINS, John & Henrietta Williams, April 1, 1817 – bdsm: John Pukins, Thomas Williams

PUPPO, Daniel & Elizabeth Stroman, August 9, 1803 – bdsm: Daniel C. Puppo, John Hoff

PURCELL, Thomas & Mary A. Creighton, May 2, 1836 – bdsm: Thomas Purcell, Thomas Davey

PURSELL, Thomas & Elizabeth Flood, Dec. 10, 1827 – bdsm: Thomas Pursell, Thomas Davey

QUANDER, Felix & Julia Ann Carter (free persons of colour), Oct. 5, 1848 – bdsm: Felix Quander, Osborn Quander. Julia Ann Carter was the daughter of Joseph Carter.

QUEST, John W. & Jane Wescott, April 24, 1828 – bdsm: John W. Quest, William S. Rodgers

QUINN, William & Louisa Whittington, April 19, 1823 – bdsm: William Quinn, Stephen Field

QUISENBURY, William P. &

QUISENBURY (continued)
Rebecca Paton, Aug. 16, 1842 - bdsm: William P. Quisenbury, Thomas Lomax

RAIBY, Bennett & Frances Frazier, Dec. 28, 1803 - bdsm: Bennett Raiby, James Nightingale

RAMSAY, George W. D. & Wilhelmina Bartleman, Sept. 30, 1839 - bdsm: George W. D. Ramsay, William Bartleman

RAND, Samuel F. & Sarah Jane Smith, daughter of John W. Smith, March 14, 1849 - bdsm: Samuel F. Rand, John. W. Smith

RANDALL, Theophilus & Ann Clifford, Feb. 21, 1816 - bdsm: Theophilus Randall, John H. Dutton

RATCLIFF, Joseph & Julia Ann Jacobs, March 14, 1825 - bdsm: Joseph Ratcliff, Thomas Jacobs

RATCLIFFE, Richard B. & Ann Demain, March 31, 1825 - bdsm: Richard B. Ratcliffe, Joal Demain (See also: Demaine)

Samuel & Matilda Wilkinson, Dec. 7, 1805 - bdsm: Samuel Ratcliffe, Spencer Jackson

RAWEN, Joseph & Nancy Rhodes, April 21, 1804 - bdsm: Joseph Rawen, Robert Laurason

RAWLINGS, John & Jane Pearson, Nov. 6, 1804 - bdsm: John Rawlings, John Pearson

John T. & Jane Brookes, Jan. 19, 1811 - bdsm:

RAWLINGS (continued)
John T. Rawlings, Jane Brookes

William S. & Frances E. Crupper, May 18, 1838 - bdsm: William S. Rawlings, Robert Crupper

REARDON, John & Elizabeth Jackson, April 13, 1830 - bdsm: John Reardon, George McClish

RECTOR, Ludwell Jr. & Rachel Satterwhite, July 8, 1829 - bdsm: Ludwell Rector, Jr., Jeremiah Satterwhite (See also: Rexter)

REDMAN, Henry & Ann Hill, Aug. 13, 1804 - bdsm: Henry Redman, Josiah Hill

REED, Ellis & Betsy Creedy, Dec. 10, 1817 - bdsm: Ellis Reed, Henry Purse

Frank (free black) & Polly Johnston, June 7, 1827 - bdsm: Frank Reed, John Grant

John C. & Caroline Kinsey, Sept. 29, 1841 - bdsm: John C. Reed, Ben. S. Kinsey

Sandford & Feilder Patton, June 20, 1816 - bdsm: Sandford Reed, George Park

Thomas & Mary Sexton, June 1, 1809 - bdsm: Thomas Reed, Joseph Dudley

William & Catharine Hutcheson, Oct. 24, 1805 - bdsm: William Reed

REELER, Samuel & Mary Harris, Feb. 10, 1820 - bdsm: Samuel Reeler, John Harris

REENY, Washington & Ann

REENY (continued)
Massey, Dec. 11, 1845 -
bdsm: Washington Reeny,
William Rotchford
REESE, Samuel & Harriot
McCuin, Jan. 7, 1823 -
bdsm: Samuel Reese,
James Atkinson
William L. & Ann Dorsey,
July 19, 1827 - bdsm:
William L. Reese, Mat-
thew Worthington
REEVES, Charles & Sarah
Ann Brooks, Dec. 25, 1828
- bdsm: Charles Reeves,
George Price
Nicholas & Mary Scrivener,
June 10, 1824 - bdsm:
Nicholas Reeves, Jesse S.
Drake
REILY, William & Sabina
Kent, Dec. 20, 1803 -
bdsm: William Reily,
John Kent
REISINGER, George & Sarah
Devaughn, June 12, 1804 -
bdsm: George Reisinger,
Samuel Hattersley
REISS, Ben & Mary Ann
Plum Sept. 9, 1844 -
bdsm: Ben Reiss, David
Appich
RENE, William & Matilda
Yeates, Sept. 5, 1838 -
bdsm: William Rene,
George Howard (Possibly:
Rone)
REYNOLDS, John & Eliza-
beth Simpson, Sept. 24,
1803 - bdsm: John Rey-
nolds, Jeremiah Eney
John & Mary Lee, Sept. 27,
1809 - bdsm: John Rey-
nolds, John Dixon
William & Margaret McAl-
lister, Feb. 15. 1821 -

REYNOLDS (continued)
bdsm: William Reynolds,
Grafton Cawood
William C. & Phebe Veitch,
Dec. 27, 1831 - bdsm:
William C. Reynolds,
John T. White
Wm. C. & Grace A. Harvey,
Sept. 12, 1843 - bdsm:
Wm. C. Reynolds,
Thomas Vowell
RHETT, Charles W. & Ma-
tilda Mason, orphan of
Thompson F. Mason, Oct.
19, 1847 - bdsm: Charles
W. Rhett, Benjamin Rhett
Thomas G. & Ann G. Mason,
June 8, 1846 - bdsm:
Thomas G. Rhett, G. W.
Lay
RICE, George & Hannah
O'Connor, Jan. 2, 1812 -
bdsm: George Rice,
Theodore Skinner
Thomas C. & Elizabeth
Dearborn, Jan. 10, 1846 -
bdsm: Thomas C. Rice,
James McKenzie
RICHARD, William B. &
Priscilla Crook, Dec. 19,
1820 - bdsm: William B.
Richard, David Price
RICHARDS, John & Rebecca
Carlin, Sept. 20. 1815 -
bdsm: John Richard,
Westley Carlin
John Jr. & Laura Peyton,
April 19, 1841 - bdsm:
John Richards Jr., John
Richards
William C. & Mary Ann
Morgan, Feb. 6, 1850 -
bdsm: William C. Ri-
chards, Luther D. Harrison
RICHARDSON, Charles &
Lucy Bennett, Aug. 13,

RICHARDSON (continued)
1840 - bdsm: Charles
Richardson, Alan Bryan
Judson & Milly Richards,
July 18, 1811 - bdsm:
Judson Richardson, Mark
Richardson
William & Margaret Mc-
Carty, July 29, 1830 -
bdsm: William Richard-
son, George Wiley (See
also: Wm. Whorson)
RICHEY, William & Ann
Maria May, Feb. 19, 1828
- bdsm: Wm. Richey,
Francis B. May
RICHTER, John & Mary Et-
ser, May 23, 1802 - bdsm:
John Richter, John Lim-
rick
RICKETTS, Benjamin &
Mary Stuart, Dec. 12, 1805
- bdsm: Benjamin Rick-
etts, Wm. Stuart
RICKS, George & Eleanor
Johnson , June 22, 1816 -
bdsm: George Ricks, Ber-
nard Bryan
RIDGWAY, Hanson & Susan
McGraw, Dec. 22, 1832 -
bdsm: Hanson Ridgway,
Benjamin McGraw
RIGGS, Elisha & Alice Lau-
rason, Sept. 17, 1812 -
bdsm: Elisha Riggs,
James Laurason
RILEY, George & Ann Tram-
mell, Feb. 22, 1833 -
bdsm: George Riley,
Lumsford Mullin
Mark M. & Mary Wiseman,
Feb. 16, 1826 - bdsm:
Mark M. Riley, James
Brooks
William & Celia Harper,
Nov. 13, 1823 - bdsm:

RILEY (continued)
William Riley, William
Harper
RIORDAN, James & Marshall
J. Rotchford, Aug. 13,
1834 - bdsm: James Rior-
dan, Bartholomew Rotch-
ford
RISTON, Benjamin & Cath-
arine Octavia Calendar,
Jan. 9, 1845 - bdsm: Ben-
jamin Riston, William
Darley
Benjamin K. & Ellen Javins,
daughter of George Javins,
Dec. 24, 1847 - bdsm:
Benjamin K. Riston,
George Phillips
John & Rachel Ann Wil-
liams, Nov. 26, 1839 -
bdsm: John H. Riston,
Thomas Williams
Thomas & Mary M. Trun-
nell, August 11, 1846 -
bdsm: Thomas Riston,
Isaac Trunnell
ROACH, James & Elizabeth
Carson, June 22, 1837 -
bdsm: James Roach,
James Carson
John & Monica Drury, June
14, 1801 - bdsm: John
Huer, John Roach
ROBBINS, Isaac & Mary D.
Howell, Sept. 2, 1803 -
bdsm: Isaac, Abel Janney
William & Mary Catharine
Donalson, Dec. 12, 1809 -
bdsm: William Robbins,
Robert Bayliss
ROBERTS, Richard & Miss
Spears, May 5, 1812 -
bdsm: Richard Roberts,
Martin Young
Samuel M. & Mary F.
Mount, Aug. 8, 1836 -

ROBERTS (continued)
bdsm: Samuel M. Roberts, Thomas Mount

ROBERTSON, Thomas Bolling & Martha Fairfax, orphan of Henry Fairfax, July 12, 1849 - bdsm: Thomas Bolling Robertson, John W. Fairfax

ROBEY, Joseph & Margaret Simpson, Aug. 15, 1822 - bdsm: Joseph Robey, Edmund Hewitt

Walter W. & E(lizabeth) A. Haynes, Jan. 26, 1832 - bdsm: Walter W. Robey, Augustine Newton

ROBINSON, Edward & Jane H. Kenner, Jan. 28, 1817 - bdsm: Edward Robinson, Powell H. Huff

James C. & Elizabeth Robinson, Feb. 4, 1835 - bdsm: James C. Robinson, John Robinson

James H. & Sarah Ann Hurdle, Oct. 12, 1843 - bdsm: James H. Robinson, Levi Hurdle

Matthew & Elizabeth Bacon, June 16, 1810 - bdsm: Matthew Robinson, Richard Weightman

Richard & Susan Jane Crupper Oct. 7, 1844 - bdsm: Richard Robinson, Richard Rotchford

ROCK, Richard & Margaret Spunnaugle, Dec. 10, 1812 - bdsm: Richard Rock, Leonard Adams

RODGERS, Corvill & Judith Ford, July 2, 1839 - bdsm: Corvill Rodgers, William Ford

William & Elizabeth Al-

RODGERS (continued)
lison, Oct. 15, 1818 - bdsm: William Rodgers, Andrew Rousavell

ROGERS, John C. & Mary Ann Rock, April 8, 1836 - bdsm: John C. Rogers, Philip Roach

William H. & Lucy Ellen Williams, March 2, 1841 - bdsm: William H. Rogers, Lucy Ellen Williams

ROSE, Capt. Henry B. & Ann R. Dunbar, Nov. 3, 1825 - bdsm: Capt. Henry B. Rose, Mountjoy Bayly, Jr.

Henry P. & Jane Shaw, Dec. 23, 1826 - bdsm: Henry P. Rose, Horatio Day

Thomas M. & Ann E. Dailey, May 1, 1834 - bdsm: Thomas M. Rose, William C. Rives

ROSS, John & Jane McDella, Nov. 18, 1840 - bdsm: John Ross, Jeremiah Frazier

John & Louisa Handy, Aug. 14, 1815 - bdsm: John Ross, Jeremiah Neil

Samuel & Sarah Hamilton, March 9, 1816 - bdsm: James Ross, Levi Pickering

ROSZELL, S. S. & Julia Ann DeButts, August 4, 1845 - bdsm: S. S. Roszell, R. W. Latham

ROTCH, George & Mrs. Susan McBride, Feb. 8, 1825 - bdsm: George Rotch, Thomas Steel

John & Melinda Rotch, May 19, 1820 - bdsm: John Rotch, Laughlin Masterson

ROTCHFORD, Bartholomew

ROTCHFORD (continued)
& Jane Carne, Feb. 4, 1815
- bdsm: Bartholomew
Rotchford, Richard Libby
(guardian)
Richard & Mary Jane Wad-
dey, Oct. 15, 1849 - bdsm:
Richard Rotchford, Thom-
as Waddey
ROWE, R. H. & Celia Bow-
den, Jan. 21, 1840 - bdsm:
R. H. Rowe, Andrew T.
Ball
ROXBURY, Jacob & Eliza-
beth M. Fisher, Oct. 30,
1840 - bdsm: Jacob Rox-
bury, Robert Fisher
ROZER, Francis E. & Hen-
rietta F. Roberts, July 17,
1833 - bdsm: Francis E.
Rozer, Peter E. Hoffman
RUDD, Charles D. & Amanda
M. F. Churchman, daugh-
ter of John Churchman,
Nov. 21, 1848 - bdsm:
Charles D. Rudd, John T.
Young
James & Belinda Wood,
Oct. 8, 1834 - bdsm:
James Rudd, John Clare
Richard A. & Elizabeth
Ward, July 26, 1821 -
bdsm: Richard A. Rudd,
Thomas Ward
Richard H. & Elizabeth
Swann, June 22, 1847 -
bdsm: Richard H. Rudd,
Daniel Bayliss
RUMNEY, Theodore S. &
Annie L. Morrell, Dec. 18,
1849 - bdsm: Theodore S.
Rumney, George Rumney
RUNKLES, David & Eliza
Gould, March 24, 1824 -
bdsm: David Runkles,
Andrew Thompson

RUSHMAN, William & Har-
riet Clarke, Oct. 14, 1836
- bdsm:
RUSSELL, J. B. F. & Cor-
nelia Peyton, Feb. 29,
1828 - bdsm: J. B. F.
Russell, Benjamin King
John & Sarah Dennison,
Sept. 21, 1829 - bdsm:
John Russell, Thomas
Dennison
W. W. & Virginia Fletcher,
Oct. 14, 1850 - Married by
J. N. Danforth
William C. & Margaret Ann
B. Brown, Nov. 30, 1835 -
bdsm: William C. Rus-
sell, Richard H. Clagett
RUSTICK, Thomas & Eliz-
abeth Pierce, June 3, 1803
- bdsm: Thomas Rustick,
John Duffy
RUSTIN, Osburn & Louisa
Lee, Nov. 17, 1835 -
bdsm: Benoni Wheat, John
J. Wheat
RUTHERFORD, Francis &
Frances Toler, Sept. 30,
1830 - bdsm: Francis
Rutherford, William Har-
per
RUTTER, Josiah & Mary
Pollard, March 21, 1832 -
bdsm: Josiah Rutter, John
S. Humphries
RYE, Jesse & Jane V. Askin,
July 30, 1828 - bdsm:
Jesse Rye, John Parsons
SAFFORD, Eliel T. of Wood
County, Virginia, & Ann H.
Hunter of Alexandria
County, Aug. 2, 1825 -
bdsm: Eliel T. Safford,
Alexander Hunter
SAGE, Charles & Sarah
Coats, June 22, 1843 -

SAGE (continued)
bdsm: Charles Sage, Samuel Piper
SALES, William & Rockey Tate, Dec. 27, 1805 – bdsm: William Sales, John Hunter
SANDERSON, Samuel & Sarah Day, Jan. 20, 1836 – bdsm: Samuel Sanderson, Horatio Day
SANDS, Robert & Catharine S. Remsey, Sept. 1, 1824 – bdsm: Robert Sands, Joseph Dodds
SANFORD, Samuel & Sarah Ellis, widow of John Ellis, Nov. 28, 1848 – bdsm: Samuel Sanford, William Thomas
SANGER, George & Ann Maria Rickey, Sept. 26, 1835 – bdsm: George Sanger, Walter Penn
Stephen & Mary Lowe, June 13, 1833 – bdsm: Stephen Sanger, John T. White
SARRATT, Dickerson & Susannah Harden, Aug. 21, 1813 – bdsm: Dickerson Sarratt, Thomas G. Harden
SATTERWHITE, Jeremiah & Mary Drown, Oct. 2, 1828 – bdsm: Jeremiah Satterwhite, Levi Hurdle
SAUNDERS, Alfred & Mary Asinath Cook, Sept. 27, 1837 – bdsm: Alfred Saunders, William Johnson
William B. & Caroline M. Anderson, Dec. 26, 1832 – bdsm: William B. Saunders, Henry Anderson
SAVAGE, George Edward & Jane Chartus Dobie, Dec.

SAVAGE (continued)
22, 1840 – bdsm: George Edward Savage, William Walker
SAX, Joseph & Lucy Yost, May 27, 1820 – bdsm: Joseph Sax, Benjamin Berry
SAYRE, John C. & Harriot Wood, Jan. 2, 1823 – bdsm: John C. Sayre, John Gemeny
SAYRS, John J. & Matilda E. Roberts, Dec. 17, 1829 – bdsm: John J. Sayrs, William H. Fowle (See also: Sayres)
SCHAPZEL, George & Catharine Hirsh, Aug. 9, 1831 – bdsm: George Schapzel, Conrad Hirsh
SCHOLL, Philip & Rachael Reardon, July 29, 1806 – bdsm: Philip Scholl
SCOTT, Allen & Mary Darne, Dec. 13, 1809 – bdsm: Allen Scott, Thomas Darne
Charles & Elizabeth Beadle, Sept. 23, 1806 – bdsm: Charles Scott, Thomas Bates
Henry & Amelia Bontz, July 2, 1824 – bdsm: Henry Scott, John Bayne
Horatio C. & Caroline Koones, June 1, 1815 – bdsm: Horatio C. Scott
James P. & Mary Adgate, Nov. 26, 1801 – bdsm: James P. Scott, T. L. Griffin, Hugh West, John Hooff
Robert E. & Elizabeth Taylor, March 10, 1831 – bdsm: Robert E. Scott, Alexander J. Marshall

143

SCOTT (continued)
Robert J. & Mary Ann Lewis, Sept. 22, 1818 - bdsm: Robert J. Scott, Henry Lewis

Thomas & Mary Chafline, July 10, 1810 - bdsm: Thomas Scott, James Kenner

William & Mary A. Walker, Sept. 16, 1845 - bdsm: William Scott, Thomas Waddy

SEAHORN, John & Catharine Goldsmith, Dec. 22, 1804 -- bdsm: John Seahorn, David Jenkins

SEAMAN, John L. & Martha Cooke, Nov. 7, 1818 - bdsm: John L. Seaman, Samuel Chard

SEARS, Hector & Sally King, April 2, 1818 - bdsm: Hector Sears, Henry Brame

SEATON, George & Maria Bryan, Oct. 6, 1845 - bdsm: George Lewis Meaton, Noah Taylor

SEGAR, William & Hester Drean, Jan. 11, 1834 - bdsm: William Segar, Jeremiah Hulbard

SEMMES, James W. & Mary A. Bailey, daughter of James Bailey, July 5, 1847 - bdsm: James W. Semmes, Henry Bailey

SERGEANT, John & Peggy Moody, Dec. 7, 1810 - bdsm: John Sergeant, James Duke

SEYMON, Daniel & Charlott Brent, Jan. 2, 1841 - bdsm: Daniel Seymon, H. W. Steets (Steits)

SHAKESPHEARE, Wm. &

SHAKESPHEARE (continued)
Susanna Price, July 27, 1801 - bdsm: William Shakespear, Lewis Simpson

SHARP, Joseph & Sally Howard, Sept. 12, 1811 - bdsm: Joseph Sharp, Charles Drew

SHARRER, James & Louisa Fry, Dec. 21, 1839 - bdsm: James Sharrer, Joseph Fry

SHAY, Samuel King & Jane Eliza Black, Oct. 19, 1831 - bdsm: Samuel King Shay, John Dunlap

SHEARFIELD, John & Merkey Payne, Jan. 10, 1818 - bdsm: John Shearfield, Robert Glenn

SHEDD, James J. & Ann R. Cannon, Dec. 31, 1841 - bdsm: James J. Shedd, John H. Baggott

William P. & Cath. M. Semmes (Simms), May 19, 1834 - bdsm: William P. Shedd, John W. Cannon

SHEEHY, Edward & Ann McLaughlin, June 22, 1816 - bdsm: Edward Sheehy, Edward McLaughlin

SHEPARD, William B. & Charlotte B. Cazenove, Oct. 6, 1834 - bdsm: William B. Shepard, C. A. Cazenove

SHEPHERD, Henry & Sarah C. Isler, May 5, 1845 - bdsm: Henry Shepherd, Robert J. T. Wilson

SHERIFF, Joshua (born Nov. 19, 1785) & Mary Locker (born Nov. 22, 1785), Feb. 18, 1811 - bdsm: Joshua

SHERIFF (continued)
Sheriff, Thomas Sheriff
Samuel & Susanna Locker,
Jan. 8, 1812 - bdsm:
Samuel Sheriff, Thomas
Sheriff
SHERMAN, Abraham & Mary
Kiteley, Nov. 17, 1802 -
bdsm: Abraham Sherman,
Joseph Bowling
SHERRER, John & Ellen
Dorbet, Sept. 25, 1845 -
bdsm: John Sherrer, William Grymes
SHERWOOD, George L. &
Jane M. Davis, Dec. 29,
1842 - bdsm: George L.
Sherwood, Peter Davis
Jesse & Sarah Brooks, Dec.
5, 1844 - bdsm: Jesse
Sherwood, Henry E. Holt
(See also: Brooke)
Joseph T. & Charlotte Hollinsberry, daughter of John
Hollinsberry, Jan. 19, 1848
- bdsm: Joseph T. Sherwood, John Hollinsberry
Lewellen & Polly Robinson,
June 20, 1815 - bdsm:
William Skidmore, Samuel
Scott
Wm. H. & Ann Bishop, June
I, 1840 - bdsm: Wm. H.
Sherwood, Joshua W.
Bishop
SHIELDS, John & Nancy
Ward, Aug. 12, 1811 -
bdsm: John Shields, Robert Hart
John & Sally Davis, May 18,
1811 - bdsm: John
Shields, Robert Hardey
Thomas & Elizabeth Stevens, April 28, 1810 -
bdsm: Thomas Shields,
George Stephenson

SHIELDS (continued)
Thomas & Mary Ann Gee,
April 2, 1807 - bdsm:
Thomas Shields, Joshua
Laur
SHINN, Robert & Elizabeth
Myers, Aug. 9, 1827 -
bdsm: Robert Shinn, John
Kerr
Stephen & Mary Muir, May
13, 1826 - bdsm: Stephen
Shinn, Benjamin H. Lambert
SHINNICK, James M. & Mrs.
Catharine Javins, Sept. 9,
1848 - bdsm: James M.
Shinnick, William R. Pettit
SHIRLEY, Charles B. &
Catharine Burchell, June
23, 1846 - bdsm: Charles
B. Shirley, Edward Burchell
William H. & Jane Winter,
Sept. 11, 1844 - bdsm:
William H. Shirley,
Charles McKnight
William H. & Marian Middleton, Dec. 3, 1831 -
bdsm: William H. Shitley,
James P. Middleton
SHORTER, Roger & Sarah
Ann Birch Hunt, Jan. I1,
1827 - bdsm: Roger
Shorter, John McFarlane
SHREEVE, Benjamin Jr. &
Mary Goodhue, June 30,
1804 - bdsm: James
Keith, Jr., Benjamin
Shreve, Jr.
Isaac & Hannah Very, April
12, 1802 - bdsm: Isaac
Shreeve, James Laurason
SHREVE, Benjamin & Sarah
Kitely, Jan. 13, 1802 -
bdsm: Benjamin Shreve,

SHREVE (continued)
Edmund Craddock
SHRIKE, Peter & Julia Furguson, Feb. 2, 1843 – bdsm: Peter Shrike, Joseph Furguson
SHUCK, Frederick & Elizabeth Bogan, March 13, 1805 – bdsm: Frederick Shuck, John Bogan
SHURMUNDINE, Lewis & Susanna Simms, April 2, 1822 – bdsm: Lewis Shurmundine
SHUTT, Wm. H. & Sarah Ann Clifton, married Nov. 3, 1850 by John L. Pascoe – bdsm:
SIDES, George W. & Jane E. V. Hudgins, July 2, 1850 – bdsm: George W. Sides, W. Bawler
SILLICK, James & Mary Ann Nicholson, Feb. 18, 1840 – bdsm: James Sillick, William R. Biers
Thomas & Chloe Mason, Jan. 7, 1825 – bdsm: Thomas Sillick, John Hill
SILVER, Washington & Sarah Hall, July 3, 1837 – bdsm: Washington Silver, Peyton Williamson
SIMMONS, Cyrus & Mary E. Edmonds, Aug. 2, 1832 – bdsm: Cyrus Simmons, Hugh Banks, (guardian of Mary E. Edmonds)
James & Matilda Penn, April 11, 1837 – bdsm: James Simmons, William Penn
Joseph & Mary J. Stevenson, April 20, 1831 – bdsm: Joseph Simmons, Samuel Church (guardian of Mary

SIMMONS (continued)
J. Stevenson)
Samuel & Euna Hunter, Jan. 25, 1827 – bdsm: Samuel Simmons, Thomas Latimer
Samuel & Jane E. Walker, June 18, 1845 – bdsm: Samuel Simmons, John H. Watkins
SIMMS, James & Betsey Lightfoot, Jan. 7, 1803 – bdsm: James Simms, Philip Conn
John & Elizabeth McGee, June 15, 1830 – bdsm: John Simms, John Beckley
John & Elizabeth Petit, June 16, 1836 – bdsm: John Simms, William Spenser
John Douglass & Mary West, Aug. 30, 1809 – bdsm: John Douglass Simms, Cuthbert Powell
Peter & Jane Darnell, Nov. 7, 1844 – bdsm: Peter Simms, Harry Darnell
SIMPSON, Alfred & Susanna Cash, Dec. 3, 1817 – bdsm: Alfred Simpson, Elijah Cash
Gerrard & Ann Benson, June 26, 1817 – bdsm: Gerrard Simpson, Samuel Atwell
Gilbert & Susannah Zimmerman, Feb. 9, 1803 – bdsm: Gilbert Simpson, Henry Zimmerman
Hanson & Sarah Randell, May 23, 1816 – bdsm: Hanson Simpson, Theophilus Randell (Also: Harrison Simpson)
Henry & Julia Ann Cross, Feb. 1, 1832 – bdsm: Henry Simpson, Richard

SIMPSON (continued)
Cross

James W. & Margaret Thompson, Jan. 23, 1834 - bdsm: James W. Simpson, Edward Smyth

Peter M. & Mary Trydell, Oct. 9, 1826 - bdsm: Peter Simpson, Elijah Spernaugle

Presley & Mary H. Riffetts, March 23 1824 - bdsm: Presley Simpson, William Harper

Thomas & Jane Moore, July 29, 1820 - bdsm: Thomas Simpson, Isaac Entwisle, Jr.

William & Elizabeth Davis, Jan. 8, 1816 - bdsm: William Simpson, Alexander Veitch

SIPPLE, Samuel & Mary Ann Hookes, April 24, 1822 - bdsm: Samuel Sipple, William D. Miller

SISSON, Jesse & Ann Hall, Oct. 22, 1835 - bdsm: Jesse Sisson, Abna Humphreys

SITLER, Philip & Eleanor Posey, May 26, 1836 - bdsm: Philip Sitler, James Allen

Philip & Sally Elizabeth Bruin, Aug. 19, 1846 - bdsm: Philip Sitler, George McCleish

SKIDMORE, Jerome & Mariah Richards, April 27, 1810 - bdsm: Gerrard Skidmore, William Harriss

Jesse & Sarah Boyd, Oct. 18, 1815 - bdsm: Jesse Skidmore, Richard D. Emberson

SKIDMORE (continued)
William & Catharine Robinson, April 15, 1814 - bdsm: William Skidmore, Jesse Robinson

SKINNER, Burditt & Margaret Cheshier, March 20, 1816 - bdsm: Burditt Skinner, John Bontz

George & Mary Mills, May 6, 1812 - bdsm: George Skinner, Henry Tatspaugh

Price & Julia Rollins, March 15, 1828 - bdsm: Price Skinner, John Rollins

William A. & Aletha Moan, March 2, 1816 - bdsm: William A. Skinner, Burditt Skinner

SLATER, John & Delila Thompson, July 19, 1824 - bdsm: John Slater, Benjamin Cawood

John & Mary E. Longdon, June 16, 1834 - bdsm: John Slater, John Demain

SLAUGHTER, Rev. Philip & Anna Sophia Semmes, June 9, 1834 - bdsm: Rev. Philip Slaughter, Capt. F. Lee

SLIMMER, Daniel & Eleanor Williams, March 10, 1810 - bdsm: Daniel Slimmer, Alexander Williams

SLOAN, James & Harriot Throop, Sept. 9, 1809 - bdsm: James Sloan, George Hare

SLY, John & Susannah Curtain, June 22, 1801 - bdsm: John S. Sly, George Singleton

Thomas & Rebecca Beech, May 26, 1827 - bdsm: Thomas Sly, John Rheem

SMALL, Noah & Lucretia Jackson, Oct. 26, 1818 – bdsm: Noah Small, James Hill

SMITH, Benjamin & Matilda R. Price, April 5, 1830 – bdsm: Benjamin Smith, Horatio Clagett

Charles & Elizabeth Loyd, Dec. 24, 1814 – bdsm: Charles Smith, John Loyd

Charles & Mary H. Bowie, Dec. 7, 1818 – bdsm: Charles Smith, Davis Bowie

Daniel & Amanda F. Bull, Nov. 15, 1842 – bdsm: Daniel Smith, William Wilson

Daniel & Betsy Stitley, Oct. 29, 1801 – bdsm: Daniel Smith, Andrew Hays

Daniel H. & Amanda A. McCarty, Nov. 1, 1838 – bdsm: Daniel H. Smith, Andrew T. Bell

David B. & Harriet Dangerfield, Oct. 7, 1839 – bdsm: David B. Smith, Cassius F. Lee

Edward & Martha Lomax (free persons of colour), Aug. 14, 1845 – bdsm: Edward Smith, George Bruce

Edward & Susan Roach, Oct. 22, 1817 – bdsm: Edward Smith, Loughlin Masterson

Francis L. & Sarah G. Vowell, April 13,1836 – bdsm: Francis L. Smith, Charles A. Thornton

George H. & Mary Ann Loyd, March 10, 1846 – bdsm: George H. Smith, Donald McDonald

George W. & Mary Norris,

SMITH (continued)
Oct. 3, 1843 – bdsm: George W. Smith, James Norris

Isaac & Mary Welsh, Feb. 26, 1806 – bdsm: Isaac Smith, John Smith

James & Rebecca Lindsay, May 17, 1832 – bdsm: James Smith, Noble Lindsay

James P. & Mary Sanford, April 11, 1837 – bdsm: James P. Smith, George H. Keightley

John & Barbara Manly, Nov. 3, 1807 – bdsm: John Smith, Thomas Mezarvey

John & Louisa House, Jan. 28, 1813 – bdsm: John Smith, David House

John & Louisa Jenkins, June 14, 1825 – bdsm: John Smith, David Jenkins

John A. W. & Julia Anna Macpherson, Oct. 18, 1827 – bdsm: John A. W. Smith, William F. Philips

John F. & Martha Kent, June 20, 1811 – bdsm: John R. Lucas, Robert Anderson

John K. & Mary Whaling, Feb. 19, 1814 – bdsm: John K. Smith, William McCally

John L. & Mary Tucker, May 27, 1843 – bdsm: John L. Smith, David Irvin

John Thomas & Sarah Ann Grimes, Dec. 26, 1826 – bdsm: John Thomas Smith, Joseph Broders

John Y. & Nancy Dorsey, Aug. 3, 1818 – bdsm: John Y. Smith, Nancy Dorsey

Joseph & Eliza Skidmore,

SMITH (continued)

Nov. Z6, 1817 - bdsm: Joseph Smith, Rezin Tayler

Joseph & Elizabeth Huddleston, Dec. 23, 1835 - bdsm: Joseph Smith, John Huddleston

Joseph & Unis Redman, Dec. 17, 1840 - bdsm: Joseph Smith, Henry Mansfield

Juliss & Mary Ann Tennison, Aug. 10, 1817 - bdsm: Julius Smith, James Hill

Madison & Matilda Delphy, Nov. 10, 1817 - bdsm: Madison Smith, Susanna Cannon

Rufus & Mary Ann Hoff, Sept. 8, 1846 - bdsm: Rufus Smith, Charles W. Blincoe

Samuel P. & Maria Wood, Nov. 28, 1825 - bdsm: Samuel P. Smith, William McCarty

Theodore E. & Eliza Ratcliffe, May 21, 1831 - bdsm: Theodore E. Smith, Joseph Dodds

Thomas & Mary C. Deane, Nov. 26, 1818 - bdsm: Thomas Smith, Samuel Lindsay

Thomas W. & Ellen Wattles, Nov. 12, 1840 - bdsm: Thomas W. Smith, Nathaniel Wattles

Wiliam & Louisa A. Baggett, April 11, 1835 - bdsm: William Smith, Alexander Moore

William & Mary Morgan, July 27, 1805 - bdsm:

SMITH (continued)

William Smith, Thomas Sanford

William & Nancy Glover, Nov. 25, 1802 - bdsm: William Smith, Thomas Glover

William & Nancy Somby, March 14, 1826 - bdsm: William Smith, David Jarboe (See also: William Smith Coldman)

William & Sarah McKee, July 19, 1822 - bdsm: William Smith, Bartholomew Delphy

William & Sarah Morgan, July 19, 1802 - bdsm: Wm. Smith, John Dunn

SMITHER, Catesby C. & Mary Webb, July 27, 1812 - bdsm: Catesby C. Smither, John Wood

SMOOT, Charles C. & Sarah W. Bryan, Jan. 21, 1823 - bdsm: Charles C. Smoot, Bernard Bryan

George A. & Elizabeth Bland, Aug. 22, 1817 - bdsm: Geo. A. Smoot, John S. Emerson

James E. & Phoebe C. Lowe, March 11, 1828 - bdsm: James E. Smoot, John Dunlap

SMYTH, William & Hannah Drinker, Feb. 28, 1822 - bdsm: William Smyth, Thomas Smith

William & Mary M. Hewes, Nov. 26, 1833 - bdsm: William Smyth, Hugh C. Smith

SNOWDEN, Richard of Prince Georges County, Maryland, & Louisa Vic-

SNOWDEN (continued)
toria Warfield, May 16, 1818 - bdsm:
Samuel & Ann Longdon, Jan. 7, 1802 - bdsm: Samuel Snowden, John Longdon
SNYDERS, Robert & Ann Howard, May 23, 1838 - bdsm: Robert Snyders, John Hart
SOAPER, Benoni & Letitia Johnson, June 9, 1851 - Married by J. J. Pascoe
SOLOMAN, Samuel & Ann Padgett, Dec. 25, 1827 - bdsm: Samuel Soloman, Thomas Davey
SOMERS, Jos. A. & Mary Charlton Atkinson, Sept. 19, 1837 - Joseph R. Somers, Charles Atkinson
SOTHORON, William B. & Ann White, March 4, 1835 - bdsm: William B. Sothoron, Samuel V. Hill
SOUTHARD, Henry & Mary E. Brian, July 26, 1849 - bdsm: Henry Southard, John J. Brian
James & Sarah West, Jan. 22, 1833 - bdsm: James Southard, William Southard
William & Sarah Beatly, Dec. 26, 1820 - bdsm: William Southard, James Dudly
SPARKS, Joel B. & Julia Ann Ogden, June 2, 1831 - bdsm: Joel B. Sparks, William C. Spillman
SPENCE, Wm. Henry & Camilla Pierce, Oct. 13, 1845 - bdsm: Wm. Henry Spence, James Garrell
SPENCER, Daniel & Eliza

SPENCER (continued)
Wiley, Jan. 3, 1833 - bdsm: Daniel Spencer, Hugh Wiley
James & Dorothy Bladen, Aug. 9, 1817 - bdsm: James Spencer, Augustine Bladen
Jesse & Nancy Spencer, Nov. 15, 1817 - bdsm: Jesse Spencer, Nancy Spencer
William & Nancy Loudoun, Dec. 10, 1823 - bdsm: William Spencer, Peter Loudoun (Both parties free Negro)
SPIDEN, John A. & Ann Martin, March 29, 1823 - bdsm: John A. Spiden, James Walker
SPILMAN, William C. & Ann Ogdon, Oct. 23, 1824 - bdsm: William C. Spilman, Willian Vernon
Wm. & Elizabeth Ogden, Dec. 14, 1839 - bdsm: Wm. Spilman, William C. Spilman, Jr.
SPOONER, Walter & Mary Ballard, June 11, 1802 - bdsm: Walter Spooner, William Ballard
SPRAGUE, Joshua & Susannah Lee, Sept. 1, 1804 - bdsm: Joshua Sprague, Johnston Jenkins
SPRINGSTEEL, Philip & Ann E. Lawrence, April 22, 1850 - Married by John L. Pascoe
STACKPOLE, William & Caroline Gerry, Dec. 28, 1841 - bdsm: William Stackpole, James Hutcheson

STANLY, George & Mary Chisel, April 19, 1804 – bdsm: George Stanly, John Duffy

STANSBURY, Joseph & Georgianna Morris, license issued April 26, 1851 – bdsm:

STANTON, Richard & Harriet Perry, Sept. 26, 1811 – bdsm: Richard Stanton, Alexander Perry

Richard H. & Asenath Throop, Sept. 19, 1833 – bdsm: Richard H. Stanton, Thomas W. Brocchus

STAPLES, Samuel G. & Mary Boyd, Oct. 3, 1829 – bdsm: Samuel G. Staples, Charles King

STARKS, Mathew & Catharine Hopes, June 27, 1833 – bdsm: Mathew Starks, Davis Bowie

STEARNS, John & Anna Harriet Lloyd, July 17, 1848 – bdsm: John Stearns, Cassius F. Lee

STEED, Robert E. & Julianna M. Lowe, May 30, 1829 – bdsm: Robert E. Steed, Augustine Newton

STEEL, John H. & Alcey Coward, Feb. 13, 1838 – bdsm: John H. Steel, Wilfred Sidebottom

Jonathan H. & Julia Ann Adams, Feb. 26, 1823 – bdsm: Jonathan H. Steel, Leonard Adams

STEPHENS, Robert & Mary Elizabeth Moseley Bowling, Dec. 16, 1824 – bdsm: Robert Stephens, James K. Plant

STEPHENSON, John & Mary

STEPHENSON (continued) Ann Hansmond Nov. 14, 1840 – bdsm: John Stephenson, Henry Hansmand

Robert A. & Malinda C. Turner, Sept. 24, 1849 – bdsm: Robert A. Stephenson, Thomas C. Craven

William & Margaret G. Hogan, July 18, 1810 – bdsm: William Stephenson, William S. Douglass

STERRET, James & Polly Mills, Oct. 8, 1803 – bdsm: James Sterret, John Davis

STEUART, Charles T. & Ann S. Deneale, April 27, 1820 – bdsm: Charles T. Steuart, Henry Fitzhugh (Charles Townshend Steuart of King George County married the same day by Rev. O. Norris)

STEUTERS, Morris & Betsey Mayhall, July 8, 1822 – bdsm: Morris Steuters, Westley Benter

STEVENS, Thomas & Mary S. Deming Oct. 21, 1835 – bdsm: Thomas Stevens, John Thompson

STEVENSON, John & Rebecca Silence, Dec. 23, 1828 – bdsm: John Stevenson, Robert Hodgkin

Robert & Mary Young, April 19, 1817 – bdsm: Robert Stevenson, James Young

STEWART, James M. & Elizabeth Tretcher, April 23, 1812 – bdsm: James M. Stewart, William Ramsay

John A. & Eliza Dunlap,

STEWART (continued)
Nov. 8, 1824 – bdsm: John A. Stewart, John Dunlap
Kensey Johns & Hannah Lee, May 5, 1840 – bdsm: Kensey Johns Stewart, John Lloyd
William & Delia Downs, July 30, 1821 – bdsm: William Stewart, Ewell Russ
William & Sarah Ann Hookes, Jan. 10, 1811 – bdsm: William Stewart, Jacob Hookes
William & Sarah Forrest, May 16, 1832 – bdsm: William Stewart, James Coates
William B. & Catharine Reed, May 3, 1815 – bdsm: William B. Stewart, Thomas Albisdeston
William Y. & Ann Maria Hodgskins, Nov. 25, 1829 – bdsm: William Y. Stewart, John Nanery
STILWELL, John & Sally Bogwell, Dec. 14, 1807 – bdsm: John Stilwell, Catharine George
STOOPS, James & Verlinda Jane Compton, Oct. 27, 1836 – bdsm: James Stoops, Emanuel Compton
Richard & Ann Compton, Jan. 24, 1837 – bdsm: Richard Stoops, Ludwell Compton
William & Elizabeth Smith, Feb. 5, 1802 – bdsm: William Stoops, Jesse Smith
William & Margaret McGraw, Jan 3, 1832 – bdsm: William Stoops, Benjamin McGraw
STORK, Richard B. & Hannah

STORK (continued)
Jane Whit, Oct. 24, 1833 – bdsm: Richard B. Stork, John Higdon
STRICKLAND, Daniel & Susannah Tracy, Sept. 10, 1803 – bdsm: Daniel Strickland, James Grimes
STRINGFELLOW, H. & Mary M. Green, daughter of James Green, July 16, 1849 – bdsm: H. Stringfellow, James Green
STUART, Charles Calvert & Cornelia L. Turbeville, Feb. 20, 1817 – bdsm: Charles Calvert Stuart, William Robinson
Peter M. & Elizabeth Rudd, May 27, 1830 – bdsm: Peter M. Stuart, John A. Rudd
STUTSON, John & Mary Clark, March 2, 1824 – bdsm: John Stutson, Richard Wood
SULLIVAN, Andrew & Maria Gallager, April 19, 1832 – bdsm: Andrew Sullivan, Horatio Day
Owen & Elizabeth Denington, Sept. 3, 1803 – bdsm: Owen Sullivan, Robert Gibson
SUMBY, John & Emeline Clarke, Nov. 8, 1841 – bdsm: John Sumby, Thomas Butter
SUMMERS, Thomas & Rachel Hooper, Sept. 2, 1802 – bdsm: Thomas Summers, William Woodcocks
Wesley & Mary Margaret Rotchford, June 8, 1833 – bdsm: Wesley Summers, Bartholemew Rotchford

SUMMERS (continued)
Wm. H. & Ellen H. Dozier, June 27, 1850 - bdsm: Wm. H. Summers, S.S. Crabb

SUPTON, Daniel S. & Sarah Lambert, June 8, 1813 - bdsm: Daniel S. Supton, Geo. Lambert

SURVOIRE, William & Mary Ramsay, April 18, 1822 - bdsm: William Survoire, Daniel Evans

SUTER, Alexander & Maria Fletcher, May 2, 1811 - bdsm: Alexander Suter, Joshua Yeaton

SUTHERLAND, David & Mary Webb, April 15, 1816 - bdsm: David Sutherland, Joseph Evans

SUTTON, John & Patience Purdie, May 20, 1817 - bdsm: John Sutton, James King

Samuel & Ann Leech, Nov. 22, 1832 - bdsm: Samuel Sutton, Samuel Cronmiller

William & Sophia Shroder, Feb. 9, 1824 - bdsm: William Sutton, George Markell

SWALLOW, John & Deliah Penn, July 5, 1843 - bdsm: John Swallow, William R. Ball

SWANN, Benjamin & Susanna Benter, Aug. 17, 1848 - bdsm: Benjamin Swann, Richard H. Rudd

John & Ann Bellford, April 21, 1803 - bdsm: John Swann, John Crawford

John Blake & Ann Underwood, Feb. 15, 1811 - bdsm: John Blake Swann,

SWANN (continued)
John B. Hill

William & Sarah Ann Dogett, Dec. 17, 1839 - bdsm: William Swann, Somersett Aubinoe

William T. & Frances Alexander, July 12, 1810 - bdsm: William T. Swann, Thomas Swann

SWAYNE, George & Mary Violett, Oct. 4, 1817 - bdsm: George Swayne, John Violett

SWIFT, William R. & Mary D. Harper, July 31, 1815 - bdsm: William R. Swift, James Harper

SWILER, Joseph & Elizabeth McFadden, Dec. 21, 1805 - bdsm: Joseph Swiler, John Greenwood

SYDEBOTTAM, Wilfred & Ardry Grady, Dec. 10, 1816 - bdsm: Wilfred Sydebottom, Townshend Baggott

SYKE, Peter & Isabella McFadden, Oct. 31, 1809 - bdsm: Peter Syke, John Lanham

TABB, John P. & Rebecca Lloyd, April 29, 1844 - bdsm: John P. Tabb, John Lloyd

TAFFE, James & Elizabeth Downs, Jan. 3, 1811 - bdsm: James Taffe, Daniel Downs

TALBOT, Thomas & Winifred Ann Rotch, Nov. 9, 1829 - bdsm: Thomas Talbot, Edward Smyth

TALBOTT, Alexander & Rachel Walker, Sept. 28, 1836 - bdsm: Alexander Talbott, Reuben Johnston,

TALBOTT (continued)
Jr.
William & Mary Lindsay,
June 5, 1817 - bdsm: Wil-
liam Talbott, Andrew
Roundsavel
TATE, Benjamin & Nelly
Smallwood, August, 11,
1803 - bdsm: Benjamin
Tate, John Duffy
Jesse & Peggy Mittchell,
Dec. 27, 1803 - bdsm:
Jesse Tate, Cuthbert
Powell
Josiah & Patsy Simms,
March 8, 1815 - bdsm:
Josiah Tate, James Evans
Simeon & Cassandra Clark,
May 15, 1822 - bdsm:
Simeon Tate, Isaac Tate
Simon & Martha Smith, July
23, 1817 - bdsm: Simon
Tate, Adam Henry
William E. & Mary Brown,
March 16, 1842 - bdsm:
William E. Tate, Simon
Tate
TATSAPAUGH, Edwin & Ju-
lia Dixon, daughter of John
Dixion, Nov. 13, 1848 -
bdsm: Edwin Tatsapaugh,
A. D. Collinsworth
John & Elizabeth O'Neal,
Oct. 31, 1815 - bdsm:
John Tatsapaugh, Timothy
Mountford
TATTERSHALL, Thomas &
Nancy Boyd, November 2,
1803 - bdsm: Thomas Tat-
tershall, William Boyd
TATTERSON, James & Ellen
Pursley, license issued
June 5, 1851 - bdsm:
TAYLOR, Augustine & Wi-
dow Charity Glover, Jan.
9, 1833 - bdsm: Augustine

TAYLOR (continued)
Taylor, Bennett Knight
Bazil & Mary Lynn, August
12, 1828 - bdsm: Bazil
Taylor, Charles Fletcher
Charles & Rosetta Tat-
sapaugh, Dec. 23, 1830 -
bdsm: Charles Taylor,
David Irwin
Charles S. & Harriet B.
Fowle, May 15, 1845 -
bdsm: Charles S. Taylor,
Harriet B. Fowle
Daniel & Eliza Watkins,
Nov. 20, 1821 - bdsm:
Daniel Taylor, Isaiah Tate
Evan P. & Rebecca Law-
rence, Feb. 16, 1813 -
bdsm: Evan P. Taylor,
Charles McKnight
George & Mary Eaton, June
25, 1801 - bdsm: John
White, George Taylor
George W. & Ann Eliza
Travis, July 22, 1846 -
bdsm: George W. Taylor,
Wm. .F Hodgkin
Harrison & Mary Dennison,
Nov. 16, 1829 - bdsm:
Harrison Taylor, Mary
Dennison
James & Catharine Mag-
lenen, Jan. 9, 1836 -
bdsm: James Taylor,
Frederick Vaccari
John & Catharine C. Mit-
chell, June 9, 1841 -
bdsm: John Taylor, Philip
Deakins
John & Mary Crook, Oct. 3,
1826 - bdsm: John Taylor,
Thompson Jordon
Joseph & Elizabeth Jacobs,
Sept. 15, 1825 - bdsm:
Joseph Taylor, Prestley
Jacobs

TAYLOR (continued)
Lawrence Berry & Virginia C. Powell, Feb. 7, 1844 – bdsm: Lawrence Berry Taylor, John S. Powell

Nora & Louisa Darnell (coloured), Dec. 9, 1844 – bdsm: Nora Taylor, Harry Darnell

Robert & Catharine Studor, daughter of Mary Studor, Aug. 15, 1838 – bdsm: Robert Taylor, Mary Studor

Robert Johnston & Maria Moore Rose, March 4, 1806 – bdsm: Robert Johnston Taylor, Henry Rose of Alexandria

Samuel S. & Martha V. Hancock, May 17, 1845 – bdsm: Samuel S. Taylor, George Snyder

Thomas & Eliza Dogan, March 15, 1837 – bdsm: Thomas Taylor, Philip Dogan

Thomas & Sarah Shuck, Oct. 27, 1802 – bdsm: Thomas Taylor, Jacob Shuck

William & Jane Lucinda Poston, March 5. 1818 – bdsm: William Taylor, Joseph Poston

TEMPLE, William Esq. of Delaware & Catharine Lowber, license granted Aug. 3, 1852 – Permission granted by John Lower, father

TENNISON, Samuel & Catharine Mankins, Jan. 4, 1802 – bdsm: Samuel Tennison & David Mankins

Samuel & Lucinda Marts, Feb. 7, 1820 – bdsm: Samuel Tennison, William

TENNISON (continued)
Mills

Samuel & Margaret M. Banon, June 1, 1840 – bdsm: Samuel Tennison, George Price

THOMAS, Bazil & Molly Lucas, March 24, 1806 – bdsm: Bazil Thomas, Samuel Henry

Benjamin & Jane George, April 11, 1836 – bdsm: Benjamin Thomas, Isaac George

Benson & Ann Tucker, Jan. 5, 1824 – bdsm: Benson Thomas, Thomas Tucker

George J. & Maria Harper, Sept. 16, 1833 – bdsm: George J. Thomas, William Harper

Joseph & Ann Farrell, April 1, 1809 – bdsm: Joseph Thomas, Richard Weightman

W. D. & Elizabeth Riggs, July 24, 1838 – bdsm: W. D. Thomas, James Jack

William & Cordelia E. Veitch, Aug. 8, 1842 – bdsm: William Thomas, Nathaniel Beach (Minister Returns reads: Cordelia E. Beitels)

William & Jane Holt, Jan. 14, 1842 – bdsm: William Thomas, Henry Williams

William & Mary Hilton, daughter of Wm. Hilton, April 25, 1815 – bdsm: William Thomas, William Hilton

William H. & Rosalie Sauls, daughter of Edward Sauls, Sept. 28, 1848 – bdsm: William H. Thomas, Ed-

THOMAS (continued)
ward Sauls
Wilson L. & Sarah Tucker, May 27, 1822 - bdsm: Wilson L. Thomas, James O. Tucker
THOMPSON, Craven Peyton & Sally Eliza Tucker, Nov. 11, 1807 - bdsm: Craven Peyton Thompson
Douglas & Eliza Cranston, Jan. 13, 1821 - bdsm: Douglas Thompson, John Furlans (Married Jan. 13, 1821 by Rev. O. Norris)
George & Rebecca Gardner, Sept. 12, 1803 - bdsm: George Thompson, Jeremiah Eney
Henry P. & Christina Lynch, July 4, 1839 - bdsm: Henry P. Thompson, Elizabth Beerford
James & Barbara Brooner, Feb. 14, 1805 - bdsm: James Thompson, Theodore Sherly
John & Anna Jackson, Nov. 29, 1806 - bdsm: John Thompson, Daniel Wells
John & Emeline Kinner, Sept. 12, 1846 - bdsm: John Thompson, William Johnson
John & Jenny Manly, November 2, 1803 - bdsm: John Thompson, Jenny Manly
John & Matty Davies, Aug. 25, 1802 - bdsm: John Thompson, John Davies
John F. & Margaret A. Walker, Aug. 27, 1832 - bdsm: John F. Thompson, John West
Richard & Elizabeth Don-

THOMPSON (continued)
aldson, Dec. 12, 1809 - bdsm: Richard Thompson, Thomas Thompson
Richard & Lydia Horner, March 27, 1815 - bdsm: Richard Thompson, John Horner
Richard & Sophia Williams, Jan. 5, 1811 - bdsm: Richard Thompson, Peter Lopton
Samuel & Emeline Slacum, Oct. 29, 1821 - (Married at St. John Church, Washington, D.C., Oct. 30, 1821 by Rev. O. Norris)
William & Manitta Monis (possibly Morris), Aug. 28. 1840 - bdsm: William Thompson, Joseph Ferguson
William & Sally Simpson, March 3, 1802 - bdsm: William Taylor, John Thompson
Woodward & Frances Baggett, July 23, 1811 - bdsm: Woodward Thompson, Thomas Steel
Woodward & Jane Mills, March 28, 1833 - bdsm: Woodward Thompson, Richard Kendrick
THORN, John & Winney Clements, Dec. 28, 1809 - bdsm: John Thorn, Henry Emerson
THORNTON, Nicholas & Susannah L. Carne, Feb. 28, 1816 - bdsm: Nicholas Thornton, Richard Libby
THROOP, Phares & Elizabeth Bonne, May 22, 1804 - bdsm: Phares Throop, Benjamin Baden

THROOP (continued)
Thomas & Mary Ann Mankin, Feb. 2, 1826 - bdsm: Thomas Throop, Charles Mankin
TIBBET, Walter & Ann Margaret Hunter, Feb. 22, 1827 - bdsm: Walter Tibbet, James Kelley
TIGNELL, Magor & Louisa Wood, June 12, 1806 - bdsm: Magor Tignell, Dixon Brittingham
TILLSON, Martin L. & Frances B. Gray, March 3, 1830 - bdsm: Martin L. Tillson, John G. Gray
TIPPITT, Jonathan & Catharine Tucker, Sept. 6, 1834 - bdsm: Jonathan Tippitt, Jesse Skidmore
TOLBERT, Henry & Sarah Wood, Dec. 24, 1803 - bdsm: Henry Tolbert, McKinzer Tolbert
TOLSON, Edward of Prince George's County, Maryland, & Susan Middleton of the same, Jan. 19, 1825 - bdsm:
George S. & Eliza R. Jones, May 14, 1839 - bdsm: George S. Tolson, Thomas H. Jones
TOMLIN, Robert & Sarah Ferguson, July 13, 1839 - bdsm: Robert Tomlin, John Green
TOTTEN, Mark & Violett Jenkins, March 29, 1824 - bdsm: Mark Totten, William Hunter (See also: Trotter)
TOWERS, James & Mary E. Cooley, Feb. 23, 1836 - bdsm: James Towers, R.

TOWERS (continued)
Mockbee
Thomas & Elizabeth Chatham, Jan. 30, 1806 - bdsm: Thomas Towers, Francis Hucorn
TOWNSHEND, John P. & Laura Dunbar, July 21, 1842 - bdsm: John P. Townshend, John Butcher
Samuel H. & Catharine Lumsdon, Jan. 25, 1823 - bdsm: Samuel H. Townshend, Singleton Townshend
TRACEY, Thomas D. & Sarah May, Aug. 14, 1817 - bdsm: Thomas D. Tracey, Lewis W. Plum
TRAMMELL, George W. & Sarah Southard, May 15, 1836 - bdsm: George W. Trammell, John Alexander
TRAVERS, Thomas & Hennretta Ann Cook, Oct. 16, 1828 - bdsm: Thomas Travers, George Coryell
TRAVIS, John & Milly Knight, May 9, 1844 - bdsm: John Travis, Thomas Berry
Robert & Nancy Williams, Aug. 23, 1820 - bdsm: Robert Travis, John Smith
TREAKLE, William H. & Jane McKew, Dec. 21, 1848 - bdsm: William H. Treakle, James Treakle
TRESISE, Thomas & Sally Morris, June 23, 1802 - bdsm: Thomas Tresise, Alexander Perry
TRESLER, Philip & Susan Ferguson, Jan. 11, 1834 - bdsm: Philip Tresler, J. Susan Ferguson
TRIPLETT, Charles H. &

TRIPLETT (continued)
Esther Ann Dunlap, Feb. 6, 1833 - bdsm: Charles H. Triplett, James P. Smith
Francis F. & Mary Ann Wheat, Feb. 10, 1845 - bdsm: Francis F. Triplett, Benoni Wheat,
George W. & Jane R. Dale, Nov. 20, 1839 - bdsm: George W. Triplett, John Richards Jr.
William P. & Kate R. Tatsapaugh, April 13, 1848 - bdsm: William P. Triplett, Henry Tatsapaugh
TRUMAN, William & Sarah Hopkins, Dec. 12, 1836 - bdsm: William Truman, William Arnold
TRUNNELLS, Isaac & Eleanor Martindall, April 23, 1822 - bdsm: Isaac Trunnels, William Green
TUBMAN, Richard J. & Selina Ann Javins,Feb. 17, 1833 - bdsm: Richard J. Tubman, Thomas C. Ogden
TUCKER, William & Ann Skidmore, Nov. 29, 1833 - bdsm: William Tucker, Jared Skidmore
TULEY, Thomas C. & Mary Ann Cohen, Aug. 22, 1822 - bdsm: Thomas C. Tuley, William Cohen
TURK, Nicholas & Betsy Neale, June 5, 1817 - bdsm: Nicholas Turk, John Marvell
TURNER, Charles W. & Jane Johnston, Oct. 15, 1839 - bdsm: Charles W. Turner, Reuben Johnston, Jr.
Henry L. & Susanna Avery,

TURNER (continued)
Jan. 2, 1840 - bdsm: Henry L. Turner, Thomas Slatford
James & Susan Colston, Oct. 5, 1805 - bdsm: James Turner, Thomas L. Griffin
John & Mary Reily, July 26, 1811 - bdsm: John Turner, John Dixon
Richard H. & Margaret S. Hooe, May 18, 1840 - bdsm: Richard H. Turner, Wm. T. Smith
William & Kitty West, July 25, 1804 - bdsm: William Turner, John Hooff
TURPIN, William S. & Ann Fortney, July 30, 1822 - bdsm: William S. Turpin, Ann Fortney
TUTTON, John & Ann Williams, Sept. 2, 1803 - bdsm: John Tutton, Alexander Williams
TYLER, Daniel & Rebecca Bines, Jan. 2, 1820 - celebrated by Rev. Oliver Norris
Henry & Mary Ann Willis, Dec. 5, 1817 - bdsm: Henry Tyler, Jeremiah Fugitt
Samuel & Mary Virginia Tyler, daughter of Thompson Tyler, July 4, 1849 - bdsm: Samuel Tyler, Thompson Tyler
Thompson G. & Mary Ann Gruver, June 21, 1827 - bdsm: Thompson G. Tyler, John Gruver
UHLER, Peter G. & Catherine Griffith, Nov. 7, 1844 - bdsm: Peter G. Uhler,

158

UHLER (continued)
George Bryan
Peter G. & Martha Ann Veitch, Sept. 21, 1842 – bdsm: Peter G. Uhler, William C. Reynolds
UNIE, Arthur T. & Elizabeth Howard, April 2, 1823 – bdsm: Arthur T. Unie, Stephen Shin
UPHAM, Giles & Ann Jenkins, Oct. 23, 1823 – bdsm: Giles Upham, George Douglas Cawood
VACCHARI, Frederick & Rosa Pearson, Sept. 17, 1823 – bdsm: Frederick Vacchari, John Brown (See also: Viecharia)
VAIS, Anthony & Sarah Stewart, March 25, 1816 – bdsm: Anthony Vais, Bennett Murrell
Van NESS, David & Julia Ann Eliza Yeaton, May 18, 1824 – bdsm: David Van Ness, William Yeaton
Van SOHNGEN, Henry & Siloam Hill (daughter of Laurence Hill), Sept. 2, 1828 – bdsm: Henry Van Sohngen, Laurence Hill
VANASSE, Ignatius & Cecelia Page, Oct. 10, 1838 – bdsm: Ignatius Vanasse, John Epps
VANSANT, James & Elizabeth Abercrombie, Oct. 31, 1816 – bdsm: James Vansant, Robert Abercrombie
VAUGHN, David & Sally Frazier, April 19, 1814 – bdsm: David Vaughn, James B. Edwards
VEITCH, E. R. & Elizabeth M. Chins, March 5, 1835 –

VEITCH (continued)
bdsm: E. R. Veitch, William C. Reynolds
William & Mary Johnston, Dec. 5, 1843 – bdsm: William Veitch, William C. Reynolds
William Conn & Sarah Childs, Nov. 15, 1827 – bdsm: William Conn Veitch, Sarah Childs
VERNEL, George & Salley Purkis, July 23, 1807 – bdsm: George Vernel, Thomas Purkis, Beale Howard
VERNON, James & Mary Ann Spencer, Sept. 2, 1847 – bdsm: James Vernon, Benjamin F. Dudley
William T. & Sarah E. Jefferson, Dec. 30, 1824 – bdsm: William T. Vernon, Warner M. Hilliard
VIOLETT, Edwin R. & Harriott E. Baggett, Nov. 15, 1845 – bdsm: Edwin R. Violett
William D. & Cloe Ann Armstrong, Feb. 28, 1832 – bdsm: William D. Violett, James E. Mankins
VOWELL, Ebenezer & Eliza Orme, Oct. 12, 1813 – bdsm: Ebenezer Vowell, Thomas Vowell
John Cripps & Mary Jacqueline Taylor, Dec. 5, 1810 – bdsm: John Cripps Vowell
Thomas & Elizabeth Mills, May 26, 1842 – bdsm: Thomas Vowell, John L. Pascoe
WADDELL, John & Lucia C. Porter, Aug. 24, 1835 –

WADDELL (continued)
bdsm: John Waddell, William Yeaton
WADDY, Thomas & Eliza Walker, May 12, 1841 – bdsm: Thomas Waddey, John Young
Thomas & Elizabeth Cox, July 22, 1829 – bdsm: Thomas Waddy, Wm. B. Cox
WADE, Hiram & Mary Bennett (free people of colour), Sept. 17, 1846 – bdsm: Hiram Wade, John Harris
Robert & Celestial Jane Cook, June 30, 1841 – bdsm: Robert Wade, Theodore Cook
Robert of Charles County, Maryland, & Elizabeth Smallwood, Jan. 17, 1811 – bdsm: Robert Wade, Elijah Marine
WADSWORTH, Charles & Elizabeth Faris, April 15, 1806 – bdsm: Charles Wadsworth, Elisha C. Dick
WAIGLEY, George & Ann Murray, April 2, 1830 – bdsm: George Waigley, Ignatius Murray
WALDEM, Thomas & Kitty Stentsman, Oct. 27, 1803 – bdsm: Thomas Walden, Garnett Haden
WALKER, Edward & Elizabeth A. Legg, July 31, 1823 – bdsm: Edward Walker, Rice C. Ballard (Married July 31, 1823 by Rev. O. Norris)
James & Ann Martin, March 29, 1823 – bdsm: John A.

WALKER (continued)
Spiden, James Walker
James & Elizabeth Wilson, July 30, 1810 – bdsm: James Walker, Simon Thomas
James & Kitty Wise, Nov. 11, 1813 – bdsm: James Walker, John Smith
John & Sarah Smith, April 25, 1822 – bdsm: John Walker, John Smith
Levin & Margaret Williams, Jan. 30, 1806 – bdsm: Levin Walker, John Bright
Reginald W. & Julia Ann Jacob, Oct. 24, 1850 – bdsm:
Robert & Sally Adams, March 23, 1805 – bdsm: Robert Walker, Ephraim Mills
William J. & Martha Javins, Nov. 16, 1846 – bdsm: William J. Walker, Thomas Norflet
WALKOM, Jonathan & Elizabeth Rowe, Nov. 15, 1820 – bdsm: Jonathan Walkom, Wm. Pomery (Married same day by Rev. O. Norris)
WALLACE, James & Eliza Fugett, Dec. 23, 1844 – bdsm: James Wallace, Robert Taylor
James & Susanna Mary Ann Douglass, Dec. 3, 1805 – bdsm: James Wallace, Charles Douglass
Jonathan & Hepsabah Martha Dodds, May 27, 1818 – bdsm: Jonathan Wallace, Isaac Entwisle
Richard & Elizabeth Hurst, June 2, 1831 – bdsm: Ri-

160

WALLACE (continued)
chard Wallace, Elizabeth Hurst
Richard & Sarah Griffith, June 26, 1816 - bdsm: Richard Wallace, Edward Tyler
Thomas & Tobitha Glanders, Jan. 19, 1804 - bdsm: Thomas Wallace, John Armstrong
William & Elizabeth Henning, Sept. 15, 1827 - bdsm: William Wallace, Edward Hart
William J. & Caroline J. Hoff, June 11, 1851 - bdsm:
WALLACH, Richard & Nancy Simms, March 2, 1813 - bdsm: Richard Wallach, John D. Simms
WANNALL, Thomas & May Roberts, May 24, 1816 - bdsm: Thomas Wannall, John Graham
WANSCHA, Martin & Elizabeth Kelly, May 20,1801 - bdsm: Vincent Kelly, Martin Wanscha
WARD, Enoch & Mary Ann Evans, Jan. 25, 1842 - bdsm: Enoch Ward, Willis Henderson
James & Hepsey Swallow, Aug. 3, 1815 - bdsm: James Ward, William Ballenger
James & Lucy Coates, March 21, 1821 - bdsm: James Ward, Ewell Rust
James & Prudence Myers, May 20, 1809 - bdsm: James Ward, Richard Lewis
John W. & Henrietta Carlin,

WARD (continued)
May 21, 1834 - bdsm: Frederick A. Koones, James McKenzie
Jonathan & Sarah Bealle, Jan. 15, 1818 - bdsm: Jonathan Ward, William Lewis
Lewis & Eleanor Lambkin & Jan. 21, 1830 - bdsm: Lewis Ward, Alexander Ardrey
Lewis & Sarah Marston, Sept. 4, 1830 - bdsm: Lewis Ward, Joseph Maskel
Thomas & Ann Young, Dec. 23, 1809 - bdsm: Thomas Ward, Jacob Heineman
William & Anna Dodds, June 10, 1818 - bdsm: William Ward, Joseph Dodds
William & Georgana Kerby, July 2, 1840 - bdsm: William Ward, Willis Henderson
William & Louisa D. Cook, March 3 1842 - bdsm: William Ward, Theo. Cook
WARDER, Richard Henry & Mary Ann Ratcliffe, daughter of Richard B. Ratcliffe, Feb. 26, 1848 - bdsm: Richard Henry Warder, Richard B. Ratcliffe
WARING, Francis & Frances Sincox, June 25, 1850 - bdsm: Francis Waring, Vincent S&nell
WARNER, John & Phebe London, July 6, 1842 - bdsm: John Warner, Samuel Williams
Samuel & Polly Reedy, July

161

WARNER (continued)
18, 1805 – bdsm: Samuel Warner, Alexander Dunbar
WASHINGTON, George & Elizabeth Hartley, July 25, 1811 – bdsm: George Washington, Robert P. Washington
Richard C. & Sophia M. Roberts, Jan. 8, 1829 – bdsm: Richard C. Washington, John Roberts
William & Rebecca W. Cracroft, July 21, 1814 – bdsm: William H. Washington, Robert J. Taylor
William H. & Rebecca W. Cracroft, July 21, 1824 – bdsm: none
WATERHOUSE, Elias B. & Alice Cartright, Feb. 5, 1818 – bdsm: Elias B. Waterhouse, James Lawrason
WATERS, Benjamin G. & Lucy J. Berkley, Jan. 17, 1843 – bdsm: Benjamin G. Waters, Reuben Zimmerman
George & Susan Calbut, Sept. 18, 1840 – bdsm: George Waters, James Jack
Jonathan M. & Maria Beckby (Beckly?), March 30, 1825 – bdsm: Jonathan M. Waters, Henry Lomax
Thomas A. & Sarah L. Wilson, Oct. 30, 1839 – bdsm: Thomas A. Waters, George H. Smoot
WATKINS, Robert & Eliza Tate, Sept. 12, 1809 – bdsm: Robert Watkins, Peter Piles
Thomas & Mary Williams,

WATKINS (continued)
Dec. 11, 1812 – bdsm: Thomas Watkins, Jacob Heineman
William T. & Mary Elizabeth Benter, July 29, 1841 – bdsm: William T. Watkins, James M. Watkins
WATSON, Cornelius & Harriet Hunter, Dec. 1, 1839 – bdsm: Cornelius Watson, Richard Bowles
John & Caroline E. Keefer, Jan. 9, 1830 – bdsm: John Watson, William A. Davis
Thomas & Anna M. Daniel, Jan. 14, 1818 – bdsm: Thomas Watson, Dozier Bennett
William & Elizabeth Uhler, Nov. 19, 1806 – bdsm: William Watson, Lewis Simpson
William S. & Julia Ann Nevitt, Nov. 14, 1836 – bdsm: William S. Watson, James P. Middleton
WATTLES, Nathaniel & Sarah Smith, Sept. 25, 1811 – bdsm: Nathaniel Wattles, Hugh W. Deneale
WAUGH, Albert P. & Rachell Atwell, Sept. 19, 1821 – bdsm: Albert P. Waugh, John Potten
Alexander & Mary T. Bucky, May 8, 1832 – bdsm: Alex. Waugh, Phares Throop
James Jr. & Nancy Hooe, May 12, 1814 – bdsm: James Waugh, Jr., Townshend Waugh
John Thomas & Mary E. Brooks, May 2, 1840 – bdsm: John Thomas

WAUGH (continued)
Waugh, Daniel H. Smith
Townsend & Rachel Judge,
June 15, 1813 - bdsm:
Townsend Waugh, Jacob
Hoffman
WAY, Frederick & Elizabeth
Shortell, Nov. 27, 1806 -
bdsm: Frederick Way,
Thomas Cooke, Margaret
Shortell
WEAVER, Emanuel & Eliza
Wilson* (see below), Nov.
18, 1823 - bdsm: Emanuel
Weaver, Alexander Bryan
*Emanuel & Eliza Watson,
Nov. 18, 1823 - (second
certificate)
Jacob & Virginia P. Preston,
June 27, 1849 - bdsm:
Jacob Weaver, Benjamin
Waters
William & Juliann Lee,
April 15, 1823 - bdsm:
William Weaver, John
Harris
William & Letty Hines, July
4, 1838 - bdsm: William
Weaver, Samuel Agee
WEBB, James & Mary
Prichard, April 11, 1805 -
bdsm: James Webb,
James Armitage
John W. & Emily Jacobs,
June 2, 1835 - bdsm: John
W. Webb, Presley Jacobs
WEBSTER, Adam L. & Sarah
H. Hand, Nov. 2, 1810 -
bdsm: Adam L. Webster,
Hugh W. Deneale
Armstead & Liddy Murray,
Jan. 2, 1822 - bdsm:
Armstead Webster, George
Murray (Married Jan. 2,
1822 by Rev. O. Norris)
James & Letiha Edwards,

WEBSTER (continued)
Nov. 14, 1838 - bdsm:
James Webster, Richard
Bowles
John B. & Sarah Latham,
June 21, 1817 - bdsm:
John B. Webster, William
Latham
WEDGE, James & Ann
Brookes, June 13, 1820 -
bdsm: James Wedge, Wil-
liam Gibbs
WEEDON, Clement & Ann
Maria Hancock, Nov. 14,
1839 - bdsm: Clement
Weedon, John B. Hancock
WEEKS, Robert & Sarah
Gasper, March 23, 1824 -
bdsm: Robert Weeks, Ed-
ward McLaughlin
WEEMS, Jesse & Nancy O.
Rickard, June 23, 1818 -
bdsm: Jesse E. Weems,
Charles Slade
WEEVER, John & Eleanor
Roberts, Feb. 20, 1806 -
bdsm: John Weever, John
Dixon
WEIR, Philip Henry given
permission to marry by P.
H. Hooff, Oct. 15, 1851 -
bdsm: none given (Weir
was a servant)
WELCH, Robert A. & Olivia
Green, Jan. 14, 1832 -
bdsm: Robert A. Welch,
John F. Green
WELLS, James M. & Mary
Ann Waygly, Aug. 16,
1838 - bdsm: James M.
Wells, William Wells
William & Sarah Sawkins,
May 21, 1811 - bdsm:
William Wells, James
Campbell (Also: Sarah
Hawkins)

WELSH, John & Ann Davis, May 11, 1833 - bdsm: John Welsh, James Davis

WENSHIER, Martin & Margaret Charles, June 19, 1807 - bdsm: Martin Wenshier, Thomas Mezarvey

WEST, Francis & Clara Jackson, Dec. 22, 1815 - bdsm: Francis West, George Russell

James & Sarah Dudley, Dec. 26, 1827 - bdsm: James West, James Dudley

Jeremiah & Eleanor Ann Swann, July ? 1832 - bdsm: Jeremiah West, John S. Swann

Martin & Catherine Burger, Oct. 27, 1831 - bdsm: Martin West

William Henry & Gertrude Moss Minor, July 29, 1841 - bdsm: William Henry West, Daniel Minor

WEYMOUTH, John & Sarah Forrest, May 18, 1825 - bdsm: John Weymouth, Sarah Forrest

WHALEY, David L. & Jennet Darne, Oct. 10, 1834 - bdsm: David L. Whaley, George Whaley

James & Harriot Gooding, Feb. 15, 1812 - bdsm: James Whaley, John Gooding

WHARTON, William A. & Virginia Scott, Oct. 28, 1844 - bdsm: William A. Wharton, Virginia Scott

WHEAT, John J. & Emily E. Dixion, Nov. 1, 1842 - bdsm: John J. Wheat, Benoni Wheat

John Thomas & Selena Pat-

WHEAT (continued)
ten, March 10, 1825 - bdsm: John Thomas Wheat, Thomas Wheat

William & Molly Fagins, June 7, 1804 - bdsm: William Wheat, William Armstrong

WHEATLEY, James H. & Selina A. J. Smith, July 29, 1835 - bdsm: James H. Wheatley, Thomas Smith

WHEELER, Ephraim & Martha E. Creighton, March 23, 1836 - bdsm: Ephraim Wheeler, John Creighton

Jabez & Louisa M. B. Meade, March 5, 1836 - bdsm: Jabez Wheeler, James P. Middleton

Richard & Elizabeth Hammontree, Nov. 20, 1810 - bdsm: Richard Wheeler, Alexander Bickerton

Samuel & Jane Summers, July 24, 1817 - bdsm: Samuel Wheeler, John C. Mandell

Samuel & Sarah Parsons, Dec. 19, 1803 - bdsm: Samuel Wheeler, Lewis Summers

Samuel & Winifred Winkfield, Aug. 14, 1805 - bdsm: Samuel Wheeler, John Brownal

Thomas & Catharine Lucas, Sept. 16, 1816 - bdsm: Thomas Wheeler, John Parlrere

Thomas & Hester B. Bryan, March 3, 1835 - bdsm: Thomas Wheeler, Bernard Bryan

William & Mary Caroline

WHEELER (continued)
Coxe, June 27, 1837 – bdsm: William Wheeler, Samuel H. Devaughn

WHEELWRIGHT, John & Caroline Eliza Payson, Sept. 7, 1815 – bdsm: John Wheelwright, Joseph Aubin

WHITE, Edward D. & Catharine S. L. Ringgold, Sept. 17, 1834 – bdsm: Edward D. White, George Brent

Gilbert & Ann M. Gloster, Sept. 16, 1845 – bdsm: Gilbert White, James N. Gloster

James C. & Elizabeth Bluffield, Feb. 8, 1816 – bdsm: James C. White, William Morgan

John & Mary Hill, June 2, 1804 – bdsm: John White, George Hill

Joseph H. & Martha Mandell, Jan. 3, 1827 – bdsm: Joseph H. White, John C. Mandell

Rezin & Faithy Cole, Dec. 11, 1815 – bdsm: Rezin White, George Russell

Samuel B. & Ann Hutcheson, Nov. 11, 1815 – bdsm: Samuel B. White, Thomas Potts

Thomas & Ann Haily, Feb. 10, 1803 – bdsm: Thomas White, James Sheely

Thomas M. & Marian Wood, Aug. 23, 1828 – bdsm: Thomas M. White, John Wood (guardian of Marian Wood)

Vachel & Mary Ann Callendes, Jan. 10, 1826 – bdsm: Vachel White,

WHITE (continued)
Gabriel Bradley

WHITING, Fabius & Louisa T. Yeaton, Dec. 1, 1821 – bdsm: Fabius Whiting, William G. Cranch (Married Dec. 3, 1821 by Rev. O. Norris)

Fairfax W. & Margaret Douglas, Sept. 11, 1843 – bdsm: Fairfax H. Whiting, John Douglas

WHITMORE, James H. & Maria A. Simpkins, Dec. 24, 1846 – bdsm: James H. Whitmore, B. Hooe

WHITTINGTON, Thomas & Margaret C. Dearborn, Dec. 28, 1825 – bdsm: Thomas Whittington, Simon Dearborn

WHITTLE, Thomas & Mary Buckland, Dec. 5, 1816 – bdsm: Thomas Whittle, Adam Lynn

WIGART, Andrew & Sally Davis, Oct. 28, 1807 – bdsm: Andrew Wigart, James Birch

WIGGS, John & Elizabeth Foreman, Sept. 5, 1833 – bdsm: John Wiggs, Samuel Simmons

John & Sarah Leary, Feb. 19, 1829 – bdsm: John Wiggs, Daniel Wright

WILBAR, John & Sarah Perry, July 9, 1816 – bdsm: John Wilbar, Alexander Perry

WILCOX, Anthony & Phebe Lacock, April 23, 1811 – bdsm: Anthony Evans, Charles Peterson

WILDER, Henry C. & Mary A. Woolls, Nov. 26, 1834

WILDER (continued)
- bdsm: Henry C. Wilder,
John Waddy
WILEY, Ephraim & Phillis
Hessen, July 22, 1802 -
bdsm: Ephraim & William
Wilson
Hugh G. & Mary Wright,
Feb. 6, 1816 - bdsm: Hugh
G. Wiley, James Potter
Jesse & Anne Hicks, Feb.
12, 1814 - bdsm: Jesse
Wiley, William Hicks
Littleton & Margaret Dea-
kins, June 25, 1803 -
bdsm: Littleton Wiley,
Ambrose Deakins, George
Wiley
Thomas & Elizabeth Gatis,
May 2, 1844 - bdsm:
Thomas Wiley, James
Javins
WILKINSON, N. Berry & Sa-
rah Ann Bahtman, Oct. 12,
1831 - bdsm: N. Berry
Wilkinson, John T.
Humphreys (Also: Batman)
WILLIAMS, Charles & Mary
Tenley, Dec. 8, 1828 -
bdsm: Charles Williams,
Robert Williams
Daniel & Maria Derrick,
April 5, 1848 - bdsm:
Daniel Williams, John M.
Turley
Evan & Ann Seldon, May 16,
1816 - bdsm: Evan Wil-
liams, George Russell
George & Betsy Beckley,
Feb. 25, 1825 - bdsm:
George Williams, John
Beckley
George & Betsy Beckly,
Feb. 25, 1824 - bdsm:
Harry & Eleanor Williams,
September 10, 1805 -

WILLIAMS (continued)
bdsm: Harry Williams,
Bernard Bryan
Henry & Elizabeth Boyer,
Oct. 27, 1806 - bdsm:
Henry Williams, John
Boyer
Hiram & Matilda W. Simms,
Dec. 21, 1820 - bdsm:
Hiram O. Williams (Cel-
ebrated Dec. 21, 1820 by
Rev. Oliver Norris)
John & Elizabeth Baggott,
Jan. 21, 1804 - bdsm:
John Williams, Alexander
Williams
Joseph & Elizabeth Knight,
June 3, 1822 - bdsm:
Joseph Williams, John
Brassington
Joseph & Priscilla Darnell,
Jan. 26, 1830 - bdsm:
Joseph Williams, Gus-
tavus Gibson
Peter & Sally Hutchins, May
10, 1833 - bdsm: Peter
Williams, George Sisson
Presly & Nelly Robinson,
Jan. 25, 1803 - bdsm:
Presly Williams, Jesse
Robinson
Robert & Nancy Martin,
April 13, 1842 - bdsm:
Robert Williams, William
Powell
Thomas & Ann Wilkins,
Aug. 22, 1818 - bdsm:
Thomas Williams, Mi-
chael Henrity
Thomas M. & Eliz. M.
Johnson, March 29, 1838 -
bdsm: Thomas M. Wil-
liams, Eliz. M. Johnson
Vincent & Chloe Selick,
Dec. 29, 1832 - bdsm:
Vincent Williams, John

WILLIAMS (continued)
Barker

Wilkinson & Mary Nash (daughter of Jane Nash), Nov. 29, 1832 - bdsm: Wilkinson Williams, Jane Nash

William & Sarah Davis, Jan. 19, 1810 - bdsm: William Williams, Alexander Williams

William A. & Ann Esleeck, June 1, 1835 - bdsm: William A. Williams, John W. King

William L. & Polly Winterberry, August 24, 1810 - bdsm: William L. Wilson, John Winterberry

WILLIAMSON, Philip D. & Mary M. Vowell, Jan. 9, 1823 - bdsm: Philip D. Williamson & Norman R Fitzhugh

WILLIANS, Gustavus & Matilda Fox, Sept. 25, 1842 - bdsm: Gustavus Willans, Tristam H. Gardner

WILLIS, Abel & Mary Ann Clusom, Dec. 14, 1813 - bdsm: Abel Willis, Henry Nicholson

WILLS, John & Ailsey Thomas, March 12, 1816 - bdsm: John Wills, William Thomas

John C. & Catharine Duffey, Dec. 9, 1847 - bdsm: John C. Wills, George Duffey

WILMER, William H. & Ann Brice Fitzhugh, Feb. 5, 1823 - bdsm: William H. Wilmer, Jacob Morgan (Married by Rev. O. Norris)

WILSON, Charles & Julia

WILSON (continued)
Ware, daughter of Kinsay Ware, July 24, 1850 - bdsm: Charles Wilson, Thomas M. McCormick

Jacob & Louisa Swann, May 21, 1844 - bdsm: Jacob Wilson, John H. Griffith

Jacob H. & Elizabeth B. Hills, Nov. 22, 1831 - bdsm: Jacob H. Wilson, Josiah B. Hills

James & Alice Fletcher, May 29, 1811 - bdsm: James Wilson, George Russell

John & Ann McFarlane, Feb. 26, 1840 - bdsm: John Wilson

Nathaniel K. & Elizabeth Moulds, July 24, 1801 - bdsm: Nathaniel K. Wilson, Wm. P. Patterson

Oliver & Mary Heineman, March 25, 1810 - bdsm: Oliver Wilson, Jacob Heineman

Richard & Fanny B. B. Coffer, April 18, 1812 - bdsm: Richard Wilson, Lyle Millan

Robert J. T. & Mary Elizabeth Ricketts, Dec. 24, 1828 - bdsm: Robert J. T. Wilson, George P. Wise

Thomas of Baltimore & Mary Cruse of Alexandria County, May 6, 1815 - bdsm: Thomas Wilson, Thomas Cruse

William & Catharine Glover, April 15, 1820 - bdsm: William Wilson, Zephaniah S. Wade

William & Deborah Chis-

WILSON (continued)
sell, May 7, 1811 - bdsm: William Wilson, John Thompson
William & Flora E. Morgan (free persons of colour), Nov. 4, 1841 - bdsm: William Wilson, John L. Harris
William Jr. & Ann Carson, Aug. 19, 1806 - bdsm: William Wilson, Samuel Carson
William K. & Anne E. Wise, Sept. 13, 1842 - bdsm: William K. Wilson, Robert Jamieson
WINDSOR, R. & Ann M. Lowe, Oct. 18, 1821 - bdsm: R. Windsor, Philip Hooff (Married Oct. 18, 1821 by Rev. O. Norris)
Robert N. & Sarah Ann H. Sheppard, Dec. 18, 1809 - bdsm: Robert N. Windsor, Eliza Taylor
William & Susanna Snell, March 10, 1802 - bdsm: William Windsor, James Gale
WINN, Timothy & Rebecca Dulany, March 7, 1811 - bdsm: Timothy Winn, Silus Butler
WINTER, Gabriel & Sarah Ann Peyton, March 17, 1818 - bdsm: Gabriel Winter, James H. Blake, Jr.
WISE, George & Ann Kirby, July 1, 1824 - bdsm: George Wise, John Kirby
George & Elizabeth Miller, Jan. 10, 1814 - bdsm: George Wise, John Boyer, Jr.
George & Margaret Greer,

WISE (continued)
April 9, 1817 - bdsm: George Wise, William Dunlap
George & Martha Newton, April 16, 1801 - bdsm: George Wise, Wm. Newton
George & Martha P. Brooks, Nov. 13, 1845 - bdsm: George Wise, Jesse Sherwood
George Carr & Ann Fulton, July 23, 1801 - bdsm: George Carr Wise, Thomas Clarke
George P. & Sarah Ann Newton, March 11, 1829 - bdsm: George P. Wise, Joseph L. Sanford
Joseph & Elizabeth Fry, July 28, 1804 - bdsm: Joseph Wise, John Duffy, combmaker
Thomas & Linney Piles, July 3, 1804 - bdsm: Thomas Wise, William Wroe
WITHERS, Addison L. & Frances T. Buckey, May 16, 1829 - bdsm: Addison L. Withers, John Buckey
WIZER, Thomas & Nancy Riordan, April 3, 1806 - bdsm: Thomas Wizer, Thomas White, Jr.
WOLFE, Dr. Thomas of Frederick County & Mary Ann Patten of Alexandria County, May 14, 1816 - bdsm:
WOOD, Benjamin & Elizabeth Hartley, April 16, 1812 - bdsm: Benjamin Wood, John Boyer
Elijah & Sarah Western,

WOOD (continued)
April 16, 1812 – bdsm: Elijah Wood, Jacob Hookes
James & Margaret Turner, June 25, 1823 – bdsm: James Wood, Joseph T. Hallowell (Married June 25, 1823 by Rev. O. Norris)
John & Elizabeth Fig, Dec. 2, 1801 – bdsm: John Wood, Bennett Raley
John & Elizabeth Myers, Mar. 21, 1810 – bdsm: John Wood, William Smith
John & Jemima Davis, Dec. 30, 1811 – bdsm: John Wood, Thomas Tattershell
John & Mary Coats, March 11, 1824 – bdsm: John Wood, Ewell Russ
Richard & Catharine Baggett, April 23, 1810 – bdsm: Richard Wood, Thomas L. Griffin
Richard D. & Mary Jane Anderson, March 3, 1845 – bdsm: Richard D. Wood, William Padgett
William & Eliza Parsons, Sept. 3, 1801 – bdsm: William Wood, James H. Hamilton
William & Susan Key Bond, Oct. 22, 1818 – bdsm: William Wood, Lewis Hoff
WOODDY, Samuel & Mary Williams, daughter of Henry Williams (persons of colour), Oct. 20, 1847 – bdsm: Samuel Wooddy, Henry Williams
WOODWARD, Joseph &

WOODWARD (continued)
Catharine Oliver, Nov. 10, 1816 – bdsm: Joseph Woodward, Thomas Carlton
WORDEN, Marmix & Sarah Curry, Sept. 5, 1825 – bdsm: Marmix Worden, Hugh M. Logan
WORTHAM, William & Mary Ann Skinner, March 15, 1841 – bdsm: William Wortham, John T. Ballenger
WORTHAN, William & Nancy Ann Patterson, June 14, 1836 – bdsm: William Worthan, Simon Dearborn
WORTHINGTON, Isaac & Catherine Rease, Jan. 27, 1821 – bdsm: Isaac Worthington, James Atkinson (Married Jan. 27, 1821 by Rev. O. Norris)
Joseph & Sarah Young, Nov. 10, 1825 – bdsm: Joseph Worthington, Robert H. Miller
WREN, James & Sarah Jones, March 4, 1805 – bdsm: James Wren, George Deneale
WRIGHT, George & Charlotte Copper, Nov. 11, 1815 – bdsm: George Wright, Joseph Nevitt
Harrison D. & Charlotte V. Douglass, Jan. 9, 1839 – bdsm: Harrison. D. Wright, Reuben Johnston, Jr.
James & Margaret Piper, Nov. 27, 1817 – bdsm: James Wright, Henry Brown
Richard & Emily M. Hor-

WRIGHT (continued)
well, March 1, 1828 –
bdsm: Richard Wright, Richard Horwell

Thomas A. & Mary Crawford, Sept. 30, 1835 –
bdsm: Thomas A. Wright, John Crawford

William & Elizabeth Conner, April 9, 1803 – bdsm: Wm. Wright, George Appleby

Zachariah & Jane Lane, Feb. 18, 1832 – bdsm: Zachariah Wright, John Dudlap

WYLEE, Andrew Jr. & Mary Caroline Bryan, March 6, 1845 – bdsm: Andrew Wylee, Jr., Daniel Bryan

YEARLY, Nathaniel & Elizabeth Smith, March 30, 1807 – bdsm: Nathaniel Yearly, Bennett Reily

Nathaniel & Nancy Boothe, July 3, 1820 – bdsm: Nathaniel Yearly, David Dicks

YOUNG, John of Alexandria County & Mary Davis of Alexandria County, June 17, 1807 – bdsm: John Young , Jacob Wisemiller

William & Ellen Sullivan, June 9, 1815 – bdsm: William Young, James Vansant

YOUST, Hiram & Nancy Brent, Sept. 19, 1825 – bdsm: Hiram Youst, Aaron R. Musgrave

ZIMMERMAN, Adam & Sarah E. Simpson, Dec. 18, 1817 – bdsm: Adam Zimmerman, John Simpson

George & Ann Simpson, Aug.

ZIMMERMAN (continued)
23, 1806 – bdsm: George Zimmerman, John Gooding

Jacob & Emily Frederick, July 8, 1829 – bdsm: Jacob Zimmerman, Lewis Hipkins

Jacob & Jane Smith, March 21, 1810 – bdsm: Jacob Zimmerman, James Gullatt

Reuben & Mary A. E. Waters, March 1, 1836 – bdsm: Reuben Zimmerman, Benjamin Waters

INDEX

ABBOTT, Ann 21 102
ABERCROMBIE, Elizabeth 159
   Elizabeth L 41 Martha Alice
   117 Mary 119 Robert 62 119
   159 Susan 73
ABERCRUMBIE, Robert 102
ADAM, Jane 10 72 Jane S 64 John
   64 72
ADAMS, Andrew H 45 Benj 61
   George R 51 79 Harriet S 48
   Jane Eliza 101 Jane S 8 Julia
   Ann 38 151 Leonard 48 59 141
   151 Margaret 7 61 Nancy 116
   Sally 67 160
ADGATE, Mary 143 Phebe 26
   Phoebe 116
ADGETE, Mary 36
AGEE, Samuel 163
AKTINSON, James W 70
ALDERY, Nancy 120
ALDISDESTON, Thomas 152
ALEXANDER, Amos 67 Ann 63
   Frances 39 153 James 104
   John 157 Marianna T S 54 Mar-
   tha 130 Mary F 105 Robert 63
ALFRED, John L 76
ALLAN, Ignatius 99 Julia Ann 99
ALLBRITTON, John 46
ALLEN, Edwin T 107 129 Hannah
   Ann 73 Ignatius 67 99 James
   120 131 147 Julia Ann 20 99
   Kyrle 107 Lucretia 26 Maria
   108 Mary 91 Matilda 21 101
   Sarah 131
ALLISON, Elizabeth 35 141 Har-
   riet 119 James 65 105 Rebecca
   65 Robert 104 William 133
ANDERSON, Alexander 74
   Caroline M 143 Frances Ann
   60 Francis Ann 7 Henry 143
   James 49 50 James H 81 Lou-

ANDERSON (continued)
   isa 118 Margaret 31 131 Mary
   Jane 169 Nancy 68 Robert 68
   123 148 Sandford 50 William
   60 61
ANDREWS, Jacob 113 Marie C 61
ANGEL, Elizabeth 65
ANNESS, Elizabeth 5 57
ANSWORTH, Wm 56
APPICH, David 58 83 90 114 139
   Mary Ann 58
APPLEBY, George 170
ARBINOE, A Louisa 52
ARDREY, Alexander 161
ARMITAGE, James 52 65 163
   Sarah 7 63
ARMSTRONG, Cloe Ann 159
   Elizabeth 31 129 Fanny 103
   Isabella 7 John 161 John J 47
   John T 97 Julia Ann 20 99
   Samuel 64 100 134 Susanna 21
   101 William 164
ARNOLD, Elizabeth 29 Martha 60
   William 158 Wm 47
ARRINGTON, Alfred 132 Eunice
   15 85
ARSHCOME, James 59
ARTHUR, Thomas 107
ASHBY, Bettie S 29 Turner W 83
ASHFORD, William 73
ASHROD, Louisa 73
ASHTON, Benjamin C 54
   Elizabeth G 28 121 Frances 18
   92 Margaret 68 Rachael 58
   Rachel 5 Verlinda 15 85
ASKER, Jane V 35
ASKIN, Ann M 32 132 Jane V 142
ATKINS, Sarah 30 127
ATKINSON, Charles 150 James
   48 139 169 Mary C 37 Mary
   Charlton 150 Ruth Ann 48

171

172

BAWLER, William 52
BAXTER, Polly 1 47
BAYLE, Lucy 9
BAYLESS, William 102
BAYLEY, Betsey 57 Elizabeth 69
   Lydia 69 Sarah 126
BAYLISS, Daniel 142 Edward 76
   Matilda 72 Robert 140 Sarah M
   8 65 William 72
BAYLY, Mountjoy Jr 141
BAYNE, Catharine B 59 Eb-
   bsworth 83 Henry 83 98 John
   143
BEACH, James 83 Nathaniel 155
   Samuel 51 76
BEACHAM, Nathaniel 82
BEADLE, Elizabeth 36 143
BEALL, Aquila 108
BEALLE, Sarah 41 161
BEAN, Jane 32 Jane B 131
BEANE, Ann E 72
BEARCROFT, Dommick 68 Sally
   85
BEATLY, Sarah 38 150
BECKBY, Maria 162
BECKLEY, Betsy 166 Jesse 73
   John 108 146 166 John A 108
   Mary Ann 73
BECKLY, Betsy 166 Maria 162
BEECH, Rebecca 147
BEEDLE, Eliza Ann 3 51
BEELER, Louis 76 84
BEERFORD, Elizabth 156
BEERS, William R 108
BEITELS, Cordelia E 155 Cor-
   delia Ellen 39
BELCHER, Elizabeth 10
BELEHER, Elizabeth 70
BELL, Amy 93 Andrew 78 Andrew
   T 148 Dolly 72 Elizabeth 22 99
   Henry 85 Precilla 15 Prescilla
   85 Robert 105 Robert H 136
BELLFORD, Ann 39 153
BENNETT, Dozier 115 162
   Elizabeth 9 67 Hannah 79 Julia
   131 Lucy 139 Martha 115 Mary
   160 Milly 4 54 Richard 79
BENNOT, Francis see BURNET,
   Francis 7
BENSON, Ann 146
BENTER, Elizabeth 42 Mary 4 55
   Mary Elizabeth 162 Susanna

BENTER (continued)
   153 Westley 151 William 55
   102
BENTLEY, Nilson 88
BENTON, Adeline 93 Elizabeth
   75
BEOKLY, Jane Eliza 6
BERKLEY, Lucy J 42 162 Maria
   E 126
BERREY, John 98
BERRY, Ann 85 Ann Eliza 18 B H
   87 Bayne S 3 52 Benj H 83 94
   Benjamin 93 143 Benjamin H
   66 126 Catharine S 72
   Elizabeth 3 52 Jane 20
   Julianna 72 Marian L 122
   Marion L 29 Mary 113 Mercer
   A 87 Nathan E 122 Rebecca S
   2 48 Richard 46 Sarah F 35
   Sarah Jane 6 61 Thomas 72
   157
BEST, Susan 10 71
BETTS, Edward 61
BETZOLD, Daric 115 Frederick
   47 Louisa C 26 Louisa
   Catharine 115
BICKERTON, Alexander 164
BIERS, William R 146
BIGGS, Sophia Ann 10 69
BILLINGSLY, Mary Jane 6 59
BINES, Rebecca 158
BIRCH, Albina 2 48 Elizabeth 77
   James 52 77 102 165 Sarah E
   102 Thomas 49 William 48
BISBEY, Sarah Ellen 1
BISBY, Sarah E 45
BISHOP, Ann 145 Eliza 135
   Joshua W 145
BLACK, Eliza 107 Jane Eliza 144
   Mary 1 46
BLACKLOCK, Elisabeth C 85
   Jane A 117 Maria 13 78
BLACKWELL, Lewis 131
BLADEN, Augustine 150 Dorothy
   38 150
BLAKE, James H Jr 168
BLAKELEIG, Aliddy 14
BLAKENEY, Liddia 82
BLAND, ELizabeth 37 Elizabeth
   149
BLINCOE, Charles W 149
BLOXHAM, Agnes 98 James 125

173

BLUE, Elizabeth 58 Henry see
    BRENT, Henry 5 Jane S 78
    John 58 135 John J 78 131
BLUFFIELD, Elizabeth 42 165
BLUNT, Joseph B 80 Sarah 17 91
BOGAN, Elizabeth 36 146 John
    68 90 146 Mary 25 112
BOGWELL, Sally 152
BOLDS, Richard 126
BOLEN, Martha 6 59
BOLLING, Polly 11 73
BOND, Susan Key 44 169 William
    89
BONNER, Robert 124
BONSALL, John 45
BONTZ, Amelia 143 Ann 3 53
    Catharine 33 135 Elizabeth 22
    51 Jacob 45 135 John 127 147
    Julia Carolina 127 Mary A 1 45
BOONE, Elizabeth 156
BOOTH, Sarah 9 67 133
BOOTHE, Ann 24 111 Helen Ann
    M 89 Nancy 44 170
BOOTS, Sarah 32
BORROWDALE, Bridget 14 82
BOSWELL, Lewis 89 Louisa 8 66
BOTTS, Kitty 78
BOWDEN, Celia 142
BOWDON, Sarah J 109
BOWIE, Alice A 135 Alice M 33
    Benjamin 103 David 61-63
    Davis 66 99 106 148 151
    Elizabeth 9 67 James 99 Maria
    37 Mary H 37 148 Reubin 136
BOWLE, Susan 17
BOWLES, Richard 162 163 Susan
    90
BOWLIN, Martha 59
BOWLING, Ann 79 Betsy 11 74
    Elizabeth 32 133 Joseph 54
    145 Mary 54 Mary Elizabeth
    Moseley 151 Sarah 79
BOWSER, Elizabeth 16 87
BOWZER, Elizabeth 16 87
BOYD, Ann 22 Catharine 47
    Catherine 2 Constantia 104
    Elizabeth 4 40 55 John 112
    Louisa 16 88 Mary 151 Mary
    Jane 134 Nancy 39 Nancy 154
    Rebecca 135 Sarah 37 147 Wil-
    liam 154
BOYER, Ann 60 Elizabeth 15 43

BOYER (continued)
    83 166 John 57 61 63 70 81 104
    137 166 168 John Jr 168 John
    L 133 Joseph 131 Margaret 61
    Virginia 81
BOYIER, Permelia W 72
BOYLE, Lucy 67
BRADDACK, Louisa 82
BRADHSAW, Eleanor 99
BRADLEY, Ann 81 C C 93 E F 45
    Gabriel 165 H 45 Harrison 101
    118 127 M Catharine 6 Nancy
    112 Sarah Ann 118 Susan A 127
BRADLY, Ann 14 Daniel 112
BRAME, Henry 53 144
BRANDT, Elizabeth L A 31 129
BRANHAM, Lucy 97
BRANN, Samuel G 109
BRANSON, Benjamin 114
BRASSINGTON, John 166
BRAWNER, Henry 78
BREART, Lucretia 126
BRENNER, Peter 102 132
BRENT, Charlott 144 Charlotte
    128 George 165 Henry 82 129
    Martha 31 129 Mary Jane 66
    Nancy 170
BRETT, Lucretia 30
BREWER, Ann 106 Henrietta M
    91
BRIAN, John J 150 Mary E 150
BRIANT, John 58
BRICKHANNON, Robert E 74
BRIGHT, John 160
BRIN, Betsey 25 113
BRITTINGHAM, Dixon 52 58 157
BROADBACK, Mary Ann 95
BROCCHUS, Perry E 129 Thomas
    50
BROCKETT, Ann 50 Robert 73
    128
BRODERS, Joseph 148
BROGDON, George 103
BROOK, Ann 90 Mary 80 98 Sarah
    135
BROOKE, John H 47 Mary J A 2
    47 Sarah 36 145
BROOKES, Ann 163 David see
    BROOKS, David 59 Jane 34
    138
BROOKS, Christian 98 Des-
    demona 106 Elizabeth 132

BROOKS (continued)
Eliza 103 Fanny 120 Frederick
130 James 107 140 Jane 18 93
Martha P 168 Mary 21 101
Mary E 162 Sarah 33 145 Sarah
Ann 139 William 96
BROONER, Barbara 156
BROWN, Alexander 108 Amie 63
Ann Elizabeth 108 Celia 125
Elizabeth 2 49 Ellen 88 George
130 Gustavus 124 Harnett 136
Henry 56 169 James 62 Jane
120 Jannete 21 John 159 Lucy
31 130 Margaret A B 35 Mar-
garet Ann B 142 Martha 1 Mar-
tha L 47 Mary 6 39 60 108 114
125 Mary 154 Mary E 120
Milly Ann 4 Polly 5 Rachael
60 Richard A 58 Robert 58
Sarah 24 48 Sophia 61 Susan 5
57
BROWNAL, John 164
BROWNE, Polly 58
BRUCE, Ann 5 57 Catharine 20 97
Cornelia Ann 114 Daniel 60 85
Daniel Henrietta 85 George 148
BRUIN, Sally Elizabeth 147
BRUNER, Catharine 45 Catherine
1 John 45
BRYAN, Alan 140 Alexander 163
Bernard 117 128 140 149 164
166 Daniel 170 Elizabeth 22
103 George 159 Hester B 164 J
C 137 James D 67 77 106 131
John 64 111 114 Maria 144
Marianna 113 Mary Ann 27 117
Mary Caroline 170 Sally 60 108
Sarah W 149 Statia Ann 55
BRYANT, George H 120
BRYCE, John 74
BUCHANAN, Aletha 54
BUCKERS, Caroline M 61 John 61
BUCKEY, Catherine 121 Frances
T 44 168 John 121 168
BUCKINGHAM, Isaac 47 125
BUCKLAND, Mary 43 165
BUCKY, Mary T 162
BUDD, Laura 19 Laura W 96
BULL, Amanda F 37 148
BULLOCK, James 125
BUNS, Thomas 92
BUNUFF, John see BUNOUF,

BUNUFF (continued)
John 60
BURCHELL, Catharine 145 Ed-
ward 145
BURGER, Catharine 42 Catherine
164
BURGESS, Lucy 3 50 Wm 50
BURK, Rebecca 56
BURNETT, Hannah 13
BURNS, Lavinia 52 Philicia 133
Thomas 111
BURRAG, Thomas see BURAGE,
Thomas 6
BUSBY, Ann 17 91
BUSH, Thomas 96
BUSHBY, Margaret E 133
BUSSELL, Rody 18 94
BUSTLE, Winifred 18 93
BUTCHER, Catharine A 97
Catherine A 20 John 115 157
Jonathan 97 Robert H 116
BUTLER, Emeline 115 John 54
Lucinda 77 Mary R 12 77
Pamelia 16 87 Robert 96 115
Sarah 77 Silus 168 Teresa 71
BUTTER, Thomas 152
BUTTES, John 51
BUTTS, Judith P 34 137 Mark 64
89 Mark Jr 82 Mary W 14 82
BYRNE, Elizabeth 5 58 Mary 17
90 William 125
CADDIS, David 50
CADERTON, John 113 Sarah 25
113
CADIS, David 49
CADY, Nancy 12 76
CAHALL, Kitty 62
CALBUT, Susan 162
CALDWELL, Josiah F 62
CALENDAR, Catharine Octavia
140
CALENDER, Eleanor 20 100
CALICO, Mary 69
CALL, Polly 14 81 William 67
CALLENDES, Mary Ann 165
CALVERT, Henry 93 Henry see
COLVERT, Henry 68
CAMPBELL, Celestial 23
Elizabeth 3 53 James 163 Jane
M 26 115 Lewis 54 Mary A 86
Nancy 18 94 William 53 106
CAMPBLE, Elizabeth 3

CANNON, Ann R 36 144 Caroline
23 107 John W 144 Margaret M
4 54 Mary 27 117 Susanna 149
CAPRON, Ann Eliza 104
CAREW, Margaret 16 87
CARLIN, Adaline 9 Elizabeth 20
97 Geo W 94 Henrietta 41 161
James H 80 Jane 135 Mary 55
70 Peggy 71 Rebecca 34 139
Sarah 4 55 Sarah H 22 103
Wesley 47 Westley 139
CARLTON, Thomas 169
CARNE, Jane 142 Mary 100
Susanna L 40 Susannah L 156
Wm 100
CARNES, Ann 129 Wm D see
CAIRNS, Wm D 62
CAROLIN, Ann 54 Caroline 68
Hugh 68 82 Julia 82
CAROLINE, Ann 4
CARPENTER, Eliza 60
CARRELL, Henry 47
CARROL, Mary 128
CARROLL, Jas 65 John B 130
William 136
CARSON, Ann 43 91 168
Elizabeth 140 George 78
James 87 91 140 Jane 87
Nehemiah 132 Samuel 168
Sarah Y 1
CARTER, Griffin 70 Hetty 23 107
John A 79 Joseph 137 Julia
Ann 137 Landon 129 Libren 63
Louisa 73 Mary Ann 15 86
Mary W 79 Nancy 71 Sarah
Ann 70
CARTRIGHT, Alice 162
CARTWRIGHT, Alice 42
CARY, Catharine 9 67 Eliza 17 89
Patsey Jefferson 30
CASEY, Mary Ann 92
CASH, Elijah 146 Susanna 10 36
146
CATHARLY, Molley 16 Molly 88
CATLETT, George W 101
CATON, James 88
CATTERTON, John 64 95
Lucretia 95
CATTISON, Lucretia 31
CATTS, Samuel 60
CAWOOD, Benjamin 100 103 147
Elizabeth Ann 82 George

CAWOOD (continued)
Douglas 159 Grafton 139 Mary
A E 87 Moses F A 66 87 125
Moses O B 64 83 93
CAYTON, Penelope 13 79
CAYWOOD, Benjamin 101 Susan
47
CAZANOVE, Harriett 112 Anna
Maria 98
CAZENOVE, Anthony C 88 C A
144 Charlotte B 144 Charlotti
Busti 36 Eliza F 16 88 Harriett
25 Octavious A 112 Paulina 15
Pauline 85 Wm G 74
CHADWELL, Fanny 33
CHAFLINE, Mary 36 144
CHAMBERLAIN, Janes S 124
CHAMBERS, Jonathan 96
CHANNCEY, John 105
CHAPIN, Julia 27 Julia Anna 124
Louise A A 22
CHAPMAN, George 65 Harriet B
13 78 Laura 103 Louisa Ann
Adilaide 103 Lucy A 135 Lucy
Ann 33 Mary J 65
CHARD, Hannah 90 Samuel 144
CHARLES, Margaret 164
CHASE, Maria 99
CHATHAM, Ann 49 Elizabeth 40
157 Fanny 12 77 Henry 56 77
Jane 7 56 Mary 17 90
CHAUNCEY, John 59
CHENAULT, Elijah 54 90
CHESHIER, Margaret 37 147
CHESHIRE, Jane 95
CHEVERILL, Catharine 17 91
CHICHESTER, Patsy 65
CHICK, William N 66
CHILDS, Ann W 24 110 Elizabeth
46 John 46 Sarah 159 Sarah A
22
CHILES, Mary 49 Sarah A 105
CHILTON, Maria 127
CHIN, Ann 94 Sophia 72
CHING, Sarah G 81
CHINN, Ann 19
CHINS, Elizabeth M 159
CHISAM, Elizabeth 2 47
CHISEL, Mary 38 151
CHISELL, Deborah 167 168
CHITIS, Mary 2
CHITTERSON, Mary 25 114

CHRISE, Eliza 13 78
CHRISTOPHE, Christian 50
CHURCH, Samuel 103 146 Sarah
32 132
CHURCHMAN, Albina V 121 Al-
vina V 28 Amanda M F 142
Ann 100 Eliz 28 Elizabeth 119
Frederick 76 133 John 119 121
136 142 Margaret 33 Margaret
J 136 Mary 12 76 Rebecca 133
CLAGETT, B W 65 Elizabeth A
101 Elizabeth Ann 132 Horatio
132 148 Mary 15 85 96 Richard
H 120 142 William 82
CLAGGETT, Elizabeth A 21
CLAPDORE, Mary Ann 65
CLARE, James 75 John 57 68 76
77 128 142
CLARK, Betsy 27 Cassandra 154
Elizabeth 9 John M 54 Joseph
M 90 Mary 152 Peyton 66
Rhody 35 61 Sarah Ann 134
Thomas 71
CLARKE, Alexander 55 Ann 137
Betsey 119 Elias see CLARK,
Elias 66 Elizabeth 19 95
Emeline 152 Harriet 35 142
John M 110 Lethe 51 Lucy 136
Thomas 168 Thompson 104
CLEARPOLE, Rebecca 54
CLEAVELAND, Ann 58
CLEMENTS, Ann 127 Mary A 9
Samuel 62 Winney 156
CLIFFORD, Ann 34 138
CLIFORD, Jane 48
CLIFTON, Sarah Ann 146
CLUSOM, Mary Ann 167
COAD, Therza 125 Thirza 29
COADE, Drury 14 81 Sarah 14
Sarah Ann 81
COAN, William 98
COANS, Ann 89
COATES, James 120 152 Lucy 41
161 Margaret 6 59
COATS, Ann Jane 79 Daniel 79
John 67 Lucinda 120 Mary 169
Sarah 142
COAX, Ann Eliza 93 William B
93
COBY, Elizabeth 48 William 48
COFFEE, Fanny B B 43
COFFER, Fanny B B 167

COFFIN, Sarah 6 58
COHAGAN, John 84 Sally 15 84
COHAGEN, John 135
COHEN, Eliza 125 Mary Ann 18
158 William 100 158 Wm 67
COLDMAN, William Smith see
SMITH, William 149
COLE, Ann 10 70 Catharine 1
Elizabeth 53 Emily 91 Faithy
165 James 70 79 Letty 112
Louisa 74 Mary 5 Mary Jane
42 William 74 105 127
COLEMAN, James P 64 92 98
Margaret 74 Susan 17 92
COLES, Faith 43 Lewis 116
COLLINGSWORTH, A D see
COLLINSWORTH, A D 68 A D
154 W P 52
COLSTON, Ann 103 Susan 158
COLUMBUS, Charles see
COLUMBAL, Carlo 68
COMPTON, Ann 152 Cyrus 68 126
Emanuel 152 Emanuel G 73
Ludwell 152 Rhoda 106 Roda
23 Susanna 2 48 Verlinda Jane
152
CONE, Catharine 74
CONGIGGIN, John 95
CONN, Philip 146
CONNER, Elizabeth 24 44 110
170
CONTEE, Sarah F 4
COOK, Celestial Jane 160 Chris-
tiana Jane 11 David 49
Elizabeth 134 Ellen 49 Hen-
nretta Ann 157 Jane 41 75 John
W 72 Leonard 112 Louisa D 41
161 Mary 51 Mary Asinath 143
Nancy 28 Rebecca C 80
Rebecca Clare 13 Rebecca H
80 Sarah A 11 72 Theo 161
Theodore 160 Wm 51
COOKE, Elizabeth Mary 75
Leonard 131 Lucretia 3 Martha
36 144 Mary 3 Nancy 120
Rebecca 98 Thomas 163
COOLEY, Martha 100 Mary E 157
COONES, Mary 12 76
COOPER, Robert 122 Samuel 87
COPPER, Charlotte 44 169
Thomas 73
CORCORN, Margaret W 19 96

CORNWELL, Cornelia 136
CORREL, Mary 31
CORRY, Eliza. 5
CORSE, John 52 106 113 Julia E
122 Montgomery D 122
CORTIN, Elizabeth Ann 93
CORYELL, George 157
COTTRINGER, Caroline 30 126
COUCHMAN, Eliza 18 93 Leticia
93
COURTS, Eliza 65
COWAN, Joseph 59
COWARD, Alcey 151
COWEN, William 80
COWHEN, Mahalan 116
COWING, Elizabeth 88
COX, Ann Eliza 18 Chas F 69
Eliza 93 Elizabeth 160 Harriot
65 Harriott 10 William B 93
Wm B 160
COXE, Catharine 11 74 Mary
Caroline 164 165
CRABB, S S 153
CRACROFT, Ann R 13 79 Maria
Rose 121 Rebecca W 42 162
CRADDOCK, Edmund 146
CRAGGINS, Charles S see
CROGGON, Charles S 70
CRAIG, Ann 124
CRAIK, Maria D 14 83
CRANCH, William G 165
CRANDELE, Sarah 11
CRANDELL, Elizabeth 97
Lucinda C 76 Sarah 74 Thomas
60
CRANDLE, Susan 28 121
CRANSTON, Eliza 40 156 John 70
Mary Ann 3 50
CRANY, Mary Ann 7 Nancy Ann
62
CRAUSTON, John 50 71
CRAVALL, Mary 75
CRAVELL, Mary 12
CRAVEN, John 134 Mary C 134
Mary E 33 Thomas 66 Thomas
C 151
CRAWFORD, Ann 17 89 John 117
153 170 Mary 44 170
CREASE, Jane E 129
CREBLE, Mary 73
CREDIT, Mary Ann 68 Nancy 13
79

CREEDY, Betsy 34 138
CREIGHTON, John 164 John T 93
126 Martha E 164 Mary A 137
CREVELL, John 59
CROCKETT, Asa 82
CROGGON, N J 61
CRONMILLER, Samuel 153
CROOK, Elizabeth 119 George 82
Margaret 34 Mary 154 Priscilla
139 William 124
CROOKE, Bernard 137 Margaret
137
CROSBY, Jesse 66
CROSS, Ann Cornelia 135 Julia
Ann 146 Reid 135 Richard 146
CROWE, Nancy 83
CRUMP, Daniel 69 126 John 50
CRUPPER, Frances E 138 Julia
Ann 21 100 Robert 100 138
Susan J 35 Susan Jane 141
CRUSE, Ann 136 Mary 43 167
Thomas 63 137 167
CRYS, Ann 55
CRYSS, Henry 99
CSYER, Patsey 1
CULLIN, Bridget 19
CULLINS, Carter 71
CUNNINGHAM, John 91 112
CUNNY, David 72
CURREY, Mary 130
CURRIE, Elizabeth 26 100
CURRY, Elizabeth 21 57 98 116
James 116 Patrick 98 Sarah
169
CURTAIN, Elizabeth 5 58 Susan-
nah 147 Susanne 37
CURTIS, C 16 Charlotte 88 Jacob
88 Mary 10 69
CUSTIS, G W P 97 George W P
114 Mary A R 114 Mary Ann
Randolph 114
DADE, Baldwin 46 Catharine 46
Chas E 67 Eliza L 7 Eliza S
64
DAGAN, George 78
DAILEY, Ann 95 Ann E 141 Ed-
ward 95 Isabella V 81
DAILY, Ann 19
DAINGERFIELD, Edward 59 John
B 59 Maria 21 Sarah F 6 Vir-
ginia B 32 134
DALE, Jane R 40 158 John R 48

DALEY, Isabella V 14 Ursula 28
121
DALY, Isabella V 81
DAMAINE, Ann 34
DANA, G B 111
DANFORTH, Emma N 61 J N 61
142
DANGERFIELD, Bathurst 115
Harriet 148 Maria 101 Sarah T
59 William H 97
DANIEL, Anna M 162 Catharine
54 Thomas 55
DARLEY, William 140
DARNE, Jennet 42 164 Margaret 5
58 Mary 143 Simon 58 Thomas
143
DARNELL, Harry 100 146 155
Jane 146 Louisa 155 Priscilla
43 166
DARNES, Nancy 1 46 Simon 46
DARRELL, Walter L 64
DATES, Ann 19 96
DAUGHERTY, Margaret 125
DAVEY, Thomas 137 150
DAVIDSON, Bazil H 103 James
49
DAVIES, Ann 4 John 156 Matty
156
DAVIS, Ann 50 51 164 Ann E 79
Benjamin 118 Betty 103 Chloe
Ann 20 Delila 51 Delilah 3
Elizabeth 36 112 147 Frances
18 73 93 George 57 Hannah
Ann 16 88 Henry 93 Henry W
118 James 164 Jane 77 Jane M
36 145 Jane M W 118 Jemima
169 John 45 47 85 151 Josiah
H 84 88 Lewis S 74 Ludwell H
48 Mary 24 27 111 118 170
Mary Ann 19 27 96 118 Matilda
20 99 Matty 40 Nancy 1 18 25
45 46 48 74 93 112 Peter 145
Richard 109 Richard W 99 124
Rosalie Higginson 80 Sally 86
145 165 Samuel H 78 Sarah 15
50 95 167 Sarah A 36 Thomas
M 69 William 57 118 William
A 162
DAVISS, Peter 52
DAVY, Elizabeth 1 Thomas 92
118
DAY, Amelia 33 136 Ann 62

DAY (continued)
Hanora 114 Hanson 108 127
Horatio 48 57 73 141 143 152
James 125 Sally 91 Sarah 35
143 Winifred 106
DEAGAN, Charlotte 105
DEAGON, Charlotte 22
DEAKENS, Mima 131
DEAKINS, Ambrose 166 Marg 124
Margaret 43 166 Philip 154
DEAN, Leantha 23 Susan O 29
William 124
DEANE, Mary C 37 149 Susan 124
Susan O 29
DEARBORN, Charles H 105
Elizabeth 139 Harriet A 81
Margaret C 43 165 Mary A T
137 Simon 81 165 169
DEBLANCE, Fanny 14
DEBLAUCE, Fanny 81
DEBLAUN, Fanny 81
DeBUTTS Julia Ann 141
DEETON, Christopher 118
Frances 58 Isabella 118
DEGGE, Robert F 116
DELPHEY, Richard 75
DELPHY, Barthol 93 Bar-
tholomew 149 Lucinda E 61
Matilda 37 149
DEMAIN, Ann 138 Grace 84 Joal
138 John 147
DEMAINE, Ann 138 Joal 138
Julius 84
DEMENT, Thomas K 118
DEMING, Mary S 38 151
DENEALA, Ann Lucretia 38
DENEALE, Ann S 151 Catherine 7
George 55 84 87 169 Hugh W
45 52 126 162 163 Hugh West
62 Julia Ann 103 Mary C 62
William 48 100
DENINGTON, Elizabeth 152
DENNESON, Catharine 25
DENNISON, Catharine 112 Maria
53 Mary 154 Sarah 142 Thomas
53 142
DENNISTOWN, Sarah 137
DENON, Eleanor 44
DERMENT, Elizabeth 82
DERRECK, James 82
DERRICK, Maria 43 166
DEVAUGH, Mary Jane 133

DEVAUGHN, John 88 Margaret
   111 Rebecca Jane 111 Ruth 84
   Samuel H 111 133 165 Sarah
   139 William 111
DEVEREUX, Elizabeth 26 115
DEWAIN, Debby 19
DeWARREN Mary 63
DEWY, Thomas 58
DICK, David 58 Elisha C 160
   Elisha Cullen 134 Julia 134
DICKENS, Matilda E 104 Mid-
   dleton Elwood 104
DICKS, David 170
DIGGS, John B 84
DILLON, Lucy Ann 103
DINMORE, Richard 77
DISNEY, Sarah Ann 129
DIXION, Emily E 42 164 George
   O 70 77 John 154 John A 63 88
DIXON, Grace 71 Henrietta 77
   Jane 49 83 John 84 89 109 114
   125 139 158 163 John B 88
   Julia 154
DOBBIN, Rachael 107
DOBIE, Jane Chartus 143
DODDS, Anna 161 Hepsabah Mar-
   tha 160 Joseph 143 149 161
DOE, Dearborn 84
DOGAN, Ann 114 Eliza 39 Eliza
   155 Jane Eliza 18 94 John 79
   114 Margaret Ann 57 Philip
   155 Philip 67 77 94 Susanna 64
   Wm 114
DOGANS, Elizabeth 79 Philip 79
DOGETT, Sarah Ann 153
DONALDSON, Andrew 46 Anna 46
   Benjamin 77 Catharine 9 68
   Elizabeth 156 Hannah 77
   Richard 71 Robert 77 Thomas
   63
DONALSON, Anna 1 Catharine
   140
DOOLEY, John J 77
DOOLY, John 93
DOOR, Milly 23
DORBET, Ellen 145
DORCEY, Elizabeth 24 69 Mary
   24 111
DORMANS, Francis 75
DORRETY, Margarret 89
DORSEY, Ann 139 Elizabeth 3 53
   110 Julia Ann 48 Margaret 83

DORSEY (continued)
   Mial 122 Nancy 148 Sarah 99
   Thomas 95 Vernon 72 Winifred
   31 96
DOUGHERTY, Arthur see
   DAUGHERTY, Arthur 73 Eliza
   33 135
DOUGLAS, Charles B R 82 Jas
   110 John 165 Loyd 90 Margaret
   165
DOUGLASS, C B R 102 Charles
   160 Charles B K 51 Charles B
   R 102 110 118 Charlotte 44
   Charlotte V 169 Eliza 32 133
   Eliza V 105 Jacob 69 75 113
   John 78 106 Louisa 113
   Susanna Mary Ann 160 Wil-
   liam S 151
DOVE, Alley 27 117 Sally 9 Sarah
   3 53 William 78
DOVER, Betsy 109 Milly 109
   Sally 69
DOWELL, Ellen 14 81
DOWNES, Delia 38
DOWNS, Daniel 153 Delia 152
   Elizabeth 153
DOZIER, Ellen H 153
DRAIN, Henry 107
DRAKE, Ann E 14 83 Jesse S 139
   William 107
DREAN, Hester 144
DREESE, Martha J 15 Martha
   Jane 86
DREW, Charles 59 144
DREWRY, Mary 39
DREWS, Nicholas 91
DRINKER, Hannah 149 Rebecca
   M 63
DROWN, Mary 143
DRUM, _____ 57 58
DRURY, Monica 35 140
DUDLAP, John 170
DUDLEY, Benjamin F 79 159
   Cloanna 14 82 James 63 70
   164 Joseph 138 Rebecca 24
   111 Sarah 42 164
DUDLY, James 150
DUFF, James 90 Jane 90 John 91
   97 Sarah 33 90
DUFFEY, Catharine 167
   Catherine 43 Elizabeth 36
   George 167

DUFFY, Elisabeth 67 John 53 67
73 89 115 124 142 151 154 168
Piles 168 Rosena 13 William
67
DUGAN, Philip 79
DUKE, James 144
DULANY, Bladen 126 James H
118 Maria H 99 Mary G 61
Rebecca 168 Rebecca Ann 79
DUNBAR, Alexander 89 120 133
135 162 Ann R 35 141
Elizabeth A 25 114 Laura 40
157
DUNCAN, Samuel 119
DUNDAS, John 134 Laura 17 91
Nancy 24 Nancy Hooe 24
Nancy Moore 109 Sophia
Matilda 33 134
DUNDASS, Laura 91
DUNLANEY, Eleanor 46
DUNLAP, Eliza 38 151 Esther
Ann 40 158 John 54 84 144 149
152 Mary 1 45 William 168
DUNN, John 149 Martha 20
DUNNINGTON, Catharine 55 Mar-
tha 11 75
DURR, Mary Elizabeth 134
DURRINGTON, Ann 15 86
DUTCHY, Cecilla 18 Ceilla 94
Leonard 94
DUTTON, John H 138
DUTY, Rebecca 22 Rebeccah 104
DUVAL, Betsey 64
DUVAUN, Debby 95
DYER, Deborah 13 80 Margaret 28
119 Thomas see DYRE,
Thomas 13
DYOR, John 127
DYSON, Hannah 6 60
EACHES, Eliza 83 James M 67
EASTON, David 109 130
EATON, Mary 39 154
EDMONDS, Betsy 101 Edmund 54
Mary E 146 Meredith 57
Roberta E 29 125
EDMONDSON, Mary 31 129
EDMONSON, Mary Ann 69
EDWARD, Mary E 36
EDWARDS, James B 159 John 52
Letila 163
EGLING, Amelia 22 102
ELLICOTT, Ann 19 96

ELLIOT, John 134 Martha E 109
ELLIOTT, Silas 78
ELLIS, Ann 28 George 95 John
143 Nancy 1 46 Sarah 143
EMBERSON, Richard D 147
EMERSON, Aquilla 71 81 95 125
132 Catherine 66 Delila 19 95
John 156 John P 81 John S 81
108 149 Sarah 14 81
EMMERSON, Aquilla 45
EMMIT, Margaret 11
EMMITT, Josiah 72 Margaret 72
ENDS, Elizabeth 6 83
ENEY, Jeremiah 139 156
ENGLISH, A Roberta 10 Roberta
70 Wm B 74
ENTWISLE, Isaac 160 Isaac Jr
147 James 129
EPPS, John 159
ERSKIN, Robert 104
ESLEECK, Ann 167
ESSEX, Billezid 66
ETSER, Mary 34 140
EVANS, Anthony 165 Catharine 4
17 90 135 Catherine 55 Daniel
153 David 74 Edward 64
Elizabeth 5 Emily 99 Ephraim
75 Hannah 15 85 Helen 82 Hen-
rietta 134 James 59 95 99 133
James 154 Jane 21 100 John
89 105 115 John T 91 Joseph
153 Louisa 47 Martha Ann 131
Mary Ann 41 161 Nancy 26 115
Rebecca 75 Susanna 3 52 Wil-
liam 53
EWING, M E 79
FADLEY, James 130
FAGINS, Molly 42 164
FAIR, Nancy 122
FAIRBUSH, Mary M 105
FAIRFAX, Briscoe 58 Eugenia
120 Henry 141 John W 141
Martha 141
FANNALL, Mary 111
FANT, John 46
FAR, Ann 33 136
FARIS, Elizabeth 160
FARLANE, John M 132
FARLTON, Hopewell Gunther 91
FARMER, Joseph 82
FARQUHAR, Mary W 24
FARR, Jacob 112

FARRELL, Ann 155
FAW, Eliza 115 Julian M 26
Juliana Marie 117 Sophia E 26
FEARSON, Joseph 119
FEBEGIN, Catherine 30
FENDALL, Benj T 119 Benjamin
T 119 Eliza C 28 119 Susan F
119 Townshend 96
FENDLEY, Susan 62
FERGUSON, Anna 8 64 Bertha
103 Joseph 156 Patty 107
Sarah 157 Susan 157 William
115
FEUGIT, James see FUGETT,
James 87
FIELD, Horace 52 57 John A 70
Jonathan 74 133 136 Kilaney
133 Stephen 116 137
FIELDS, Oliver 121
FIG, Elizabeth 44 169
FIGG, Matilda 88
FINCH, Elizabeth 102
FINDLEY, Sarah 9
FINDLY, Sarah 67
FINNIK, Linn y 8 Linnay 64
FISHER, Elizabeth M 142
Frederick 88 Robert 142
FISS, Matilda 23
FITZGERALD, Ann 10 71 Celia
12 77 Julia 76
FITZHUGH, Ann Brice 167 Ed-
mund 75 Henry 151 Margaretta
10 Mary Lee 72 Norman R 167
William 72 William W 104
FIZALL, John 61
FLANAGAN, Mary Ann 123
FLANAGEN, Cleary 21
FLANNAGIN, Cleary 101
FLEMING, Alcinda 127 Andrew J
68 Isabella 96 Margaret 13 78
FLEMMING, Ann 89
FLETCHER, Alice 43 167
Charles 154 Edward 123 Maria
8 66 153 Rebecca 24 111 Vir-
ginia 35 142 William 55
FLOOD, Elizabeth 137 James 92
103 Margaret 58 Thomas 69
FLOWERS, Ann H 101
FOARD, Danial see FORD,
Danial 15
FOOTE, Jane 31
FORD, Daniel 59 Elizabeth Ann

FORD (continued)
74 Judith 141 William 141 Wm
121
FOREMAN, Elizabeth 165
FOREST, Joicey 5
FORGERSON, Ann 51
FORREST, Joicey 57 Sarah 38
152 164
FORRESTER, Lucy 61
FORTNEY, Ann 158
FOSTER, Mary Ann 3 50 123
FOSTERS, Mrs 3
FOUCARD, John 90
FOWLE, Anne Carolin 76 Anne
Caroline 12 Esther Jane 6 59
George D 72 76 Harriet B 39
Harriet B 154 Rebecca H 18 92
Susan L 112 William H 143
FOWLES, Polly 23 108
FOX, Isaac 100 Lucinda 54
Matilda 167 Sarah 134
FOY, Patrick 110
FRANCIS, Mary 85
FRANK, Elizabeth 31 130
Jeremiah 49
FRANKLAND, Thomas 115
FRANKLIN, Elleanor P L 71 El-
lenor P L 10 Margaret 12 76
Phebe 10
FRANKS, Ann N 91 Lucinda 90
Robert 91
FRAZER, Elizabeth 101 Henry 86
William 76
FRAZIER, Anthony 104 Frances
138 Henry 116 Jeremiah 141
Sally 41 159 Sarah 94
FREDERICK, Eliz A 8 Elizabeth
A 66 Emily 44 170
FREDERICKSEN, Eva 12 Eva C
76
FREEMAN, Ann 8 65 Cecilia 90
Eleanor 107 Nancy 18 92 Wm
65
FRENCH, Mary E 32
FREY, Louisa 36
FRIGNETT, John 63
FRIZZELL, John 92
FRULING, John 87
FRY, Elizabeth 168 Joseph 144
Louisa 144 Thomas 74
FUGATT, Mary Ann 47
FUGETT, Eliza 160 James see

182

FUGETT (continued)
  FEUGIT James 14 15 Thomas
  102
FUGGIT, Peggy 6
FUGITT, Ann O 59 Gustavus 47
  Jeremiah 158 Lucinda 30 125
FUGUSON, Joseph 86
FUIER, Lewis 65
FULLER, Jane 26 77
FULLERTON, Peggy 11 75
FULTON, Ann 168 Eliza 122
  Mary Ann 44 Virginia 125
FUMPUSON, Mary 53
FURGUSON, Bertha 19 Joseph
  146 Julia 146
FURLANS, John 156
FURLEY, Maria 52
GADSBY, John 65 Margaret S 64
GAENOLDS, Mickey 25
GAITHER, Greenbary 109
GALE, James 168
GALES, Elizabeth 24
GALLAGER, Maria 152
GALLAGHER, Patrick 63
GALLAHAN, Eleanor 110 Samuel
  110
GALT, James 53 81 Mathew W
  60
GANETT, Martha 43 108
GANTT, Charles see GANT,
  Charles 16
GARDENER, Constance T 11
  John L 73
GARDNER, Ann Eliza 25 114
  Constance T 73 Michael 102
  Rebecca 40 156 Tristam H 167
  Will C 85 William 56 William
  C 112 William G 98
GARLIC, Mary Ann 16 87
GARNER, Margaret 99
GARRELL, James 150
GARRETT, Enoch 128 Nancy 136
  Richard 124
GASPER, Sarah 163
GATES, Elizabeth 111 Emelia 99
  Margaret 39 Mary 21 Mary A
  101 Thomas 111
GATIS, Elizabeth 166
GAVIN, Mary 123
GEE, Mary Ann 36 145
GEIGER, Ann 1 46
GEMENY, John 73 143

GEMINY, John 121 Navine 121
GEORGE, Catharine 152 Isaac 88
  155 Jane 155
GERRY, Caroline 38 150 Reuben
  101
GIBBS, John H 88 William 163
GIBSON, Augusta 115 Daniel 88
  Emily 94 Gus 69 88 99 Gus-
  tavus 52 71 95 108 166 Henry
  55 66 131 Hester E 8 Hestor
  Elleanor 66 Jas 95 John H 77
  Mary Ann 73 Richard H 106
  Robert 152 William 107
GIESTA, Susan 108
GILBERT, Isabella 21 100
GILBRETH, Henry 69 Jane 9 69
  Joanna 17 89 John 69 Mary 6
GILLBRETH, John 60 Mary 60
GILLIEZ, Lucinda 129
GILLINGHAM, Lucas 12
GILLWITH, Joanna 17 89
GILMAN, Ephraim 95 Gshraim
  131
GIRD, Eliza Mary 51 William F
  69
GLADDEN, Dianna 91
GLADDIN, Susan 2 49
GLADEN, Cloe 120
GLANDERS, Tobitha 41 161
GLASGOE, Geo W see
  GLASSGOW, Geo W 89 Mary 3
GLASSFORD, William 101
GLASSGOW, Cath A 103
  Catharine A 22
GLASTER, James N 84 Mary
  Jane 84
GLAUVILLE, Mary 11
GLENN, Robert 144
GLOSTER, Ann M 165 James N
  165
GLOVER, Benjamin 47 Catharine
  43 167 Charity 154 Joseph 89
  Nancy 149 Thomas 149
GLUYAS, William 118
GODARD, William 105
GODWIN, Ann 25
GOFSON, Mary Ann 3
GOING, Ann 19 94
GOLDSBURY, Susan 124
GOLDSMITH, Catharine 144
  Catherine 43
GONSOLVE, Margaret Ann 63

GOODHUE, Mary 145
GOODING, Ann 25 Harriot 164
  Harriott 42 John 113 164 170
GOODRICH, Sarah 49
GOODRICK, Ann 97
GOODS, Ebby 13 Eliza 78 James
  C 137 Susanna 99
GOODWIN, Hebziba 128 Hepzaba
  31
GOPOM, Thomas M 51
GORDEN, Nelly 104
GORDON, George 90
GORMAN, John B 71
GOSSEN, Mary Ann 3 4 53
GOSSER, Emeline 69
GOTARE, Dorcas 17 Dorcus 90
GOULD, Eliza 35 142
GOWEN, Joseph 123 Mary 123
GOWINGS, Louisa 46
GRADY, Ardry 39 153
GRAHAM, John 132 161 Libby
  Ann 132 Penelope 18 94
GRANT, John 99 138 Nancy 19 95
  Sarah 94
GRANVILLE, Patrick 64
GRASON, Letty 11
GRAY, Alfred 58 Bridget 74
  Catharine 41 Frances B 157
  George W 115 Georgianna C 31
  130 Helen M 115 Helen Marion
  26 Hezekiah 93 Jacob 111 Jane
  18 93 John G 105 157 Nancy
  105 Precilla 18 Priscilla 93
  Robert 109 Sarah 22 105
  Thomas 49 William 91
GRAYSON, George 107 Jane 58
  Letty 11 72 Sarah 80
GREEN, Dorcas 32 133 Edward
  120 Eliza Ann 30 128
  Elizabeth 9 49 69 Elizabeth H
  9 67 Isaac 130 James 128 152
  Jane B 125 John 157 John F 91
  114 125 163 Margaret 44 Mary
  25 114 Mary M 152 Olivia 163
  Robert 86 Sarah 32 83 132
  Susanna 3 Susannah 50
  Thomas 50 William 83 158
  Wm P 73
GREENE, Mary M 38
GREENWOOD, Benj 127 Jane
  Eliza 134 John 79 93 135 153
  Mary Ann 94 Rebecca 79

GREENWOOD (continued)
  William S 127
GREER, Margaret 168
GREGG, Jacob 87
GREGORY, Elizabeth L 2 Matilda
  12
GRETTER, Mary G 6 59
GREW, Rebecca H 11 72
GRIFFIN, Frances 5 Franky 56
  James 117 T L 143 Thomas L
  95 129 137 158 169 William
  Harper 91
GRIFFITH, Catherine 158 Elisa L
  102 Eliz L 21 John H 167
  Sarah 41 161
GRIGSBY, Mary Ann 8
GRIMES, Elizabeth 50 James 152
  Mary 78 Mary Ann 34 137
  Nancy 11 73 Sarah Ann 37 148
  Sylvester 92
GRIMSLEY, Ann 19 96 James 103
  William 129
GRINELLS, Sarah A 135
GRINNAGE, Fanny 33 136
GRINNOLDS, Mockey 113
GROVERMAN, Maria 106
GROVES, Nancy 24 110
GRUMBLE, Margaret 13 80
GRUNDELL, Sarah A 13
GRUVER, John 158 Mary Ann 158
GRYMES, Ann 28 120 Maria 65
  Mrs 120 William 145
GUATT, William 69
GULATT, Mary 67 William 67
  108
GULLAT, Catharine 10
GULLATT, Catharine 69 James
  74 170
GURNEY, Hermon 111
GUSS, Charles Edward 105
GUTHRIE, Lucretia 11 75 Mary
  13 Mary Ann 78
GUTHROW, Joseph 109
GUY, Elizabeth 22 105 George 82
  James 75
GWYTON, Geo B see GUYTON,
  Geo B 93
HACKETT, Dennis 114
HADEN, Garnett 160
HAILY, Ann 165
HAIR, George 91
HALE, Lucinda 78

184

HALEY, Daniel 67 Jane 84
HALL, Ann 147 Delia 93
  Elizabeth B 25 James 56
  Jemima 44 Mary H 40 Sarah 83
  146 Susan 47 Zebediah 93
HALLEY, Jane 15 John 117
HALLOWELL, Benj 24 Joseph T
  168
HALLS, Nancy 27 117
HAMACK, Sarah 12 76
HAMILTON, Alexander 80 James
  H 169 Jane 7 63 Jane L 3 52
  Lucy 7 62 Mary E 23 Mary El-
  len 108 109 Philip 52 Sally C
  80 Sarah 35 141 Wesley 109
HAMMATT, John B 70
HAMMETT, John B Jr 94
HAMMITT, John B Jr 94
HAMMOND, Jane 32 131
HAMMONTREE, Elizabeth 164
HAMPSON, John B 106 Joseph H
  50
HANCOCK, Andrew 96 Ann Maria
  163 John B 84 163 Martha V
  155 Mary Elizabeth 84
HAND, Sarah H 42 163 Tryphasa 9
  68
HANDLESS, Frances Ann 112
  Sarah 66 Susanna 112
HANDY, Louisa 141
HANEY, Elizabeth 16 87 M A 107
  Mary Ann 107
HANSMAND, Henry 151
HANSMOND, Mary Ann 151
HANSON, Elizabeth E 92 Grace
  19 94 Marbury 136 Mark 94 104
  William 77
HANTZMON, Henry 108 Louisa
  108
HARBIN, Joseph B 106
HARDEN, Susannah 143 Thomas
  G 143
HARDEY, Robert 145
HARDING, Bettice 107 Lettice 23
  106 Lewellin A 59 Sarah 102
HARE, Elizabeth 128 George 147
HARLE, Ann 52 Brittania 52
HARLEY, Eunice 103
HARPER, Catherine A 4 55 Celia
  140 J W 61 James 153 Julia R
  96 Maria 39 155 Mary D 39 153
  Nancy 1 76 95 Rachael Wells

HARPER (continued)
  53 S F 61 Sarah 26 117 Sarah
  Wells 120 Virginia 53
  Washington T 101 William 76
  96 117 140 142 147 155 Wil-
  liam A 96
HARRE, Frances 49
HARRINGTON, Mary 65 Mary A
  18 Mary Ann 93
HARRIS, Ann 90 107 Cornelia 39
  Elizabeth 7 33 63 135 George
  W 75 George Washington 122
  Hannah 29 125 James 95 John
  89 98 107 138 160 163 John L
  168 Joseph 64 135 Lucy 105
  Margaret E 38 Mary 8 64 138
  Mary C 46 Mary E 51 Matthias
  see HARRIS, Maulias 96 Selia
  61 William 56 William A 109
HARRISON, Elias 68 117 122
  Elizabeth 126 Hannah C 131
  Jane Bell 122 Jemina 134 John
  D 53 Luther D 139 Margaret A
  53 Martha 118 Mary 24 66 109
  119 Robert 59 Sally 126
  Theodocia 51
HARRISS, Ann 33 Anne 135
  James 135 John 72 William
  147
HART, Edward 161 Elizabeth 113
  John 150 Robert 145
HARTLEY, Elizabeth 162 168
  Letitia 26
HARTLY, Latitia 116
HARVEY, Grace A 139
HARWOOD, B 108
HASCUM, Priscilla 70
HATTERSLEY, Samuel 76 87 139
  Sarah 90
HATTON, Louisa 15 84 William
  90
HAWKE, Thomas A 97
HAWKINS, Charles 66 94 Samuel
  96 Sarah 42 163
HAWXHURST, Walter 86
HAYES, Andrew 45 65 Jane 2 49
  Mary 45 Sarah 65
HAYNES, E(lizabeth) A 141
HAYNIE, Presley 57
HAYS, Andrew 86 148 Jane 86
HAYSON, John 133
HEAD, Benjamin 107

HEADON, Garret 133
HEATH, Adeline 62 Eleanor 109
  Ellinor 24 William 109
HEBB, Sarah T 89
HEBLE, Sally 17
HEIKLING, Phoebe 31
HEINEMAN, Jacob 161 162 167
  Mary 43 167
HEISKELL, Mary Lark 117
HEISSE, Louisa 88
HEISSON, Elizabeth 11 74
HELLRIGEL, Catherine 125
  George 125
HENDERSON, Dorcas 79 James
  Louis see HENDERSON,
  James L 20 Mary Ann 82
  Nancy 23 106 Sarah 7 62 Wil-
  lis 161
HENKLIN, Phoebe 129
HENNING, Elizabeth 161
HENRICKSON, Catharine 23 105
HENRITY, Michael 166
HENRY, Adam 154 Ann 56 Nancy
  2 49 Phillis 56 Robert 46
  Samuel 155
HENSON, ELizabeth 74
HEPBURN, Alexander 104
  Isabella 22 104 Latitia 18 92
HERBERT, Mary 47 Noblet 85
  Sarah Fairfax 130 William 68
  William Jr 98 William Sr 130
HERNDORE, Traverse D 75
HERSE, Isabelle 130
HESSE, Louise 16
HESSEN, Phillis 43 166
HETHERINGTON, James 64
HETHRINGTON, Mary 65 Mary
  Ann 8
HEWES, Eliza Ann 20 98 Ellicott
  89 Mary M 37 149
HEWETT, Edmund 53 Peter 108
HEWITT, Edmund 99 141 Rosalie
  116 Virginia C 34
HIBBARD, Jeremiah 133
HICKEY, Ann D 4 55 56 Rebecca
  91
HICKMAN, Mary 10 70
HICKS, Anne 166 George 114
  Maria 91 William 166 William
  Jr 97
HICKY, Rebecca 17
HIGDON, Elizabeth 10 70 John 58

HIGDON (continued)
  78 152 Mary Jane 48 Sally 13
  78
HIGS, Eleanor 95
HILL, Ann 138 George 69 105 165
  George Jr 100 James 47 86 108
  125 148 149 John 59 99 146
  John B 99 116 153 Josiah 138
  Laurence 159 Lucretia 105
  Mary 32 132 165 Richard 119
  Robert see HILLS, Robert 100
  Samuel V 150 Sarah 15 86
  Siloam 159
HILLIARD, Warner M 159
HILLMAN, Lucy 33 134
HILLS, Eliz 23 Elizabeth B 43
  167 Elizabeth J 106 Josiah B
  115 167 Mary A 15 85 Robert
  see HILL, Robert 21
HILLYARD, Mary 10 70
HILTON, Mary 155 William 62
  155 Wm 155
HIMERDENGER, Christian 133
HINES, Alfred 84 128 Letty 163
  Maria 3 52 Wm 66
HINGERTS, Sarah 121
HIPKINS, Lewis 56 85 106 109
  132 170 Louisa 56 Mary
  Augusta 132 Susannah 109
HIRSH, Catharine 143 Catherine
  84 Conrad 84 143
HITLER, Rebecca 109
HITTON, Mary 39
HOAKES, Elizabeth 16
HOBBS, Henry 94
HODGKIN, Mary 19 95 Robert 99
  151 Wm F 154
HODGKINS, Ann Maria 38 Susan
  24 111
HODGSKINS, Ann Maria 152 Mar-
  garet 107
HODGSON, Wm 101
HODSKINS, Robert 92
HOFF, Caroline J 161 John 137
  Lewis 169 Mary Ann 149
HOFFMAN, Jacob 163 Peter E
  104 142
HOGAN, Margaret G 151
HOKES, Elizabeth 85 Jacob 71
  Richard 71
HOLLAND, Thomas 91
HOLLINSBERRY, Charlotte 145

186

HOLLINSBERRY (continued)
John 145
HOLLOWELL, Joseph T 128
HOLLOWOOD, Rhoda 50
HOLLY, Elizabeth 59
HOLLYWOOD, Jane 7 64
HOLT, Henry E 89 145 Jane 40
155
HOLTON, Elizabeth 26 89
HOLTZMAN, Martha M 62
HOOE, Anna M H 19 95 B 165
Bernard 95 108 112 131 Ber-
nard Jr 126 Clarissa B 126
Eliza T 85 Jane Cecelia 12
Jane Cecilia 76 Margaret S 158
Mary E 23 Mary Elizabeth 108
Nancy 162 Sarah Ellen 15 85
HOOFF, Caroline J 41 John 117
143 158 Lawrence Sr 53 Lewis
112 P H 163 Philip 168
HOOKES, Jacob 152 168 Mary
Ann 37 147 Sarah Ann 152
HOOPER, Rachel 38 152
HOPES, Catharine 151
HOPEWELL, Julia 10 69
HOPKINS, Mary 47 R S 103 Sarah
158 William 135
HORNER, John 101 John 156
Lydia 156
HORSEMAN, Mary A E 41
HORWELL, Amanda R 4 Ar-
manda M 54 Edward C 48 69
Emily M 169 170 Nancy E 15
Richard 121 170 Sarah M 28
121
HOSKINS, James O C 133
HOUGH, Edward S 137 Sophia 137
HOUSE, David 55 148 Elizabeth
55 James 126 Louisa 38 148
HOUSTON, Mary 122
HOWARD, Ann 102 150 Ann L
102 Beal 118 Beale 58 84 117
159 Catharine L 84 Elizabeth
27 29 63 117 125 159 Eugenia
102 George 139 Isaac 71 Jane
31 131 John 109 Mary 24 109
Mary E 87 Mary J 67 Mary
Jane 67 Nancy 63 Sally 28 121
144 Samuel 114 121
HOWELL, Mary D 35 140
HOWISON, Harriet G 126
HOWLAND, Thomas 81 Thomas

HOWLAND (continued)
H 126
HOY, Francis 117 Nelly 61
HUBBALL, Eletia 55
HUBBLE, Polly 13 78
HUCORN, Esther H 17 91 Francis
157
HUDDLESTON, Elizabeth 149
HUDDLETON, Jane 120
HUDGENS, Jane E 36
HUDGINS, Jane E 146
HUDSON, Julia Ann 57 Mary Ann
128 Sarah 50
HUFF, Powell H 141
HUGHLEY, Matilda Lee 3
HUGHNELY, Matilda Lee 3 52
HUGHS, Benjamin see HEWS,
Benjamin 99
HUGNELY, Semphonica 12
HUGUELY, Elishaba Harris 5 57
HUGUELY, Geo F 77 Semphonica
77
HULBARD, Jeremiah 144
HULL, Mary 19 95
HUME, C Ann 115 Catherine Ann
26
HUMPHREY, Mary 82
HUMPHREYS, Abna 147 John 90
John T 166
HUMPHRIES, Abner 66 Ann 86
John 142 John S 60 86
HUNGER, Catharine A 49
HUNT, Elizabeth 110 Mary A 11
Mary Ophelia 73 Sarah Ann
Birch 145
HUNTER, Alexander 93 142 Ann
H 142 Ann M 40 Ann Margaret
157 Eliza 73 Elizabeth C 88
Euna 146 Hannah 31 Harriet
162 John 73 119 143 Margaret
13 80 Mary A 89 Mary W 28
119 Robert 80 Robert W 119
William 157
HUNTINGTON, Sabina 23
HURDLE, Levi 68 103 136 141
143 Sarah Ann 141
HURDLESTON, Jane 28 120
HURLEY, Eunice 22
HURSE, Betsey 108
HURST, Elizabeth 41 160 161
John 50
HUSTON, William 124

HUTCHESON, Ann 165 Catharine
34 138 James 101 150
HUTCHINS, Mary Elizabeth 124
Sally 166 William 73
HUTCHINSON, Ann 43 George 109
HUTCHISON, George 63
HUTSON, Elizabeth 52 Mary Ann
63
HYNEMAN, Jacob 130
HYNEMAN, Margaret 31 130
HYNES, Alfred 118
INGRAHAM, Maria 46
INGRAM, Hannah 29 123
IRVIN, David 148
IRWIN, David 154 Frances F 18
Sarah 86
ISAAC, Samuel 132
ISAACS, Samuel 87 93
ISABELL, Jonah 85 92
ISLER, Sarah C 144
JACK, James 155 162
JACKSON, Ann 14 Anna 156 Clara
42 164 Elizabeth 138 Endora A
7 Flora 7 Isaac 68 John 51
Lucretia 37 148 Mary 52 Spen-
cer 138
JACOB, Ann G 59 Julia Ann 160
JACOBS, Ann G 6 Caroline 69
Elizabeth 39 154 Emily 163
Hannah Ann 17 89 John 109
Julia Ann 138 Margaret 123
Presley 123 163 Prestley 154
Thomas 138 Thomas E 75
Thomas Sr 97
JAMES, Margaret 5 56
JAMIESON, Andrew 68 Robert 46
66 92 168
JAMIESSON, Mary R 42
JANNEY, Abel 140 Hannah Ann
103 Lucretia 133 Maria 104
Phineas 104 Rachel E 101
Rebecca 21 Tacy M 23
Thomas 133
JANSON, Caroline 16
JANUARY, Catharine 113
JARBOE, David 149 George 77
JARBOUR, David 78
JARVINS, Sarah 22
JARVIS, David 65 Thomas 99
JAVENS, Elizabeth 131
JAVINS, Catharine 2 48 145 Den-
nis 87 106 Ellen 140

JAVINS (continued)
George 140 James 91 John 64
Julia A 23 106 Martha 160
Mary 96 Sarah 64 Selina Ann
158 Susan 14 15 87 Thomas 97
Thompson 106 William 48
JAVIS, James 166
JEFFERSON, Ann 12 77 Ben-
jamin 122 Henry 129 Mary 129
Mary Ann 32 132 Nancy 12
Sarah E 159 Susan 122
JEFFERY, Ann 82
JEFFRIES, Eugenia 23 106
JENKINS, Ann 159 David 57 144
148 Emeline 21 100 Johnston
150 Joseph 45 Louisa 37 148
Lydia B 22 104 Mary Ann 4 25
112 Sarah 30 127 Uriah 100 104
Violet 40 Violett 157 William
60
JENSON, Carline 87
JEROME, Elizabeth 7 63
JERRO, Mary 12 77
JETT, Arrianna 113
JEWELL, Elijah 128 Fielder 47
JEWETT, Joseph G 70 Mary Al-
ton 32
JINKINNS, Ann J 55
JOHNS, John 82 Peter 121
JOHNSON, Aquilla 86 Becky 128
Bryant 112 122 E J 28 Eleanor
140 Eliz M 166 Elizabeth 28
111 121 Elizabeth Jane 120 El-
len 31 131 Ellenor 34 35 Flora
61 George 52 133 Jane 100
John M 104 120 John T 130
Letitia 150 Martha 30 Nancy
117 Polly 34 Rachal 106
Rachel 23 Reuben 110 Sarah 6
Sarah A 133 William 98 121
143 156
JOHNSTON, Agnes 7 Elizabeth 29
123 Fanny 48 Hezekiah 107
Jane 158 John 108 119 Mar-
garet A H 119 Martha 127 Martha D 98 Mary 159 Philip P 60
Polly 138 Reuben 98 Reuben Jr
46 50 53 54 61 69 94 118 128
153 154 158 169 Reubin Jr 62
Sarah 59 Sarah Ann 32 Selina R
70 Theophilus see JOHNSON,
Theophilus 23

JONES, A P 84 Ann 30 127
Eleanor 116 Eliza R 157
Elizabeth 9 28 67 122 Ezekiel
127 Ezikiel 46 George 123
Helen 67 Jane 135 John see
JOHNS, John 107 Letty 105
Mary 6 59 Mary H 5 57 Milly
Ann 71 Moses 67 Paulina 48
Rebecca 104 Sarah 109 169
Stanfield 117 Thacker 108
Thomas H 84 157
JORDON, John 73 Sarah 46
Thompson 46 154 46
JOURDAN, Rebecca A 60
JOURDOUN, Elizabeth 89
JUDDLESTON, John 149
JUDGE, Rachel 163
JUDSON, Julia Ann 5
JULIUS, Elizabeth 61 Milly 62
JURNO, Margaret 126
KAIN, Emmit 91
KANE, Rebecca 114
KARKEEK, Elizabeth 27 118
KEACH, Elizabeth 6 60
KEASER, Eliza 24 109
KEATING, Edward 97 Elizabeth
49 George 129 J N 116 Mary
116 Olivia 130
KEATLY, Jane 30 127
KEATON, Lucy 122
KEEFER, Caroline E 162 Chris-
tian 81 Sarah 104
KEENE, Nancy 4 55 Newton 76
KEFFER, Caroline E 42
KEIGHTLEY, George H 148
KEITH, Catharine C 109
Catherine C 24 James 61
Thomas R 109
KELL, Alesanna 7 63 Isaac 63
121 126
KELLEY, James 157 William 72
KELLY, Elizabeth 42 161 James
129 Jeremiah 122 Martha 32
131 Mary 98 Mary Ann 16 88
Robert 74
KELTON, Eliza 18 Georgeanna
126 Georgiana 30
KENADY, Sarah 89
KENDRICK, Richard 156
KENNEDY, Elizabeth 133 John
121 Patty 2 50 Susanna Maria
24 109

KENNER, George 51 James 144
Jane A 35 Jane H 141
KENSEY, William 130
KENT, John 139 Malinda 15 Mar-
tha 37 148 Nancy 1 46 Sabina
34 139 Stephen 136
KERBY, Georgana 161
KERR, James D 74 John 145
KERRY, James D Jr 122
KESLEY, Margaret M 88 Obediah
76
KESSNER, Elizabeth 21
KETLING, Mary 26 116
KEYS, John A 107
KIDWELL, Chloe 11 72 Elijah 72
Harriet A 9 James M 48 John
66 Louisa 65 Mary E 2 Pres-
cilla 48
KIGGINS, Ann 123
KIGHTLEY, Matilda 74 Susanna
74
KILHAM, Elizabeth 16 88
KILLIUM, Sally 115
KILTON, Eliza M 93
KILY, Mary 83
KINCAID, Eliza 13 78 George 50
100 Joanna 32 Sarah Elizabeth
84
KING, Aminta 107 Ann 3 52 Anna
123 Arminta 23 Benjamin 56
142 Charles 66 151 Elizabeth
33 136 James 59 153 John 131
John J 125 John W 167 Mar-
garet 98 124 Mary 10 54 69 100
Nancy 8 66 Patrick 50 Richard
H 48 Sally 144 William 72 123
KINNER, Emeline 156
KINSEY, Adaline 82 Ben S 121
138 Benj S 63 Benjamin S 120
Caroline 138 Hannah 80 Lucy
86 Mary E 121 Rebecca 26 115
Zenas 80 99 110 Zenus 82
KINZER, J Louis 60
KIRBY, Ann 168 Eliz 20
Elizabeth 59 John 59 168
Nancy 73
KIRK, Ann 5 57 Hariet 22 Harriot
104 Mary 5 56 Samuel 56 57
William 104
KIRKPATRICK, William 124 125
KIRSH, Catherine 16
KITCHEN, Elisha 87

189

KITELEY, Mary 145 Mary Ann 85
 Matilda 11 74
KITELY, Rachel 43 Sarah 36 145
KITTY, Jane 127
KLINE, Catharine 88 Gabriel 88
KNIGHT, Bennett 154 Elizabeth
 43 166 Milly 40 157
KOONES, Caroline 36 143 David
 69 Frederick A 117 161
KORN, Elizabeth W 117 John 63
 117 Margaret 63 Mary Ann S
 109
KORNE, Mary Ann 24
KRAUTH, Julia H 24 111
KRONES, Frederick A 112
KUNE, Elizabeth 32 133
LACEY, Laurence 72
LACOCK, Phebe 43 165
LADD, Joseph B 75
LAFERTY, Elizabeth 133
LAMBERT, Benjamin H 145 Geo
 153 Mary 10 69 Sarah 38 153
LAMBKIN, Eleanor 41 161
LAMPHIER, Harriet 120 Robert G
 120
LANE, Jane 170 Mary 85
LANGFORD, Sarah J 6
LANHAM, Altheir 122 Elias 113
 Harriet 112 John 122 153 Mary
 30 126 Sarah 14 82 Susannah
 17 91
LANNEGAN, Mary 124
LANNON, Letitia 18
LANNUM, John 92 Letitia 92
LANPHIER, Elizabeth 100
LANSDALE, Caroline D 13 79
LARMOUR, Mary 21 102 Samuel
 B 102
LASKEY, Mary 30
LATHAM, Catharine 101 130 Ed-
 ward see LATHRAM, Edward
 25 Elizabeth 109 Ellinder 62
 Maria 92 R W 141 Rosa 27 123
 Sarah 42 163 Susan 111 Wil-
 liam 62 123 163
LATHRAM, Elizabeth 61
LATIMER, Thomas 146
LAUR, Joshua 145
LAURASON, Alice 140 James 115
 140 145 Jas 83 Nancy Buleher
 115 Robert 136 138
LAURENCE, John 55 Judith 23

LAURENCE (continued)
 106
LAUSON, John 136
LAVENDER, Martha 108
LAWLESS, Joanna 30
LAWRASON, Alice 35 James 115
 122 162 Mary Anne 35 Mary
 Miller 115
LAWRENCE, Ann E 150 John 113
 Rebecca 39 154
LAWS, Ann 95 131 Ann E 68
 Bolitha 100
LAWSON, Elizabeth 96 John 56
 81 121 Mary 136 Rachael 104
LAWYER, Margaret P M 117
LAY, G W 139 Henry C 111
LEADBEATER, John 83
LEAP, Ann 30 125 Jacob 125
LEARY, Andrew 56 130 Frances 4
 56 Hector 103 Nancy 22 Sarah
 165
LEATHRUM, Maria 6 59
LEAVY, Nancy 102
LEBREY, Elizabeth 82
LEDDY, Owen 101
LEE, Alfred 103 Ann 12 77 Ann
 Hennrietta 116 Casius F 151
 Cassius F 107 148 Cecelia 33
 Cecilia 136 Cornelia 101 Ed-
 mund J 55 Edmund J Jr 97
 Elizabeth 27 118 Ellen 3 F 147
 Hannah 152 John 97 103
 Juliann 163 Lewis 136 Louisa
 142 Martha 78 Mary 34 139
 Nancy 94 Philip 77 78 Phillip
 114 Richard H 91 Richard
 Henry 114 Robert E 26 114
 Sidney S 114 Sophia 98 Susan-
 nah 38 150 Zenobia 96
LEECH, Ann 153
LEEDER, Thomas 59
LEGG, Elias P 97 Elizabeth 8
 Elizabeth A 160 Margaret 6 60
 Sarah J 27 119 William G 119
LEGGE, Elizabeth 64
LeGRAND Mary C 107
LEONARD, Rebecca W 111
 Sophia E 117
LESLE, James W 115
LETHGON, Alexander 96
LEVERI, Septimus see LEVER-
 ING, Septimus 115

190

LEWIN, Joseph 89
LEWIS, Helen 27 119 Henry 144
Judith 29 Margaret G 63 Mary
Ann 36 144 Mary Elisa Angela
9 Richard 161 Samuel 51 86
William 161
LIBBY, Richard 142 156
LIGHTFOOT, Betsey 36 146 Wm
116
LIMRICK, Anna 20 98
LINDSAY, Elizabeth 105 Ellen 68
86 Ellen C 99 John 118 Martha
A 93 Mary 154 Nancy 88 Noble
148 Noblet 62 Rebecca 148
Salley 118 Samuel 53 149
Sarah 47
LINSLEY, E 65
LIPSCOMB, William 57
LITHCOE, Jane 28 120
LIVINGSTON, John 92
LLOYD, Anna Harriet 151 Edward
91 John 136 152 153 Paulina
60 Rana 41 Rebecca 153 Selina
136
LOCKE, Thomas 136
LOCKER, Mary 36 144 Susanna
145 Susannah 36
LOGAN, Hugh M 169 Rachael 20
100 Randolph 76
LOGGINS ,Janney 105
LOMAX, Elizabeth 135 Henry 162
John 131 Martha 148 Stephen
135 Thomas 138
LONDON, Phebe 42 161
LONG, Linny 23 107 Mary D 92
William 107
LONGDEN, Kitty 3 53 Lucy 97
Ralph 97
LONGDON, Ann 37 150 Elizabeth
5 58 John 150 John A 58 Julia
95 Lucy 31 Maria 55 Mary E
37 147 Olfehair 113 Olphair 25
Sarah 86 Walter 113 122
LOPTON, Peter 156
LOUDOUN, George 117 Nancy 150
Peter 150
LOVE, Elizabeth 56 Julia Ann 4
56
LOWBER, Catharine 39 155
LOWE, Ann M 168 Christiana 4
55 James R M 49 James Rec-
tor Magruder 105 Julia 38

LOWE (continued)
Julianna M 151 Mary 35 143
Phoebe C 37 149
LOWER, John 155
LOWRY, Robert 86
LOYD, Elizabeth 37 148 John 148
Mary Ann 148 Rebecca 114
LUCAS, Catharine 42 164 John R
148 Molly 155 Rebecca 31 130
Wilhelmina 83
LUCKETT, Ann 17
LUDL..., Thomas H 112
LUDLOW, J R 104
LUKE, Eliza 2 50
LUMSDON, Catharine 40 157
LUNT, Betsey 6 Betsy 59 Ezra
115
LUPTON, Daniel L 69
LUTZ, Ann 13 80 Sophia 21 100
LYLE, Elizabeth 113 William 68
LYLES, Elizabeth 55 Isabella F
51 Julia Ann Maria 131
Rachael 55
LYNCH, Christina 156
LYNN, Adam 165 Martha Ann 24
Mary 154
LYNTON, George L 134
McAFEE, Mary 64
McALLAN, Alice 16 87
McALLISTER, Margaret 34 139
McATTEE, Chloe 129 Samuel 129
130
McBRIDE, Margaret A 126 Susan
35 141
McBROCKLIN, Sally 57
M'CALLESTER, Margaret 8
McCALLY, William 148
McCARTHY, Michael 123
McCARTY, Amanda A 148 Mar-
garet 43 140 Michael 123 Milly
3 53 Nancy 81 Timothy 70
William 149
McCLEA, Elizabeth 26 116
McCLEAN, Hannah A 67 Lucretia
110
McCLEISH, George 147 Margaret
11 75
McCLEREN, Ann 101
McCLERY, Indiana J 16
McCLIFF, Wm 71
McCLISH, Archibald 83 George
138 Margaret 11 75 William 85

McCLOUD, Mrs 35
McCOBB, John 52 Mary W 73
  Rachael D 84 Rachel 15
McCOLLESTER, Margaret 65
McCORMICK, Martha 67 Thomas
  M 167
McCOY, Mary 113
McCUE, Mary 24 111
McCUIN, Harriot 139
McCUTCHENS, Martha 69
McCUTCHESON, Ellenor 29
McDANIEL, James 103
McDEARMONT, Edward 110
McDELLA, Jane 141
McDELLER, Ann 86
McDEMICK, Ann 7
McDENNICK, Mary Ann 61 Wil-
  liam 61 129
McDILLER, Ann 86 Sarah A 15
McDONALD, Donald 148 Eliza 20
  97 James 129 Margaret 31 129
McDONGALL, Elizabeth B 113
McFADDEN, Ann 25 113
  Elizabeth 39 153 Isabella 39
  153
McFARLAIN, Benny 110
McFARLANE, Ann 167 B 24 John
  110 127 145 Margaret 127
McFARLEN, George 110
McFARLIN, John 127 Margaret 30
  127
M'FAW, Mary 8
McGEE, Elizabeth 146 Samuel
  133
McGLENNIN, Rose 33 135
McGRAW, Benjamin 140 152
  Margaret 152 Susan 140
McINTIRE, Catherine O 18 Mary
  19 Sarah Eliza 26 115
McINTYRE, Catherine O 93 Mary
  94
McKAY, Elizabeth 113 Susan 20
  99
McKEE, Sarah 37 149
MACKELROY, Jane 2 50
McKELVEC, Catharine 23
  Elizabeth 107
McKELVIN, Catharine 107
McKENNEY, John 98 Sarah B 20
McKENZIE, Harriotte 82 James
  139 161 Lewis 82
McKERVEN, Mary 3 52

McKEW, Jane 157
McKEWIN, Mary 29 Nancy 123
  Robert 123
McKINNEY, Henrietta 26 116
  Mary 5 58 Sarah B 98
McKNIGHT, Catharine A 70
  Catherine A 10 Charles 50 70
  77 117 125 133 145 154 Mar-
  garet S 111 Margaret Susan 24
  William H 111 Wm H 69
McLAUGHEN, Edward 115
McLAUGHLIN, Ann 144 Edward
  144 163
McLEAN, Eliza 45
McLEOD, Mary Ann 92
McMACHEN, Henry 98
McMAHAN, Isabella 109
McMAHON, Isabella 24
McMECHEN, William 134
McMEHEN, William 129
McNAMARA, John 90 Mary 121
  Sarah D 77
McNAUGHTEN, Peter 124
McNEAL, Lucinda R 120
McNOTON, George see
  McNAUGHTEN, George 124
McPHERSON, Julia Ann 37 Julia
  Anna 148 Sarah 28 121
McQUEEN, M E 115 Mary E 27
McREA, Ann A 4 78 Kitty 5 57
McSHANE, Charles 55
MADDEN, Mary F 134 Sally R 8
  64
MADDOCK, Ann R 97
MADDOX, Ann 21 102 Elizabeth
  Ann 125
MADELLA, Susan 22
MAGEE, Mary Ann 64
MAGER, Bernard 97
MAGHER, Matthew 111
MAGIE, Mary Ann 8
MAGLENEN, Catharine 154
MAGOR, John M 105
MAGRUDER, Maria 7 62 Rachel 8
MAHANNY, Maria 59 Mary 6
MAHAUNY, Maria 59
MAHONEY, Ally 110
MAHONY, Sarah 106 Thomas 70
MAJOR, Ann 33 136 John 54 Mary
  6 54
MANDELL, John C 96 164 165
  Martha 165 Mary E 96 Mary

MANDELL (continued)
Eliz 19
MANDEVILLE, Ann 63 Joseph 63
113 Joseph Jr 130 Maria 36
Susan 25 113
MANDLEY, Elizabeth 33 135
MANERY, John 49
MANKIN, Charles 55 110 157
Elizabeth 75 James E 91 134
Mary Ann 40 157 Mathew 69
Wm 75
MANKINS, Betsy 56 Catharine
155 Catherine 39 Charles 53
David 103 David 155 James 96
James E 159 Mary Jane 133
William 95
MANLEY, John H 49 68 Matthew
75 Sarah 2 47
MANLY, Barbara 148 Jenny 156
Jenny 40 Mathew 94
MANN, Elizabeth 53 Zachariah
105
MANNING, Margaret M 30 31 128
MANOUGH, Joanna 7
MANSFIELD, Emeline 105 Henry
57 102 105 149 James 101
Julia A 15 Julia Ann 86 Wil-
liam 122
MARBURY, Elizabeth C 29 124
Henry 124 Leonard 80 Lucy 27
MARCEL, Israel 84
MARIE, Elizabeth 33
MARINE, Elijah 160
MARK, Eliza 12 106 Elizabeth 23
106 Hortensia H 68 John Jr 135
Mary L 18 Samuel 106 134
MARKELL, George 74 153 George
H 84 Sarah Ann Charlotte 74
MARKLEY, Elizabeth 75 Mary L
11 75 Sarah A 105 Susanna 26
MARKLY, Elizabeth 11 Susannah
116
MARLE, Elizabeth 135 Joseph
135 Rebecca 25 113
MARMADUKE, ELizabeth 77
MARO, Catharine 130
MARR, Eliza 106 Matthew 106
MARROW, Milly 136
MARSH, Phebe 116 117
MARSHALL, Alexander J 143 Ann
D 22 104 Henry 131 Patty 3 50
Richard 127 Robert P 129

MARSTELLER, Elizabeth 68
MARSTON, Ann M 102 John 105
Sarah 28 161
MARTIN, Ann 150 160 Ann G 113
Elizabeth 71 James 112 Jane 5
58 Mary E 105 Nancy 17 89
166 Susan 6 59 Thomas L 88
113
MARTINDALL, Eleanor 158
MARTS, Lucinda 155
MARVEL, Betsey 79 Henry 132
MARVELL, John 158 Nancy 134
MASHERSEAD, Elias 132
MASKEL, Joseph 161
MASON, Aminta 22 102 Ann G
139 Anna M 114 Anna Maria 25
26 Chloe 146 Elizabeth 99
John 102 Matilda 139 R C 120
Sally E 77 120 Sarah E 62
Sarah G 89 Thompson F 110
139
MASSEY, Ann 138 139 Jane 129
Mary 27 118
MASSIE, John W 85 121 Marian
133
MASTERS, Eliz 23 Elizabeth 107
MASTERSON, John 99 L 89
Laughlin 57 114 141 Loughin
121 Loughlin 90 148 Loughton
119
MASTIN, William 91
MATHANEY, Thomas 118
MATTHEWS, Edmonia 126
Mildred 110
MATTOCHS, Mary 49
MATTOX, Eleanor 26 Eleanor A
115
MAUNCEY, Mary 109
MAY, Ann Maria 34 140 Elizabeth
25 Francis B 137 140 Mary 5
58 Sarah 40 137 157
MAYHALL, Betsey 151 Betsy 38
MAZARVEY, Thomas 113
MEADE, Edwin Theodore 124
Louisa M B 42 164 Sarah Ann
C 125 Theo 114 Theodore 125
Theodore see MEADE, Edwin
T 124
MEADS, Elizabeth 2 48
MELLEN, George 135
MERCHANT, Mary Ann 98
Thomas 98

MERRICK, Priscilla 9 69
MERTLAND, Susannah 29 124
METCALF, Dwight 134
Thomas 98 148 164
MIDDLETON, Harriet 95 James P
86 97 124 131 145 162 164
Marian 145 Sarah 40 Susan 157
MILBURN, Stephen 66
MILES, Abraham 96 Lucretia 96
MILLAN, George 102 121 James
107 Lyle 167
MILLBURN, Stephen see MIL-
BURN, Stephen 125
MILLER, Charles B 125 Cornelia
38 Elizabeth 44 55 98 168 H 59
Harriet 128 Jane Douglass 57
R H 38 Robert H 133 169 Wil-
liam D 85 147 Zetisha 128
MILLES, Benjamin see MILLAS,
Benjamin 29
MILLON, George 59
MILLS, Amelia 14 81 Eliza 4
Elizabeth 41 159 Emeline 110
Ephraim 160 Harriet R 21 102
Jane 156 Mary 14 72 147
Nancy 107 Phebe A 18 Phebe
Ann 92 Polly 38 151 Rebecca
53 Rebecca Jane 16 88 Wil-
liam 155 William 87 110
MINOR, Catharine Ann 114 Daniel
56 70 100 164 George Jr 50
Gertrude Moss 164 Hunter H 77
Mary F 8 65 Mary Francis 65
Sarah A 130 William 130 Wm
114
MITCHEL, Catharine 39
MITCHELL, Ann 128 Ann Eliza
47 Catharine C 154 Catherine 8
66 Deborah 35 Judson 47
Richard B 45 William 67
MITCHUM, Mary 8
MITTCHELL, Nelly 71 Peggy 154
MITTCHUM, Mary 65
MOAN, Aletha 37 147
MOCKBEE, R 157
MOFFETT, John 92 John see
MOFFIT, John 30 Robert 126
MOFFITT, John 87
MOHLER, Mary 36
MONIS, Manitta 156
MONROE, John M 48 Sarah A E G
12 76

MOODS, Ann Maria 134
MOODY, Peggy 36 144 Sarah 14
83
MOORE, Alexander 50 70 91 149
Ann 22 Ann Caverly 105 Bar-
bara 25 113 Elizabeth 39 56
107 Jane 147 Jane J 70 Julia
Ann 20 98 Robert 133 Sarah 14
78 80 William 57 79
MORE, Barbara 25
MORGAN, Alexander 132
Elizabeth 67 Flora E 43 168
Hannah 22 105 Henry 137
Henry see MORGAN, Hiram 30
Hiram 109 Jacob 167 Jane E
100 Margaret Virginia 137
Mary 37 149 Mary Ann 107 139
Polly 95 Sarah 37 149 Thomas
67 William 105 107 119 127
165 Wm 100
MORRELL, Annie L 142
MORRIL, Mariah 17
MORRIS, Ann 9 69 Eleanor 128
Georgianna 151 Henry 56
James 50 John H 93 Julia 50
Levin 108 Manitta 156 Maria 2
Sally 157 Susan E 11 74
MORRISON, William 90 William
M 48
MOSS, Obediah 73
MOTHERSEAD, Elias 104
MOTHERSED, Stephen 83
MOTHERSON, Christopher 102
MOULDEN, Ann 66
MOULDS, Elizabeth 167
MOULDY, George 51
MOULDZ, Elizabeth 43
MOUNT, Mary F 140 Thomas 141
MOUNTFORD, Timothy 57 154
MOXLEY, Benjamin 72 74 Maria
70 Martha Jane 72
MUIR, James 119 Jane 91 Mary
145
MULLEN, Elizabeth 9 68
Emeline 66 Emiline 8 Em-
meline 66 Lucy 47 Mary 128
Samuel 128 Wm 47
MULLIN, Lucy Ann 2 Lumsford
140 Mary 30
MUNAY, Mary Ann 134
MUNROE, Thomas 67
MURPHEY, Margaret 126

MURPHY, Ann 122 Edward 61 110
MURRAY, Ann 41 160 Ann O 57
  Edward 128 George 85 163 Ig-
  natius 69 84 160 James 80 126
  129 Liddy 163 Lucretia 1 46
  Lydia 42 Margarett 64 Mary
  Ann 134 Thomas 58
MURRELL, Bennett 159
MUSGRAVE, Aaron R 170
MUSGROVE, Margaret 8 Margaret
  W 64 Maria 132
MYERS, Barbara 30 127 Catharine
  91 Catherine 17 Elizabeth 44
  145 169 Fanny 17 89 Mary 92
  Prudence 161 Rebecca 7 61
NAIRN, Margaret 4
NALBY, Sarah Ann 104
NANERY, John 152
NASH, Jane 71 167 Jane Ann 58
  Mary 167 Robert 82 89
NEAL, Christie 56 Jane Christie
  5 John 56
NEALE, Betsy 39 158 Catharine
  118 Catherine 27 Christopher
  114 Margaret 4 56 William 82
NEIL, Jeremiah 141
NEILL, Betsy 127
NEILLE, Christie 56 Jane
  Christie 5 John 56
NELSON, Henley 47 John 100 135
  Nancy 9 67 Sally 2 51
NEVELL, Joseph 123
NEVETT, Ann Virginia 49 James
  C 49
NEVITT, Joseph 169 Julia Ann
  162 Rosanna 55
NEWTON, Augustine 70 78 141
  151 Catharine C 125 Jane 10
  70 Maria C 122 Martha 168
  Mary R 1 45 Sarah Ann 44 168
  William 45 William C 126
  Wm 168
NICHINGS, William see
  NICHENS, William 130
NICHOLAS, Ann T 94 Mildred
  Ann 91 Zachariah 94
NICHOLLS, Matilda 77
NICHOLS, Matilda 12
NICHOLSON, Henry 167 Jane 108
  Mary 25 Mary Ann 36 146
NICOLL, Harriet V 112 Harris 112
NIGHT, Mariah 29 124

NIGHTINGALE, James 133 138
NOLAN, William 128
NOLAND, Hariet 60 Susan 128
  Thomas J 133
NOLLOWOOD, Rhoda 2
NORFELT, Thomas 160
NORFOLK, Priscilla C 33 136
NORRIS, Eliza W 14 Francis 52
  James 148 Mark 120 Mary 37
  120 148 O 46 56 60–62 66 67
  74 85 92 102 108 109 111 114
  116 126 127 132 133 137 151
  156 160 163 165 167 168 169
  Oliver 70 83 85 113 158 166
  Rev 79 Sarah 33 135 Theo 80
NOWELL, James 55 James see
  KNOWEL, James 111
NOWLAND, Margaret 84 Nimrod
  H 59 William 131
NUTT, Elizabeth 75 Mary Ann 68
  Wm D 75
O'Brien, Matthew 73
O'CONNELL, Margaret 90
O'CONNER, Hannah 34 William
  53
O'CONNOR, Hannah 139
O'DAYE, Mary 64
O'NEAL, E 28 Elizabeth 154
  Mary 86
O'NEALE, Ann M 104 Elizabeth
  120 Mart T 111 Mary 25
O'NEIL, Ann 101 Ferdinand 101
O'NEILLE, Eleanor 3 51
O'REILEY, Eliza H 50
OAKLEY, Ellen Ann 10 Margaret
  124
OARD, Joseph 119
ODEN, Nathaniel 93
ODLETON, Maria 21 100
OGDEN, Elizabeth 150 Julia Ann
  150 Thomas C 158
OGDON, Ann 150
OGLE, Richard L 101
OLIVER, Catharine 44 169
ORD, Nancy 11 74
ORME, Eliza 41 159
OSBURN, Anne 17 91
OSWALD, Henry 90 94 116
OTHRAM, Susan 122
OVERMAN, John 75
OWENS, Mary Eliza 86
PADETT, Susan 19

PADGET, James 67 Mary A 67
　Mary C D 36 Mary P 9
PADGETT, Ann 150 Catharine 30
　127 Catharine Ann 124
　Catherine Ann 29 Charles 127
　Elizabeth M 60 Geo 110
　George 110 James 67 Jane Ann
　15 86 87 John 88 John G 124
　John W 53 Mary A 67 Rebecca
　80 Sarah 32 132 William 127
　169 Wm Jr 129
PAGE, Ann 8 66 Ann Catharine 94
　Cecelia 159 Charles 66 82
　Delia 19 Delilah 94 Eliza 118
　Elizabeth 27 Martha Ellen 40
　Washington C 66 118
　Washington G 94 William 57
　96 Wm Byrd 62
PAGET, Mary 8 64
PAINE, Maria W 87
PALMER, John 99 116
PARK, George 138
PARKER, George 90 Jenny 99
　John 82 Polly 25 114
PARLRERE, John 164
PARMER, Margaret A 104
PARRY, Edward 50
PARSON, Ann Eliza 125
　Catherine 15 Cathrine 86
PARSONS, Eliza 169 Elizabeth 16
　50 67 87 John 53 59 132 133
　142 M 13 Margaret 80 Mary
　Ann Elizabeth 59 Sarah 4 42 54
　164 Sarah A 129 Thomas 64 67
PASCOE, Charles 49 57 58 95 120
　130 J J 150 John L 128 146
　150 159 Mary 19 95
PATON, Ann B 104 Mary Ann 44
　Mary Jane 77 Rebecca 138
PATRERELL, Susanna 31 130
PATTEN, Mary Ann 44 168
　Selena 164
PATTERSON, Ann M 21
　Catharine 17 Catherine 91
　Henry 46 James 114 Martha 84
　Nancy Ann 169 Sarah 51 Sarah
　Jane 76 Sarah M 32 Sarah
　Matilda 134 Susan Ann Maria
　102 William 91 94 102 118 126
　134 Wm P 167
PATTISON, Caroline 60
PATTON, Ann Feilder 34 Feilder

PATTON (continued)
　138 Hezekiah 72 James 133
　Rosalie C 115 Susannah 107
PAYNE, George 92 Horace 87
　Isaac 103 Jane 61 Maria 30
　127 Mary 92 Merkey 144 Nancy
　32 133 Thomas H 80 William
　80
PAYSON, Caroline Eliza 165
PEAK, Mary E M 56
PEARSON, Jane 138 John 128 138
　Milly 128 Rosa 41 159 Sarah
　17 90 Thomas W 89
PEEK, William 113
PEIRCE, Eliza. 35
PELTON, Enoch 48
PELTY, Sally 51
PENDAL, Mary 129
PENDALL, Mary 31
PENN, Daniel K 125 Deliah 153
　Delila 39 Elizabeth 20 99
　Francis Ann 88 Matilda 46 146
　Walter 99 143 Walter L 88 108
　131 William 146 Zachariah 73
PEPPER, Sarah 22 97
PERCY, Maria 50
PERDRED, Ellen 108
PERNAL, Thamer 24
PERNEL, Thamer 109
PERRY, Alexander 75 100 112
　151 157 165 Ann 3 Anne 53
　Charlotte 13 80 Harriet 38 151
　James 136 Jane 100 Maria A
　123 Sarah 43 136 165
PETERSON, Charles 165
PETIT, Elizabeth 146
PETITT, Elizabeth 36
PETTIT, Jane Ann 116 John 116
　William R 145
PEYTON, Ann Maria 110 Cornelia
　35 142 Francis 110 114 Laura
　34 139 Sarah Ann 44 168
PHENIX, Ann 21 101
PHILIPS, Eleanor 137 Elizabeth
　23 85 106 James see PHIL-
　LIPS, James 135 John 111
　Mary Elizabeth 131 Polly 10
　71 William 106 William F 148
PHILLIPS, Elizabeth 106 George
　140 John 124 Mary Elizabeth
　31 131 William 106
PICKENS, Rebecca 86

196

PICKERING, Levi 61 96 118 137
141 Mary Ann 99
PICKING, John 116
PIDDIT, Susan 94
PIERCE, Camilla 150 Elizabeth
142 Thomas 117
PIERCY, Maria 2
PILES, Anna 125 Elizabeth 38
102 124 Linney 168 Peter 124
162 Sarah 121
PINDRED, Ellen 108
PIPER, Betsey 56 Catharine 15
86 James E 64 Margaret 169
Samuel 143 Sarah A 6 Sarah
Ann 59
PIPSICO, Catharine 76 Henry 135
John 74 76 Lucinda 11 74
PIPSICOE, George 120
PIPSICS, Catherine 12
PITCHER, Eliza 108
PITTEN, Elizabeth 77
PITTMAN, Edward 95
PLANT, James K 151
PLUM, Lewis W 70 157 Lewis
Wilson 111 Mary Ann 139
PLUMB, Joseph 113
POLLARD, Ann Elizabeth 97
Henry 103 Jane 53 Mary 142
William 97
POMERY, William 68 Wm 136
160
POOR, Charles 71 Mary E 71
POPLER, James 56
PORCELL, Frances M 25 Francis
M 114
PORTER, Imogen 19 Lucia C 41
159 Peggy 2
POSEY, Benjamin 75 Eleanor 147
Eliza 46 Elizabeth A 128 Sarah
4 54 67 Sarah Ann 12 76
POSTON, Ann Lucinda 39 Jane
Lucinda 155 Joseph 136 155
POTTEN, John 56 162
POTTER, James 166 Margaret
Ann 19 95
POTTS, Abraham E 65 Anna H
100 Harriot 1 47 Thomas 60 74
85 165 Wilhelmina D 97 98
Wilhelmina S 20
POWELL, Cuthbert 146 154 Edith
22 104 Frances 129 Harriet E
132 John S 155 Margaret 50

POWELL (continued)
Midred 121 Mildred 28 Virginia
C 155 William 106 120 166
POWERS, Elisa 76
PRACTOR, John J 47
PRATT, Emily 93 Harriet Louisa
31 Harriet Louise 130 William
130
PRESCOTT, Catharine 47 Wil-
liam 47
PRESTON, Margaret 16 87 Vir-
ginia P 163
PRETTYMAN, R F 109
PRICE, Alfred 65 Charles 137
David 71 105 139 Elizabeth 13
79 Ellis 55 Ellis L 137 George
54 74 139 155 Hannah 22 102
Harriett 22 Jane Ann 71
Jeremiah 127 Julia A K 127
Marietta 75 Matilda R 148
Susanna 44 144 Susannah 36
Virginia 110 William 75 Wm
75 Wm B 89
PRICHARD, Mary 163
PRITCHARD, Stephen 129
PROCTOR, John J 47
PURDIE, Patience 39 153
PURKINS, Rhode 18 92
PURKIS, Salley 159 Thomas 159
PURSE, Henry 138
PURSLEY, Ellen 154
QUAID, James 60 101
QUANDER, Osborn 137
RADCLIFF, Catherine A 14
RADDEN, Onnar 92
RAIN, Mary Ann 119
RALAY, Bennett 136
RALEY, Bennett 169
RAMSAY, Alice L 9 67 Amelia 3
50 Ann M 54 Catharine R 15 84
85 Eliza 4 Eliza J 54 G W D
85 106 George W D 84 Jesse T
54 Mary 132 153 Robert T 117
Sarah 8 65 William 45 151
RAMSEY, Ann M 4 Mary 36
RANDALL, Theopolus 108
RANDELL, Harriet 82 Sarah 36
146 Theophilus 82 146
RANSOM, Patty 30 127
RAPLEY, Charlotte M 112
RATCLIFF, Ann 25 111 Ignatius
111

197

RATCLIFFE, Eliza 149 Mary Ann 161 Richard B 161
RAWLING, John 85 Julia Ann 85
RAWLINGS, John 126 137 Julia Ann 15
REARDON, Elizabeth 122 John T 125 Rachael 143 Sarah A 119
REARY, Bennett 83
REASE, Catharine 44 Catherine 169
REASON, Sarah 20 98
REDMAN, Sinthy 135 Unis 149
REDMONDE, Edward 128
REED, Catharine 38 127 152 Harriett G 32 132 William 105
REEDER, Ann Clifton 133 Richard 56
REEDY, Polly 161
REEFE, Elizabeth 90
REELER, Samuel 94
REESE, Mary 103
REEVES, William 77 84
REID, Elizabeth Ann 82
REILY, Bennett 170 Mary 40 158 William 83
REINBER, Joseph 110
REISE, William L 79
REMSEY, Catharine S 143
RESLER, Eve 16 87
REUXBERRY, Reuben 74
REXTER, Ludwell Jr see RECTOR, Ludwell Jr 138
REYLY, Mary Ann 27 117
REYNOLDS, Elizabeth 12 77 Ellen M 94 Emily 17 Martha Ann 5 57 Mary 29 122 Rebecca 20 Rebeckah 99 William 122 William C 159
RHEEM, John 147
RHETT, Benjamin 139
RHODES, A E T 115 Anthony 51 71 97 104 121 Jane 47 Maria A 104 Maria W 73 Nancy 138 Susan 3 51
RICE, George 111 W H 93
RICHARDS, Ann 14 Carey 54 Catharine 63 John 139 John Jr 158 Kitty 29 123 Mariah 147 Milley 34 Milly 140 Wm B 119 Wm B Jr 84
RICHARDSON, Agnes 26 115 John 132 Mark 140

RICKARD, Nancy O 163
RICKETTS, Mary Elizabeth 167 William S 61
RICKEY, Ann Maria 143
RIFFETTS, Mary H 147
RIGGS, Elizabeth 155
RILEY, Mary 114 Sarah A 114 Sarah Ann 25
RINGGOLD, Catharine S L 165
RINKER, Sarah A 110
RIORDAN, Nancy 168
RISENER, Catharine 114
RISINGER, SALLY 16 Sally 88
RIVES, William C 81 141
RIXTER, Elisa 68 Eliza 9 Mary 68
ROACH, John 140 Philip 141 Susan 148
ROBBINS, Isaac H 55 104 Jane P 12 78
ROBERTS, Bridget 22 105 Eleanor 163 Henrietta F 142 John 162 Mary 41 Matidae 35 Matilda E 143 May 161 Rebecca S 89 Robert 53 Sophia M 162
ROBERTSON, Delilah 64
ROBEY Joseph see ROBY, Joseph 35 Stacey 117
ROBINSON, Ann 14 83 Ann Louisa 32 132 Catharine 147 Deliah 8 Elizabeth 141 James H 81 Jesse 147 166 John 141 John W 132 Lydia 30 128 Mary Ann 15 84 Matthew 97 Nelly 43 166 Polly 36 145 William 152
ROCK, Mary Ann 73 141 Richard 81 119 122 131 William W 71
RODGERS, Benjamin 94 Carroll 68 Jane 19 94 William S 137
ROGERS, Sylvia 114
ROLLINS, Elizabeth 80 John 147 Julia 147 Martha Ann 133
RONE, William see RENE, William 139
ROOE, Maria 12 67
ROOKER, Jobez 50
ROSE, Charlotte E 95 Henry 121 155 John 87 Maria Moore 155
ROSH, Mary Ann 11
ROSS, Ann 78 Catharine 20 96 Charles 77 96 Elizabeth 110

ROSS (continued)
Jane 90 John 78 86 125 Mary 29
125 Walter 115
ROTCH, Melinda 35 141 Susan 48
Winifred Ann 153
ROTCHFORD, Bartholemew 85
152 Bartholomew 140 Marshall
J 140 Mary Margaret 152
Richard 92 141 William 139
ROUNDSAVEL, Andrew 154
ROUNDSAVELL, Elizabeth 21
ROUNSAVELL, Andrew 83 97 102
Elizabeth 102
ROUSAVELL, Andrew 141
ROWE, Elizabeth 41 160 Maria
90
ROXBURY, Elizabeth 130 Jane 89
ROZIER, Eliza B 75
RUDD, Charles D 89 136
Elizabeth 152 Helen 103 John
A 60 152 Marian 136 Richard
111 Richard A 103 136 Richard
H 153
RUMNEY, Eliza 90 George 142
John 127
RUNNELLS, Jane 51 Sarah 100
RUSHMAN, William 136
RUSS, Ewell 152 169
RUSSELL, Catharine 128 George
58 72 86 94 95 96 105 106 109
127 164 165 166 167 Martha 30
125 Sarah Ann 10 71
RUST, Ewell 161
RUTTER, Josiah 53
RYAN, Ann 14 82
RYE, Lucy 101 Milly 87
SALES, Susan 4 56
SALOMONS, William 53
SANDFORD, Elizabeth 26 116
Theo 89 Thomas 60 106
SANFORD, Ann 26 115 116
Catharine 98 Catharine Porter
106 Esther W 76 Joseph L 123
168 Mary 148 Samuel 81 Sarah
29 Sarah E 123 Thomas 149
SATTERWHITE, Jeremiah 57 138
Jeremiah W 94 Mary A E 62
Rachel 34 138
SAULS, Edward 51 155 156
Rosalie 155
SAUNDERS, Mary 118
SAVERY, Rose 16 87

SAVOY, Louisa 71 William 71
Wm 71
SAWKINS, Sarah 163
SAX, Joseph 102
SAYRE, John J 57
SAYRES, John J see SAYRS, John
J 143 Sarah 92
SAYRS, John J see SAYRES, John
J 35
SCHAKESPEAR, William 50
SCHEARMAN, Mary 58
SCHROPSHIRE, Elizabeth 136
SCOTT, Allen 42 Alley 101 An-
denetta Jackson Anna
Allmassi Gertrude 60 Charles
51 60 117 Eliz 10 Eliza 72
Elizabeth Ann 27 117 Harriot
12 75 Horatio C 143 James S
72 77 Jesse 46 Lucinda 98
Mary 46 Milly 80 Mitty 13
Samuel 145 Thomas 86 135
Virginia 164
SCRIVENER, Mary 139
SEARS, Jane 82 William B 87
SEATON, Anna Maria V 107 Eliza
W 27 Eliza Wise 118 George
94 Hannah A 94 Hannah Ann 19
Rebecca 27 118
SEETEN, John 77
SELDEN, Eliza Armistead 26
Eliza. A 116
SELDON, Ann 166
SELF, Eliza 83 Sarah 81
SELICK, Chloe 166
SELLERS, Ann Eliza 29 122
SELVEY, Dorothy 22 105
SEMMES, Anna Sophia 147 Cath
M 144 George 82 Mary
Elizabeth 85 Thomas 85 89 92
100 102 William H 111
SEMMS, Eliza 27 118 George H
49 Margaret T 49
SETTLE, Frances E 21 102
SEWELL, Joseph 122 Matilda
116 Rachel Ann 28 122 Richard
122
SEXTON, Ann 108 Mary 34 138
SHACKELFORD, James 75 John
77
SHACKLEFORD, John 99
SHAKES, Cecelia 7 John 111
Mary Eleanor 111

199

SLADE, Charles 81 163 Mary 81
SLATER, Delila 5 Delilah 56
SLATFORD, George 68 George
   William 48 James 54 Sarah 2
   9 48 68 Thomas 158
SLEIGH, Susan 21 102 William
   102
SLY, John S 147 Rebecca 76
   Susannah 58
SMALL, Susanna 43
SMALLRIDGE, Gertrude 83
   Guertrude 14
SMALLWOOD, Eleanor 65
   Elizabeth 41 160 Nelly 154
   Nelly 39
SMEDLEY, Alice 95 Elizabeth 7
   62 Lydia I 102 Susan 27 119
SMELLING, Loudoun 115
SMITH, Adeline 68 Alexander 93
   Ann 8 33 65 68 134 Ann Maria
   107 Boyd 134 Cassandra 27
   123 Catharine 29 Cordelia 3 52
   Daniel 130 Daniel H 163
   Drucilla 19 95 E H 28 Elihu
   117 Eliza Ann 50 Elizabeth
   152 170 Elizabeth Harriot 119
   George H 60 Hannah 27 118
   Hugh C 149 James 134 James
   P 76 158 Jane 44 170 Jane A
   120 Jesse 58 152 John 82 115
   120 148 157 160 John K 76
   John L 119 John W 95 138
   John Y 55 Joseph 102 120 128
   Madison 54 Martha 154 Martha
   J 94 Martha Jane 18 Mary 6 8
   60 66 Mary Ann 102 Mary Ann
   Harrison 103 Mary Jane 47
   Mary W 6 Nancy 6 60 72 R E
   104 Rebecca 12 13 73 Rebecca
   E 22 104 Robert 60 101 112
   Sally 128 Samuel 45 47 48 50
   Sarah 41 160 162 Sarah Jane 34
   138 Selina A J 164 Thomas 46
   78 83 124 129 149 164 Vic-
   torina 106 Virginia 20 Wil-
   hemina 66 William 67 169
   Wm T 158
SMITHER, Julia 120
SMITHERMAN, Elizabeth 22 103
SMOOT, Ann Caroline 5 57
   Elizabeth 132 George H 87 162
   Mary E 14 87 Mary Eliza 16

SMOOT (continued)
   Susan W 29 Susana W 122
SMYTH, Edward 147 153
SNELL, Catharine 25 113 Susanna
   168
SNOWDEN, Allevy 13
SNYDER, George 57 100 155
   Polly 20 97
SOLERS, Henrietta 33
SOLLERS, Henrietta 33 134
SOLOMON, Caroline 92 Sarah 5
   58
SOMBY, Nancy 9 149
SOMERS, Daniel 91 Joseph R 150
   Lucinda 97 Mary 126 Mary Ann
   121 Simon 126
SOMES, Francis 55
SOMMOKS, Jeremiah 97
SOUTHARD, Eliza G 91 Sarah 40
   157 William 91 150
SOUTHERD, John 130
SOUTHERN, Elenor 77
SPARKS, Julia A 23 109
SPEAKE, Mary C 57 Mary G 5
SPEAKS, Rosanna 33 136
SPEAR, Hannah C 24 110 Joseph
   88
SPEARS, Miss 140 William 70
SPENCE, Teresa Ann 90
SPENCER, Mary Ann 159 Nancy
   150
SPENSER, William 146
SPERNAUGLE, Elijah 147 Elizah
   46
SPIDEN, John A 150 160
SPILLMAN, William C 150 Wm
   C 86
SPILMAN, Ann Maria 83 Susan G
   64 William C 83 William C Jr
   150 Wm 150
SPINKS, Elizabeth 126
SPRIGGS, Jane 4 55
SPUNAUGLE, Catharine 45 Mar-
   garet 35
SPUNNAUGLE, Margaret 141
STABLER, Rich H 23 Susan 83
STANTON, Amanda 129 John H
   73 Maria 11 73 Richard H 100
STAPLES, Sarah 5
STAPPLES, Samuel J 92
STEDECORN, Simon 110
STEEL, Catharine 21 Horatio N

STEEL (continued)
100 Nancy 112 Thomas 110–112
141 156
STEELE, Cath 100 H N 79 Sarah
C 13 Sarah Catharine 79
STEETS, H W 144
STEINER, H M 73
STEITS, H W 144
STENTSMAN, Kitty 41 160
STEPHENS, Mary J 125
STEPHENSON, Ann 2 47 50
George 145 James 74 John 123
Nancy 123 Rachael 113 Rachel
25
STEPHESON, Ann 2
STEPNAY, Endine 24
STEPNEY, Emeline 109
STEUTER, Morris see STUER-
TEN, Morris 38
STEVENS, Charles 123 Elizabeth
36 145
STEVENSON, Ann 2 Margaret 31
129 Mary J 146 Susan 103
STEWART, Elizabeth 7 53 Hugh
119 John A 68 115 Margaret 10
Mary 46 Mary Ann 70 Sarah
159 Susannah 117
STIDOLPH, Sophia Ann 25 112
STITHLEY, Betsy 37
STITLEY, Betsy 148
STODDER, Mary 51
STOKELEY, Margaret 78
STOKEY, Cornelius 64
STOKOLY, Margaret 13
STONE, Eleanor 1 47 Elizabeth
58 Joseph 68 Mary Ann 28 120
William 47 120
STONELL, Vincent 161
STONEMET, Mary 9
STONEMETS, Mary 67
STONER, Daniel 80
STOOPS, Eliza 58 William 116
STOTT, Polly 7 62
STRAIT, Sarah 10 70
STREET, Ann 101 Daniel 101 128
Eliza 128
STRIDMORE, Gerrard 96 Nancy
96
STROMAN, Elizabeth 34 137
STUART, Mary 140 S 40 William
B 102 Wm 140
STUDOR, Catharine 155 Mary 155

STULL, Ann M 52
STUPPAR, Barbara 47
SULLIVAN, Ellen 44 Owen 46 62
99 124 Owne 86
SUMMERS, Charlotte 25 114
Eleanor 86 Elizabeth 71
George 86 Jane 42 164 Jane M
13 78 John 80 John D 105
Lewis 164 Marion W 80 Mary
Jane 53 Samuel 55 William 78
SURVAY, William 54
SUTER, Elizabeth 69 Endocia C
14 81 John 54
SUTHERLAND, Ann 76 Hopey 104
SUTTON, John 110 Samuel 127
SWAIN, George 131 Julius 84
SWALLOW, Hepsey 41 161
SWANN, Eleanor 123 Eleanor Ann
164 Elizabeth 142 Ellenor 29
John S 164 Judith 27 117
Louisa 167 Mary 29 124 Sarah
3 51 Sarah A 54 Thomas 153
William 46
SWAYNE, Julius G 110
SWEET, Margaret 9 68
SWITZER, Ann 97
SWODEN, Elizabeth 132
SWORD, Anna 24 110
SYLVIA, Dorothy 22
SYPHAX, Amelia 46 William 109
TAFFE, James 117
TAITE, Isaiah 61
TALBOT, Eliza 5 Helen 54 Julia
G 69 Lucy 33 Lydia 29 Mary
27 Matilda 3 52
TALBOTT, Eliza 5 57 Helen 4
Josiah 54 Mary 56 123 Nancy
23 107 Rebecca 4 54
TALBUT, Lydia 123
TALBUTT, Nancy 4 54
TARLETON, Peggy 75
TASTEPAUGH, Peter 76
TATE, Eliza 42 162 Isaac 154
Isaiah 154 Rockey 143 Simeon
48 Simon 154
TATSAPAUGH, Caroline R 98
Henry 158 John 88 98 104 Kate
R 158 Mary Ann 88 Rosetta
154 Zoretta 39
TATSEPAUGH, Henry 49
TATSPAUGH, Henry 147 John 87
Mrs 34 Peter 88

WATSON, Ann 3 32 37 52 Anna
132 Elizabeth 117 Jane 14 81
Sarah 3 52 Thomas 52
WATTLES, Ann 7 62 Caroline 33
135 Chloe 42 Ellen 37 149
Nathaniel 135 137 149 Sophia
Elizabeth 34 137
WAUGH, Albert P 109 Lawrence
124 Letitia 82 Letty 14 Sally 3
52 Townshend 162 William 52
132
WAY, Frederick 131 Margaret 13
80 Salome 26 115
WAYGLY, Ann 42 Mary Ann 163
WEAVER, Jane Ellender 134
Martha 74 Mary 84
WEBB, John 90 Mary 149 153
Verlinda 45
WEBSTER, Catharine A 70
George 135 Henry A 69 134
Henry H 96 Mary Ann 80 Rev
37 William L 103
WEED, Prescilla 17
WEEDEN, Henry 91 Priscilla 91
WEEKS, Joseph 51
WEIGHTMAN, Richard 141 155
WEILEY, Sarah 49
WELBORNE, Jane 73
WELLBORNE, Jane 11
WELLS, Daniel 61 156 Mary A
116 Mary E 7 Mary Elizabeth
62 William 163 Wm Henry 116
WELSH, Debrah 108 Mary 37 148
WESCOTT, Jane 34 135
WESLEY, William Woodcocks
152
WEST, Ann M 126 Desdemona
134 Desdemonia 32 Hugh 96
143 John 89 156 Kitty 158
Mary 146 Sarah 38 150
WESTCOTT, Mary Ann 25 111
WESTERN, Sarah 168
WESTON, Ann F 51 Eliza 115
Sarah 28 29 122
WEYLIE, Ephraim 46 Neily 1 46
WHALEY, George 164
WHALING, Mary 148
WHEAT, Adeline Bond 112
Benoni 60 119 142 158 164
John J 142 Martha J 63 Mary
Ann 158 Thomas 164
WHEATLEY, Ann 47

WHEATLY, Ann 1
WHEATON, Catharine 19 83
WHEELER, Charlotte 59 Dolly
118 Eleanor 130 Richard H 66
Samuel 125 127 Sarah 136
WHERRY, Margaretta H 1 45
WHIT, Jane 152
WHITE, Ann 37 150 Ellen 7 62
Hannah J 38 John 54 John T 86
116 139 143 Judith 93 Mary
119 Robert L 63 Sarah 77
Thomas Jr 168
WHITING, Lucy 59 Maria F 133
Sophia 52 Thacker see JONES,
Thacker 108
WHITINGTON, Mary Ann 15
WHITMORE, Mary 23 108 Mary E
35
WHITNEY, Sophia 3 52
WHITTINGTON, Louisa 34 137
Mary Ann 15 84 Thomas 51 84
104 128
WHORSON, Wm see
RICHARDSON, William 140
WIGGINS, William 118
WILBAR, Sarah 16 88
WILES, Mary 128
WILEY, Ann 2 49 E 47 Eliza 150
Elizabeth 83 Geo 106 George
49 140 166 Hugh 128 150
Matilda 128
WILKES, Barbary 12 76
WILKINS, Ann 43 166 Mary Ann
122 S M 133
WILKINSON, Adeline 117 Matilda
138
WILLIAM, Betsy 28 Catherine 14
Nancy 96
WILLIAMS, Alexander 81 88 89
92 147 158 166 167 Ann 40 158
Bazil 66 Betsey 121 Catharine
81 Eleanor 147 166 Eliza 19 96
Elizabeth 26 116 Ellinor 37
Evan 72 Henrietta 137 Henry
73 155 169 Hiram O 166 James
121 Jane 17 74 89 John 80
Lucy Ellen 141 Margaret 41
160 Martha 107 Mary 18 42 66
92 162 169 Nancy 8 9 40 66
157 Rachel Ann 140 Rebecca
Ellen 111 Robert 166 Samuel
161 Sarah 32 41 65 132 Sarah S

WILLIAMS (continued)
16 88 Sophia 7 40 63 156
Thomas 58 123 137 140 Vincent 113 Wilkinson 98 William 80 107 William A 55 62
WILLIAMSON, Elizabeth 99
Peyton 146 William 52
WILLIE, Nancy 20
WILLIS, Abel 88 Eleanor 68 Ellenor 7 Mary Ann 40 158
Robert 68
WILLS, Francis 99
WILSON, Ann C 84 Charles F 134
Eleanor 56 Eliza 163 Elizabeth
41 160 Ephraim 166 Frederick
106 Jacob 92 Jacob H 100
James 57 Louisa A 27 117
Melvina A 62 Mercy A 100
Robert J T 62 144 Sarah L 162
William 148 166 168
WINDSOR, Mary G 84 Robert N
71 Susan 32 Susan H 71
WINKFIELD, Winifred 42 164
WINTER, Jane 145
WINTERBERRY, John 167 Polly
167
WISE, Anne E 168 George 59 64
111 George P 167 Kitty 41 160
Margaret G 111 Mary Ann Martha 64 Nathaniel S 107 Peter
65
WISEMAN, Mary 140 Nancy 29
124
WISEMILLER, Jacob 170
WITHERS, John 113
WOOD, Belinda 35 142 Benjamin
103 111 113 Eleanor 18 93
Elijah 78 Fanny 19 96 Harriot
143 Isaac 101 Jane E 80 John
45 63 73 77 80 100 123 149 165
Louisa 157 Louise 40 Lucy 28
121 Maria 37 123 149 Marian
165 Mary 22 Mary Ann 68 Mary
C 103 Mary E 19 Richard 120
134 152 Sarah 157 Susan 45
WOODROW, Mary 28 120
WOOLEN, John 111
WOOLLES, William 52
WOOLLS, George 106 Mary A 165
WORKMAN, Catharine 12 76
Degina 76 John 92
WORTHAN, William R 136

WORTHINGTON, Julia A 41 Matthew 139 William 80
WRIGHT, Betsey 74 Charles M
62 108 119 Daniel 73 165
Elizabeth S 124 George 50 Harriet 108 Harriett 23 Mary 43
166 Phebe 16 87 Sally 11 74
Thomas 89 William 98 Wm 95
WROE, Eliza 1 Elizabeth 45
Samuel 80 William 168
WYATT, George Williams 134
WYER, Mary A 75
WYLEY, Mary E 113 Thomas 113
YARDLEY, Mary 57
YATES, Francis L D 93
YEARLY, Ann 21 102 Maria Ann
B 97 Mary Ann B 20 Nathaniel
63
YEATES, Matilda 139
YEATON, Joshua 153 Julia Ann
Eliza 159 Louisa T 43 165 W
C 45 53 96 William 159 160
Wm C 116
YOST, Lucy 35 143 Rebecca 22
103
YOUNG, Ann 41 161 Elizabeth 30
83 127 Elizabeth M 29
Elizabeth Mary 83 George 122
James 59 90 123 151 John 160
John Q 108 John T 142 Martin
140 Mary 11 38 74 151 Nancy 5
58 Sarah 169
ZIMMERMAN, Eliza 20 97
Emeline 130 George 130 Henry
146 Jacob 66 86 134 Julia Ann
62 Reuben 162 Susannah 36
146 Wm H 62
_____ Slave Margaret 115